'Shapiro and Eyers tell the entertaining and illuminating story of how Afterpay emerged as a global, online-retailing power in a few short years. It's a fascinating study in entrepreneurship, modern-day retailing and stubbornness in the face of skepticism.'

**Gregory Zuckerman, *The Wall Street Journal***

'A fascinating read of the journey behind one of the biggest Australian entrepreneurial successes of our time!'

**Jane Lu, CEO and founder, Showpo**

'Like it or not, Afterpay has, in a remarkably short period, become an important participant in consumer finance markets in Australia and the world. This book explores in detail how this occurred and who made it happen. It is well written and well worth reading.'

**David Gonski AC, company director**

D0932608

*To my parents for encouraging me to write, my brother and sister for believing I could, my wife for tipping me off about Afterpay ('I think these guys will be big') and my boys ('I think these guys will be big!').*
**Jonathan Shapiro**

*To my family and friends, who are always there to motivate, debate and disagree. Thanks for inspiring me to question, investigate and puzzle over the change-makers in our world.*
**James Eyers**

# buy
# now,
# pay
# later

the extraordinary story of
# afterpay

## JONATHAN SHAPIRO
## and JAMES EYERS

ALLEN&UNWIN
SYDNEY·MELBOURNE·AUCKLAND·LONDON

Allen & Unwin
83 Alexander Street
Crows Nest NSW 2065
Australia
Phone: (61 2) 8425 0100
Email: info@allenandunwin.com
Web: www.allenandunwin.com

 A catalogue record for this
book is available from the
National Library of Australia

ISBN 978 1 76087 946 4

Index by Puddingburn
Internal design by Midland Typesetters
Set in 12/16 pt Adobe Garamond LT by Midland Typesetters, Australia

10 9 8 7 6 5 4 3 2 1

# CONTENTS

# PROLOGUE

'TREPIDATION' IS THE word we both had scrawled and underlined in our notepads after a half-hour Zoom call with Anthony Eisen and Nick Molnar, the founders of Afterpay.

The call was held on Tuesday, 19 January 2021, when most of Australia was enjoying a summer holiday after a traumatic 2020, which had seen the world ravaged by the coronavirus pandemic.

Nick dialled in from 'Nicko's iPhone'. He was unshaven and crouched under a staircase in his holiday house in Byron Bay. The scheduled time of 1 pm coincided with the nap time of his second child, who was only a few months old. Anthony logged on from his desk at Afterpay's Melbourne office, in a Collins Street tower with views of the city in the background.

The purpose of the call: to tell them about our project. We were going to write a book about Afterpay. We were quite excited, so much so that we kept interrupting each other as we explained why we thought the timing was right for this extraordinary tale to be told. But even through our screens, we could detect a distinct lack of enthusiasm from the Afterpay camp.

Once we finished rambling, Eisen explained, politely and methodically, that he and Molnar weren't all that keen on the book. They'd never contemplated the story of Afterpay being written. If they were ever going to tell it, now was not the time. They figured they were only in the early chapters of any Afterpay treatise.

Nicko's iPhone blacked out intermittently as he received other messages. He said little for most of the call. When he spoke, it was to tell us that he wasn't all that keen either. He didn't want 'egg on their faces'. They had a lot of work to do over the next two years to deliver on the plan they'd laid out. The notion of marking the first six years of the company with a book, and the idea of being associated with it, made both of them anxious.

But they did indulge in a brief moment of satisfaction. Was the fact that we were writing a book some recognition that their model had been validated? That wasn't a question two scruffy banking reporters could answer. But the stock market certainly thought so. That day, Afterpay's market valuation would touch $40 billion, making it Australia's twelfth-largest listed company. Never in the history of the Australian stock market had so much wealth been created so quickly.

Molnar had, six months earlier, become Australia's youngest-ever billionaire. The very first Afterpay backers were $7 million richer for each $10,000 they'd invested. Even if that amount had been invested in mid-March 2020, during the depths of the pandemic-induced panic, it would have generated a very healthy gain of $130,000.

There was plenty of smart money willing to validate the model. Silicon Valley's top venture funds, Wall Street's most sophisticated hedge funds, and Chinese technology goliath Tencent had all invested in Afterpay.

But they hadn't been there from the start. Afterpay was not launched with money from vaunted venture capital funds but from private individuals, friends, associates and stockbrokers' clients. It is they who were offered golden tickets, which they accepted, or turned down or traded in way too early to their eternal regret.

At the time that first capital was raised, Afterpay was little more than an idea. Initially, Afterpay offered exactly what the name suggested. Shoppers buying goods online could buy something, try it and then, if it was what they wanted, pay for it within 30 days. But a simpler, more elegant model triumphed: the consumer would pay four equal instalments over six weeks, while the merchant would pay the cost of the short-term credit facility to Afterpay.

Afterpay's idea was hardly revolutionary. It was a modern twist on lay-by, a method of instalment payment introduced in the frugal depression era of the early 1930s that had endured, to the frustration of retailers. But it was reinvented at the right time, because millennials and Gen Xers were turning their back on credit cards and driving new trends in ecommerce.

That simple idea was more powerful than Nick and Anthony could ever have imagined. It compelled shoppers to shed the guilt associated with an impulse buy, and allowed them to be able to afford it before their next pay cheque arrived.

Shoppers loved the free service, while merchants experienced a boost in sales that more than justified the cost. Afterpay had unlocked a win-win model that rebooted the interest-free instalments industry—now dubbed 'buy now, pay later'.

And against the odds, Afterpay had cracked America. That triggered an epic land grab in a $US300 billion online retail market, forcing payments giants and big banks to follow.

Yet despite its rapid and incredible success, few companies had been more divisive and elicited more emotion than Afterpay. Suburban hairdressers, fashionistas and young millennials used the product and absolutely loved it. To them, the founders had almost messianic status. Afterpay didn't just have customers, it had diehard fans who spread the gospel on their behalf, accelerating growth at no cost. Unsurprisingly, the amateur investors who made spectacular gains loved it, too. But professional investors in Australia, by and large, hated Afterpay. The company was over-hyped and overvalued, and by their assessment could never realistically make a large enough profit to justify the enormous valuation the share market was assigning to it. To grizzled credit analysts, Afterpay was like a speedboat cutting across Sydney Harbour: the moment it slowed, a wake of bad debts would swell up from behind and dump on it. But the more the Afterpay stock price went up, the more it made them look bad—and the more costly it became not to have purchased shares in it.

Then there were the consumer advocates, who for decades had strived to protect ordinary Australians from debt traps. To them, Afterpay was exploiting a loophole, skirting the definition that it was lending money and fooling customers with its pay-in-four model into believing they could afford whatever they wanted. Bestselling personal finance author Scott Pape compared the service to marijuana, a gateway debt drug.

As Afterpay gained in popularity, the virtues and the vices of its model were debated not only in the share market but also in the halls of Parliament House in Canberra. The lucrative contest for financial and political capital sucked in stockbrokers, lawmakers, lobbyists and influencers. In the United States, that extended from the Kardashians to former treasury secretary Larry Summers.

By the time it was only a few years old, Afterpay had already left a mark. It had changed the way a university student bought sneakers, and the way the prime minister delegated control of the financial system. It had tested the minds of the nation's sharpest investors, the existing rules of finance and the fortitude of the most powerful bankers to future-proof their century-old institutions. Almost everybody had an Afterpay story. There'd been no business like it in Australia, and there probably never will be again. That was why we had to write this book.

That was our pitch, anyway. Whether Nick and Anthony agreed wasn't clear; at least, they agreed they couldn't stop us. As we concluded the call, they told us they were prepared to help. They didn't want to be part of the book, or endorse it. They would grant no on-the-record interviews; they made that clear. But they wanted to ensure we got what we needed, and understood as much as we could of the history of the business. They would respond to questions and grant access to a handful of Afterpay staff who we asked to interview. Those discussions could be used as background information, but would not be on the record.

• • •

When we organised a follow-up call on Monday, 8 February 2021, it was a far more relaxed Nick and Anthony who dialled in.

Nick called from Afterpay's Surry Hills office, while this time Anthony was at his home in Melbourne. Nick was in jeans and a white Afterpay T-shirt. He joked about the tech issues he was having that day, and he had his feet on the desk for most of the interview. He had just turned 31 the previous weekend. Anthony was in a black hoodie and stared down the camera.

For an hour and a half they took our questions, which we had carefully prepared to help us fill in the gaps of the Afterpay story we'd pieced together through hours of interviews, research and years of frontline coverage as corporate reporters at *The Australian Financial Review*, a national, daily publication. Anthony spoke candidly about his late father's business and his time at Guinness Peat Group.

The precise moment when the Afterpay idea was born was hard to nail down. But the moments of serendipity, fortune and inspiration where the story changed were clear. So, too, were the moments when all seemed lost and the forces of gravity, long defied, threatened to pull everything apart. They'd survived a multitude of existential threats as underdogs, and were inevitably going to face them as one of the emerging titans of the new payments order.

Nick's enthusiasm and will to succeed made him resilient beyond his years. Anthony, meanwhile, wore the scars of a gruelling career of corporate battles. Anthony had run his career in reverse, taking a moonshot bet in the middle of his corporate life. He admitted to momentarily 'bearing his soul'.

This time, we detected warmth and an element of nostalgia when the two founders spoke about the days before Afterpay became a verb. When we probed Eisen about those darker, more difficult moments, he grinned and deferred to his preferred euphemism: 'It was a journey.'

Like no other before. And no other since.

# 1

# RAGS TO RICHES

Zoltan Kaufman lived with his young family in a large three-bedroom apartment in Budapest, Hungary. It had a luxurious lounge room with soft velvet couches, a long hallway and a maid's quarters. Every morning, breakfast would be rolled in on a mobile tray. Three times a week, a personal trainer would teach Zoltan's glamorous wife, Lilly, gymnastics. On special occasions they would dance to the Pearl Fishers duet that played on the gramophone.[1]

Zoltan made a good living supplying raw materials to a nail factory, but in the evenings he worked on his other, more lucrative business: leasing jewellery on a pay-as-you-wear arrangement to wannabe aristocrats. A man of honour, Zoltan had built up a network of clients across the cosmopolitan city.

Then war broke out in Europe. Everything changed for Zoltan and his middle-class Jewish family. Hungary allied itself with the Axis powers. In 1942, Zoltan was taken from his home to serve in a labour camp in Lipinszkaja, on the western border of Poland.[2] A year later, on 20 November 1943, Zoltan tried to escape; he was shot and killed.

But Zoltan's side hustle had saved his family. The gold and diamonds he kept in the apartment became the currency Lilly used to buy Christian identity papers from the cleaning lady, whose daughter was a similar age to Susie, the Kaufmans' eight-year-old daughter. The gold was also used to pay off the hotelier of a mountain resort, a customer of Zoltan's, when suspicious locals forced them to flee the city.

The war was devastating. But post-war Hungary remained hostile to those Jews who had survived the Holocaust. They had no place there. Lilly and Susie were smuggled onto trucks that stopped short of the Austrian border. They crawled through potato fields. The final payment was Susie's accordion, donated to the family living on the farm, who directed them to safety.

At the Rothschild Hospital, a de facto refugee camp in the district of Vienna that was occupied by the Americans, Lilly met her second husband, Joe, a skilled tailor. They caught a train to Paris, lugging aboard Joe's heavy sewing machine, testing his patience and the young family's resolve.

Two years later, in 1949, they arrived in Sydney, sailing through the Heads on a voyage paid for by an American charity. A family friend named Leopold, or 'Kisci' (Hungarian for 'little', as he was short), helped with the sponsorship. The family of three spent their first few nights on Edgecliff Road, in the Eastern Suburbs, before moving to cheaper digs on Orwell Street, Kings Cross. They slept in a single room. There was a kitchen and a toilet shared with fellow lodgers. Susie slept on two uneven packing cases. But the bohemian neighbourhood, with its coffee shops and late-night spots, including various cabaret clubs, sustained them with a taste of the Europe they had left behind.[3]

Joe bought a new sewing machine with an interest-free loan from the Jewish Welfare Society, and put his skills to good use. Working day and night, he made men's and ladies' suits.

Life was a little tougher for ten-year-old Susie Kaufman, who could barely speak English. But she got by at Double Bay Public School thanks to the kindness of girls such as Faye Bolton, who showed her where the toilets were and helped her memorise the periodic table of elements. The headmaster, Mr Hurrigan, stayed after school to help her with her English, but once reluctantly had to cane her after discovering she had taught the other kids Hungarian swear words.

The dark beginnings of Susie's life turned brighter in Australia. Her stepfather opened a factory on Burton Street, Darlinghurst, and then menswear stores across the city. She holidayed in the Blue Mountains, rode horses in Centennial Park and gathered on warm days with her friends at Little Jerusalem, the nickname they'd given to the steps on the Bondi Beach promenade. Her parents took out a mortgage to buy a big house in Vaucluse. Susie eventually got married, got divorced and retrained as a social worker, working at the children's hospital in Randwick.

The sun shone on Australia and on the hardworking immigrants and refugees who had arrived on its shores. Some of Sydney's Jewish refugees had re-created the life of prosperity the Nazis had torn apart, stitch by stitch. Synagogues and Jewish schools were built as the community flourished.

Susie herself had two children, Ronald and Vivian, and some years later had four grandchildren. Once a month on the Sabbath, the grandchildren decided that dinner should be limited to them and the grandparents. That allowed for intergenerational bonding and all-night tile rummy. The idea was thought up by Susie's eldest grandson, Nick Molnar, a jewellery salesman of the digital age.

• • •

Susie's son, Ron—Nick's father—attended Rose Bay Public School, before her stepfather, Joe, offered to pay for tuition at the prestigious Sydney Grammar School in the city, where Susie would often meet Ron for lunch. Ron was smart but only worked hard enough to get the commerce degree his mother had insisted on. He accepted his grandfather Joe's request to help him run his stores across the city, but upon Joe's retirement they were closed.

Ron and his younger uncle, Johnny, went into business, opening a jewellery store in a city arcade, but then Ron married Michele and they went overseas. When he returned, they opened their own jewellery store together in the prime location of Wynyard Station. A redesign of the city's transport routes had created more retail hubs and a thoroughfare a few blocks back from Circular Quay.

In February 1990 and February 1992, Ron and Michele gave Susie two grandsons, Nick and Simon; Susie already had two granddaughters born to her daughter, Vivian.

The boys were enrolled at Moriah War Memorial College, a Jewish school that in 1994 had shifted from a small campus in Bellevue Hill to a much bigger site on the other side of the Bondi Junction shopping centre, down the hill in Queens Park. Moriah had secured a lease from the New South Wales government after it closed the old Eastern Suburbs Hospital; the new campus represented 'the largest investment—in money, time and effort—ever made by the Sydney Jewish community', barrister and Jewish community leader Robert Goot told students at their last assembly before the move in 1994.

The school's governors had found a desirable location, nestled alongside Centennial Park, a swamp that had been landscaped into rolling parklands between Sydney's central business district and its famous Eastern Suburbs beaches. That location was just a few hundred metres from another Jewish campus, Temple Emanuel, which had relocated from Woollahra. The liberal Emanuel Synagogue had been set up in 1939 after a wave of Jews fled Nazi Germany in the 1930s before the outbreak of war.

Moriah College had come a long way since its foundational headmaster, Harold Nagley, arrived from Mount Scopus, a Jewish school in Melbourne, in 1968 and found Sydney's Jewish community in the wilderness. In Melbourne, a strong post-Holocaust survivor community had grown among immigrants from Poland. They were more traditional than Sydney's mostly Hungarian Jewish immigrants, many of whom were disenchanted with religion, after being scarred by their experience of war.

Nicole Strasser, a young refugee at Double Bay Public School, was packed ham sandwiches for lunch and sent to school on the Jewish holidays by her mother, who had hid her during the war in Paris. When other kids at the school told her they were Jewish, she had an identity crisis. Susie had a similar experience at the same school. She was made a member of the Church of England, but when she noticed other kids attending Jewish scripture class without being bashed or taunted, she had a revelation. Mr Hurrigan told her she was not alone: other parents had also hidden their children's religions to protect them. But over time, they regained their identities, both individually and collectively.

Many Hungarians preferred to sit in the Jewish social club, the Hakoah Club in Bondi, drinking coffee and watching football, rather than to attend synagogue. Jewish religious customs played a peripheral part in their lives. But they were slowly rediscovering their identities as they became more prosperous and confident. An influx of other immigrants from South Africa and Russia expanded the Sydney Jewish community and encouraged more openness.

Nagley felt he could help rebuild the community's Jewish identity by building a new school. He worked tirelessly to establish Moriah College, an institution that would compete with the exclusive private schools dotted around it, while recognising Jewish history, however uncomfortable it was.

But there were also monuments of triumph and prosperity in this new land—a literal rags-to-riches tale. The names of Sydney's prominent Jewish business leaders, men who had docked in the harbour city penniless, adorned the orange-brick buildings on the Moriah campus as benefactors to the college.

One was Harry Triguboff, founder of the Meriton property-development company and one of the ten richest people in Australia. He supported the school's auditorium, which was named after his late father, Moshe Triguboff. Students would eat their sandwiches alongside a garden donated by Agnes and Berel Ginges, who had founded Best & Less, a popular women's fashion retailer.

Other giants of Australian retail also loomed large. John Saunders, one of the co-founders of Westfield, sponsored the science building, while Westfield's other co-founder, Frank Lowy, dedicated the synagogue at Moriah to his father, Hugo Lowy, who had died at Auschwitz.

Westfield wasn't merely ingrained in the buildings around the school, it loomed large on the skyline. As they played at lunchtime, Moriah students could see the distinctive red Westfield logo emblazoned on the top of its shopping centre at Bondi Junction, while its global headquarters were just a short drive away on William Street. Frank Lowy's grandkids all attended Moriah College.[4]

The generous financial contributions to the school reflected a sense of giving something back to a country that had offered immigrants security, and taught the students, even if by osmosis, that Australia, like the United States, was a land of opportunity.

The epitome of Australia as a place of hope, fortune and opportunity was Westfield. Frank Lowy and John Saunders had arrived penniless as survivors of the Holocaust. Lowy drove a smallgoods delivery truck, and Saunders, eight years his senior, ran a hole-in-the-wall delicatessen at Sydney's Town Hall Station. They went into business together, setting up a deli in Blacktown, 35 kilometres west of the city. A condition of the partnership was that neither would say 'I told you so' if things didn't work out—and also that their wives would not be involved in the business.

At Blacktown Station, Lowy and Saunders sold devon sausage and ham to Anglo-Australians and salami to the 'new Australian' immigrants as they returned to their homes after a hard day's work, craving a taste from their previous life. They extended the deli with a lounge and pavement seating, and sold decent coffee—hard to come by in their new land.[5]

Soon they realised the area was in the middle of a property-development boom, and this prompted them to buy up and subdivide fields and farmland. When another Hungarian émigré purchased land and put up a row of shops, Saunders got the idea to do something similar. They sold their deli for $20,000 and used the cash to buy nearby land, but rather than build a row of shops, they built a mini-mall like the ones that had become popular in the United States. As the land was a field in the west of Sydney, they called it Westfield Place.

The pair were on to something—and soon were developing malls all over the countryside and in the city. Sydney was a town that loved to shop. Westfield knew how to position, build and manage the centres that brought customers to the merchants who were willing to rent space from them. In 1960, they listed their company on the Sydney stock exchange. By 1976, they'd outgrown Australia, and had the chutzpah to chance their arm in the United States, buying a mall in Connecticut. Within three years they had purchased two more, as they rapidly and successfully expanded their global empire.

In Australia, the success of Jewish immigrants was rapid and significant. By the mid-1980s, a quarter of the families in the *Business Review Weekly* Rich 200 list were Jewish. And more than a quarter of the families with wealth of more than $200 million were Jewish. But any mention of wealth was viewed with trepidation among the community.[6]

'Those Jews who are uncomfortable, sometimes downright apprehensive every time the wealth of some Jews is highlighted may be right to a point. They fear it encourages envy, the breeding ground for anti-Semitism through the ages,' wrote Simon Lipski, a columnist for the *Australian Jewish Times*.[7]

That the 1980s and early '90s were economically tough for Australia made the community particularly uneasy about the wealth they had accumulated. 'But on balance the success some Jews have had in creating wealth, considering how they came as poor refugees or as survivors after World War II, is a matter for pride not unease— pride in their achievement, as well as in Australia's comparative freedom as a country that adopted them,' Lipski wrote.

Several of the new arrivals became entrepreneurs in the fashion industry. Peter Hallas arrived in Sydney from Hungary in 1956 and felt an incredible sense of freedom. After living in communist Hungary, his reflex when he saw a police officer was to scurry across the street. And while he learned not to fear Australian law-enforcement agents, his father, who arrived in 1970, still lived in fear.[8]

In 1975, Hallas and his wife, Yvonne, started a company called Seafolly, which made aerobic wear just as Jane Fonda's exercise craze was taking hold. Seafolly's advertising was striking, and featured healthy, bronzed Aussie women. Among the wealthy Jews there were some cultural quirks. The predominantly Polish Jews in Melbourne tended to keep their companies private, while Sydney Jews ran public companies that tapped the share market for funds. That was most likely because 'Hungarian Jews were more cosmopolitan and less paranoid than Eastern European ones, who have experienced more direct anti-Semitism in the *shtetls* (villages) of Poland and arrived in Australia with more a small town mentality,' explained Hungarian émigré and trucking magnate Sir Peter Abeles.[9]

There were a few recipes for their success. One was an ingenuity and resilience that those who had survived the Holocaust and fled Europe had developed. Another was partnerships, based on trust and common backgrounds that bind migrant communities together.

The refugees found friends and families whose skills, knowledge and characters complemented their own. Like Lowy and Saunders, they pooled their talents, problem-solved and shared the profits. There was Ted Lustig and Max Moar, who together developed the Chase shopping centre in the northern Sydney suburb of Chatswood and the Grand Hyatt hotel in Melbourne, and Albert Scheinberg and John Hammond, who met before the war but later joined with refugee Ervin Graf to form another property company, the Stockland Trust.

Most of the entrepreneurs of that age credit their success to Australia's free and open society, which 'did not erect any barriers, allowing fair and equal opportunity for all'.[10]

The soul of Jewish commerce was the *schmatter* or rag trade, which itself has become a part of the Jewish identity, not just in Australia but around the world. The Jewish community has been involved in the Australian rag trade for as long as Europeans have settled on the continent. From 1788 to 1830, 463 Jews arrived in Australia, of whom 384 were convicts, 52 free settlers and 27 children. One-third of those settlers were in the retail trade: second-hand clothes dealers, furriers, tailors, hatters and shoemakers.

The World War II refugees could begin making clothes the moment they stepped off the boat. They didn't need money, equipment or even a command of the English language.

'You needed credit,' explained George Bloomfield, who founded clothing retailer Wraggs. 'So I could go to Joe Blow, buy five yards of fabric, make the samples, go and sell it to Joe Bloggs, get the order come back, make it and get paid before you pay for the fabric. That's how most people got started in the clothing trade. There's a long list of them who came with no money and became millionaires.'[11]

Max Ginges arrived before the war, in 1929. He sold ladies' dresses from a knapsack and a suitcase, using just two words—'possible' and 'impossible'. His son, Berel, founded Best & Less with an overriding principle to keep prices low and not expand margins.[12] 'I had salesgirls I didn't know I had!' he said. 'When a woman went to David Jones to try on a coat, the salesgirl told her, "Don't buy it here, love, go over there, they've got them at a third of the price."'[13]

Auschwitz survivor Gitta Gold and her husband, Fred, ran a lingerie store called Belle's in Bondi. Her real drawcard wasn't the items behind the counter. She offered her customers ice-cream, coffee or a cigarette.[14] 'Everybody needs to talk and they couldn't go to a rabbi or a priest or neighbour or a psychiatrist,' she said. 'I was a neutral person so they poured their hearts out.'[15]

While many parents chose to send their children to public schools or prestigious non-Jewish private schools, the establishment of schools such as Moriah College firmed up the community's roots. The next generation would have access to a top education and the opportunity to join the professional class—as doctors, lawyers and financiers.

Harold Nagley died in 1989, the year before Nick Molnar was born, but a family connection lived on at the school: Nagley's daughter, Stephanie Schwarz, was teaching computing studies there. A first-class honours graduate in chemistry, Schwarz had witnessed the dawn of the computer industry up close before becoming a teacher. She had joined IBM in 1969, the same year its technology helped land the first man on the moon. It was also the year 'big blue' launched its Customer Information Control System, which used remote terminals and servers—the birth of the age of computing networks.

Schwarz had stumbled into teaching when IBM refused to let her work part-time after her first child was born. She initially taught at TAFE, a professional education college, and then moved to Moriah in 1989, the same year her father died. There she got to work, building one of the best computer-studies programs in the state, and perhaps the country.

Schwarz taught the building blocks of programming by getting students to play games and build simple programs. In the early 1990s, a favourite game was Lemonade Stand, which had been made for the Apple II computers and taught the foundations of building a business. She helped students focus on problem-solving by breaking things down into steps. Don't think about the endpoint but the inputs, she said. Build what you have learned and you will see it develop in front of your eyes. Technology is not an end of itself, she told her pupils. They had to understand the basic building blocks. 'If you understand that, you can do anything with it.'

Sitting in her computer-studies class in 2006 and 2007, when he sat the Higher School Certificate, was Nick Molnar.

• • •

While Jewish day schools were lauded as centres of academic religious scholarship, they were hardly temples of sporting excellence that would rival the surrounding private schools. At business they excelled; at sport not so much. That was the one drawback for Nick Molnar, who was a keen and talented rugby player.

While most Sydney private schools fielded competitive rugby union teams, Moriah didn't play Saturday-morning sport, recognising that some families would be observing Shabbat. So Nick played for the local club, Eastern Suburbs.

The Beasts, as they are known, are the oldest district rugby club in Australia, tracing their history back to 1900. They had many famous players, including Dally Messenger, World Cup winners Tony Daly and Jason Little, and the valiant number eight Tim Gavin. The club's headquarters along the tree-lined O'Sullivan Road was just a few hundred metres from the Molnar family home, on the border of the exclusive suburbs of Bellevue Hill and Rose Bay.

Molnar's love of rugby was showcased on the invitation for his bar mitzvah—the Jewish boy's coming of age at thirteen, when he is deemed old enough to read directly from the Torah scrolls. It carried an image of the mouthguarded Molnar in Easts rugby gear with arms raised in triumph. The reading took place at the South Head Synagogue in Rose Bay, while the function afterwards was held at the Woolloomooloo Bay Hotel, a traditional Aussie pub on a wharf, with housing commission flats behind it.

Molnar had some triumphs on the rugby pitch. In 2008, he was part of the Australian squad that won the gold medal at the World Maccabiah Games, as the team fended off other rugby-playing nations with sizeable Jewish diasporas. The final was a nail-biting three-point triumph over Great Britain. Molnar, just eighteen at the time, was regarded as a small but skilful player by his teammates. Ron would entertain Jewish rugby legends at the family home, including the former Maccabi coach and Wallaby Rupert Rosenblum.

In his final year of school, Nick switched codes to rugby league, which had initially been created as a professional alternative to rugby union but over a century had grown to be a bigger sport in Australia. He signed up to play at the Eastern Suburbs Roosters, the famed local club that many of his friends watched play. Molnar trained intensively, working so hard that he regularly threw up at training. But he missed the cut for the team that would contest the SG Ball Cup, a national competition for under-18s, and a feeder for the elite National Rugby League clubs.

Nick was gutted. But the very same day he'd taken the call from the Roosters and been told it was over, he attended rugby union practice at The University of Sydney and was recruited to their club.

Molnar had done well enough in the Higher School Certificate exams to be accepted into commerce at The University of Sydney, putting him in the top 10 per cent of school-leavers in the state, but as university began and thousands of new students flooded the sandstone campus, his mind was still on becoming a professional footballer.

At the University Rugby Club, Molnar joined the elite development squad and was awarded a rugby scholarship. Four weeks later he was playing in the Sydney University First XV, alongside Bernard Foley and a handful of other current and future Wallabies, including Sam Carter, Will Skelton, Nathan Charles and Paddy Ryan. Molnar mainly played fullback, a tough position where he was his team's last line of defence.

On his days off from university and football, Nick worked in his parents' jewellery shop where Ron and Michele had alternated shifts for years. Nick had already developed a knack as an eBay seller, importing headphones from Japan and marketing them. He had developed a reputation as an eBay expert after selling the motorbike belonging to his Business Studies teacher, Mr Manocchio, on the website.

Simon Molnar, meanwhile, had wanted to be a vet but was now pursuing a career in IT. He and Nick convinced their parents that they could sell some jewellery stock online to supplement the store's revenue. Other major jewellers, such as Michael Hill and Goldmark, weren't doing online sales all that well, they argued. Michele agreed, and suggested her sons give it a crack.

'I started to list a few pieces on eBay and it started to move quite well but I was in Year 11,' Simon Molnar told Fairfax. 'I handed the keys over to [Nick] and he really ramped it up and became the top seller of jewellery for eBay Australia.'[16]

As Nick's studies neared an end, he started eyeing a career in investment banking, influenced by the lectures and his fellow students in his commerce degree. He'd also struck up a friendship with his neighbour, Anthony Eisen, who was half-suspicious, half-curious about Molnar's nocturnal business activities.

Eisen brokered an interview for Molnar at Lazard, the global investment bank run by Eisen's former boss, John Wylie. Molnar missed out on the role, but Wylie referred him to his former business partner and mate from Oxford University, Mark Carnegie, who had run Lazard's private-equity business for a few years before setting up his own shop, M.H. Carnegie & Co. Carnegie had a venture capital fund that was operating out of a warehouse-style space in Underwood Street, Paddington, and was recruiting talented young analysts to help him identify and manage start-ups.

The interview was robust. Carnegie asked him what he wanted, to which Molnar replied, 'Work at a venture fund like yours.'

Carnegie ignored the attempt to suck up. 'Well, let's say I tell you to go away right now, what are you going to do?'

Molnar tried to bluff, saying he had a job at another bank and would just head there.

Carnegie persevered. He opened up Nick's CV and asked him about his eBay business. 'What are your projections for next year, the year after? You, my friend, are leaving something on the table here—this is a big opportunity and you need to take it seriously.'

Carnegie told him he would not hire him. But to provide the young man with some motivation to take on some risk, he agreed to hold the job open for a year. Nick's assignment until then was to scale up his online jewellery business.

A week before his University of Sydney graduation ceremony in April 2011, Molnar devised a plan. There was a big North American jewellery industry conference approaching, and he decided to seek a meeting with Shmuel Gniwisch, who was online jewellery retailing royalty. He sent off an email in the dead of the night:

Hi Shmuel,

Apologies for the cold email. For some context, my name is Nick Molnar, I am a 21-year-old entrepreneur and I currently sell the most jewellery on eBay in Australia out of my bedroom.

I am coming to Las Vegas next week for the jewellery conference, and if you are there too, I would love to meet for a coffee.

Kind regards, Nick.[17]

Shmuel 'Sam' Gniwisch was an ordained but a non-practising rabbi from Montreal, Canada. His mother, Julie, was born in the Carpathian Alps as her mother fled Nazi-occupied Eastern Europe during the war for the safety of Canada. His father, Isaac, also survived the Holocaust.

Julie was the matriarch of Delmar, a private company that was Canada's largest jewellery manufacturer. Shmuel, his brothers and his brother-in-law, all ordained rabbis, had started selling some of the brand's jewellery online in the late 1990s as the internet was in its infancy. The low-cost items suitable for everyday wear were well suited to selling over the internet, and by the time the 1999 tech boom was in full swing, they'd attracted funding from Californian venture capitalist Bill Gross.

Gross's incubator fund, Idealab, offered to buy 60 per cent of their internet company BuyJewel.com, which was averaging $30,000 worth of sales a month, for a price tag of $7 million. They couldn't refuse and the company was relocated to Pasadena, where Gross put them up in a mansion. But the Gniwisches, with their beards and yarmulkes, were out of place. 'Walking around, I saw there were all these young, beatnik-looking kids with jeans and earrings on,' Julie told *CNN Money*. 'Stuck in the middle of this place were my boys. They looked more like a rabbinical seminary than an Internet start-up company.'[18]

The oddest thing, in the eyes of Isaac, was Idealab's idea that they shouldn't actually make a profit. Isaac insisted that Ice.com, the name the website assumed in May 2000, needed to make money from each transaction. 'I always stressed the bottom line, but the thinking of that period was that you didn't worry about it,' Isaac said. 'So I kept saying, "What's happening to the bottom line?" And they kept saying that the guys who run the company don't worry about the bottom line at this point.'[19]

In the wake of the 2000 tech bust, Bill Gross's grand vision of uniting all his ecommerce websites was abandoned. The Gniwisches negotiated to return to Montreal but incurred a $600,000 debt. They went back to their original strategy of focusing on sales rather than eyeballs.

They devised some clever new ways to attract customers. It was Isaac who came up with a plan to sell pearls for $4.95, a $2 loss, and he argued about it with Shmuel. But the promotion gained the business 170,000 new customers in a cheap and practical way, more than covering the cost of the deficit. Ice also added a financing program, as most of its sales were under $500, and came up with discount offers for browsers. The business was back on track and re-established itself as North America's top online jewellery retailer. But the lure of easy money had almost destroyed it.

'Everybody was in dreamland for a while,' Isaac told *CNN Money*. 'All balloons look good when they have air in them.'[20]

Shmuel replied to Molnar's email within a day: 'Sounds great, see you on Monday.'

Now Nick had to scramble. He wasn't really going to Las Vegas, and now he had to explain to his mortified mother that he would miss his own graduation, and ask his father to come with him. Nick wasn't actually 21 yet and wasn't sure he'd be granted access to the casino where the meeting might be held.

When the Las Vegas meeting did take place, it was after the day's exhibitions in a hall the size of several football fields. In a sponsors' booth deserted by its minders, Nick, Ron and Shmuel agreed that the Molnars would sell jewellery in Australia under the Ice Online brand.

# 2

# ASSET STRIPPERS

IN OCTOBER 2013, Anthony Eisen turned out the lights at Guinness Peat Group's offices by Sydney Harbour. The 42-year-old Eisen was among the younger members of Ron Brierley and Gary Weiss's band of accounting sleuths and legal tacticians. But he was the last man standing, as one of the most feared and admired corporate partnerships Australia had ever produced met its end.

Brierley and Weiss styled themselves as the closest thing the Antipodeans had to Warren Buffett and Charlie Munger: an odd couple of bookish investors who embraced both the art and the war of investing more than the outcome. Both were New Zealanders, and while Weiss was a doctor of law and Brierley a knight of the realm, they were outsiders to the clubby boardrooms they had set out to shake up.

Weiss and Brierley had joined forces in the 1980s. Ever since then, their maverick approach to investing had rattled the bones of the old boys' clubs that had presided over the nation's august corporations as they hunted for legal loopholes and assets of hidden value. Their cunning raids on the blue-chip companies of the day, Woolworths and Australian Gas Light, were the stuff of legend.

The pair differentiated themselves from the larger-than-life corporate characters such as Christopher Skase, Alan Bond and Robert Holmes à Court who rampaged through the stock market with large lines of credit. Yet they, too, had experienced a boom and bust, as the 1987 crash split apart their empire. In 1990, Brierley began putting it back together when he acquired control of a London-listed shell company called Guinness Peat Group.

Weiss had spent the interim period at a merchant bank, Whitlam Turnbull, formed by the son of past prime minister Gough Whitlam, a young lawyer with leadership aspirations, Malcolm Turnbull, and former New South Wales state premier Neville Wran. Weiss was the self-proclaimed 'fourth Beatle' but soon rejoined Brierley in 1992.

By 2004, Brierley and his band had grown GPG's assets by ten times to £500 million.

The GPG game was to identify deeply undervalued assets whose worth could be realised by shaking things up. That often meant dismantling boards, management teams and companies themselves—stripping them apart and flogging the parts for more than the sum implied by the share market's price. 'GPG looked for companies that were "better dead than alive", or potentially worth more than what they were trading at if their assets were sold,' wrote Anthony Hughes, Geoff Wilson and Matthew Kidman in their 2005 book on investing strategy, *Masters of the Market*.[1]

By 2010, the hunter had become the hunted yet again. Several large New Zealand shareholders had decided that GPG itself was worth more dead than alive. They'd used GPG-style aggression to get some seats on the board, and that board eventually determined it was in all shareholders' interests to effectively kill GPG. The order was for $1 billion worth of investments in 55 businesses across the world—from honey farms to technology companies—to be sold, and the funds returned to shareholders.

Eisen, who had risen through the ranks in his six years at the company, had the thankless task of unscrambling the GPG omelette. In February 2011, when chairman Rob Campbell made the order official, Eisen began the two-and-a-half-year process of finding and negotiating with buyers, often with hostile counterparties, given the markets were still stressed following the global financial crisis.

It was the antithesis of the job he'd instantly accepted from Gary Weiss six years earlier when invited to join GPG. Eisen had up until that point spent his career on the sell side of investment banking, hustling for work. The idea of working on the buy side, finding and investing in businesses, appealed to him. But now he was once again a seller. In his early forties, Eisen should have been at the pinnacle of his career. But in fact he was working himself out of a job. How had it come to this?

• • •

Anthony Mathew Eisen was the grandson of Holocaust survivors Simon and Rose Adler, whose daughter Anita had married Malcolm Eisen. They had two children, Anthony and Natalie.

Like many immigrants at the time, Adler took a job at the Australian Consolidated Industries (ACI) glass factory in the industrial suburb of Waterloo, in Sydney's south-east. The large sand dunes, which are now the Moore Park Golf Course, supplied the sand for the glass, and the bottles ACI made were sent to a nearby brewery.

Anthony's father, Malcolm, was a man with a big, soft heart. He followed the path of many Jewish immigrants in the *schmatter* trade. The family business, Malcolm Distributors, was based out of a warehouse in Surry Hills. The inner-city suburb was the hub of Sydney's thriving textile industry by virtue of its proximity to Central Railway Station, the wharfs of Pyrmont and the city's department stores.

Surry Hills had undergone many transformations by the time it became the centre of the booming textile industry. In the early 1800s the sandy, swampy and windswept hills were granted as farmland to two captains, John Foveaux and John Palmer, but the latter hastily sold off his plots to settle his debts. In the 1820s, the area was literally gentrified as colonial gentry and wealthy ex-convicts built large homes. Within the 50 years to 1870 the population doubled, breeding slum-like conditions akin to those of Glasgow or London. Opium dens, brothels and speakeasies littered the alleys, while disease spread in the dark underbelly of an already edgy city.

But by 1915 the area had been repurposed for commercial use, with department store David Jones setting up a purpose-built factory in the suburb to assemble clothes for its nearby flagship stores, the first of which had commenced trading in 1838 on the corner of George and Barrack streets, opposite the General Post Office, before a second CBD store opened on Market Street in 1927.

By the 1950s, Surry Hills was becoming an area of light industry. The deteriorating buildings and lack of demand for office space meant rents were low. The goods were delivered weekly—rag traders began to buy up old terraces and build two-storey factories, which were suited to the fashion industry, as clothing was naturally light and easy to carry down a flight of stairs. The relatively small floor space across two levels wasn't suited to large-scale manufacturing, but it was ideal for making clothes, and for printing pamphlets and newspapers.

Max Glass, a women's fashion proprietor, ran his business from the top floor of his building and rented out the bottom floor for £1500 a month—making a good return on his £30,000 investment. The booming real-estate market lured many Jewish immigrants to expand their business empires into property development, where even larger fortunes could be made.

This was the world in which Malcolm Eisen worked. When his young son Anthony wasn't studying, he was helping Malcolm load dresses into a van, to be sold under the family's popular label

Neater Fashion. But Anthony was not destined for a career in the *schmatter* trade, and his father enrolled him at the prestigious Sydney Grammar. One of the city's best, the boys' school sits in a prime position, its sandstone facade looking over Hyde Park. Anthony then did an accounting and finance degree at the University of New South Wales, but spent only a month at accounting firm PwC before he entered the investment banking industry.

The first few months of his professional career were marked by tragedy. His father, Malcolm, passed away at the age of 51, when Anthony was just 23. Anthony had been close to his father, who was a mentor to him and instilled in him a strong work ethic. His mother, Anita, had taken over the family business when Malcolm had become too sick, and ran it after he passed away. Before and after Malcolm passed away, she was the rock of the family, supporting and encouraging Anthony and his sister.

At Hambros chartered accountants, Eisen worked on some nation-building deals. Sydney was in a state of giddiness since 4 am on the morning of 24 September 1993, when IOC chief Juan Antonio Samaranch uttered the word 'Syd-e-ney', awarding the city the right to host the 2000 Olympic Games. Eisen was among the young bankers advising Stadium Australia, the company that was to build and operate the main 115,000-seat stadium in the Western Suburbs.

Eisen was also part of the team advising Telstra, the government-owned telecommunications company that had partnered with News Corp to set up Foxtel, a pay-TV provider. At that time, in 1997, Telstra was earmarked to be privatised via an initial public offering (IPO). The deal, known as T1, would offer a third of the company to the public.

Prime Minister John Howard and his treasurer, Peter Costello, who'd been elected the previous year, had continued a trend of floating key government assets to cut public-sector debt in an attempt to restore Australia's sovereign credit rating. In 1991, the Commonwealth Bank had floated, followed by pharmaceutical Commonwealth Serum Laboratories (CSL) and Tabcorp in 1994.

The government had hired talented dealmaker John Wylie, of Credit Suisse First Boston, among others, to advise on the Telstra float. Eisen had been recruited by Credit Suisse in 1998 to bolster their team. To convince public officials they were worthy of hiring, the investment banks had made a habit of turning up in Canberra with a large posse of analysts in a demonstration of their manpower. Wylie had been involved in a range of privatisations, including a $665 million placement of Qantas shares to British Airways, and several poles and wires and coal station sales that netted billions of dollars for the Commonwealth and the states. In the process, he had earned his bank over $100 million in fees.

The Telstra float was tense because of the political sensitivities involved in selling off an operator of vital infrastructure. T1 was billed as 'the people's privatisation', and there was an imperative to assign the bulk of the shares domestically. But some banks fought to get large US and European clients allocations they wanted, and to price the shares attractively. Ultimately, finance minister John Fahey—who as New South Wales premier in 1993 had famously leapt into the air when Samaranch made his Olympics announcement—held his nerve and set the pricing at the expensive end of the range, raising $14 billion. The majority of the investors were ordinary Australians: some 1.8 million new investors were thus introduced to the share market.

In November 1998, as the excitement of T1 died down, Eisen was sent to New York by Credit Suisse. There he had a front-row seat as Wall Street fell in love with technology stocks, before the collapse left the finance industry decimated and the economy staring at a recession. Eisen was in New York during the 11 September 2001 terrorist attacks, and was ready to move back to Australia. He was headhunted by a small independent advisory firm called Caliburn Partnership.

Caliburn was a top-tier outfit, founded by a trio of investment banking stars in Simon Mordant, Ron Malek and Peter Hunt. Their pitch was to deliver trusted objective advice, and corral the conflicted investment banks into working for the client. The firm paved the way for other star bankers to go out on their own, as the model proved that companies were willing to pay tens of millions for unconflicted counsel.

In 2003, Caliburn's services were hired by one of the poster-child companies of the 1999 tech-stock bubble: Solution 6. Their mandate was to come up with a strategy to realise value in the beaten-up accounting software firm, which had been abandoned as the tech euphoria turned to disdain.

It had been quite a ride for Solution 6, a business software company that in March 2000 was on the verge of being taken over by another tech darling, Sausage Software, which would have valued the combined business at $4 billion. But the looming tech wreck had threatened the deal—and then some juicy revelations about Solution 6's visionary founder all but killed it. The 42-year-old Texan Chris Tyler had dazzled institutions with his vision for the business during his three years in charge. They had enthusiastically backed his $400 million acquisition spree of smaller companies that culminated in the Sausage Software offer. But an *Australian Financial Review* article by Nick Tabakoff uncovered the fact that the CEO had left a trail of corporate disaster in Canada, and had been given a ten-year suspended sentence for marijuana possession. After that he earned the nickname 'Two Bags Tyler', a reference to the two garbage bags of cannabis Dallas police had caught him holding.

Tyler soon vanished from the corporate scene, and the appropriately named former head of Star Casino Group Neil Gamble stepped in. Telstra, in its initial enthusiasm for new technology, owned 25 per cent of the shares of Solution 6, and planned to increase that to 40 per cent. But Telstra eventually unloaded half of its shares to another accounting software firm, Craig Winkler's Mind Your Own Business, or MYOB.

In March 2002, GPG snapped up around 19 per cent of the company's shares, while media tycoon Kerry Packer's Consolidated Press later acquired a 7 per cent holding. By 2004, in true GPG style, they were calling for a break-up of the company on the basis that the assets of the company were more valuable if they were spun on. Caliburn's job was to explore the options on behalf of the board, and Eisen was soon interacting frequently with Gary Weiss.

After nine months, Caliburn did its job. A long search for a buyer for Solution 6's enterprise software business yielded a result as Francisco Partners paid $34 million for the division. The main consumer unit merged with MYOB in a deal welcomed by the market, with both shares appreciating.

Eisen proved to be a well-presented, well-credentialed and intelligent investment banker. His skills were soon enlisted to help GPG make a play for insurance group Tower Limited. For two months he became a fixture at the firm as they tipped $90 million into Tower.

But shortly after GPG made its investment, Tower's accountants slashed the value of their assets, forcing the company into an emergency share issue to keep the bankers at bay.

Brierley thought the $90 million was dusted but Weiss convinced him that the group should support the share raising. Eisen was once again called in to help. As the work on the investment reached its culmination, Eisen was ready to move on. His wife, Samantha, was desperate to move back to Melbourne to be closer to her family, and he visited Gary Weiss in his office near Sydney Harbour to ask his advice on what roles might be available. Weiss had come to know Eisen well. He'd also known his late father, Malcolm, through Weiss's close friend, Dov Spiro. Spiro had married into the Brender family, one of the most successful of the Jewish rag-trader families. Malcolm had suppled dresses to the Brender's Katie's brand, which was later bought by Coles Myer. Eisen had sought Weiss's counsel about which advisory firm to approach. But Weiss had different plans, making Eisen an offer to join the 'dark side' of investment management. He felt his talents could go further as an investor of capital, rather than an adviser to others. Eisen accepted almost instantly—and then had to convince his wife that they should stay in Sydney.

• • •

For Eisen, the opportunity to join the famed and feared Guinness Peat, the most cunning investors in the country, was too good to turn down. There were no restrictions, no geographical hard lines or sector limitations. Weiss and Brierley instilled an entrepreneurial spirit in their employees to create value in a way that was ethical, even if GPG's approach put a few noses out of joint along the way.

Gary Weiss was widely respected as an astute corporate tactician, but also as a man of integrity who in every deal left something on the table. His most distinctive feature was his hair—an afro visible from some distance. He also played the guitar for the band Gary and the Asset Strippers.

Weiss was the child of Holocaust-survivor parents. His father, Ali, had been sent first to Auschwitz and then to Buchenwald. His mother, Lotti, had endured 38 months of unimaginable physical and emotional trauma at the concentration camps of Auschwitz and Theresienstadt, after she and her sisters were ordered from their home in Bratislava. Her bravery, ingenuity and endurance had helped her survive the worst of conditions and the worst of human cruelty.

After the war, Lotti and Ali met and married. They left Czecho-slovakia, with great difficulty, to start a new life in Wellington, New Zealand, where Ali's brother Leo had settled. Ali and Leo were taught to make covered buttons and started their own business supplying local rag traders. In New Zealand, Lotti raised two sons. Gary, the younger, trained as a corporate lawyer. Weiss climbed the ranks at Wellington law firm Scott Morrison Dunphy & Co and was made a partner. But he wanted to move his young family to Sydney, where he could give his children a Jewish education. His law firm's client was the auditor of Ron Brierley's investment company and he asked them to pass on his CV. Weiss figured that Brierley, who was now primarily based in Sydney, may need an in-house lawyer.

That impressive CV, which included a doctorate in law from Cornell University, had led Brierley to expect a far more conservative individual to walk through his door.

'When I first saw him, I couldn't reconcile it with the mental picture I had from these excellent references,' Brierley told *The Age*.[2]

Brierley had a lot in common with Weiss. Both had lived in the Wellington suburb of Wadestown and attended the same high school, Wellington College. In Sydney they were both outsiders with points to prove and so they agreed to work together. In 1984, Gary Weiss showed up for his first day of work at Industrial Equity Limited. The decision to abandon a career in law horrified his former senior partner, Sir Michael Hardie Boys, who thought he was destined for a career on the bench. Sir Michael was a judge of the High Court of New Zealand and became the governor-general of New Zealand.

Brierley had the demeanour of an old man even when he was young. But he hardly ever wore suits, opting for polo shirts, shorts, white socks and running shoes. In school he'd collected stamps, but not for the love of them. He preferred buying cheap bags of old stamps in the hope of unearthing one that was worth ten times the lot rather than paying top dollar for a rare collector's item. He'd also buy as many of a single stamp as he could to corner the market.

Brierley started a share-market tip sheet and began investing in the share market when he was still a teenager, and in 1961, while still in his twenties, he registered his own investment company. He soon discovered the value of agitating boards to realise value by breaking up their companies. By the 1970s, he'd matured from a pesky corporate gadfly to a feared asset stripper and corporate raider, wrote Yvonne van Dongen in a May 2011 feature on Brierley. 'In the "greed is good" 1980s, he was recast more favourably as an entrepreneur, made a knight of the realm and chairman of New Zealand's largest bank, Bank of New Zealand,' van Dongen noted.[3]

Brierley Investments had become the largest company in New Zealand, with investments in 300 companies including Galeries Lafayette in Paris and Air New Zealand. His Australian-listed investment firm Industrial Equity Limited (IEL) was the third-largest company on that exchange. For a fleeting moment it was the market's largest company, surpassing the country's big banks and miners.

The corporate stunts of Weiss and Brierley have lived long in the memory. In 1984, Weiss identified a loophole in the corporate constitution of the Australian Gas Light Company, or AGL: it wasn't actually created as a company but established by an act of parliament. This meant the requirements to disclose substantial holdings didn't apply. Over several months, Weiss and Brierley set up proxy companies—the Gary Sobers Indoor Cricket Club, the Countess of Naples and the Cessnock Flying School—and snapped up nearly 40 per cent of AGL. On Christmas Eve, Brierley's IEL revealed the stake to a stunned AGL board of directors.

'These fuckwits at AGL have made us look stupid,' the Minister of Energy fumed to a 33-year-old Weiss, who was hauled in for an emergency meeting in January 1985.

In 1986, Weiss and Brierley managed to snap up 20 per cent in the struggling grocer Woolworths and a further 20 per cent through the acquisition of a company in New Zealand that owned a stake.

Weiss's legal knowledge could also be weaponised to humiliate and frustrate his adversaries. IEL had teamed up with Kerry Packer and had been trying to buy Bell Resources, a company controlled by rival Robert Holmes à Court. When Holmes à Court sold his stake to another raider, Alan Bond, he pushed back the annual general meeting in Perth from Monday afternoon to Tuesday morning. But Weiss's legal assessment was that the manner in which the meeting items were changed meant that the notice given was insufficient. He showed up to the empty ballroom at the Parmelia Hilton in Perth on the Monday afternoon. He went through the motions, adjourned to the bar and sent the company the tab. A West Australian court ruled that Weiss's meeting had been the valid one. The battle was a morale booster, as Brierley's consortium had sold their shares in Bell to Alan Bond for a profit.

The ingenious raids on Woolworths and AGL had done more to showcase Weiss and Brierley's intelligence than to create meaningful wealth for investors. IEL itself was in strife as a result of the 1987 crash. Brierley had been warning of a major correction, and the group was loaded with the debt it had needed to make major acquisitions such as Woolworths. 'You can't do that; you would be selling the lifeboats,' Brierley lamented when his management team urged him to sell some of the stakes he'd built to pare back IEL's debt.

As Brierley and Weiss battled to contain the fallout, a civil war within the firm had broken out between the management team and the investment team. The latter—Brierley, Weiss, Graeme Cureton, Blake Nixon and Peter Pedley—all walked. But within a couple of years the band was back together. Weiss reunited with Brierley and gained control of the London-listed Guinness Peat Group.

Brierley snapped up the merchant bank from Alan Hawkins, whose Equiticorp business empire had crumbled. But he had to fight off publishing tycoon Robert Maxwell in a tense corporate battle.

Guinness Peat Group had an interesting history. It had made the bold decision to invest in a passenger jet financing business formed by Tony Ryan, a manager at Irish carrier Aer Lingus. Within 15 years of its founding, Ryan had built Guinness Peat Aviation into one of Ireland's most successful companies as it helped to finance the national carriers of poor nations and expand the fleets of wealthier ones. GPA also lay the foundations for Ireland's tax-friendly framework. After Guinness Peat Aviation collapsed, Ryan later formed the budget airline Ryan Air.

The new owners of Guinness Peat were determined not to repeat the mistakes of the past.

'After some near-death experiences with huge takeovers in the 1980s, the former IEL boys are seeking a profitable but less dangerous life,' wrote *AFR*'s Trevor Sykes. 'They're also enjoying too good a life to ruin it by sinking the company. They might make larger takeovers than they have to date, but it would be foreign to their whole carefully developed policy to bet the whole company on a single investment.'[4]

Weiss, Brierley and their small but highly skilled band of analysts invested cautiously, applying their deep-value approach of buying distressed assets in easy-to-understand old-economy companies. They were still able to sniff out loopholes and exploit them to embarrass large corporations. In May 1995, the target was oil and gas company Ampolex, which had incorrectly drafted the conversion terms of its listed bond issue. Weiss had been made aware that the trust deed, the legal document governing the securities, prescribed far more generous terms than had been communicated to the market by a factor of six. Brierley rang the appropriately named CEO Peter Power who didn't take his call. Later when GPG requested conversion on their terms, all hell broke loose. As a dispute lingered, GPG cut a deal with Mobil, who had launched a takeover for Ampolex.

Brierley's distrust of accountants and particularly actuaries meant they could identify hidden value in the insurance industry.

One of the firm's bigger investments was Tower, which linked back to one of New Zealand's oldest life insurance companies. GPG had made about $100 million of paper gains from the Tower investment as it spun off its financial planning trustee business to create Australian Wealth Management (which later became IOOF).

But Guinness Peat wasn't averse to dabbling in new-age technology stocks if there was an angle suggesting deep value. They had an investment in Solution 6. The younger analysts in the team regarded accounting software firm MYOB as undervalued even though Brierley did not.

GPG had also recruited the former head of Sausage Software, Wayne Bos, to run the remnants of Mid-East Minerals, a defunct mining company that had no operations but a pile of cash in the bank. The listed company was renamed Tomorrow Ltd, and given a mandate to buy tech stocks. The Mid-East Minerals acquisition from Alan Bond's Dallhold Investments also brought Mike Jefferies, a skilled accountant, into the GPG tent. As GPG encircled the group, Jefferies shrewdly had a clause inserted into his contract that he was entitled to a payout if Mid-East was moved within a certain distance from the Perth General Post Office. But once Weiss had finished bartering with Alan Bond over his final rights—including a price for his famous white Land Rover—Weiss told Jefferies he wanted to keep him on. Jefferies would be posted on the western front to keep an eye out for opportunities.

Jefferies had actually been against hiring Eisen, even though he was an admirer. Eisen's talents, he felt, would be too limited by GPG's approach of targeting distressed or unloved companies and pulling them apart.

But Eisen fitted right in. He worked on some interesting investments. He tried to convince the GPG elders that new-economy companies such as MYOB were undervalued. Eisen also explored putting a consortium together to buy record label EMI. But enthusiasm for the transaction petered out.

'The market has been hypnotised by the conversion of Brierley, a professed old-economy investor, into a high-tech speculator,' wrote Trevor Sykes, a GPG shareholder, in *The Australian Financial Review* in 2000.[5]

There was no stock more 'old-world economy' than thread-maker Coats. The company had been in existence since 1795 and business had boomed after 1806 when the Napoleonic Wars cut silk supplies to the British Empire. In 1879, a Coats thread was used in Thomas Edison's electric lamp experiments. Coats had been the second-largest company in the world in 1900, and was a founding member of London's FTSE 30 index of industrial companies in 1930. Decades later it still dominated the textile industry. Coats made 350 million balls of knitting yarn a year, while its threads held together 10 billion garments.

GPG had been building a stake in London-listed Coats since 2000. The investment had been spotted by London director Blake Nixon, and by 2002 GPG owned almost a quarter of the company. Westfield founder Frank Lowy's private investment firm, Lowy Family Group, had also accumulated stock as the wealthy South African retailing Lewis family cut their stake. Weiss was close to Lowy, and was appointed to the board of Westfield that year.

In April 2004, GPG made its play for Coats. It offered to buy out the Lowys and the Rothschilds, who had formed a consortium with GPG to acquire Coats, in addition to minority shareholders. Once the deal was consummated, a total of £218 million had been invested in the company. The move didn't seem all that risky to Weiss, given the company's two-and-half-century existence, its 25 per cent market share and the fact that human fashion trends were unlikely to regress all the way back to the Neanderthal age.

'Unless nudity is embraced in a very large way globally, the clothing industry—or the textile industry more generally—will continue to grow,' he said in the 2005 edition of *Masters of the Market*. 'The simple logic of the acquisition is that thread holds the world together. It is essential in everything from car seats to clothing to teabags to tampons. Coats is the world leader in the global apparel market (22 per cent to 25 per cent) and spins enough thread every four hours to reach the moon and back.'[6]

The logic to GPG's turnaround plan for Coats was simple: relocate its manufacturing from high-cost countries such as Britain to lower-cost regions. But the execution was wickedly hard, given the company had tens of thousands of staff in 67 countries. 'Restructurings are easy to do from an academic standpoint—that's probably an absolutely trite observation—but far less easy to implement in a practical way,' Weiss said in the same *Masters of the Market* interview.

So GPG had its hands full with Coats, but some of its other investments had soured. In 2005, metal group Capral had halved in value, while Greens Foods fell by a third as it missed its profit targets twice. Eyebrows were also raised about Guinness Peat's tame treatment of Premier Investments, the investment company run by retailer Solomon Lew that had a 5.7 per cent stake in Coles Myer, which operated grocery and department chains.

'Brierley and the GPG of old would have pounced on Premier and its lazy balance sheet years ago, slit its corporate throat and handed out the assets to shareholders to turn a quick profit,' wrote the *AFR*'s Eli Greenblatt. 'Far from attacking the prey, though, Brierley and Weiss sit on the Premier board and show no sign of winding it up.'

'Certainly the [GPG] board believes it's been a very rewarding vehicle for shareholders and anticipate it being so for some time yet,' Weiss told Greenblatt.

'He can't see the incompatibility between this attitude and GPG's more usual approach,' Greenblatt observed.[7]

For GPG, which had tended to invest in companies run by others, it had crossed its own Rubicon by taking full operational control of Coats. But there were signs their bold plan was working. By mid-2007, the business was humming. Coats' profit margins—earnings before interest and tax—had tripled from 4 per cent to 12 per cent.

Ron Brierley's past missteps had led him to the view that investment companies have a finite life and so he instructed the team to explore options to divest assets. Coats was in a position where it could be sold to another industry player or relisted. One day in September 2007, Goldman Sachs bankers were called in to begin the sale process. But that night, Coats' chief executive Mike Smithyman called Weiss with some unwelcome news.

Coats stood accused by the European Union of conspiring to corner the needled and haberdashery market in the late 1990s. The fine was €140 million, and even if it was to appeal the decision it would be forced to outlay tens of millions of Euros. There could be no sale until the situation was resolved.

The prospects dimmed further as the 2008 financial crisis ravaged global markets. GPG's shares fell sharply, and continued to trade below the $1 billion value of its portfolio of assets.

Coats soon had another problem. The actuaries at the British pension regulator had determined that there was a shortfall at the three pension funds tied to Coats and had dispatched a warning notice. GPG had told the regulator it would kick in an extra £124 million to satisfy them that they could make good on their pension obligations.

But that wasn't nearly enough to appease the regulator, which battled it out with GPG. The process added to Brierley's already strong disdain for actuaries.

Coats wasn't the only British company with pension issues. Long-established corporations had set up pension schemes to attract staff during the boom years of the 1950s, promising them an income in their retirement. But the schemes had taken on a life of their own and now presented large risks to the core operations of large companies. The regulatory pendulum had swung from favouring corporations that could raid these pension plans at will, to favouring workers and the sanctity of the obligations made to them. In London people joked that British Airways was 'a gigantic pension fund with an airline attached to it'. But with Coats there was nothing for GPG to laugh about. The additional capital call would drain money out of the company and all but obliterate GPG's chances of turning the business around.

The global financial crisis led Guinness Peat to sell out of some of its technology investments. In April 2008, GPG punished MYOB founder and chief executive Craig Winkler for rejecting a $735 million bid from private-equity firm Archer. GPG used its 15 per cent stake to block a lucrative options package. Archer returned in October, after the markets had cratered following the collapse of Lehman Brothers, with a vastly lower bid of $440 million. The hurt of being forced to agree to sell the highly successful company he'd spent years building at a distressed price to private-equity buyers was too much for Winkler to bare. By then Winkler had already stepped down as CEO. But in February 2009 he left the company altogether, and in April 2009 he ploughed $14.7 million into a rival accounting software start-up called Xero, giving him a 24 per cent stake.

For Brierley and Weiss, the crash of 1987 seemed to be repeating. The escalating Coats problem and other misfiring investments had made GPG vulnerable, and there was growing tension in the boardroom over how to deal with it, and what to communicate.

GPG's New Zealand–based institutional investors AMP Capital and Milford, backed by Investors Mutual, began pushing for the board to take action as the share price fell substantially below the $1 billion value of GPG's portfolio of assets. An already volatile situation intensified when disagreements at the GPG board level emerged. Veteran of the New Zealand operations Tony Gibbs had initially backed a planned demerger in which the GPG empire would be carved up by region. That plan would involve Gibbs running the New Zealand operations. Weiss would oversee the Australian operations before handing over the chief executive role to Anthony Eisen who had proved himself capable of taking command.

But then Gibbs publicly denounced the plan. In a defiant statement to the New Zealand stock exchange, he called for cash to be returned, putting him in direct confrontation with Weiss and other directors.

In 2010, Brierley flew to Auckland to meet the institutional investors face to face. To appease the institutions, he agreed to allow them to appoint more independent directors to the GPG board—including three New Zealanders, Mike Allen, Rob Campbell and Gavin Walker, and an Australian, Mark Johnson.

But that was the beginning of the end. In February 2011, chairman Rob Campbell announced that the board had determined that GPG should sell all its assets to return value to the company's shareholders. The only asset that would not be sold would be Coats, which would remain the sole asset of GPG, and which would rename itself such.

'I think this is a good case where the board and management of the company have listened to their shareholders and responded accordingly,' Guy Elliffe, head of equities at AMP Capital Investors in Wellington, told Tony Boyd of the *AFR* on 12 February 2011.[8]

Brierley was furious. He described the sales as self-destruction and madness. 'That instantly put GPG into the lame-duck basket,' he said. 'As soon as the announcement came out, the switchboard here was jammed with bargain hunters.'[9]

Gary Weiss left soon after the announcement, as did Mark Johnson. For Anthony Eisen, his path to the top lay in ruin. GPG's board had become dysfunctional while the assets they had accumulated over the years were now on the block. His short-term future was troublesome, his long-term plans uncertain. The GPG empire had been toppled by the short-termism Brierley had railed against. Eisen, too, did not see the logic in flogging its assets. GPG had no debt, so there had been no financial pressure. But now there was no choice. The shareholders had spoken. Unwinding all the investments that GPG had made over the years was a hollow, unrewarding experience. But for Eisen it was a big responsibility that armed him with valuable skills. Along with Brierley and Jason Ters, he would slowly liquidate GPG's 55 investments: they ranged from a 250-year-old business worth $500 million to a small punt-on-a-peanut company.

In 2012, GPG accepted an offer of $3.2 million for its minority stakes in four promising egg, honey, milk and peanut companies. Eisen had also found a consortium of buyers to take the 56 per cent it owned in a payments company called TAFMO off its hands for $5.6 million, after a large bidder walked away. But the deal hit a few snags as the Australian Takeovers Panel intervened to block one of the bidders.

About halfway through the process, in June 2012, Eisen found himself up against his mentor. Weiss had teamed up with a private-equity firm, Crescent Capital, to bid for a GPG asset, financial services company ClearView. Weiss had known ClearView well and the consulting actuary he hired convinced him it was of value. The company's CEO, Simon Swanson, had also become frustrated with the prolonged uncertainty as its main investor plotted an exit.

The ClearView business was one of the larger assets in the portfolio, but the Crescent proposal seemed like a lowball bid, valuing the firm at $220 million. Eisen was forced to publicly dismiss the hostile advance of his mentor. 'It doesn't represent fair value at all for ClearView shares,' he told the media. 'The company has got substantial value in its book of life insurance and wealth management. The price is wholly inadequate.'[10]

In August 2012, the consortium sweetened the offer in a bid valuing the business at $262 million. That was still well below audit firm KPMG's assessment, which meant the board couldn't recommend the offer. But Eisen and GPG accepted.

On 1 October 2013, the long and arduous process was complete. GPG hired New Zealand stockbroker FirstNZ Capital to find buyers for its one-third shareholding in Tower Insurance. Harbour Asset and AMP Capital, the GPG institutional investor that led the calls for the GPG liquidation, were the buyers. GPG netted $106 million. From February 2011, the asset sales had raised £698 million, or $1.4 billion, above the £677 million accounting-book value of GPG when chairman Rob Campbell had announced the restructure. But there was a tinge of regret that some substantial sums had been left on the table.

In a matter of months, the discarded companies began finding their way back to the marketplace. Capilano Honey floated on the ASX at a valuation of $20 million. Tasmanian Pure Foods was rebranded to Bellamy's, and also listed with a $125 million valuation. Touchcorp's new shareholders, which included GPG alumni, also plotted a quick sale at ten times the price they'd paid for the stake. The bargain hunters had been successful.

As far as Eisen was concerned, his job was done. He'd been given a task by the board, on behalf of shareholders, to turn the investments into cash. The asset sales had realised more than their accounting values. Eisen had spent eight years working alongside the most brilliant and eccentric corporate minds in Australia. He'd bought businesses and sold more. He'd been party to board blow-ups, to systemic financial crises, to existential threats. The period had been gruelling and he had little to show for it, other than an intense education of the inner workings of corporate Australia and an expanded network. He was the last man standing. But for GPG, the lights were out.

# 3

# LAY-BY

EVERY YEAR ON the second weekend of August, 80,000 runners make their way along New South Head Road through Rose Bay. The 14-kilometre route of the City2Surf then takes them up 'Heartbreak Hill', towards the end of the peninsula, before turning towards Bondi Beach. The runners pass the Rose Bay Marina and then several roads on their right. These streets run perpendicular to the harbour promenade, and converge 700 metres up Bellevue Hill. And that is where Anthony Eisen and Nick Molnar met in 2010.

Eisen, at the time, was in the eye of the storm at Guinness Peat. He was managing its investments, which were spread across the globe, and was keeping odd hours. In the dead of night he noticed the light on in the large window in a house across the street. Then in the morning he noticed a boy in his late teens loading parcels into a car. Eisen started to think the neighbours might be drug dealers— they were definitely dealing in something. Some mornings he'd inadvertently tailed the car into which the parcels had been loaded as it made its way to the post office at Bellevue Hill.

One day Eisen met the father of the house, Ron Molnar, as both took out their bins for the weekly pick-up. The two would chat as

Ron took his labrador out for a walk while Eisen was tinkering with his boat in the driveway. Eisen's curiosity soon got the better of him and he asked what sort of operation Molnar's son was running. Ron told Anthony that Nick, his digital native son, had mastered the art of selling stuff on eBay, and was applying his talents to the 30-year-old family jewellery business.

In time, Anthony introduced himself to Nick and they got on well. The common interest was business, and Eisen would ask him how sales were tracking. Eisen was impressed enough to give the young Molnar an internship at the shrinking operation he was managing at Guinness Peat.

Molnar showed up for work at the Gateway Building, the glass skyscraper at Circular Quay directly in between the harbour city's world-famous landmarks, the Sydney Harbour Bridge and the Opera House. Molnar was on his L-plates: Eisen would ask him to build him a financial model, but would then have to redo it. He'd ask Molnar to write a reference letter—but would rewrite it. Molnar had found a role model. 'This is a person I want to become,' he thought to himself as he observed the highly articulate Eisen in action.[1]

Eisen had patience, though, and enough faith in Molnar's talents to vouch for the young man as he sought a career in investment banking. Molnar didn't make the cut at Lazard, where Eisen's old boss, John Wylie, worked after the US investment bank bought out the boutique firm he founded with Mark Carnegie. Wylie had sent Molnar to see Carnegie, who had held a position for him for a year on the proviso he build his confidence as an entrepreneur and build up his online jewellery business.

Carnegie's pep talk had inspired Molnar. That was the motivation for his cheeky but successful attempt to bring Ice Online to Australia. The financier had also persuaded Molnar to shift from selling high-end jewellery to cheaper mass-market products, along the lines of the Ice Online model. Molnar had studied Sam

Gniwisch's strategy after that meeting in Las Vegas. Ice in the United States was selling everyday jewellery that retailed for between $50 and $500. As a result of these tips, sales at Ice Online Australia had increased from $2000 a day to $10,000 a day.

In May 2012, Molnar began work at Carnegie's venture fund, where he spent the following twelve months. By night he was still trying to figure out ways to boost sales, as his younger brother, Simon, and his mother, Michele, spent more time on the Ice Online operation.

'We realised buying jewellery online was not like buying a dress,' Michele Molnar told *The Sydney Morning Herald*. 'People were getting to the checkout and not confident to complete the transaction. We used to sit around the dinner table and work out how to make the transaction easy.'[2]

Molnar thought some form of credit might be the answer. The Ice parent company had an instalment product that accounted for 50 per cent of sales. Surely a similar offering in Australia would boost sales? In Europe, too, a 'try before you buy' service had been established by Swedish company Klarna, which allowed customers to receive a product and try it out before the first payment was due in 30 days. But Molnar was not aware of anyone offering this sort of service in Australia.

Carnegie had stirred Molnar's entrepreneurial spirit—but perhaps a little too much. He was increasingly spending his time on coming up with ideas to enhance his family's online jewellery business.

Looking at data from Ice Online, Molnar was puzzled by low conversion rates: only one out of every 100 customers that came to the website would actually make a purchase. He knew instinctively that members of the millennial generation—those born between 1981 and 1996—were not keen on using credit cards: growing up in the shadows of the global financial crisis, they had witnessed how damaging excessive debt could be. The Reserve Bank of Australia had found in 2013 that people under the age of 30 were making

80 per cent of card payments with a debit card, compared to 50 per cent in all other age groups. But without a credit card, buying online could be difficult, as many customers weren't keen on paying for something in full before it had been received.

During their regular catch-ups, Molnar would pitch ideas to Eisen. A man of structure, Eisen asked Molnar to formally write up business plans for his bright ideas. The first involved renting airspace in shopping centre car parks to retailers, to make announcements in the same way a radio signal can be interrupted by toll-road operators to transmit an important safety message. Eisen didn't think much of that idea. The second was the 'try before you buy' model, which he was prepared to consider.

Eisen and Molnar talked about lay-by, which allowed something to be bought without a credit card using instalment payments. But the technique required all payments to be made *before* the item was taken home. Eisen recalled its popularity before the arrival of credit cards, and the two discussed its ongoing use. In 2012, almost 10 per cent of Australians had bought something on lay-by but the product appealed to an older demographic. Lay-by was almost unheard of by Molnar's generation. It typically required a 10 to 20 per cent upfront deposit and a service fee of perhaps $5 or $10, and then customers would pay the remainder over several weeks or even months. But if they stopped making payments, they'd often lose the deposit.

The conversations with Eisen piqued Molnar's interest. Lay-by wasn't appealing to the new generation because it didn't satisfy a desire for instant gratification. The internet offered immediacy. Millennials wouldn't want to wait until they'd made all their payments to get their goods. So if they were offered an option to get the product right away and to repay for it in instalments, without having to take out an expensive credit card or even be subjected to formal credit assessments, this might help retailers sell more goods.

• • •

While Nick may not have appreciated it at the time, the use of credit had ebbed and flowed over the last two centuries. At various points in history, the pendulum had swung from customers not having access to funds to buy the goods they wanted or needed, to merchants not generating the sales they needed from their customers. At certain times their mutual desires for credit had converged, fostering a boom in consumption. But the balance was a delicate one. Too little credit meant shoppers couldn't get what they needed or desired. Too much credit overwhelmed consumers and left them heavily indebted and in hardship.

In 1807, a furniture store in New York named Cowperthwaithe & Sons was the first to allow its customers to pay in instalments. The benefit for the store was that it could repossess the item if payments were missed. But the true pioneer of instalment payments was Isaac Singer, the proprietor of Singer sewing machines. He persuaded women that they would quickly pay off their sewing machine either by sewing for profit or through savings as they made clothing for their families.

'Singer's machines were neither the best nor the cheapest products on the market. But the firm's innovative credit plan, inspired by piano showrooms near company headquarters, tripled sales in just one year,' Harvard Business School historians wrote. 'By the 1890s, Singer Sewing Machine agents were notorious for their hard-sell "dollar down, dollar a week" tactics. The company's aggressive salespeople and easy payments made Singer one of the first multinational corporations.'[3]

Around the turn of the century, Australian merchants began offering their wealthy customers credit. In fact, it was the customers who demanded it, as they didn't want to carry large wads of cash into town, nor did they trust their servants, who sometimes did their shopping. But credit wasn't fashionable for the masses. There was a sense of frugality and value among those who had set up their own homes—three good meals and a couple of well-made suits were adequate reward for an honest worker's toil. They shopped for value, not luxury. And with World War I raging in Europe, it was not a time for extravagance.

The rise of chain stores—which mass-produced standard items and cut out the frills of advertising, marketing and home delivery—accelerated a trend away from credit. It also prompted more merchants to come up with new ways to compete. They focused on high-end customers, and the extension of credit was a bonus.

That changed with the arrival in Sydney of Yorkshireman William Buckingham. Around the 1920s, he introduced a form of financing that had been used in the north of England called cash orders, fuelling a surge in sales for his company, Buckingham Ltd, which he floated on the Sydney exchange. Cash orders were similar to the system of 'check trading' first used in England in the 1890s.

Buckingham's main department store was situated on the corner of Riley and Oxford streets, just beyond the Sydney CBD towards the Eastern Suburbs, but his salesmen also took merchandise to the terrace houses in Surry Hills and Redfern. They collected orders and later returned to collect instalment payments. The easy credit system encouraged more spending among the working classes, who weren't used to shopping for anything other than necessities. The retailer paid the sale price of the goods directly to the manufacturer, and then allowed the customer to pay for it in instalments, plus pre-agreed interest. The manufacturer, meanwhile, paid the retailer a commission based on the sale price.

The first Sydney retailer to adopt cash orders with gusto was RH Gordon & Co, a home furnishings business that had set up at the southern end of George Street, among a group of furniture retailers that spread across to Pitt Street. Its 'easy payment plan' allowed weekly payments on orders from £5 to £150. By the mid-1920s, cash orders proliferated as other retailers adopted the model. A finance company called Cash Orders Amalgamated was established, and allowed a customer to buy goods up to a certain value at an accredited store. The financier paid the store and then collected the amounts, plus interest, from the customer via instalments.

The Australian Guarantee Company was also on the scene, having been formed in 1921 to finance the purchase of small items for the house, before widening its remit to fund loans for the emerging automotive industry under a partnership with the Ford Motor Company. Renamed the Australian Guarantee Corporation in 1925, it listed on the stock exchange in 1928 and was funded by issuing debentures to the early investing public. It would take an infamous place in the history of Australian credit, especially after the Bank of New South Wales first invested in the company in the 1950s.

The Great Depression of 1929 turned an era of excess back to one of frugality, and it became tougher to get credit as lending standards tightened. In response, the large department stores came up with a service called 'lay-by', in order to help customers keep shopping through the downturn. Lay-by allowed customers to secure a purchase and pay for it through instalments; once the item was paid off, the purchaser could take it home.

On 10 October 1930, department store Anthony Hordern & Sons advertised a payment arrangement called D-P-S (standing for Deposit Purchase System), which encouraged customers to 'leave a deposit, pay as it suits you'. The product did not charge interest. Within the week, Hordern ran a poster campaign for its customers to 'avail yourself of our lay-by service', and in 1932 another large chain, Farmers, embraced the lay-by model to encourage its shoppers to spend: 'Begin tomorrow and lay away a gift each day until your list is completed. Farmers grant you ample time in which to pay the balance without any hardship on your purse.'

The lay-by method proved an enduring and very Australian way for spendthrift households to buy things while avoiding the pitfalls of interest payments.

By the 1950s, the big department stores—Grace Bros and David Jones in Sydney, and Myer in Melbourne—operated credit schemes for valued shoppers. Those who qualified were given metallic charge plates embossed with their names and addresses, that were laid into an imprinter to produce a charge slip—the earliest form of the credit card. But the enthusiasm of retailers to promote credit as a means of driving sales was waning by the 1960s. 'Retailers began to perceive that credit did not really gain them much even in goodwill or customer loyalty and that their credit schemes were expensive to maintain and administer,' wrote Beverley Kingston in her 1994 history of shopping in Australia, *Basket, Bag and Trolley*.[4]

But credit at this time was even less appealing to customers, who risked being trapped in high-interest loans. Credit managers assumed the role of social workers, helping indebted shoppers through personal and financial crises, which led to a renaissance of the lay-by method. 'It had become clear that the retailers more than consumers needed a system of widespread easily available credit where the risks were distributed elsewhere than into their individual pricing policies,' wrote Kingston.

In the early 1960s, another trend arrived in Australia from overseas: the consumer protection group. The Australian Consumers' Association had been formed to counter the outlandish advertising that had been deployed to flog aspirins and cigarettes, and to call out the deceptive sizes and prices of toothpaste and soap powder. The ACA had signed up tens of thousands of members—mainly house-wives, scientists, lawyers and other middle-class professionals. Its magazine, *Choice*, helped readers buy a car, choose children's shoes, make coffee, assess a diet and care for woollen fabrics. Over time, consumer groups such as the ACA helped establish codes for car sales, credit and door-to-door selling. But the wheels of commerce made it hard for them to keep pace.

'It is one of the surest indications of human ingenuity that ways are constantly being found to circumvent the most sophisti-cated legislation protecting consumers,' wrote Kingston. 'It is not possible for the law to keep abreast of the initiatives of designers, manufacturers and retailers. Human memory and experience in these matters is never long and the rate of change in modern society makes it easy to fool some of the people most of the time.'[5]

Credit made a storming comeback in the mid-1970s with the introduction of the Bankcard scheme, which amalgamated the various instore credit offerings under one banner. There was money to be made for financiers. The major Australian banks had formed an alliance to introduce the Bankcard in 1974, sixteen years after the first credit cards had been launched in the US market. The credit card was created by Bank of America in 1958, which sent out the BankAmericard in the mail to residents of Fresno, California, kicking off a consumer finance revolution aimed at the middle class that would catapult spending on consumer goods.

Bankcard encouraged more households to run up debts. The result was a large drop-off in the use of lay-by, from 6 per cent of sales to just 1 per cent. The credit card provided the convenience of taking the goods home right away—although for customers who didn't pay the sale price back at the end of the interest-free period, which could run from 28 to 55 days, there was a sting of around 20 per cent per annum interest.

By the 1990s, the introduction of the EFTPOS direct-debit system made credit cards attractive again, but more as a convenience than a form of financing—it was easier to make large purchases without lugging around large wads of cash. The global card schemes Visa and Mastercard had been issuing credit cards for the major banks since the mid-1980s, and these had the added convenience of allowing their holders to shop and withdraw cash overseas.

In the United States, lay-by existed under another name: 'layaway'. In the age of credit cards, the concept made little sense, given retailers charged an administration fee. The shopper might be better off paying the interest charged on the credit card, or saving up the money themselves before purchasing the goods.

But as *The New Yorker* columnist James Surowiecki explained, layaway was not a form of payment but a 'commitment device'. It was 'a way to get yourself to do something that you want to do but know you'll have a hard time doing if left purely to your own devices'— and this explained why it was back in vogue in 2012. 'What the revival of layaway makes clear is that, while many shoppers are prone to spend what they don't have on what they shouldn't buy, they can also be sophisticated about their weakness, and savvy about finding ways to control it,' wrote Surowiecki.[6]

When the birth of the internet gave rise to ecommerce, retailers were soon trying to come up with ways to digitise lay-by. The first company in Australia to both digitise the lay-by product and create a merchant-funded instalment plan that was interest-free for the customer was Transax, the United Kingdom's largest cheque-guarantee company, which in 1996 was acquired by US credit data giant Equifax. Transax's cheque-warranty system allowed merchants to accept a cheque after obtaining a 'guarantee code' by calling in the details of the cheque via the phone to Transax. Transax did not have access to customer bank account information, but used its own risk assessment model to approve cheques up to $10,000, usually in 60 seconds.

In its Australian operations, Transax saw that the writing was on the wall for cheques, and started to look for new ways to deploy its customer insights and risk systems for merchants. This led it to discussions with merchants about digitising lay-by in the late 1990s.

DEKA, a general merchandise retailer in New Zealand that had been taken over by the Farmers Trading Company in the early 1990s, was an existing Transax customer and became the first to automate its lay-by service in the year 2000. Lay-by was costing it a lot, both in storage and in staff time, as customers came into stores and paid off bits and bobs. At first, the new system was merely a direct debit transfer service. The merchant still waited until all four repayments were made before releasing the goods. It helped with payment logistics, and from Equifax's perspective there was no risk. Merchants weren't charged for the product, which was being used to retain the business of those who used cheques, even if this was a diminishing segment. To Transax's surprise, however, there was latent customer demand, as 3000 retailers applied for the service.

The corporate entity morphed, as Equifax's US parent split into two companies, Certegy and Equifax Ezi-Pay Australia. Certegy's Australian unit came up with a loan agreement where it used funding to develop a 'take-home lay-by payment plan'. The merchant was paid upfront for the good and paid Certegy up to 6 per cent of the sale price. The term for the customer to pay the instalments ranged from three to eighteen months, with amounts of up to $3000.

The buy now, pay later industry—if we can define it as merchant-funded, short-term credit for the customer without interest—was thus born at Certegy. The first retailer to use the product was Freedom Furniture, in late 2003. Freedom wanted to release the goods sold on lay-by because its high warehouse costs made it uneconomical for it to hold items while customers paid them off. So Certegy did a deal: it would pay Freedom for the goods there and then—allowing the customer to take them home—if Freedom covered the cost of the funds. It started charging merchants 5 to 6 per cent of the cost of the goods, to cover the credit risk and a business margin it could pay back to the US office that provided the funding lines.

The next shift for Certegy was into jewellery. One of the pioneers was a Jewish immigrant from Egypt, Albert Bensimon, who ran Shiels Jewellers in Adelaide. Bensimon was highly respected as a retailer, and once he had signed on, Rob May, the head of sales and marketing at Certegy, was able to convince national jewellery retailers Michael Hill and Prouds to get on board as well.

'Getting rid of lay-by was a win for them,' May said, 'as they didn't need stock sitting in safes for six or eight weeks, and customers coming in hassling staff making small payments, and the back-end accounting and insurance—it is worth giving up 6 per cent of the margin. People don't realise how much lay-by was costing the retailers. Not only did they manually have to accept the instalments coming in, they had to hold on to the stock.'

And not all stock was picked up. Many toy stores ran lay-by sales in September, to allow parents to spread the cost of their Christmas purchases into the holiday season, but sometimes the goods were never collected. The New Year sales were instituted to clear unclaimed lay-by stock.

Retailers immediately recognised, too, that they could now upsell to customers. They considered this a win-win situation: there were no imposing credit checks, and customers took home a better-quality product, which would also deliver a higher margin for the retailer. A $100 vacuum might have a $50 margin, but if a customer could walk away with a higher-quality $500 machine, the merchant might pocket $300—more than enough to cover the cost of the service.

Between 2005 and 2007, around 4500 Australian merchants signed up to the Certegy service, which was available at over 10,000 checkouts. As a customer-acquisition tool, the model was rapid. Within just a few years, all the major jewellers and furniture stores in Australia were on board. Certegy—whose parent company had, by this time, been acquired by Fidelity Information Services—then expanded into fashion, homewares, auto goods, hardware, roofing and home repairs. Dentists were keen on paying the margin to allow customers to come into the chair for costly procedures and pay it back over a year as a cashflow-management tool.

What's more, the product had a positive impact on sales. Godfreys, the large vacuum cleaner retailer, had approached Certegy when the average sale of a machine was $150. This went up to $380 once Certegy was added, as the product encouraged customers to buy more expensive machines, and the service represented around 30 per cent of all transactions. When Godfreys was purchased by a private-equity consortium in 2006, they looked to cut costs and, regarding the Certegy payment as a financing cost, slashed it. Now Godfreys started losing the higher-margin sales.

From the get-go, there were concerns among consumer groups about facilitating credit and encouraging vulnerable customers to buy more than they could afford. The product was unregulated— it did not charge interest, so fell outside the Australian states and territories' credit acts, which were merged into a federal law in 2009. Certegy battled with consumer groups, the Australian Securities & Investments Commission and the Australian Competition & Consumer Commission. Certegy also prevented merchants from passing on the cost of the financing to the consumers, known as surcharging. This was an issue the Reserve Bank, as regulator of the Australian payments system, would later pay a lot of attention to. Merchants were loyal, and over time the 6 per cent fee crept higher. Eventually Certegy would process 25 per cent of sales for some of its major clients.

The company had a close relationship with Harvey Norman, for which it passed cheques. However, Certegy didn't regard furniture and whitegoods as suitable for the instalment product, because it considered their margins weren't large enough to cover the cost of funds, while Harvey Norman wasn't keen on paying away 6 per cent of its margin. But the stores' co-founder, Gerry Harvey, understood that point-of-sale financing was a crucial source of sales growth. Harvey Norman adopted other forms of financing, including consumer leases and 'no-interest' loans. The consumer-lease product was pitched to Gerry Harvey by FlexiRent co-founders David Berkman and Andrew Abercrombie, who had created the business in 1991 to finance digital handsets. By 1995, it was in every Harvey Norman store nationally and became a popular way to finance computers because it allowed purchasers to benefit from tax deductions for office equipment.

Abercrombie had trained as a lawyer, and started his first firm two years after graduating from Monash University in Melbourne. Its specialty was film finance deals, which at the time had access to some attractive tax breaks. One of his clients was INXS, Australia's biggest global rock band in the 1980s, led by the flamboyant Michael Hutchence.

Flexi's products would sit alongside the interest-free offerings provided by GE that were heavily promoted at Harvey Norman checkouts. The finance arm of General Electric had expanded in Australia through the noughties, after buying the personal finance and car dealer finance arms of the Australian Guarantee Corporation (AGC) from Westpac in late 2001 for $1.7 billion.

AGC's history went back to 1921 as a financier of small household items before a relationship with the Ford Motor Company saw it finance the arrival of cars in Australia. But AGC had expanded into property development, retail finance, corporate finance, bill acceptance and a range of other areas. The Bank of New South Wales bought AGC in the 1950s before changing its name to Westpac in 1982. A decade later, AGC would almost bring Westpac to its knees, after the property slump of the early 1990s felled its large commercial property developments: AGC accounted for around half of Westpac's $1.56 billion loss for the six months to 31 March 1992.

Around the same time as GE bought AGC, Harvey Norman turned to GE Finance to provide loan products to customers, in competition with FlexiGroup. General Electric's high-flying global chief executive, Jeff Immelt, would meet with co-founder Gerry Harvey on his visits to Australia. The loans were advertised as being 'interest-free', which they were for a period, but if customers missed payments they could be stung with extortionate penalty interest charges of around 28 per cent.

When the global financial crisis struck, the sands of the point-of-sale consumer finance market shifted again. Fidelity decided to offload its global assets to focus on its financial processing core and sold Certegy to FlexiGroup for $31 million. The buy now, pay later product, funded by the merchant, would remain a very profitable business line for FlexiGroup. As the new energy era emerged, Certegy-Ezi-Pay became a popular way to finance rooftop solar panels, with costs funded by installers rather than households.

By the time the Molnar family had embraced online retailing for their jewellery business, the credit and consumption pendulums were swinging again. A younger generation were now earning money. Many of them were suspicious of credit cards—which they feared were mechanisms to lure them into high-interest loans—and of credit in general. Others had yet to grasp the concept. The increased aversion to using plastic, which had been taken up by their parents with gusto, the lay-by mentality of their grandparents, and their own desire to spend on themselves had created the conditions for the next instalment in the history of consumer credit.

• • •

Anthony Eisen was still working out what he was going to do next. He was finishing up at Guinness Peat and was exploring a few options. One was to team up with David Hancock, a career banker who had a track record of running and organising businesses. The plan was to make a play for a New Zealand–based mortgage insurance business, which allowed borrowers with insufficient deposits to take out loans from the banks. But the usually conservative Eisen was interested in Molnar and had been captivated during many conversations with his neighbour about creating a new way to pay, especially for millennials who shunned credit cards. He'd modelled the numbers and felt there was something to it.

On 5 May 2014, Nick Molnar filed papers with the corporate regulator to register a business called Innovative Payments. That would be the commercial shell of his and Eisen's ideas, which were still taking shape and involved different product options. Eisen told Hancock about it, and the three of them met for dinner at a seafood restaurant in Woollahra. Hancock had managed big teams and J.P. Morgan and Citigroup, and after the financial crisis had been recruited to the Commonwealth Bank to build its capital market functions. He'd also sold instalment derivatives as an investment banker. Hancock liked Molnar and the instalment idea straightaway. He was prepared to back it financially and do what he could to make the idea work.

At the time, Hancock was the chief executive of Tower Insurance. He'd been appointed just months before Anthony Eisen divested GPG's stake in the business. Hancock had been commuting between Sydney, the country town of Bowral, where his family home was, and New Zealand. To source the $500,000 he was prepared to invest, he and his wife sold their house, alongside Centennial Park in Sydney. He promised his wife, Fiona, that one day he would buy it back with the profits he would make from the payments start-up. Meanwhile, Eisen and Molnar also decided on a new name—Afterpay—officially registering it in November 2014. The name was thought up by Nick's aunt. But it was already in existence—in the Netherlands.

In 2010, a company named AfterPay had started a pay-on-delivery business, which invoiced customers and allowed them to receive goods purchased online before they parted with their money. The company had actually existed since 2005 as a unit within a debt-collection agency. The pay-on-delivery model was so successful that AfterPay's creator, Stefan van den Berg, set it up as an independent start-up.

By 2012, it had become a leading Dutch brand and expanded into Belgium. In 2014, Arvato, a unit of German media giant

Bertelsmann, acquired the company, which had a 6 per cent share of all online transactions by volume in the Netherlands and had 1.5 million active users, rivalling PayPal. The name was simple, catchy and described the product in the Netherlands.

Molnar had been keen to come up with a business name that was a verb, after being impressed by the way the name 'Google' had been absorbed into the modern lexicon. 'Afterpay' would likely do the same in Australia. It wasn't likely the two brands would ever compete.

In their living rooms, the small team drafted various business models, but without the technology they were nothing more than a PowerPoint operation.

Molnar and Eisen considered flying to Israel to assemble a team of software engineers to build the payments platform they needed. But there was one man already in Eisen's network who could help: Touchcorp's Adrian Cleeve. GPG had a long-held investment in the payments company run by Cleeve. Mike Jefferies was the director at GPG responsible for the investment in the payments business and had the most frequent interactions with Cleeve. Eisen had got on well with Cleeve. He could debate operating details and grand corporate visions with him. Eisen regarded Cleeve as an inventor, a businessman, an architect and an intellect.

Eisen and Molnar presented their instalments payment concept to him for his input and feedback. They tapped his knowledge of the payments industry and his interest in technology to help design the product. Cleeve had a philosophy that if technology could be used to take risk responsibly, it could unlock value for customers— and if it could be done at scale, it could create wealth. That was the essence of Touchcorp, which had agreed to take on the fraud risk for its major client, Optus. Cleeve had repositioned the company to do deals with large telecommunications companies in which its technology would be used to prevent fraudulent transactions. Touch would take on the risk and keep the difference.

There was no formal agreement other than a handshake between Cleeve and Eisen in the early days—just a commitment to help. As the Afterpay idea progressed, workshops, case studies, screenshots and website wireframes were created. Cleeve cut through the corporate bureaucracy to make the idea happen. Touch had something that was invaluable to Afterpay: a large, capable team of development talent, who had the capacity to take on a new project. Better yet, their expertise was in payments systems. Molnar and Eisen would not have to go to the trouble of recruiting developers to build their platform.

In a matter of weeks, the team of fifteen developers had customised their technology for Afterpay's use. Paul Connolly was the project manager, with Lulu Young on strategy. Craig Baker and Ian Asham were the lead architects. John Nguyen, Harley Bailey and Shaun Jackson were senior developers. Gerhard Hanneman was senior systems engineer, Enno Davies senior systems administration, Francis Sy Lei Chen and Nesta Xu were the assigned developers, Rebecca Ferrington the tester, and Fetzie Walburgh the service desk manager.

In February 2015, Eisen and Cleeve nutted out a formal arrangement. The value of the platform they would build for Afterpay was agreed at $13 million. It would be paid in the form of $3 million in two instalment payments and $10 million worth of equity when Afterpay did its first capital raise, which would have to be at least $6 million. Touch's ownership stake in Afterpay depended on how much money Afterpay could raise and at what price. Touch would earn ongoing transaction fees and would provide support for customers.

In some ways, the arrangement suited Touch, which was preparing its initial public offering. The cash component of the fee could be booked as revenue, boosting the earnings upon which its bankers would sell its shares. But there was a risk that Afterpay would stall, or fail to raise the cash.

Afterpay could now begin its beta testing, which Nick used on the Ice Online website.

The initial marketing was similar in name and concept to the Dutch AfterPay. Molnar commissioned an advert to explain how Afterpay worked. It showed a young female shopper browsing the internet for shoes, jewellery and sunglasses from her sofa.

'Buying online should be fun, simple and risk free,' the voice-over said with uplifting music playing in the background.

'At Afterpay we believe you should be able to shop in the comfort of your own home and receive the order without having to pay a cent. Then try it on, make sure it fits and is exactly what you expected when you ordered. Love it? Keep it and pay within 30 days. Not perfect? Return and pay nothing. No catches.

'Smart online shoppers only pay after they know the items are perfect.' 'Try before you buy' was the tagline.

The early signs were encouraging. But Nick and Simon soon realised that of the two payment methods they offered, one was a dud. 'There were two versions of the product—there was one "pay after" division and one was "pay before".' 'Pay after' allowed a customer to pay in full after 30 days, whereas 'pay before' allowed for four instalment payments.

'When we launched Ice Online nobody was using pay on delivery,' Simon Molnar told Fairfax.[7] Nick made the call then to kill the pay after option. Other merchants, too, hated the idea, which left them open to the hassle of dealing with a greater volume of returns. But this caused some serious apprehension, as it wouldn't technically be 'after pay' then.

By now Molnar had secured a key client on which he could test his idea: Edible Blooms, an online store that sold and delivered gifts for special occasions—hampers, flowers and chocolates. They had agreed to add Afterpay to their website in the run-up to Valentine's Day. It was a failure. The company pulled Afterpay off its website because of a lack of interest.

'Don't worry, Ant, we got this,' Molnar told Eisen, attempting to project confidence. But in reality his confidence was in danger of evaporating altogether.

# 4

# TOUCH POINT

On a crisp autumn evening in 2015, Adrian Cleeve invited trusted corporate advisers to a celebratory dinner at his apartment in Melbourne. Cleeve, 61 years old, lived in a three-level penthouse protruding from a ten-storey office building on the corner of La Trobe and Russell streets. The building, which sat behind the State Library and directly opposite the old gothic-style Magistrates Court, was designed by architect Nona Katsalidis and financed by the Cleeve family in 1991, in the middle of a nationwide depression.

Adrian was one of the youngest of five sons and two daughters born to Irish Catholic parents in the Victorian town of Bendigo. The siblings had for years pooled their money to provide for the growing clan of Cleeves, guided by Adrian's entrepreneurial spirit. A confirmed bachelor, Adrian, or 'Uncle A', had enjoyed mixed success in real estate, along with his flamboyant friend Adrian Valmorbida, and Katsalidis. The trio had formed syndicates that developed some of Melbourne's most iconic buildings, including Melbourne Terrace Apartments, where Valmorbida famously hired a crane to place his Ferrari in the penthouse apartment.

But in October 2001, Cleeve's career hit rock bottom as he and his younger brother, Keith, were sacked by an anxious chairman from the company they had formed. Then Adrian had battled with the tax office and lost, forcing him to borrow hundreds of thousands of dollars from the family to repay his debt to the Commonwealth. Cleeve had also been embroiled in a dispute or two, about commissions relating to business sales he'd brokered.

But on this evening years later, those tough times were behind him. He was toasting his new status as the chief executive officer of Touchcorp. The payment company had just completed its initial public offering, which valued it at $160 million.

There by Cleeve's side was his fiancée, Wendy Ng. The 30-year-old daughter of a wealthy Malaysian property investor, Wendy was half his age. Cleeve's family and friends thought he would never settle down. In August 2014, Cleeve bought Wendy a $118,000 engagement ring. The glamorous destination wedding was to take place on the shores of Italy's Lake Como the following May.

Dinner that night was Cleeve's opportunity to thank the financiers who had made his arrival onto the exchange possible. Among his guests were Hugh Robertson, the erudite stockbroker with the best connections in town; Tom Cribb, a young Goldman Sachs banker eager to prove himself; and Anthony Eisen.

While Mike Jefferies was the main point of contact for GPG, Eisen and Cleeve had known each other for about seven years. Now their fortunes had become deeply intertwined. Two years earlier, Eisen had overseen Cleeve's purchase of a large block of Touchcorp shares, giving him a bigger stake in the company he was running. Eisen had also worked in the background, advising Cleeve on the IPO. In January 2015, Eisen was preparing for an important fundraising of his own and approached Cleeve with an unusual invitation: for Cleeve's company to help him and his young partner build the tech for their new start-up, Afterpay. Both his and Cleeve's reputations depended on it.

That night they feasted on lamb catered by Il Bacaro, the Venetian restaurant in nearby Little Collins Street, and drank bottle after bottle of fine Tuscan wine. The discussion centred on the successful IPO and the array of investing personalities they'd encountered on the roadshow. The IPO had been a triumph. At the end of the first day of trading, the Cleeve family's 18.7 per cent shareholding had gained almost $4 million, for a total worth of $34.3 million.

Cleeve himself was in a reflective mood. It was almost a lifetime ago, in the mid-1990s, that Keith had left his job at gas retailer Mobil, convinced that his idea to develop a digital sales widget would work. Mobil didn't agree, but Adrian did, and he'd joined Keith on a mission to commercialise his idea.

Their eldest brothers, Laurence and Damien, both specialist medical doctors in their late forties at the time, were always prepared to back their younger brothers' various ventures—which until then had mainly been property developments in Bendigo and Melbourne. They invested $6 million into a family trust over the next five years, which helped get the business off the ground.

The name 'Touchcorp' alluded to a concept rare at the time but that has since become commonplace: using touchscreen interfaces to navigate menus. But the company's play was less futuristic. In 1999, Touchcorp secured its first major client, Mobil's rival fuel retailer Shell. Touchcorp set up electronic self-service kiosks that could be used to prepay road toll and mobile phone carrier charges. About 30 kiosks had been set up at Coles Express stores, offering about 30 products.

Encouraged by this early win, and with the hubris of the prevailing dotcom era, Touchcorp began approaching investors. With Rupert Murdoch's brother-in-law John Calvert-Jones acting as chairman and Adrian Cleeve as managing director, Touchcorp incorporated as a public company. Blueblood brokerage firm JBWere helped the business raise $14 million with an eye on an ASX listing.

But as the dotcom boom turned to bust, investors turned their attention to cash burn. In the case of Touchcorp, the speed with which money was being spent was alarming. On 3 October 2001, Calvert-Jones took the drastic action of dumping both Adrian Cleeve as managing director and Keith Cleeve as chief operating officer and director. The chairman, a significant shareholder in his own right, lamented the harsh realities of a start-up and put the decision down to cost-cutting. 'Failure to match income to expenditure rates, and thus depleting available cash reserves to unacceptable levels, can place the future of the company in jeopardy,' Calvert-Jones told fellow shareholders in a letter announcing the changes.

Although Adrian had been stripped of the leadership, he remained a director of the company. In 2003, he told his brothers that he still believed their investment in Touchcorp would provide for their retirement, and was worth at least $10 million.

It was around this time that Guinness Peat Group, directed by Mike Jefferies, made a play for a fifteen-year-old ASX-listed payments company called Intellect.

The investment group paid $8.2 million for a 19.9 per cent stake. 'We see this company as being a world-class player in quite a large market,' GPG's investment manager, Jefferies, said in June 2003. The business Intellect sold the point-of-sale terminals used by stores to process card payments. It was listed in Australia but its global operations were in the Belgian town of Zaventem.

Intellect was a mid-tier player in the market. The top two firms had research budgets that were larger than Intellect's revenue, which meant its sales team often lost out on tenders. But Jefferies and Guinness Peat were attracted to the idea that the company made a certain type of terminal that was compatible with a new global standard that was on the verge of being introduced. The hope was that Intellect was on the brink of a surge in sales.

But prior to that, the company needed a strategy to deliver recurring revenue—so that Intellect could charge customers on an ongoing basis, not just for the sale of the brick.

In late 2001, Phil Course, an Australian within the firm, had an idea. On a napkin he illustrated his plan for his boss, Wens Brinkman. In essence, it was to build an interface to connect merchants selling everything from movie tickets to mobile phone credit with payments systems and devices that could process payments, such as terminals, landlines, phones and web browsers. If it worked, a clunky terminal could do more than just process Bankcard payments. It could communicate with other servers and be a means of selling other products.

Brinkman gave Course his blessing to develop the middleware—which they called Trusted Access For Multiple Organisations, or TAFMO. Internally, the project was known as Then A Fucking Miracle Occurs. When the board found out the alternative name, Brinkman was summoned by the chairman, Jos Haag, who was not known for his sense of humour. CEO Jan de Smet insisted the project be based in Belgium, and Course assembled a team of seven developers who worked fourteen-hour days that often ended in a late dinner at the Oude Market in Leuven, where they lived. There was a cultural divide among the hardworking but jovial Australians and the clock-watching Belgians, who fought over car-spot allocations. But the fate of Intellect depended on the TAFMO project. This was no time for petty office politics.

The technology developed by TAFMO had powerful applications. The Australian payments system was old, clunky and prohibitive for new players to access. The new TAFMO technology had immense and underappreciated potential. The crack team of payments experts had built a widget that allowed new players to access the system and add functionality. By connecting to other hosts, a point-of-sale payments terminal could offer mobile phone credit, process healthcare claims and even sell movie tickets. But in the dawning era of cloud computing, the technology did not need to live on a physical terminal. It could be incorporated into mobile phone applications so customers could top up credit on their handsets remotely. TAFMO could also incorporate functions to manage fraud and chargebacks, or disputed sales, by cross-referencing a centralised database. This not only cracked open the payments system, but also levelled the playing field for new entrants.

TAFMO was well ahead of its time. In the context of the enormous payments industry, it had the potential to become one of the most valuable pieces of technology Australia had ever produced.

On a trip to Melbourne, Course met Adrian and Keith Cleeve. They struck a deal to offer Touchcorp's content through Intellect's point-of-sale terminals. But soon after, in October 2001, the Cleeve brothers were removed from their roles. Adrian was replaced by Frank Ajzensztat.

The tie-up between Touch and Intellect seemed to be working well. Intellect signed up Bankwest and St George to roll out its services on their large terminal fleets. Commonwealth Bank, too, was at the negotiating table. The revenue began to flow. Patents were filed by TAFMO to protect their intellectual property, with Course and Greg McCreath listed as inventors. From November 2002 to October 2003, the dollar value of products sold on Intellect's terminals grew by ten times to almost $5 million.

The Touch business, however, was running dangerously low on funds. Adrian Cleeve called Course and asked him to try to convince Calvert-Jones to sell the business to Intellect. Course jetted off to an exclusive golf club in the English countryside to meet Calvert-Jones, who agreed to sell Touch to Intellect in exchange for a percentage of the future revenue derived from Australia. A few weeks later the deal was consummated.

Shortly after the paperwork was signed in 2003, Intellect's CEO Jan de Smet asked Course to meet with Mike Jefferies of his large shareholder, the Guinness Peat Group. At the Sydney office he was introduced to Gary Weiss, Graeme Cureton and a young consultant from a small investment bank, Caliburn, named Anthony Eisen. Intellect had been a lacklustre investment, but GPG was prepared to show patience. The problem was that Intellect, too, was running low on funds.

Jefferies asked Course to become CEO of Intellect, but he declined. That role would divert him from the project he was working on at TAFMO. Jefferies said he had no choice but to raise money to extract the TAFMO business unit out of Intellect. In June 2004, the TAFMO spin-off was announced, with Course appointed CEO of the newly created unlisted public Australian company. GPG had invested a further £6.6 million to take a 56 per cent stake in TAFMO.

Intellect shareholders retained 28.6 per cent. Calvert-Jones and the Cleeves, in the form of Cleevecorp, owned about 3 per cent each after a loan they made to the original Touchcorp, renamed XTCL,[1] couldn't be repaid. The 28.6 per cent stake in TAFMO retained by Intellect, however, soon fell into the hands of convertible note financiers led by the intensely private fund manager Duncan Saville. Saville, a South African accountant who had previously worked for Ron Brierley, was skilled at identifying distressed opportunities and profiting from them. When Intellect couldn't service the notes, the company's assets were transferred to the noteholders.

At the freshly incorporated TAFMO, Course had to put together a board of directors. He aimed high and reached out to Hatim Tyabji, a rock star of the payments world who had created billion-dollar valuations out of thin air at VeriFone, Saraide, Bytemobile and

Jasper Wireless. Tyabji had also served on the board of US$25 billion US electronics retailer Best Buy.

He flew to Australia and, to Course's surprise, accepted the role. Jefferies told Course he'd 'hooked a marlin on a five-pound handline'. A board was formed, comprising Jefferies as chair, Adrian Cleeve back in the fold as vice-chair, Denis Calvert (a former merchant banker at Citi), Tyabji and Course.

The business continued to grow, attracting enterprise customers 7-Eleven, Tobaccoland Australia, Commonwealth Bank, St George and four mobile operators: Optus, Telstra, Vodafone and Virgin. Touch offered over 300 products, from Medicare payments to fishing licences, and 60 per cent of Australia's electronic payments terminals carried TAFMO technology.

In 2008, Course resigned from the company and Adrian Cleeve was appointed CEO. A year later, in 2009, the TAFMO name was changed to that of the Cleeves' original firm: Touchcorp Holdings Ltd. There was, however, no corporate lineage between the companies.

By 2011, it was the company's major shareholder, Guinness Peat, that was in strife. The directive from the GPG board was that the group had to liquidate its entire $660 million portfolio of investments. The $6.6 million Touch represented a 1 per cent position, and so was hardly worth the time of Anthony Eisen as he negotiated complex exits from insurance and wealth-management businesses the group owned. But the diligent Eisen appointed an advisory firm to assist with the sale.

A large listed company showed an interest in Touch, but that had cooled by October 2012. With GPG running short of suitors, an opportunity arose for some of the existing directors of TAFMO, including Adrian Cleeve, to snap up the holding at a bargain-basement price. On 8 October 2012, a three-member 'syndicate' delivered a term sheet to Eisen to buy the 56 per cent stake for $5.6 million, valuing TAFMO at just $10 million.

As part of the bid, Adrian Cleeve hastily set up a company called ATC Capital that would buy 20 per cent of GPG's 56 per cent stake. Under the arrangement, the family trust Cleevecorp would own 8 per cent. Two other entities with apparent associations to Saville would buy the remaining 28 per cent.

But it wasn't a smooth process, and the former CEO Course cried foul. He suspected two of the directors—Saville and Cleeve—had orchestrated the purchase from GPG without seeking the required approval of all other shareholders. The Australian Takeovers Panel agreed—but only in part. In May 2013, it ruled that the Cleeve entities were related, which meant the purchase did have to be rubber-stamped by other shareholders. But the shareholders connected with Saville were not associated.

There was a dissenter on the Takeovers Panel committee: lawyer Laurie Shervington. He pointed out that the funding to purchase all the shares had been provided by a New Zealand insurance company where Saville was a director. The loan accounted for almost all the insurer's capital.

While the Cleeve-related sales were reversed, shareholder approval for the original deal was a formality, given the other syndicate members were allowed to keep their shares. Cleeve's ATC Capital acquired 18.6 million shares in TAFMO for $1 million while Cleevecorp bought a further 7.4 million shares for $430,000.

The Takeovers Panel process was an expensive and time-consuming annoyance, but nothing more. In December 2013, the company, which still had over 300 individual investors, reincorporated as Touchcorp Ltd in Bermuda, where the protections for minority shareholders and responsibilities of directors were reduced. In 2014, ATC Capital and Cleevecorp sold 4.65 million of those shares to former TAFMO director Mike Jefferies. He also bought shares from the other syndicate members, making him one of the larger shareholders in the company. In January 2014, Adrian Cleeve was looking to cash out of the investment. 'I hope we can pull some money out progressively now whilst continuing to increase the size of the business,' he told his brother, Damien, in an email referred to in court documents. 'I think everybody would enjoy a bit of free cash. Despite all the ups and downs, I think our brand of communism hasn't worked too badly.'

Adrian was plugging away in the hope that his tech payday would come in the form of an exit from his investment in Touch. He told his brother Laurence later that year that Touchcorp was probably worth between $105 million and $175 million, which he said meant the family's stake was around $30 million. That amount, he told Damien, would be 'enough for our long term needs if coherently managed but not if split and spent'. The exit path he chose involved floating on the Australian Securities Exchange. Just before Christmas in 2014, Adrian told Damien he was heading on a well-earned holiday as he readied for a listing.

Cleeve's plans to take Touch public began with a phone call from Tyabji to bankers at Goldman Sachs. He had a longstanding relationship with Goldman Sachs, which advised Best Buy, which he had chaired, and Tyabji used his clout to ensure Goldman managed the float. Mike Jefferies and Eisen, too, had worked closely with the investment bank in the past and were eager to appoint the Wall Street giant to manage the float.

The sale was a far less illustrious prospect than the biggest brand in investment banking typically pitched for, and the deal was passed to Tom Cribb, a young banker who had just returned home to Australia after a seven-year stint in the United States.

Cribb had been at Deutsche Bank as the global financial crisis was unfolding, but soon joined the venerated private-equity firm KKR. At Goldman, he'd done a good enough job handling the sale of an $8.4-billion book of loans by British bank Lloyds to local lender Westpac. Cribb added Touch to his list of clients, which included only one other name: non-bank financier Pepper.

While Goldman was on the float for the prestige, Hugh Robertson fought to get a role for his brokerage firm, Wilson HTM. The pairing was a mismatch but doubled Touch's chances of success, as Robertson tapped his pool of wealthy family clients to back the float.

But it was Goldman Sachs that was putting its name to the deal, so it was Cribb's responsibility to ensure that the due diligence process was thorough. He would have to take responsibility for any mistakes. Cribb spent hours at the office of lawyers Clayton Utz, making sure the information in the prospectus was correct. A constant presence in the room was Anthony Eisen, who had finished up at GPG but had returned to do a deal with Cleeve for a new start-up he was involved with.

When corporate Australia returned from its vacation in early February 2015, Touchcorp's float was being pitched to institutional investors. The story was that Touch's technology could detect potentially fraudulent payments that were costing large mobile phone carriers millions. Touchcorp would get paid to take on the risk of chargebacks, and if their technology worked, they'd profit, and seek to win more contracts. Elana Rubin, the former chair of Australia's largest pension fund, Australian Super, was recruited to the board by Jefferies. Rubin had connections to GPG, having served as a director at one of the group's larger holdings, Tower Limited.

Touchcorp, meanwhile, pushed on with the IPO. Some fund managers said the deal was rushed, which meant they didn't have time to do their homework on Touchcorp's three customers: Optus, the 7-Eleven chain and a convenience store network in Europe called Valore. There were also question marks about how Touch reported revenue and development costs. Some analysts queried the high listing multiple of 22 times earnings. The brokers selling were asked one question repeatedly: 'What the fuck is Afterpay?'

The answer was there on page 83 of the 168-page prospectus, in the key risks section, which lawyers at Clayton Utz had helped to draft.

Marked at point 5.2.8—'Afterpay development fee.' That paragraph outlined that in February 2015, Touch had struck an agreement with a business called Afterpay to customise a payments platform for it to use. A development fee of $3 million was owed to Touch, but the payment was conditional on Afterpay raising the money from private investors.

Touch had assumed Afterpay would come up with the cash, but there was a risk it would fall short that it had to spell out in the document. If Afterpay failed to pay, it would lose its rights to the platform. But more relevant for investors was the admission that 'this forecast revenue for FY2015 will not be received by Touch in that period, which may materially adversely impact Touch's FY2015 revenue and profitability'.

In the legalistic language of an offer document, Afterpay was not a hidden gem. It was a dubious credit, a low-grade customer that had been given a service without paying because it didn't have the money. As for the investment itself, it was such an early-stage venture that it was deemed worthless by analysts.

'How do I put a value on it?' one asked. 'It's not even an idea. It's not even a concept.'

But brokers Goldman Sachs and Wilson HTM had no trouble filling the order book, and on 31 March 2015 Touchcorp floated on the ASX at a $162 million valuation, popping a further 10 per cent on the first day its shares traded. For the syndicate that bought the 56 per cent stake from GPG at the $10 million valuation, the float marked a gain of seventeen times their investment. The spoils accrued to Duncan Saville's investment firms, Utilico and Vix Investments, which owned around 25 per cent of the company; the Cleeves, who owned about 15 per cent; and Jefferies, who now owned over 6 per cent of Touchcorp, having bought shares from the Cleeve entities. The original TAFMO shareholders also retained a trace of the business.

Adrian Cleeve's fortunes had turned around. He'd be able to pay his debts to his family, he'd surprised them by avoiding his fate as a confirmed bachelor, and he was now the chief executive officer of a listed technology company. On the evening of the IPO, he emailed his brothers, Damien, Laurence, Keith and Terence, and his sisters, Linley and Audrey, to tell them precisely how much money had been made that day. The family's 21.7 million shares, or 18.73 per cent of the company, were valued at the close of trading at $34,318,101, up $3,909,657 on the day.

'It has been a satisfying debut and the family's finances have taken a turn for the better,' he concluded.

# 5

# LITTLE KING

HUGH WALTER ROBERTSON had two epiphanies on his path to becoming a stockbroking king of little companies. The first was when he crutched his fiftieth lamb[1] on the family farm in rural Victoria. Sheep farming was not for him.

So Robertson headed to the big city of Melbourne to pursue a career in law, but got tossed out of law school. His next option was a career in the cut-throat world of stockbroking. He was well suited to the industry. Robertson was educated at the prestigious Geelong Grammar School, and had joined the exclusive Melbourne Club at a relatively young age—'because I wouldn't get in when I'm old,' he told friends. But he battled to get a chance. After knocking on the doors of 24 firms unsuccessfully, the 25th finally hired him—and Robertson soon found that he had a talent for selling stocks.

In the mid-1980s, brokers were caught in the middle of a David versus Goliath battle as Robert Holmes à Court tried to take control of mining giant BHP. Nicknamed 'the Big Fella', the Broken Hill Proprietary Company was Australia's largest and oldest company. The prospect of it falling into the hands of Holmes à Court, a Rhodesian corporate raider armed with a loan from US investment bank Merrill Lynch, was too much for the mining establishment to bear.

In 1986, in the middle of the battle, Robertson and other brokers were summoned for drinks at BHP by chief executive Brian Loton, and lectured about the company's wisdom and why Holmes à Court was a 'scheming satan'. As they toasted, Robertson thought, 'Fuck, if this is the rest of my life . . .' That was his second epiphany: big companies were unbelievably boring. For him, excitement was to be found in identifying small or emerging companies that weren't on the radar of the broking houses or investors. And so Robertson descended down the market capitalisation ladder to maintain his sanity and satisfy his ambitions. 'I subscribe to the Jesuit philosophy: get them while they are young and ride them through,' Robertson later told *The Australian*.[2]

Robertson discovered more than his fair share of duds, but he also unearthed a few gems. His big win was Perth engineering firm Monadelphous, which made investors 100 times their money. Monadelphous had been acquired in the early 1990s by entrepreneurial engineer John Rubino and three other partners. Robertson made a lot of money for himself and his valued clients, who tended to be private investors rather than big institutions. As a result, the brokerage firm that employed him, Faulkners, punched above its weight and was snapped up by a larger rival, Bell Potter.

Robertson gravitated away from the big institutional investors and towards cashed-up private individuals, whom he believed were far more insightful and skilled investors. He became a favoured broker to Kerry Packer's senior investment lieutenant, Ashok Jacob, and to Alex Waislitz, the former son-in-law of packaging mogul Richard Pratt.

Robertson's affinity for independently minded and unconstrained investors meant he was close to the Guinness Peat mob, and in particular to senior analyst Graeme Cureton. The broker served as a director of a firm called Ratoon Holdings, which GPG and

Waislitz controlled. In 2004, Ratoon had purchased shares in Tatter-salls, the private company that operated Victoria's lotteries, from the estate of the founder, George Adams. But four years later Ratoon was forced to dump its shares because of the global financial crisis, an equine flu crisis and the government's decision to end the existing duopoly concessions by forcing the main industry players to bid for ten-year contracts.

The single most important insight Robertson garnered from private investors was to pay attention to people. Investing in a good company run by bad people was a way to lose money. If you made an investment in a bad company run by bad people, you'd lose every-thing. But a bad company run by good people might do okay, and an investment in a good company run by good people could make you a fortune.

It didn't all go Robertson's way. He'd pushed some self-proclaimed shockers to his clientele, including the float of a crane operator called Verticon. And while Robertson was important to the brokerage firms that courted him to work under their brand, there was a feeling that he was living off his past glories, in particular Monadelphous.

'It is a bit like sleeping with the most beautiful girl, first time around. You will never find one that compares to that performance,' Robertson told *The Australian*. 'They are the ones that hide the cracks. They cover up the ones you don't get right. Because by its nature it is a very imperfect science. Shit happens.'[3]

By the autumn of 2015, Robertson was still hustling. He'd angled to get his firm, Wilson HTM, on the float of Touch. It was under those circumstances that Eisen and Molnar showed up to the Wilson board-room to meet with Robertson. It was no secret why they were there: Afterpay needed to raise $8 million to pay Touchcorp for building the platform it was using to offer its buy now, pay later product.

For Robertson, one of the tough selling points of the Touch IPO was whether this little start-up Afterpay could pay the money it owed Touch. If it couldn't, Touch would miss the earnings forecast laid out in the offer document—a cardinal sin for a recent float.

So Robertson had a motive to help Afterpay: to ensure the Touch IPO wasn't a post-market flop. And he'd known Eisen and GPG. But he was putting his reputation on the line every time he pitched an investment, especially for an idea like this that had a high chance of failure. What's more, GPG was no longer the feared and respected institution it once was. The gravitas had largely gone. Investors that followed the so-called smart money weren't convinced the GPG money fitted that description.

Eisen delivered the Afterpay story in the methodical, measured way to which Robertson had become accustomed over the years. He thought to himself that 'measured' might be the word inscribed on Eisen's tombstone. 'We think this is an interesting opportunity and we have the processes in place,' Eisen told Robertson.

Then the kid spoke. Nick Molnar, who was dark-eyed and focused and spoke with a high-pitched giggle, was in the zone. Robertson had seen entrepreneurs of all ages in all industries come begging for money. They all tended to be nervous. But Molnar was supremely confident.

He told Roberston how his generation was turning their back on credit cards: they had come of age during the global financial crisis and had seen the havoc excessive credit had created. They didn't trust the banks and didn't want a credit card, even if they could be approved for one. Later Robertson asked his 23-year-old daughter Hannah if that was true. In fact, he asked all her friends. Yes, none of them had credit cards, nor did they want one.

• • •

Afterpay already had some financial backers. David Hancock had already agreed to tip in $500,000, while Eisen would tap the old GPG network for funds.

But what they needed more than funding was a banker: someone who understood how to lend money, and—more importantly—how to get it back. Hancock tapped his banking contacts, but few were willing to risk giving up their senior roles and high salaries to join a start-up. Eventually he settled on one name: Richard Harris.

Through his contacts, Hancock knew Harris was commercial enough to give this little venture a shot, but conservative enough to make sure it didn't blow up.

Harris was a young banker from Lake Macquarie, a working-class area an hour north of Sydney. While he'd worked at the staid institution of the Commonwealth Bank, he'd also taken his fair share of adventurous postings.

In 2007, he'd moved to Tokyo to set up a unit selling home loans into the Japanese market, as Japanese lenders made it excruciatingly difficult for expats from Australia, Singapore and Hong Kong to get a loan. Within months, the CBA was writing millions of dollars of mortgages, mainly for properties on the ski fields. The customers were bankers, businessmen from around the region—and even the odd Major League Baseball player. In an uncontested market, Harris was writing pristine loans to credit-worthy borrowers. For a while, business was booming. Despite the high quality of the loan book, the 2008 global financial crisis put an end to the adventure.

In 2011, Harris was seconded to Hanoi to help run Vietnam International Bank, a lender the CBA had partially backed. It was small but growing, and in a dynamic economy. His Vietnam experience forced Harris to think on his feet. Only one in five Vietnamese had a bank account, but one in three had smart phones. Electricity bills were still paid in cash to a representative who made house calls. If the customer wasn't home on the third visit, the power was cut. The country was plagued by fraud, which meant that relying on documents such as payslips to judge whether a customer could repay a loan wasn't going to work. Harris and his team had to think of new ways to decide who to lend to and how much, and to digitise the banking system. They also created a bill-paying app for utilities.

When he returned to Australia, Harris was given a less exciting task. The Commonwealth Bank was falling behind in offering cash and broking accounts to customers who were setting up their own self-managed superannuation funds. His job was to streamline the process so the bank wouldn't lose more business to its rivals.

On a Friday afternoon in February 2015, a meeting was organised between Harris and Molnar at a cafe in Bondi Junction, a kilometre up the hill from the famous beach. Harris had just become a father and wasn't sleeping. But Molnar made enough of an impression for him to follow up the next week. Over sandwiches near Sydney Harbour, he was introduced to Anthony Eisen.

That evening, Harris returned home to Crows Nest. His exhausted wife, Jen, asked if anything interesting had happened. He told her about the meeting and the Afterpay instalments model. 'I'd use that,' she said.

Harris was a little surprised: Jen wasn't the product's target audience. She could pay for items outright without difficulty. But she explained that she spent $200 a fortnight on something for herself. If she wanted to buy something for, say, $600, she could now break it up.

Why didn't Jen just use a credit card, Harris asked. That wasn't the same, she told him. There was still a guilt factor associated with buying a large item on credit. The model would help overcome a mental barrier.

Thanks to his wife, Harris had a light-bulb moment: maybe Molnar was on to something. He decided to give this start-up a crack and asked his bosses at Commonwealth Bank if he could take a twelve-month sabbatical. They agreed—as soon as Harris finished his work on the superannuation project for CBA, he would be free to join the start-up world.

• • •

When the sun is out, there are few better spots for a business meeting than Bondi Beach. Bookended by ocean pools, the surf serves as a magnet for the city's beautiful people and travellers from all over the world, who come to play volleyball, sunbake and swim in the majestic Pacific Ocean. It's a vista few other major working cities on the planet can compete with. But when the weather turns, Bondi can be windy, exposed and hostile.

It was on one of those cold, wet winter mornings, in July, that Brazilian Fabio De Carvalho showed up at Harry's, a trendy cafe that spilled out onto the street opposite Bondi Public School. De Carvalho had worked in sales at two of the world's largest digital brands, eBay and PayPal. But in a heart-to-heart talk, he had told his colleague and mentor Andrew Rechtman that he was itching to have a crack in the start-up world.

It turned out that Rechtman was another neighbour of the Molnars, and Michele Molnar had just told him her son was desperate to find someone to help him sell his new payments product. Andrew had met Nick and thought he was smart; at the very least, he told Fabio, it was worth his time to have a meeting.

At first he didn't believe the kid surrounded by papers and notes was the founder he would have to dazzle, but there was no one else there, so it had to be him. The meeting got off to an awkward start, but ultimately they had a long conversation and Fabio was impressed by Nick's vision for his start-up.

Molnar had tried to sell Afterpay to merchants and had had some success after the Edible Blooms disaster. He had just snared Princess Polly, a fledgling online fashion brand, whose founder, Wez Bryett, had reached out via the contact page on Afterpay's website in May 2015. Bryett knew many of his customers—16- to 24-year old women—didn't own credit cards and was interested to know more about what this new company was offering.

'They sent out a press release and I was intrigued by this new payments scheme,' Bryett told *The Australian Financial Review*

*Magazine.* 'We've always been very experimental and it just sounded like a good concept.'

Molnar was anxious not to disappoint Eisen, so initially he didn't tell him about Princess Polly: better to underpromise and overdeliver, he thought.

But the Princess Polly experience showed there was some merit to the pay in four instalment product. Soon after it was switched on, Afterpay was being used to fund one in five of its online purchases. Shoppers were buying more and completing more transactions.

'It was a totally new concept when we launched it and it took off straightaway,' Bryett said. 'We didn't have to explain it or push people into it. As soon as we had it as a payment option, the demand was there. It was like people had been waiting for it.'

For Molnar and Eisen, the early deal created its own challenges: they were fronting the funds from their own bank accounts. 'They will pay us back, Nick?' a half-joking Eisen asked.

The early success of Princess Polly proved Afterpay had potential. But beyond that, it had been a struggle to sell. Signing up merchants was a critical mission for Afterpay. They needed someone with Fabio's skills to bring in the merchants. He agreed to take the role and expand the small team.

Afterpay also recruited the self-proclaimed grandfather of online retailing, Paul Greenberg. In his late fifties, Greenberg and had set up the NORA network, an online retailers' association, shortly after he left online discount department store DealsDirect in 2013. He'd met Molnar, whom he considered an eBay sales expert, in that context. Greenberg had launched the DealsDirect brand in 2004, and customers had often asked for an online version of lay-by, which had been so popular in physical stores. DealsDirect was PayPal's largest Australian merchant, and Greenberg had asked the local leadership team to come up with a solution. PayPal later acquired Bill Me Later in the United States, but the product left Greenberg underwhelmed.

When Molnar told Greenberg about his payments idea, Greenberg was still feeling the sting of his DealsDirect days, where the lack of online lay-by meant lost revenue. But Molnar's pitch was about more than lay-by, he soon realised. Traditional lay-by had been aimed at an older, lower-income demographic, people who were terrified of debt and of consuming anything before they'd paid for it. Molnar was targeting younger consumers who needed credit but didn't want a credit card. Greenberg agreed to join as an adviser.

• • •

Hugh Robertson had been impressed enough by the Eisen and Molnar combination. He decided he would wheel out his rolodex of private investors and wealthy families to get Afterpay over the line.

There was no denying it—the investment was an outright punt, an idea. There were no guarantees it would work. Anyone tipping in funds was backing the man, or repaying a past favour.

The fundraising effort, which kicked off in June 2015, needed a pitch deck—a set of well-curated slides that step a potential investor through the investment opportunity. Attached to the emails were two PDF documents: a short pitch and a more detailed 65-page deck for investors who were prepared to consider backing Afterpay's first-ever funding round. It was the kind of document that had drained the youth out of generations of investment banking graduates. These took consecutive all-nighters to draft, check and produce. And they were often just skimmed over, or binned without a second thought. But Eisen wasn't averse to the back-breaking work of pitch decks. In fact, he'd mastered the art of communicating a company's worth to investors. For his fledgling business, this was make or break.

The clear blue cover had the company name and logo—two white triangles with arrows in the negative space, the left pointing up and the other pointing at an angle to the right.

The deck was split into five chapters: an introduction to Afterpay, the market it was targeting, its tie-up with Touchcorp, how Afterpay works, and how it will make money. The first line: 'Afterpay is a technology and consumer finance company.' It had been founded in 2014 by executives with experience in finance and retail, and in combination with Touch. The platform it built performed 'real-time fraud and credit assessment'.

The mission was laid out. Today it was to 'foster the growth of online commerce by making the process of transacting easier, more flexible and affordable for consumers and merchants'. Tomorrow it was to 'use its proprietary technology, develop credit profiles for the online transacting populace to allow us to responsibly offer low-risk, individually tailored credit products in real time and without application'.

The problem Afterpay was solving was how to 'make purchasing things online more affordable, flexible and convenient', and how to 'improve the way credit is provided to individuals on a low-risk, real-time basis'. The solution was to 'allow consumers to make full payment for their online purchases—after they receive their items, over time in instalments, at no extra cost, and without providing any additional "check out" information'. For merchants, Afterpay would deliver 'incremental sales, converting customers that would have abandoned the sale, increase basket sizes, guarantee upfront payments and reduce chargebacks'.

The deck presented evidence that Afterpay was working. Princess Polly had increased its sales by 25 per cent and boosted revenues by as much as 15 per cent.

What were Afterpay's products? They came in two forms, one that would be available when it officially launched later in 2015, and another down the track. The first was described as 'Buy Now—Pay Later', and there were two options. Customers could pay after delivery of the goods, thirty days after purchase, or payments could be made in four equal payments, every fourteen days, over 42 days. Neither of these products would charge interest, or charge customers in other ways. In the future, Afterpay planned to offer a second product, which would charge interest over twelve months. That was essentially a variation of a credit card product, but it was not pursued. Afterpay would also drop the 'pay in thirty days' product to concentrate solely on the 'pay in four instalments' offering.

The strategic steps were well thought out. Afterpay's buy now, pay later product did not require credit checks to finance online purchases: the short-term loans, which did not charge interest, fell outside the definition of credit products in the credit laws.

Afterpay then outlined its edge: the cost of acquiring customers was low. That was because the merchants marketed the product to help drive their own sales. As Afterpay provided a service to consumers, it would increase customer lifetime value and merchant revenue, while also encouraging merchants to actively market Afterpay during the purchase process. That, combined with its self-titled 'Transaction Integrity Engine', would provide the payments platform with a competitive advantage.

Details around the Transaction Integrity Engine were a little vague. A score was assigned to customers based on the product they were buying, the information about them and other rules. 'Afterpay verifies if a customer is who they say they are and allocates them a personal credit limit in real time,' the deck explained. 'The Transaction Integrity Engine can utilise an unlimited number of rules.'

The message was clear that Afterpay would be doing things differently to credit cards, which approved customers for a limit— say $1000 or $3000—but didn't judge them, or even know what funds were spent on. In contrast, Afterpay would study each transaction individually, and its systems would decide whether to approve each and every purchase, which would be based on criteria including the type of product and the device it was being purchased with. The second chapter of the Afterpay pitch deck focused on the market the company could target. Australians spent about $30 billion a year buying stuff online—of which $1.8 billion was fashion. That was growing at 11 per cent a year. The offline market was larger, at $245 billion, while the entire consumer payments sector was valued at north of half a trillion dollars. Afterpay thus had the 'scope to become a disruptive force in the Australian credit market'.

Consumers relied on credit to fund purchases, to pay for education and to buy cars. In fact, credit card debt had doubled in ten years to $50 billion, while transaction values had also doubled to $22.2 billion. Average outstanding balances had increased by 30 per cent over the decade to $3147. There was a huge opportunity for Afterpay, given the 20 per cent interest rates charged on credit card debt to a nation of consumers who were largely good payers. 'Despite widespread consumer acceptance of credit in Australia, the online point of sales credit market is underpenetrated in Australia,' Afterpay said.

There were peers and competitors, both in Australia and overseas, and Afterpay named three big ones. There was Bill Me Later, a business acquired by PayPal in 2008; ten-year-old Swedish fintech Klarna; and Affirm, which did real-time, fixed-term loans at the checkout.

Some of the biggest venture funds were playing in the space. Andreessen Horowitz had just supported a US$275 million debt and equity funding round by Affirm, which had been started by one of PayPal's co-founders, Max Levchin. Meanwhile Klarna already had 35 million customers and 50,000 merchants, and over the decade since it had been founded in Sweden had accumulated a 10 per cent share of the ecommerce market in Northern Europe, helping retailers sell more than US$9 billion of goods. As the Afterpay deck noted, Klarna had recently raised over US$300 million at a US$1.4 billion valuation, with investors including Sequoia, General Atlantic, Atomic and DST.

Australia, too, had a nascent industry. ZipMoney offered customers an option to apply for loans at the online checkout, while Touch Payments—which had no connection to Touchcorp—had a pay-after-delivery product that issued an invoice to the customer.

Potential Afterpay investors were told the business model was to offer its buy now, pay later products—it would be a 'profitable transaction-based business'—before evolving into a 'highly profitable transaction-based consumer finance business'.

How would it make its money? The merchant would pay Afterpay 3.5 to 5 per cent of the purchase amount, plus a 30-cent transaction fee. Afterpay's costs were the transaction processing fee it paid to Touchcorp, and the cost of fraud and bad debts. Then there were fixed costs such as sales, administration and governance.

In the second phase, if the consumer took up the interest option for higher-value purchases, Afterpay would charge between 15 and 20 per cent interest. For a $100 buy now, pay later purchase, Afterpay would earn a margin of between 1.2 and 2.2 per cent. For a bigger-ticket $400 item that was funded by interest-bearing loans, Afterpay would earn a margin closer to 7 per cent. The company's five-year plan was for buy now, pay later to account for 70 per cent of revenue, and consumer finance 30 per cent. To offer its lending product, Afterpay said, it had applied for a credit licence in the second half of 2015. That would allow it to offer credit as it sought to convert 'selected' Afterpay customers.

Ultimately, it would not pursue the interest model, given how quickly customers embraced pay in four instalments once it was offered by the early retail adopters.

Afterpay expected customers to use the system more frequently, and for repeat transactions to double over five years. That would result in a decline in write-offs from non-payment from 1.9 per cent to 1.3 per cent.

Afterpay also estimated how much money it would make. In year one, the 2016 financial year, it projected that it would process

$36 million of sales, earning $1.5 million of revenue. By year three, it forecast $677 million of sales to earn $27 million of revenue, and by year five it forecast $2 billion of sales and $82 million of revenue. That assumed Afterpay would capture 2.4 per cent of the online market. If it could achieve a 6 per cent market share, its sales would top $3.5 billion and derive $240 million of revenue. On that forecast, it could achieve gross profit of $100 million.

Afterpay was keeping its costs tight. It owed Touchcorp $3 million but would get a $1 million research and development credit from the Australian Tax Office. The company budgeted $900,000 in year one to pay staff, travel costs, rent and board fees. The operating costs were forecast to increase to $2.3 million in year two, and to upwards of $8.4 million by 2020.

The final slide showed the Afterpay team. The inclusion of Touchcorp executives and its fifteen-strong team of developers who were developing the platform presented the company as quite an operation. Afterpay's advisory board consisted of Touchcorp chair Mike Jefferies, Anthony Eisen, Nick Molnar, Paul Greenberg and David Marshall. There were eight vacant positions, of which four had been identified: a sales director, a chief operating officer, a chief information officer and a group business director. Afterpay was still searching for a marketing manager, two sales directors and a business development manager.

The pitch was compelling—but, then again, all pitches are. Ron Brierley only needed one data point: Anthony Eisen. He was bright and a terrific operator, so Brierley didn't need to think twice and was good for $500,000. The largest investor was a shadowy firm based out of Barbados called Sidereal Holdings, which invested $1.1 million. Sidereal, it emerged, was a Canadian-based hedge fund.

Brierley's $500,000 was matched by GPG veteran Ron Langley. Graeme Cureton invested $250,000. Jason Ters, who had battled through the sell-down, was good for $75,000. Mike Jefferies put in

$50,000. All up, Eisen's former GPG colleagues had fronted around $1.8 million.

Cliff Rosenberg, who'd met Molnar at a luncheon hosted by Investec, was impressed by his enthusiasm and the simplicity of the concept. He put in $200,000 to help the Afterpay cause. CVC Capital, the ASX-listed private-equity fund, was the third-party institution in the deal, with a $200,000 investment. It already owned a stake in Touchcorp, but liked the Afterpay concept. Duncan Saville's Utilico Holdings, as it often did, followed where the GPG money went, investing $200,000. Saville's funds were already large shareholders in Touch. Adrian Cleeve's future father-in-law, Jeffery Ng, invested $250,000.

Hugh Robertson had brokered several of the GPG investments, and now he worked his client list hard. That included wealthy private families in the agriculture and property sectors. Ashok Jacob, the Ellerston chief and Kerry Packer's long-time trusted adviser, put in $50,000. So, too, did fund manager Anthony Aboud, a former Ellerston portfolio manager who had jumped ship with Paul Skamvougeras to Perpetual in 2012 to run the firm's hedge fund unit. Former Goldman Sachs bankers Sean Hogan and Steve Sher invested $200,000 and $50,000, respectively.

Another large investor was Brisbane-based Troy Harry, through his fund Trojan. Harry, a former stockbroker at Morgans, was a skilled investor with an eye for a low-risk trade. He'd stayed close to Guinness Peat over the years, and along with Hugh Robertson was an investor in TAFMO. He'd also bought a further 1 million shares in 2013 after the company had been renamed Touchcorp. Harry paid just 7 cents for a consideration of $70,000 after chairman John Calvert-Jones sought to sell some of his investments. When Touchcorp listed at $1.45, he made a cool $1.38 million profit, or twenty times his money. Mike Jefferies had made Harry aware of the Afterpay raising. Harry didn't typically invest in early-stage start-ups, but he liked the concept and was more enthusiastic than the other investors in the round. He was good for $300,000.

But Robertson had to work hard to reach the $8 million target. He'd personally invested around $200,000. One of his most valued clients—the world-renowned Melbourne gynaecologist Professor John McBain—had also agreed to write a $500,000 cheque.

The 66-year-old McBain was nothing short of medical royalty in Australia, having arrived from Scotland as a young doctor. He had pioneered in-vitro fertilisation and was part of the team that delivered Australia's first and the world's third IVF baby when Candice Reed was born in Melbourne in 1980. By 2015, IVF was responsible for the birth of one in every 33 babies in Australia.[4] And McBain was lauded as giving new hope to infertile couples, even as he and others raised concerns about possible over-reliance on the new fertility technologies.

In June 2015, it was McBain's capital that was needed, rather than his medical expertise. Robertson called in a favour and asked him to up his investment by $200,000 to $700,000 in total. His investment company, Fifty Second Celebration, upped the cheque. Now Robertson had the funds he'd said he could deliver.

Overall, 41 investors had invested in Afterpay's first raising, which valued the business at $28 million. Touchcorp's effective $10 million stake meant it owned 35 per cent. Eisen and Molnar owned 17.5 per cent each, while the new investors accounted for the remaining 30 per cent.

The raising had been a battle. Eisen had drawn on the trust he'd built up over his years at GPG, while Robertson had stretched the limits of his rolodex. Touchcorp issued a statement on 29 June 2015, the last day of the financial year, assuring its investors that Afterpay had raised the minimum amount required to pay the $3 million development fee it owed Touch. It had been a little messy, but Afterpay had been birthed.

Once the funding came through in July 2015, Afterpay signed a lease for 30 square metres in a building in Holt Street, Surry Hills, in the same street as Rupert Murdoch's infamous News Corp headquarters, and just three floors above the Cue fashion group's stylish new digs.

Molnar had decided that Paul Greenberg's Online Retailer Conference & Expo would be the perfect place to officially launch Afterpay in late July. Molnar himself would man a booth serving ice-cream from the popular Messina chain. The flavours had corny names such as 'Salted Caramel Conversion' and 'Triple Choc Fraud Free Fudge'.

• • •

When Fabio showed up for his first day, he may have had expectations that he'd signed up for a highly professional outfit. But there was no desk. Nick and his fiancée, Gabi Shulman, were unpacking IKEA boxes. 'Fabs, you can still call merchants while you unpack the boxes,' Molnar told him. This was the start-up life he had signed up for.

Fabio hit the phones, but it was hard going. The majority of merchants had no interest in what he was selling them. They questioned why they should pay Afterpay, and why the customer would pay in four instalments when they could pay once with a credit card and not be charged interest if they paid off the balance within 60 days. Fabio's pitch was that this was the chance for merchants to curry favour with their customers. Afterpay was a service the customer wouldn't have to pay for—the merchant would cover the cost. But the purchaser could have the goods straightaway, and wouldn't get into perpetual debt. The merchant could position themselves as their customers' heroes.

Within two weeks, Nick was on Fabio's back, as he'd yet to close a deal. Eisen jokingly questioned the wisdom of hiring a head of sales whom he could barely understand, given De Carvalho's thick Brazilian accent. But both founders knew Fabio had connections to the very merchants Afterpay was targeting, and he lived and breathed online payments.

By October 2015, Richard Harris had finished his project at CBA and showed up at the new office in Holt Street. By this time Eisen had moved to Melbourne, and was working out of the Touchcorp office. There was no internet in the new Sydney digs so the staff tethered their phones and used mobile data.

Afterpay's loans were maintained on a spreadsheet, and Harris's first job was to ring up the customers who were late with their payments and ask them why they were behind. That was a job he was over-qualified to do but it gave him some insights into the product and its customers.

Meanwhile, Fabio finally had a breakthrough. He'd had a good relationship with Paula Mitchell, the head of ecommerce at General Pants, and convinced her to give Afterpay a go. The two made a bet: if Afterpay delivered the results Fabio promised—driving more conversions, more sales and more revenue—she'd have to wear an Afterpay T-shirt at the next industry conference, and explain why.

In time, Fabio won the bet, and Mitchell honoured it. But the question she most often received was 'how much was Afterpay paying her to be its walking billboard?' The answer was nothing: this was guerrilla marketing at its finest.

Afterpay had also convinced premium fashion brand Cue to sign on in December. Earlier in the year, Eisen had met Justin Levis, Cue's executive director—and Eisen's cousin—who worked three floors below, to pitch the business. Justin's mother, Lynette, was the sister of Anthony's father, Malcolm. She'd married Rod Levis, who founded Cue Group in the late 1960s after he returned from London's Carnaby Street with Beatles T-shirts that sold out in an instant. Cue is well known in Australia for its commitment to local manufacturing and its niche positioning between high-street fast fashion and high-end designer wear.

The family connection didn't make the deal any easier. Cue had met Zip Money months before and wasn't comfortable with the idea of marketing credit to its customers. They were equally apprehensive about alternatives.

While Eisen was pushing the potential for bigger orders and new customers, Justin thought the idea could help him save money by potentially ditching the cumbersome lay-by process. Many of Cue's customers used lay-by, not as a budgeting tool, but to guarantee the size and style they wanted at the best price. A customer would put down a deposit to secure a particular size but then seek to renegotiate when items were put on sale. If Cue could offer the equivalent of lay-by that was better for the customer, it could solve the problem.

Justin also recognised that the 'pay in four instalments' product was better for the customer than pulling out a credit card. He was prepared to give Afterpay a shot. But even then it had taken Eisen and Molnar a long time to convince Shane Lenton, Cue's chief information officer, to turn Afterpay on.

Getting such a mainstream brand on board was a major coup. Cue soon found many of its customers were spending more to get a 'whole look' by buying multiple items.

In November 2015, Molnar took time off to get married. A year earlier he'd proposed to his girlfriend of five years, Gabi. They had met while travelling overseas after high school. Gabi had moved to Brisbane from Johannesburg, South Africa, with her family in 2008. But after meeting Nick, she was persuaded by her friends to move to Sydney and studied interior architecture at the University of New South Wales.

He defied her instruction to not attempt to choose an engagement ring, and even though he'd run a jewellery business, he realised just how difficult it was for prospective grooms to get the high-stakes purchase right. He nailed the selection of the oval halo diamond ring, which he presented to Gabi on a beach in California.

Molnar helpfully shared his experience to help other grooms make the right call. His advice: set a strict budget and buy the best stone you can afford. If you can't find what you're looking for in a store, try online.[5]

When Molnar returned from his honeymoon, Harris revised his financial models and presented them to Molnar and Eisen. At their forecast rate of growth, they would run out of funds early in the new year.

Molnar had to have a word with his salesman. Fabio was closing too many deals with merchants. Molnar and Eisen were funding the sales with private capital, and now they were running low on funds.

If Fabio signed up any more merchants, they'd soon be out of cash. Afterpay's problem had turned on its head. They desperately needed funding.

Molnar, Eisen and Hancock, who by now had finished up at Tower, began the search for capital. The Afterpay team dusted off the pitch book and looked for strategic partners that could provide the funding they desperately required to sustain their early success. The pitch went out to the banks, only to be met with a mixture of apathy and ridicule.

Next Molnar reached out to the Catch Group. It had built a successful online retail business called Catch of the Day, which had been acquired by Wesfarmers. Gabby and Hezi Leibovich agreed to a 30-minute coffee meeting. 'We were dubious whether Nick's tiny software start-up could go up against the likes of Visa, PayPal and other established giants in the sector. We said, "Thanks Nick, but it's not for us, good luck,"' Gabby Leibovich wrote in his book, *Catch of the Decade*.

Afterpay still held out hope of snaring a big fish. Molnar had gone to school with the Lowy grandkids, and Afterpay next reached out to the Westfield Group, which had set up a unit dedicated to investing in early-stage technology companies; the move was designed to help Westfield offset the digital threat posed to their global mall empire. There was interest, but Westfield wasn't known for leaving much on the table in negotiations, and no deal could be reached. Other private investors, such as David Shein, had already decided to back Zip Money, at a lower entry point.

While Robertson had argued for a public listing, as any good stockbroker naturally would, Eisen was hesitant to list Afterpay so early in its life. But he and Molnar gradually determined that it was the only way they could raise the quantum of funds they needed in the time they needed it. They told their advisers, including Cliff Rosenberg. There was never a 'right time' to list, but he had every faith in Molnar and Eisen.

So on 22 February 2016, Afterpay showed its hand when Touch issued a statement to the Australian Securities Exchange: 'Touchcorp is pleased to advise that its associate, Afterpay Holdings, has experienced rapid expansion since June 2015.'

By now Afterpay had over 100 merchant websites onboard—including Optus, SurfStitch and Cue Clothing—and had a strong pipeline. Its customer numbers had grown tenfold from 3000 to 35,000, and it had processed over 100,000 transactions.

'An IPO on acceptable terms to the Afterpay board is one of several alternatives available to Afterpay to fund the expected ongoing growth in transaction volumes and other product and strategic initiatives,' Touchcorp announced.

In a little over two years, Afterpay had gone from a coffee-shop concept to being on the verge of becoming a publicly listed company.

# 6

# GOING PUBLIC

MACQUARIE STREET RUNS uphill for just over a kilometre from the carpark entrance of the Sydney Opera House, along the city's Botanical Gardens up to Hyde Park. A collection of low-rise, 1980s office blocks overlooking the gardens are now overshadowed by the glass skyscrapers behind them—buildings such as Chifley Tower, Governor Phillip Tower and the Renzo Piano–designed Aurora Place—which assert the authority of the law firms, banks and government agencies that inhabit them.

The dazzling harbour views from the boardrooms of these glamorous buildings and the art collections in their foyers are impressive. But the smaller, older and humbler office buildings are not to be overlooked as they are the headquarters for a cluster of the city's scrappy 'small cap' fund managers, who fish beyond the largest 100 companies for share-market winners.

The combined value of all the companies listed on Australia's share market is about $2.7 trillion, and that figure is top-heavy. The leading five companies, four of which are banks or miners, have a worth of more than $500 billion. That's the same as the bottom-tier 430 companies in the All Ordinaries Index combined.

The high concentration of large companies used to be unique to Australia. But the unstoppable rise of Silicon Valley's top five has changed that. Amazon, Facebook, Apple, Microsoft and Google have defied the laws of market gravity. As they have grown, their ability to generate sales and profits has not slowed. They now account for 15 per cent of the US share market's value. But these dominant companies have a very different character to those of the Australian share market. That these giants are technology innovators, and that they're growing, has meant there's less loathing of their share-market dominance, even as their questionable use of customer data comes into the spotlight.

In contrast, the Australian share market is dominated by banks and mining companies, which confirms the self-deprecating description of a nation built on 'houses and holes'. Australia's miners dig iron ore and coal out of the ground and ship it to China, while our banks provide the mortgages to prop up Australia's seemingly never-ending growth in house prices. Houses and holes fuel our prosperity.

The uneven composition of Australia's stock market has consequences for our superannuation funds, and for the investment firms they hire on behalf of their members. If they choose to invest money broadly into the share market, the outcome will be a function of a few key variables. These include, on the one hand, the health of China's economy and Australia's relationship with it; and on the other, the demand for mortgages and the interest-rate settings, which influence the profit margins the banks can earn.

Investment firms that are hired to beat the broader market index dominated by banks and miners must also decide how greatly they are willing to risk deviating from the target return. If they are downbeat about the miners and then the price of iron ore surges, they'll underperform, which means they risk forfeiting their performance fees and face the prospect that superannuation funds or advisers will take their capital elsewhere. This factor is what makes tech investing a riskier proposition in Australia than in markets abroad.

While large investment firms are still tied to these traditional markets, in the world of small caps the possibilities are far greater. These funds aren't judged against how the 100 largest companies perform, but against the companies that rank from 101 to 300.

They still have a target to beat, but with more companies to choose from, and a broader suite of industries, the outcomes can be more dispersed. The big fund managers in the smaller pond can throw their weight around more. Stockbrokers and analysts can influence share price moves more, as can charismatic executives that woo investors. Sydney's and Melbourne's hedge funds back themselves to discover undervalued companies and to bet against overvalued companies by shorting them.

The epicentre of Sydney's small-cap community is 139 Macquarie Street, which has been dubbed by traders as 'Fund Manager House'. One day in March 2016, Tobias Yao of Wilson Asset Management (WAM) made the short stroll from that building to the offices of stockbroker Wilson HTM for a lunch presentation (this is a city where names are sometimes duplicated).

The long, boozy midday feasts in dark Italian restaurants that were once commonplace in the city are now all but extinct. Younger, more health-conscious analysts squeeze workouts into their days and usually eat a salad at their desk; if the opportunity is compelling enough, they will take in a corporate pitch at a broker over trays of sandwiches.

That day, Wilson HTM's dealmaker, Hugh Robertson, who had recently plotted his defection to rival brokerage firm Bell Potter, was parading Afterpay's management duo in preparation for its initial public offering. Eisen put in long hours to get the prospectus ready in time. But the task was complicated by the Epson printer in the Surry Hills office that had been seconded from Nick's bedroom. Each draft took at least an hour to print, which meant long lags for Molnar and Harris to read and update Eisen's mark-ups. When Mike

Roth, the business operations manager, arrived with a more suitable printer, the relief was palpable.

The prospectus showed that Afterpay had 100 merchants and almost $3 million of sales in February. The corporate regulator had taken exception to certain statements, but the company's prospects were good, and with stockbrokers and wealthy clients among the shareholders, every effort would be made to ensure a smooth listing.

Some small-cap managers knew of Afterpay. A handful had invested or looked at Touchcorp, and been charmed by Adrian Cleeve. They were aware that when Touchcorp floated, Afterpay owed it money.

Yao was born in China and had moved to Sydney while in high school. In 2014, Yao joined Geoff Wilson's Wilson Asset Management. He'd been hired from Pengana Capital, a boutique funds-management group also based in Macquarie Street where he'd analysed Asian tech stocks.

Geoff was one of the most recognisable names in funds management, growing his investment firm through a unique brand of activism that involved gobbling up smaller, underperforming listed funds. He did this primarily by using the higher currency of his funds, which had been listed on the ASX in a structure known as a 'LIC', or listed investment company. They traded at prices that were above the underlying value of the share investments they owned, allowing Wilson to buy shares of listed funds that changed hands below the value of those investments. When his position was big enough, he'd threaten to unwind the investments.

The Wilson team were small-cap specialists, and were often happy to back young companies. They had funds at hand that they could provide to help get deals done if the price was right. Yao heard the Afterpay pitch with three other managers. Once it concluded, he chatted to Molnar and Eisen.

A friend of his named Jane Lu, the founder of online retailer Showpo, had told Yao about Afterpay, and how it was driving sales on the website. Lu, the daughter of Chinese immigrants, had walked from an internship at accounting firm Ernst & Young to create a woman's fashion label. She used data to work out what items were selling and to predict what would sell in the future. She was an instant success with young Australian women. At 31, Lu was estimated by the Financial Review Rich List to have a net worth of $32 million.[1]

Yao and the team of Wilson analysts mulled over whether to invest in the Afterpay float. They were impressed by the traction Afterpay was having with retailers and customers, and decided to bet that it would snowball into something significant. WAM asked for as much stock as they could get.

Yao did not know it at the time, but WAM was one of only a small handful of institutional funds that backed the float; the others were Cyan Investment Management in Melbourne and Matthew Kidman's Centennial Funds Management.

'They were balanced and reserved and never hyped it up—which is unusual for tech entrepreneurs,' said Cyan's Dean Fergie.[2] He had tried Afterpay to buy his thirteen-year-old son a Culture Club hoodie online, and it had worked seamlessly. Afterpay had underappreciated potential, he decided, so he bid into the float.

In 2016, after the experience of some technology bubbles, there was little appetite across the broader market to invest in speculative, early-stage concept companies that had yet to generate a profit. A year before, Afterpay had been little more than an idea. Now it was pitching itself as a start-up worth $100 million. Was there space in a crowded market for a new platform? Could a company like this garner trust when mainstream banks were losing it?

The approach to start-ups was at odds with a market that had been built up on speculative miners. Australian share-market investors, generally, weren't afraid to take a punt. The tail of the ASX was littered with mining prospectors that had lured smaller investors dreaming of untold riches.

The Poseidon bubble of 1969, when a small listed prospector's nickel discovery led to a share price surge that made it three times more valuable than the Bank of New South Wales, had left an indelible mark. The euphoria of Poseidon had lured scores of shady miners that inevitably collapsed.

'Australia is not only well endowed with minerals. It is also generously endowed with share manipulators,' read one letter to the editor of *The Wall Street Journal* in October 1969. Half a century later, few would disagree that neither resource had been depleted.

In fact, nearly three decades of uninterrupted economic prosperity that began in the 1990s, and a housing boom, meant that the masses were cashed up. There was no shortage of people willing to try their luck in the share market, and no shortage of promoters able to source the stock to play whatever the hot theme was.

The institutions, however, were more reserved. They were answerable to financial advisers or pension funds that hired consultants to monitor and screen their decisions. The funds had to demonstrate a repeatable process—and that made it hard to justify investing in speculative concept stocks.

But an evolution was underway. Globally, technology stocks were taking off, and Australia didn't have many. Hamish Douglass, a former investment banker turned fund manager, was dazzling financial planners around the country with his pitch about how Big Tech was changing the world, and why Australians simply had to own a piece of these profit machines.

The ASX only had a handful of successful tech companies that were worth over $1 billion: accounting software firms Xero and MYOB, enterprise software maker Technology One and construction software company Aconex. But the ASX was generally seen as an investment backwater devoid of tech and innovation, and investors who failed to ditch their home bias risked losing out. Brokers sensed an opportunity, while the ASX went into promotional overdrive to encourage tech listings to play on the 'fear of missing out'.

In April 2016, as Eisen, Molnar and Harris were doing the rounds with prospective investors, logistics software firm WiseTech Global went public, with shares priced to value the business at $1 billion. There was nothing new or sexy about WiseTech, which was formed all the way back in 1994, when VHS had triumphed over Betamax. It had built a system to monitor supply chains and logistics. Its founder, Richard White, was a creature of the pre-internet technology era. He used to repair guitars for rock band AC/DC.

The company also made money, which was so unusual among tech firms that it could be said to be unfashionable. WiseTech was forecasting a $25 million profit over the next twelve months. But WiseTech's management was aware of what the market really wanted: revenue growth. Its share-market listing would give it the currency and the access to capital to make that possible, as it prepared to snap up competitors around the world.

Afterpay's float did not attract the same attention as WiseTech's, which was managed by brokers of prestigious global investment banks Credit Suisse and Morgan Stanley.

Whenever an Australian company lists on the stock exchange, thrown in free with the listing is a ceremony at the ASX headquarters to commemorate what is sometimes the proudest day in a founder's corporate life. There's no confetti parade, but there's the placard, the champagne and the photo opportunity of the executives ringing the bell in a function room behind the screens where members of the public can drop in and see the market's equity prices.

If the listing of Afterpay was the beginning of something new and exciting, there were no clues. Molnar and Eisen broke with so-called tech bro tradition, too. They opted against bright T-shirts, posing for photographs at the ASX satellite office in Melbourne in conservative dark suits.

The pair struck a slightly awkward pose as Eisen, who kept one hand in his pocket, gestured to Molnar to pull the rope of the bell. Nick yanked it with a sheepish grin before Eisen put out his hand to shake Molnar's—only for him to lift it up so he rang the bell, too. They both smiled, patted each other on the back and walked away, unsure as to whether the photo opportunity was over.

At a dinner that night, Molnar told his team that he was no longer scared of failure. Eisen had been apprehensive about listing. He'd initially been against the idea, arguing that it was too soon for Afterpay to be exposed to the scrutiny of the public markets. At Guinness Peat Group, he'd experienced firsthand the trials and tribulations of life as a public company.

In fact, a two-year-old start-up listing on the ASX could have been a reason to mourn, rather than celebrate. In 2016, the best and brightest businesses of the future weren't creating wealth for the public on the stock market, but for venture capital funds in private.

In the late 1990s, the last golden age of tech, which culminated in the dotcom bubble, founders were coming to the share market early in the hope of attracting investors that could make their big dreams a reality. Cisco, Amazon, Microsoft and eBay had all floated with a market value of less than US$1 billion, allowing public share-market investors to enjoy incredible wealth creation as their stocks headed into the stratosphere. That's what the share market was intended for—and had been ever since the first public companies were created back in Amsterdam, where speculators could bet a little money that a sea voyage would return with untold riches.

But that was now the purpose of venture funds, not the share market. In the 2010s, Facebook, Twitter and Snap were delaying their IPOs until their valuations were well into the billions, and both the founders and their venture capital investors made a hundred times their money. There was an abundance of private capital, and the venture capitalists had mastered the art of the 'up-round', in which backers can get rich and get out long before the IPO. And the IPO had nothing to do with raising funds to grow, but to create a 'liquidity event' so staff could access the shares they were promised and sell them to new shareholders to realise some profit.

For Afterpay to go public so early meant the growth-hacking venture funds had deemed the business unworthy of their moonshot money, and had allowed it to pass through to the uneducated masses.

And the measures of success had changed. A company's prospects were no longer its profit potential, or even (in some cases) its ability to generate sales. This was the age of the opportunity. If the 'total addressable market'—which analysts refer to as TAM—was large, then any attempt to capture a share of it was considered worthy of backing.

Australia's community of venture capital funds were particularly vocal about their abilities and the role they played in driving the economy forward. Most had a limited track record, given the nascent industry, but they demanded a voice, and capital, as an economic imperative.

Afterpay did present a compelling TAM. In its prospectus, it noted that Australians had spent $19.1 billion in online retail in the year to December 2015, which was 6.5 per cent of the total retail market of $293 billion. But the company had fallen through the cracks, even though all the venture capital funds had been pitched the opportunity. Even Mark Carnegie's enthusiasm for Molnar's entrepreneurialism had reached its limits. He declined the chance to invest. CVC, which had former GPG executive Sandy Beard as chair, had been the only one to write it a cheque. CVC was a shareholder in Touchcorp, but Hugh Robertson had shown them the deal.

Others passed. In part this was because the generous tax breaks afforded to venture capital funds in the form of capital gains tax exemptions and offsets were not available for investing in fintech: the Australian federal government's 'Early Stage Venture Capital Limited Partnership' (ESVCLP) scheme excluded financial services start-ups and lenders. A bet on Afterpay would not come with these incentives.

Afterpay's early rival Zip Money had met with a similar lack of interest from angel investors, which provide funding to early-stage business ideas. Co-founder Larry Diamond had tried to attract venture funds, but beyond a small handful of wealthy individuals who liked him more than his lending business, he got little support. A few investors suggested he find a business partner with credit experience, and a recruiter had uncovered Peter Gray, ten years Diamond's senior, who knew the ins and outs of selling credit to someone when they're in a shop—but he came from a world that relied on paper forms.

Over meetings at a pub in North Sydney, the pair had discussed how the model of 'interest-free' finance being supplied by GE Finance at Harvey Norman stores was broken, but they realised they couldn't compete with Australia's banks in issuing cards, so they had to find an unfair advantage: partnering with retailers. They saw the win-win elements: a sale for the retailer, spread-out payments for the customer, and a customer for Zip.

In 2013, they'd decided to pull the trigger and create Zip, setting up in Bondi Junction, at the top of the hill from the famous beach and just a short drive from where Eisen and Molnar had met three years before. In another coincidence, Diamond and Molnar had both attended the same school, Moriah College, but Diamond is eight years older than Molnar so their paths had not crossed.

Diamond and Gray spent these early days pitching to small retailers. Chappelli Cycles was the first to come on board, using Zip to sell a $500 bike. Diamond had tipped in money from a T-shirt business he had been running after being made redundant from Deutsche Bank in 2012, but by early 2015, after operating on the smell of an oily rag, Zip needed more funding.

Short on cash, he'd turned to his stockbroker friend John Winters at Shaw and Partners. With limited options, they sought an ASX listing—but not through the front door. A business can list on the ASX via a reverse merger, in which an existing, semi-defunct listed company agrees to raise money to buy a more valuable private business with better prospects. Provided the shareholders and directors agree, it's possible for a doomed goldminer to transform into a trendy fintech.

Winters had called on his client, Rubianna Resources chairman and barrister Philip Crutchfield QC, to provide the necessary boardroom support. Rubianna was a goldminer with Western Australian tenements that had turned out to be duds. Zip was soon on the ASX.

The initial reaction to the listing had been frosty. 'A start-up that gives interest-free loans to online shoppers for anything from boob jobs to bicycles will raise $5 million via a backdoor listing to take the fight to established rivals like GE Capital and FlexiGroup,' wrote Fairfax's Shaun Drummond on 30 June 2015, three months before the float. The headline writers did Zip no favours: the banner of the article read 'Meet the $5 a day boob job lender'.[3]

If Australia's tech starlets were listing, it was not in Australia. In late 2015, Australia's most successful tech start-up had shunned the ASX for the US Nasdaq. Atlassian, a business that made the proverbial picks and shovels for the IT departments to build their own corporate software tools, had grown impressively since it was founded by Mike Cannon-Brookes and Scott Farquhar. Farquhar had attended New South Wales' best-performing selective public school, James Ruse Agricultural High, while Cannon-Brookes hailed from Cranbrook College in Sydney's Eastern Suburbs, a few hundred metres from where Eisen and Molnar lived.

In its early days, Atlassian had the backing of Silicon Valley venture fund Accel Partners, which had helped steer it towards a Nasdaq listing. Its impressive journey from basement to US$55 billion enterprise has made the pair Australia's wealthiest technology entrepreneurs. The Nasdaq is a favoured exchange for tech stocks, and most of Atlassian's backers, and indeed its customers, were based in the United States. The company had flown a group of its teamsters from Sydney to New York to revel in the moment as confetti rained onto the trading floor. 'TEAM' was chosen as the four-letter trading ticker.

There was another benefit for Atlassian in listing in the United States rather than in Australia: the ability to put a dual-class share structure in place. This would allow the founders to raise money without giving as much control to new shareholders. After the IPO, Cannon-Brookes and Farquhar had a 66 per cent economic interest in Atlassian but controlled 86.6 per cent of the shareholder vote, as they owned Class A voting shares.

The dual-class structure was contentious. Some investors viewed it as an undemocratic dictatorship that gave the founders too much power. Others said the evidence suggested otherwise: the founders could run the company according to their vision, and the non-voters could enjoy the economic success that their interference might have diluted. Facebook and Google, two of the most powerful and profitable companies of all time, had dual-class structures. Apple, Amazon, Microsoft and Twitter did not.

Eisen and Molnar had, from the very first private raising, diluted their ownership of Afterpay to less than 40 per cent. But they still had a tight grip on the destiny of the company. Afterpay's early ASX listing meant they would have to pursue domination the old-fashioned way, courting the stock-market analysts and brokers, and selling their story to investment institutions in Australia and around the world. Every step would be taken in full view of the public, and they would be subject to continuous disclosure requirements. Any information—good, bad or ugly—would have to be shared with shareholders immediately.

Stockbroker Hugh Robertson had urged Molnar and Eisen to float. The share market, he argued, would give them the funds they needed to suck the oxygen from their competition. Eventually, Eisen and Molnar came to the same conclusion, and a national investors' roadshow was set up in March 2016. Although many investors turned down the offer, convinced that credit cards would continue to dominate online shopping, Molnar began to grow more confident that the product was gaining traction when, in between meetings in Melbourne, he checked his Facebook advertising impressions and hits on the Afterpay website: the numbers were surging.

At midday on Wednesday, 4 May 2016, Afterpay shares, trading under the ticker 'AFY', hit the ASX at $1 a share. 'What we're pioneering in Australia is buy now, pay later online, in real time,' Eisen told Shaun Drummond, who reported on the listing for *The Australian Financial Review*. Molnar described how Afterpay was 'purposefully very customer friendly. If you're buying a pair of jeans for $200, the end payment is still $200,' he said, while for the merchant, sales increased. 'In the first week Afterpay was live on General Pants Co, we accounted for 20 per cent of online sales.'[4]

The shares closed at the end of that first day 25 per cent higher. Afterpay had arrived on the ASX.

• • •

David Allingham's first job out of university was a marketing role at record label EMI. He had completed a commerce degree at The University of Sydney in 2002 after finishing high school at Sydney Grammar, where his father, Robert, taught English. Allingham's brief was to come up with a marketing plan to boost the record sales of EMI's international and Australian artists, via press releases, pushing the songs onto the airwaves, selling to retailers and arranging tours.

In many ways EMI was his dream job: he worked with Australian grunge rockers Silverchair, the funk- and Latin-influenced Cat Empire and country singer Kasey Chambers. He also hosted American singer-songwriters Jack Johnson and Ben Harper, both regular fixtures at Byron Bay's Splendour in the Grass festival. But Allingham was frustrated. His grunt work added little value. If the songs got airtime, the records sold—it had nothing to do with him. So he began looking for something more fulfilling.

With no investing experience, Allingham showed up at the door of the Eley Griffiths Group, an investment firm Ben Griffiths and Brian Eley had set up two years before, in 2002. Allingham was taken on as an analyst, and soon proved his worth. Eventually, he was given his own funds to manage.

Eley Griffiths was on the hunt for undervalued companies, and Touchcorp had caught its eye. The company was generating decent profits, and it had a stake in Afterpay. The Eley Griffiths team liked Afterpay's prospects, but was apprehensive about investing in a start-up that made no profit. So investing in Touchcorp was a more sensible way to bet on it.

Allingham and the other analysts began digging into the company. They'd been to Touchcorp's office in La Trobe Street, which runs across the northern side of Melbourne's CBD, where Adrian Cleeve mapped out on the whiteboard how Afterpay would grow.

As it happened, Allingham had met Eisen as a boy. Anthony was a pupil of Allingham's father at Sydney Grammar, and one summer day Eisen's family had invited him on their speedboat for a cruise around Sydney Harbour. For Allingham's parents, both schoolteachers, and young David, who tagged along, it was quite a treat.

Almost 30 years later, he sent Eisen an email to reintroduce himself and remind him of their day on the boat. Shortly after, he got a warm reply from Eisen, who recalled the influence Allingham's father had had on him. They agreed to meet for a coffee when Eisen was next in Sydney.

Ben Griffiths also did his scouting. He'd run into Ron Brierley, and asked him about Afterpay: why had he chosen to invest? 'Anthony is the most backable bloke I know,' was Brierley's response. But later, Brierley told Griffiths he didn't understand the business, and had banked a tenfold gain for having faith in his understudy when the shares were released from escrow.

In early May 2016, Allingham met Eisen for a coffee near their office at 139 Macquarie Street.

The pair chatted about where life had taken them since that day on the harbour, but also about Eley Griffith's investment in Touchcorp. Eisen said he'd regretted selling GPG's stake back in 2012 at the price he had. The sale had valued Touchcorp at $10 million; after the float and a run-up in the share price, the company was now worth closer to $250 million.

Allingham had a better sense of the Touchcorp business, Afterpay's prospects and its management. He returned to the office to run the numbers and consider the investment.

Shortly after his meeting with Allingham, Eisen was due to present at a conference hosted by Goldman Sachs, in the investment bank's office in the nearby Governor Phillip Tower. His 26-page presentation outlined the Afterpay business and the potential of the buy now, pay later sector. Afterpay was more than a payment method: it was increasing the sales and the basket sizes of the merchants that offered it, while reducing non-payment risk.

Over 160 merchants had already signed up. SurfStitch had initially figured the pay in four instalment offering would allow it to sell more highly priced surfboards online, but had instead seen sales of T-shirts and shorts rise.

Afterpay had processed $5 million of sales in April 2016, generating almost $200,000 in merchant fees—representing an average fee paid to Afterpay of 4 per cent of the sale. Young customers who could not trust themselves with credit were flocking to the service, which would start them on a few hundred dollars of credit and lift the limit as they showed themselves capable of repaying. It would also block them from spending too much and not allow them to use the service again unless all their payments were up to date. It was a product construct fundamentally different to that of the credit card, which allowed customers to pay just a minimum balance only to accumulate much larger debt as compounding interest was charged.

Molnar had also made an important strategic call to require the Afterpay logo to appear on the website of every retailer, not just at the checkout page, where credit card and PayPal logos were typically seen. This ingrained Afterpay into the experience of buying the product, rather than just of making the payment, and so developed a closer bond with users. The 20 per cent jump in sales at General Pants and Princess Polly helped Molnar encourage other retailers to sign up, and inbound inquiries started to pour in.

The addressable market was large. Almost $300 billion of retail purchases were made by Australians, of which $30 billion were online. While the online segment was growing by 11 per cent a year, the offline market was also there for the taking.

On 12 July 2016, Afterpay had good news to deliver to its investors. The number of merchants who had signed up for Afterpay had doubled to over 300 in just three months, while the number of users had surpassed 100,000. Afterpay was now processing over $20 million of sales a quarter, raking in over $800,000 in fees. The losses per transaction, a measure of write-offs divided by the number of financed sales, were also trending down. Afterpay shares popped 10 per cent to $1.79. The potential was beginning to be appreciated.

During the 21 July trading session, the shares touched $3 for the first time before settling to end the month at $2.30.

By the end of August, retailers had doubled from the number reported in July, to over 600. In its inaugural full-year results presentation as a listed company on 27 August, Afterpay pointed to the impact its product was having on some big retailers. At Veronika Maine, the average online order value had increased by 22 per cent while total online sales were up 21 per cent; at General Pants, the numbers were even better, with the average order value rising 25 per cent and total online sales up 32 per cent.

The doubling of Afterpay's share price made new capital more affordable, and in late August it tapped institutions and wealthy investors for funds, raising $36 million at $2.40 a share. Bell Potter was hired to source the funds, and existing institutional investors backed the deal, but several new funds took advantage of the placement to get involved. Among them was Eley Griffiths. Allingham and the team decided to switch their investment from Touchcorp to a direct bet on Afterpay.

Dean Fergie of Cyan was pleased with his decision to back Afterpay. The share price had more than doubled since the IPO, and he touted the company's business model to *The Australian Financial Review*'s markets editor Vesna Poljak in an August interview. He identified the relatively small value of purchases, which limited credit risk, and the high-margin products that it was being used to buy, which made the high fee compared to traditional payment methods an easier sell.

'The consumer says, "That's great"; the merchant says, "This is great, we're selling it for full price to a guy we otherwise may not have sold it to"; and Afterpay takes a bit of credit risk, but they know it's not much,' Fergie explained. Afterpay was processing lots of small transactions. It wasn't financing new Aston Martins. 'Would you rather sell a [$100] product for $96, or not at all? I guarantee the margins on board shorts are not 4 per cent, they're probably closer to 100 per cent. They're seeing massive growth.'[5]

But there were a few early hiccups for Afterpay. One involved Visa threatening to prevent Afterpay using its payment network. Afterpay works by having its customers link their debit or credit cards to their Afterpay account. This means payments are sent via the Visa or Mastercard networks, depending on which card is issued by the customer's bank. While most customers link up debit cards, the ability to use credit cards to pay back the instalments raised eyebrows at Visa.

While Afterpay and Australian law did not view its short-term loans as credit, because they do not charge the customer any interest, Visa did—and, under its rules, credit couldn't be used to pay off credit. It had introduced this policy to prevent a problem known as 'kiting', whereby a customer would take out a new credit card to pay off a previous one. Now Visa was trying to work out whether this new business model could be in breach of these rules. If Visa blocked Afterpay from using its network, it might be fatal for the young company.

A call by David Hancock to a senior Visa executive—who was at the Rio Olympic Games at the time—convinced the payments giant to consider its commercial interests: for every Afterpay transaction, Visa's payments switch would be hit four times, as the instalment set-up created four separate repayments. This would earn Visa four times the fee revenue from what was really a single transaction. A compromise was reached: Afterpay could stay on the network and a potential disaster was averted.

Afterpay was also nearing the end of lengthy and difficult negotiations with an Australian bank that it had not publicly named, which had begun a year earlier, on 11 February 2016.

That was when Eisen, Hancock and Richard Harris headed to the Sydney headquarters of National Australia Bank at 255 George

Street, directly opposite Ron Molnar's jewellery store. There they met Tony Carr, the director of its institutional diversified financial clients. Carr's unit banked firms that were in the business of lending money but fell outside the oversight of banking regulators.

Carr was regularly approached by start-up lenders seeking financing, and almost always turned them down, mostly on the basis that they were under-capitalised variations on the same theme. But he took an immediate interest in Afterpay. The model was simple and elegant, and he felt that he management team were both transparent and trustworthy. Carr left the meeting a champion of the Afterpay cause.

But he met with resistance. The senior decision-makers in the bank, including the credit department, discouraged him from spending more time on a small potential client whose assets weren't what NAB wanted—which was home loans, vehicle-financing, personal loans and credit cards. Afterpay was also thinly capitalised with founder money, and the idea of backing a player that wanted to compete for its credit card customers was another reason to let it go. Finally, like Visa, the bank harboured concerns that the product was a form of credit on credit. But Carr kept at it, and convinced his colleagues to push the bank's credit managers to consider approving a loan to Afterpay that it urgently needed. When Afterpay had first met Carr, they were banging on the doors of retail merchants—but now merchants were ringing them, and their capacity to provide funding was running thin.

The IPO was the barrier breaker for Carr. NAB's bankers now had more faith that Afterpay could raise the capital they might need to buffer any losses. The process that had initially been held up was fast-tracked. NAB's credit team didn't give Afterpay the green light, but there were no red flags and a lending agreement could be set up.

Establishing a loan facility wasn't straightforward. Afterpay's loans didn't fit a template. It didn't charge interest, while funds could be refunded, or repaid over time. And there were a lot of loans. While the amounts were small, the sheer number of loans rivalled that of a regional bank. Harris had to work hard to set up the systems that laid the groundwork for future funding agreements.

Afterpay was eventually granted a $20 million secured loan facility that sat on NAB's institutional loan book. The loan was backed by about $4 million of Afterpay's capital, but effectively gave Afterpay the ability to finance $200 million of sales a year.

For Carr it was a breakthrough, but for Afterpay it was a pivotal moment. Not only did the loan provide funding for the growth they could see ahead of them, but it also gave more merchants faith that the model was viable. And with the backing of one of Australia's 'big four' banks, and the biggest lender to business in Australia, Afterpay's management now had a far better story to tell the share market.

• • •

On 7 November 2016, Molnar appeared on a panel at the annual investment conference of UBS. The Swiss bank was Australia's dominant investment bank, leading the deal-making and brokerage league tables, and its conference was a key event on the calendar for its corporate and investment clients. Sydney in early November, when spring is in full swing, helps entice clients from their frosty Northern Hemisphere locations.

Michael Walsh, a veteran salesman at UBS with close ties to Australia's top investors and wealthy families, was sensing an increased interest in investing in technology and had helped shape the conference's agenda along those lines. The keynote speaker was Alec Ross, an adviser to Hillary Clinton; he had written a bestselling book on disruption in 2016 called *The Industries of the Future*, which examined big data and blockchain technologies. But the main game of the conference each year is the one-on-one 'speed-dating' sessions held in the meeting rooms of the five-star Sheraton on the Park hotel between investment analysts and the corporate representatives—usually the chief executives and chief financial officers—of over 100 top companies.

Molnar used his panel slot to provide information about Afterpay, which by now had more proof points that its instalment payments model was becoming an indispensable sales hack for online retailers. The venture was helping companies such as Veronika Maine and General Pants to increase both the number of customers who finished an online order, and the number of items each customer put into their digital shopping trolley. Overall, the Afterpay effect was a 20 per cent increase in sales: almost like magic, the psychological effect of splitting a payment into four made the customer willing to spend an extra $1 in every $5. 'We aren't just changing how people pay, we're changing how people shop,' Molnar said.

But the conference was marked by tragedy for the Afterpay team. Touchcorp CEO Adrian Cleeve was scheduled to present at 2.30 pm in the Hyde Park ballroom, along with representatives of other emerging companies. But he never made it. That morning, he collapsed while exercising, and the following day the company confirmed his sudden passing at the age of just 62.

There was also a sense of unease hanging over the conference as the 800 attendees mingled on the mezzanine level of the hotel. The first Tuesday in November of a leap year meant a US presidential election. Donald Trump, the reality TV star, had defied all conventional wisdom to win the Republican nomination. He could win the race to White House, but the betting odds suggested he would fall short. As the conference was winding up, and guests were jetting home or heading to Sydney's bars and high-end restaurants, Americans were heading to the polls.

On Wednesday, 9 November, as the results rolled in, traders in the Asian time zone had to anticipate the outcome. In the course of a Sydney lunch, the race turned in Trump's favour and the markets soured. US stock futures plunged nearly 10 per cent. As Australians returned home from work later in the day, Hillary Clinton conceded. Most watched Trump's victory speech in disbelief. But as they did, the collective global markets had an epiphany: Trump was good for stocks. A real estate developer who loved debt would spend money, cut taxes and slash red tape. Market screens turned emphatically green.

The economy would run hot, and perhaps too hot. Bond markets now had to contemplate that a strong economy would lead to a shortage of workers, forcing up wages and prices. Bond yields cranked up, and as they did, the pendulum swung away from new-world tech stocks, which thrived in an environment of low-interest rates, and towards old-world banks and industrial corporations that had once seemed to have been left behind.

For Afterpay, the macro didn't matter too much. The dawning of a new age of political strongmen and the level of the ten-year bond rate had no bearing on how a university student would pay for the clothes she bought online. These were forces that were only exerted on the largest companies on the exchange.

For other investors, it was time to get involved. Alex Waislitz, the billionaire investor, had been watching Afterpay from the sidelines. Waislitz was known for his extravagant parties and shrewd investments. The 58-year-old, who lived like a prince in a mansion in Toorak, Melbourne, famously rewarded the individual who brought him his most lucrative idea with a gift at his annual party. The prizes ranged from a sportscar to a trip on the Trans-Siberian Railway. Recently, Webjet CEO John Guscic had won a Tesla, and jokingly lamented it wasn't a Ferrari. He then gifted the car to his daughter.

Waislitz had set up the investment firm he controlled, Thorney, alongside Ashok Jacob, and had an early win in Monadelphous, the engineering group. But unlike Jacob, he had passed on the Afterpay seed-funding round. Now that Afterpay was more than an idea—it was already a fast-growing listed company—he was prepared to invest aggressively.

The brokerage firms that had helped Afterpay raise capital—Wilson HTM and Bell Potter—had committed to formally covering the stock by assigning their analysts to publish research. The analyst reports and price targets helped drum up interest in the company and encouraged more trading of Afterpay shares. They also gave overburdened institutional investors more comfort that the business's activities were being scrutinised and factored into the share price.

Bell Potter's financial analyst Lafitani Sotiriou initiated coverage of Afterpay in mid-November 2016 with a speculative buy rating and a price target of $3.53. The brokerage firm had its own fiefdoms, but Sotiriou had won the respect of the firm's brokers for making the call with high conviction that traditional wealth managers would be disrupted by newer, more nimble players. He was no pushover, but he liked what he saw in Afterpay and was willing to put his reputation on the line. Sotiriou was encouraged by the fact that Afterpay could generate a profit, which meant this was not a cash-consuming start-up but a viable operation.

Wilson HTM's Mark Bryan was already covering Afterpay, and had a $3.20 target price. Afterpay, he said, was worth $1.82 if it could capture 5 per cent of online retail sales, or $5.50 if it could grow its share to 15 per cent.

An even bigger opportunity existed if Afterpay could crack payments in physical stores. Despite the growth in ecommerce, online sales made up only 10 per cent of business at most fashion retailers. Cue had made the leap and switched on Afterpay in its retail stores in August, allowing customers to pay by taking a photo of a barcode with their smartphone. Veronika Maine and Topshop were also rolling out instore capability. But as the year drew to a close, Molnar realised he'd need to find more retail experience if Afterpay was to convince others to adopt the service, where the vast bulk of sales were still made. He tapped Paul Greenberg to make some connections.

The outlook for capturing a rising chunk of online and instore sales was firming up as groups of loyal customers started linking up on social media to tout their shopping experiences. They were essentially doing Afterpay's marketing for it. One Facebook group, called 'We Love Afterpay', was created on 9 November 2016. It would grow to have more than 100,000 members. Another was 'Afterpay Obsession'. The groups popped up organically, surprising Afterpay, validating its bet that customers would love both the flexibility its interest-free instalments provided and the experience of using the service.

But some fund managers were taking the view that Afterpay's share price, which ticked above $5 in early December, had got ahead of itself. Mike Taylor, of New Zealand–based Pie Investments, picked Afterpay as his stock to bet against, in an annual *Australian Financial Review* survey at the end of 2016.

'With a market cap of $500 million and revenue of $12.3 million forecast for June 2017, it is truly priced for perfection,' he suggested. 'We like the payments space and Afterpay has done a great job signing up quality merchants, but on an enterprise basis Afterpay is trading close to 40 times forward revenue. These revenue forecasts may or may not prove conservative, but there is no question that the multiple has got ahead of itself.'

Taylor also expected online payments to become more competitive, and he was worried that Afterpay did not conduct any external credit checks on its customers. 'This is a young company and it remains to be seen where bad debts will level out, especially with a weaker economic backdrop.'[6]

# 7

# THE UNSUSPECTED
# SECRET

On 7 November 2016, Adrian Cleeve made the short trip to the gym of his penthouse apartment in Melbourne for a workout ahead of a trip to Sydney that day. He collapsed on the treadmill and later died. On the morning of Tuesday, 8 November, his family announced that, at the age of 62, he'd passed away after a short illness. The stock market was informed via a release by Touchcorp, the company he had been associated with for almost twenty years.

Cleeve's death shocked Eisen, who had known him since his GPG days. The two men had become even closer as their companies partnered together. Moments before Cleeve began his morning workout, he'd sent Eisen a text message. Cleeve had been tracking Afterpay's sales volumes and shared his excitement with Eisen about how they were growing. Cleeve had been enthusiastic since the Afterpay journey began. But, tragically, his own journey had been cut short.

The future of both companies was now highly uncertain. To further complicate matters, Cleeve had died without leaving a will. His years of corporate manoeuvring meant his shareholdings in Touchcorp were held by three entities: Cleevecorp, his family investment trust, which had existed for two decades; ATC Capital, created to buy shares from Guinness Peat Group; and in his own name.

Cleeve's young wife, Wendy, was several months pregnant when he died. She sent Adrian's brother Terence, an accountant, a spreadsheet outlining his assets. It seemed most of the shares were Adrian's, which meant they would likely pass to her.

Mike Jefferies was a GPG veteran, and a shareholder and director of both Afterpay and Touchcorp. After a long and gruelling career, he had little interest in managing the operations of a listed company. But circumstances left him with little choice, and so he agreed to take on the role of CEO. The grief at Touch rendered many of the senior staffers incapacitated. But Jefferies found himself relying on the steady hand of general counsel Sophie Karzis, chief financial officer Nadine Lennie and Elana Rubin in the boardroom. One of his first duties was to confess to investors that Touchcorp's full-year revenues would fall well short of the $42 million it had achieved in 2015, its first year as a listed company. The profit would be $14 million, all of which related to a gain in the value of its Afterpay investment. Touchcorp had tried to repeat its success and had backed another start-up, Change Up, that wasn't delivering.

Its main business, Touchcorp now conceded, was below expectations and it would have to hire more sales staff. The market didn't take kindly to the big miss and the shares plunged 40 per cent, to below $1. Almost $75 million was wiped off the company's market value in a single brutal session. Investors, some of whom had just tipped money into a $26 million raising, had lost faith in Touchcorp, which had demonstrated strong potential but also entered into unprofitable contracts that lifted revenues but did little to create value for shareholders.

Afterpay by contrast was going well. The investors that had backed Afterpay in its first raising were on track to make ten times their money. They were bound by an agreement not to sell their shares until one year after the IPO and, as that date approached, Eisen gathered them together to provide an update.

On Tuesday, 21 February 2017, over sandwiches at Bell Potter's offices at Sydney's Aurora Place, he told them he wasn't going to talk them out of selling, but that he owed it to them to demonstrate how well the business was tracking. Some investors, including Brierley, had been itching to sell early and cash in on their good fortune. They'd tried to come up with workarounds to evade the escrow. CVC and Ron Brierley's Mercantile prepared to sell out, as did the mysterious Barbados-based Sidereal Holdings, which had 5.5 million shares.

Others, such as Troy Harry, were falling more in love with the investment and remained committed to the cause.

But despite Afterpay's undeniable success, it was in a tricky spot. Afterpay was heavily reliant on Touchcorp to maintain its platform, and the faster it grew, the greater the risk that Touchcorp would struggle to deliver. Touchcorp had spawned a child that was in danger of consuming it.

As well, Afterpay was now dangerously exposed to raiders, who could snap up shares in the vulnerable Touchcorp, which was still Afterpay's largest shareholder. The terms of its agreement meant that if Touch was acquired it would still be bound by its contract. Rumours were swirling that Andrew Abercrombie, the chair and founding director of FlexiGroup, an ASX-listed leasing and finance company, was circling. FlexiGroup engaged banker Simon Mordant to explore its options. Its interest was in Touchcorp, not Afterpay.

The promising start-up faced another existential threat. Eisen and Jefferies met in a coffee shop in La Trobe Street in Melbourne and determined that the best solution was to merge. That proposal was announced to shareholders on 23 February 2017, with a 60:40 split in favour of Afterpay.

On 17 May 2017, the merger booklet was dispatched to investors. For Cleeve's widow, Wendy, that coincided with tragedy and joy. She'd just given birth to Cleeve's daughter, but the date also marked what would have been her first wedding anniversary.

The Cleeve estate had yet to be divided between Wendy and the extended family, which comprised six siblings and 27 nieces and nephews. The entire Cleeve family holdings, including the estate, owned 17.5 per cent of Touchcorp shares, worth $25 million at the time of the bid.

But the extended Cleeve family was apprehensive about the merger. They still considered Touch the senior partner. They had engaged with Citigroup to consider alternatives, including selling their shares in Touch for cash. One interested buyer was Latitude Financial, which was considering the share purchase as part of a plan to acquire Touch. Latitude's management proposed the plan to its shareholders Deutsche Bank and private-equity backers Varde and KKR, who considered it, but passed. The prospect of complex cross-holdings in a promising but unprofitable company simply wasn't compelling enough.

The merger left the Cleeve estate with holdings in the combined group worth about $34 million. The apprehension of the Cleeve camp was shared by some institutions that prepared to dump the shares after the merger.

Once the paperwork was signed, Eisen and Molnar owned 11.6 per cent each of the newly formed Afterpay Touch, Duncan Saville's investment firms owned 9.7 per cent, while Adrian Cleeve and his estate owned 6.8 per cent.

• • •

Afterpay, meanwhile, was still selling its story. Eisen may have had years of financial-markets experience, but he still felt that he and

Molnar weren't doing enough to convince the big end of town of just how bright the company's prospects were.

On Monday, 3 April 2017, at the recently refurbished QT restaurant next to Sydney's State Theatre, Molnar attended a fund manager marketing lunch as a guest of honour. The speaker was Gary Hui, the manager of the Arowana Australian Opportunities fund, and the topic was a 'unicorn opportunity' in the small-cap market—Afterpay.

Hui, who had relocated to San Francisco, set the scene by revisiting how financial deregulation in the 1980s had made it possible for more Australians to get a mortgage. That led to a boom in bank profits, as a large unmet demand was able to access finance. Finance, he said, was an enabler to allow consumption to be shifted in time. That is to allow people to have use of what they couldn't yet afford or purchase outright.

'Whenever a clever business model is able to provide financial capacity to an underserved segment, there is the potential for large profits . . . provided the credit costs of doing so can be controlled,' Hui told the small gathering.

Afterpay was created at a time when online sales were booming. But the growth in online sales had led to an acceleration of card fraud. One type of fraud, known in the payments industry as 'card not present', had exploded from around $125 million in 2010 to over $350 million in 2015. Card-not-present fraud was often the result of the buyer using a stolen card or stolen credentials. But under the credit card scheme rules, it was the merchant who carried the risk for such a fraudulent transaction, not the bank that had issued the card. If a payment is disputed, the bank that issued the consumer's card can order a retailer to reverse the transaction and repay to the legitimate cardholder the amount that had been taken off the card, a process known as 'chargeback'. This creates a difficult and costly process in which the merchant often ends up forfeiting the value of the sale.

Hui's pitch to invest in Afterpay centred around its willingness to take this 'chargeback risk' back from the merchants, which was becoming increasingly problematic and expensive. For a merchant, that made Afterpay's fee of 4 per cent of the cost of the goods a no-brainer. Under Afterpay's model, it paid the merchant within 48 hours, and trusted its approval process and anti-fraud technology to limit chargebacks. That, in addition to the boost the instalment model provided to order values and conversion rates, as well as its ability to lift total online sales by more than 20 per cent, made it a very attractive proposition. Afterpay had well and truly gone viral.

Australians are quick to adopt new payment technologies, such as 'tap and go' functionality using plastic cards, which had been rolled out by the banks in around 2007, a few years earlier. But perhaps not since the introduction of the Bankcard in 1974 had Australian consumers flocked so quickly to a new credit offering. The Bankcard, the first mass-market credit product, attracted over 1 million users within eighteen months; within ten years it had 5 million accounts. Afterpay already had over 500,000 customers in just two years, but the viral growth rates and the huge market meant it had the potential to acquire 'unicorn' status—which is venture capital shorthand for a start-up business with a valuation of over $1 billion.[1]

Hui was first made aware of Afterpay by a former colleague from his broker days, David Hancock. Hancock, who had hired Hui and placed him in a trading role at J.P. Morgan, was an early investor and had talked Hui through the business model. Initially Hui wasn't convinced. The Arowana fund had invested in Touchcorp on the basis that its share price was cheap, he reasoned, while its indirect stake in Afterpay gave it some exposure if Hancock was right. But the data his team assembled showed just how rapidly Afterpay was being adopted. Arowana bought into Afterpay in September 2016, and had recently topped up its position, which accounted for 6 per cent of the fund's assets.

In the eyes of early stock-market investors, the March quarterly update—issued on 13 April 2017—was the moment Afterpay arrived. Over $150 million of merchant sales had been processed, blowing past Bell Potter's bullish estimate of $121 million. A business that had not existed three years before now accounted for 3 per cent of all online sales in Australia, and about 15 per cent of online fashion transactions. The numbers were jaw-dropping.

Afterpay's growth had been extraordinary. When it filed its prospectus in February 2016, it had 38,000 customers, 100 merchants and $35 million of underlying sales. By the time of its annual general meeting in August that year, it had 250,000 customers, 1500 merchants and $300 million of annualised sales. Now, just eight months later, every metric had more than doubled: Afterpay had 575,000 customers, 3700 merchants and annualised sales of $700 million.

'The product is gaining mainstream acceptance and awareness and it appears as though this rapid growth rate is set to continue,' wrote Bell Potter analyst Lafitani Sotiriou as he enthusiastically upgraded his price target from $4.06 to $4.24 and forecast a doubling of the share price. The small profit of $2 million Afterpay made in the half-year to December 2017 had Sotiriou excited that the business could in theory fund its own growth. Afterpay's financiers were also encouraged: NAB agreed to double its lending facility from $20 million to $40 million.

More analysts were growing intrigued by this fast-growing company, which was either fooling the market or had found a way to exploit an untapped or overlooked aspect of point-of-sale credit.

In April, an anonymous blogger called Find the Moat, who had built up a following among small-cap investors for his prescient analysis, published his thoughts on Afterpay. This, the blogger said, was one of several fast-growing companies where the valuation did not make any sense under a traditional framework, but it was gaining so much traction in the real world that it could justify its worth. Facebook, in its early stages, may have fitted this description: people all around the world were signing up, but there was no clear pathway for it to monetise the social network it was creating. The mantra of 'ubiquity first, profits later', which had propelled many a venture-backed start-up to untold riches, could apply here, too.

Find the Moat quoted Silicon Valley doyen and early Facebook investor Peter Thiel, who wrote, 'Great companies can be built on open but unsuspected secrets about how the world works.' Afterpay not only had customers but fans who rhapsodised about how it was changing their lives by allowing them to buy things immediately without having to sign up for a credit card while still allowing them to defer repayment. This helped them to manage tight budgets, freeing up cash flow to pay bills or rent that might be due the next week, while also reducing the feeling of guilt that can come from spending a bigger amount in one hit. And retailers were seeing a meaningful bump in sales that they could not afford to do without. Value was 'being injected into the system to the benefit of *both* retailers and customers', wrote Find the Moat. It did not 'appear out of thin air', but leveraged 'an unsuspected secret about how the world works—i.e. that conventional wisdom over-estimates the credit risks of Afterpay's consumer demographic'.[2]

So what could a business like this possibly be worth? One way for investors to get comfortable with a high-growth company that isn't yet turning a profit is to pull apart the unit economics. If each transaction could wash its own face, that meant Afterpay had the ability to turn a profit eventually. The question, then, is how much it should spend chasing growth to dominate its market and defeat its competitors.

Afterpay's transaction economics appeared highly attractive. For a $100 sale, the merchant would pay $4. Then 80 cents would be paid to Touchcorp for processing the transaction. About 70 cents would be lost in the form of bad debts and failed payments, arrived at by netting off total bad debts with late-payment fees received to calculate an average net loss per transaction. The remainder would be the net transaction margin of $2.50, or 2.5 per cent, on $100 of capital.

But Afterpay would lend out that $100 to a shopper and have it returned within six weeks. Over a twelve-month period, that $100 of fund would come back and be loaned out about twelve times, earning $2.50 each time. The implied annual return on $100 was therefore not $2.50 but twelve times that amount, or a highly attractive $30, or 30 per cent.

If Afterpay borrowed funds from a lender, the returns were even higher. Assuming Afterpay borrowed $50 of the $100 required to pay the merchant for the goods at the rate of 6 per cent, the $50 of remaining shareholder capital would generate a $30 return, less the $3 of interest, for a total return of $27, or 56 per cent.

The key to these juiced-up returns was the provision of a loan facility by National Australia Bank. It had made $40 million available to Afterpay in this form. But since the loans were short-term, like a credit card, the $40 million would be loaned out and returned twelve times throughout the year. The $40 million could therefore finance $480 million of sales over twelve months—and that would generate Afterpay a net margin of $4.4 million.

So even if Afterpay was not yet turning a profit, each transaction was profitable. Crucial to the calculus, however, was the net transaction loss ratio of 0.7 per cent of sales. Afterpay was telling the market that the amount of money that was not being repaid was very low—just 70 cents for every $100 of sales. The collection of late fees was netted off as a recovery. The 0.7 per cent loss rate appeared to be lower than the 2.6 per cent loss rate for major banks on credit cards, but the banks' number related to losses on total loans, not sales processed.

The reason for its low losses, Afterpay explained, was its Transaction Integrity System, which assessed a payment risk based on each individual transaction, including the product the buyer was trying to purchase. Some goods, such as electronics, are sometimes stolen and resold at close to their original value—but that was less likely to occur for apparel, the value of which plunged as soon as it left a store.

This was counter to expectations that young millennials without access to traditional credit, such as a credit card, were in aggregate unlikely to service their debts. The conventional wisdom, at least among analysts, was that the losses would rise well above 0.7 per cent of sales—which would make Afterpay only marginally profitable, or perhaps not profitable at all.

There was also a degree of suspicion about the net transaction loss ratio that Afterpay was presenting to the market. Most financing businesses calculate their bad debts as a percentage of their book of receivables. Afterpay's rapid growth meant it was hard to get a static picture of the ratio of customers who were servicing their debt on time. If a loan book increased by 25 per cent in six weeks, the losses would lag and appear lower than a measure that tracked the performance of all loans made at a certain point in time.

Afterpay claimed that its net transaction loss measure was more explanatory for this reason. Because its loan book was turning over so quickly, due to its short repayment cycles, and because it was growing at a rapid rate, Afterpay argued the standard way of measuring bad debts was less applicable. It would be able to tell in a short space of time if it wasn't going to get paid. In this, Afterpay may have uncovered an unsuspected secret.

Those who trusted Afterpay formed the view that the 0.7 per cent of sales as losses was a sign that small, short-term loans were less risky than unsecured consumer finance, even though credit card losses, when calculated over total sales rather than loans made, were closer to 0.3 per cent—less than half the level of Afterpay.

The doubters weren't convinced. Their view was that the net transaction loss figure was made up by Afterpay to game the market and serve its own purposes, and that the company had the discretion to tweak some of the inputs. The measure netted off losses with late fees, and it wasn't clear whether those late fees had actually been recovered or just been assumed to be recovered. And even if the credit risk was low, it had yet to be tested in a stressed environment.

Find the Moat told readers Afterpay was in the 'too hard basket' but he kept an open mind. 'Ultimately, investing in a start-up that is attempting to execute a brand-new business model necessitates that you are comfortable investing in uncertainty—and with this risk comes tremendous potential rewards (and our economy can only advance when there are people willing to make such a trade-off).'

• • •

Afterpay's stock had run hard, but it stalled after the Touchcorp merger was announced as investors waited for the deal to be consummated.

Tobias Yao of Wilson Asset Management, however, still had faith. On 17 May 2017, his boss Geoff Wilson hosted an investor forum for the Future Generations fund, a listed fund in which well-known investment firms collectively managed a pool of capital, donating the fees to charity. Wilson introduced the presenters, who were going to share their top investment ideas. But to kick things off, he chimed in with one of his own.

Wilson had just returned from Omaha, Nebraska, where he attended the Berkshire Hathaway annual general meeting. The meeting had become a pilgrimage for followers of Warren Buffett, the world's most successful investor, who chaired the company. Each year dozens of Australian professional and amateur investors made the trip and queued up at dawn to get a decent spot in the 18,000-seat CenturyLink Arena.

Early that May morning, Wilson lined up with Troy Harry and Gary Weiss. In the cold Omaha morning, Harry couldn't contain his enthusiasm for Afterpay. He predicted it was going to $100. Weiss hadn't invested as early as Wilson or Harry but held shares in the company co-founded by one of his protégés. He'd also helped make introductions to prominent retailers as Afterpay battled to win merchants over.

Harry's enthusiasm rubbed off on Wilson, who pitched Afterpay as his idea for the Future Generations forum.

'I remember when I was growing up, Mum used to use lay-by,' Wilson told the audience. 'This is the leader, and the only one in its field that does lay-by online. It could be the REA and has all the REA-type qualities. You can judge me in twelve months' time.'

REA Group, which operates the website realestate.com.au, has been nothing short of a stock-market phenomenon. It is the first place many renters or prospective home buyers go to check out a property, and it makes its money by charging the advertiser a commission to place their advertisement on the website. In 2009, it rejigged its business model, and its value multiplied by ten times in the four years that followed.

REA, along with online job ads company SEEK and carsales.com. au, made a trio of online classified firms that up-ended the media industry and made a fortune for their founders and shareholders. REA and SEEK drained the so-called rivers of gold that had flowed to media companies such as Fairfax, which published *The Age* in Melbourne, *The Sydney Morning Herald* and *The Australian Financial Review*, before it was bought by broadcaster Nine Entertainment Co. in 2018.

These print-media giants had lived off the largess of jobs, auto and real-estate classifieds, but the migration of these boards to the internet up-ended the model. With lower revenues, media companies could no longer support their cost bases, and a period of painful adjustment ensued. Fairfax embarked on round after round of redundancies. Media mogul Rupert Murdoch's son Lachlan and billionaire James Packer, whose father Kerry had owned Nine, toasted their competitor's demise as the three classifieds titans all but hollowed them out.[3]

But the online classified trio had awakened Australian share-market investors to the immense profit potential of platform businesses, arguably before the rest of the world had cottoned on. Unlike Fairfax, these companies did not have expensive overheads. They did not require large offices, a network of unionised journalists creating content, a printing press or a means of distributing their product to Australians every day. All they needed was to build a website and market it. Once the eyeballs had been attracted, the fees they charged advertisers was pure profit.

For globally minded Australian investors, REA was a template for a money-making machine. Sydney-based hedge fund Caledonia, which managed about $4 billion of money belonging to Australia's wealthiest families, made it a mission to scour the globe to find the next REA. In November 2014, it unveiled a massive investment in US real-estate portal Zillow. At an investment conference at London's Grosvenor Hotel, Caledonia's 32-year-old partner Mike Messara explained that its 20 per cent stake was the biggest bet the fund had made in its 22-year history, by a factor of three. 'We have all seen how this vertical has played out in Australia since 1998,' he said, explaining why Australians were key players in the US property portal industry. At the time, REA's market capitalisation was $5 billion, slightly larger than that of Zillow—even though the US real-estate market was ten times bigger than Australia's.

Was Afterpay the next REA? That depended on who you asked.

REA, Amazon and Google were indeed platforms that had economies of scale, argued fund manager Investors Mutual. Once the platform was built, the cost of adding a new user was zero. That meant profit margins were consistently high, while the network effect, as the company's size and reach became self-perpetuating, made it harder for competitors to overtake it, making it even more valuable.

But Investors Mutual took the view that Afterpay was a consumer finance company that required capital to grow, and that capital would come at a cost to present-day shareholders as it issued more shares or raised more debt. Its profit margins would not expand in the same way as those of a platform company. If it made a $2.50 profit on $100 of sales, it would make a $25 profit on $1000 of sales, and a $250 profit on $10,000 sales. A platform company's profit margin could grow to, say, $50 on $1000 of sales because most of its costs were fixed.

Other analysts came to a different conclusion. Chris Prunty, a former Investors Mutual analyst who had co-founded QVG, took a good hard look at Afterpay. He'd met with Molnar and asked him how he'd built so much of Afterpay in such a short space of time. Molnar's answer: 'We're relentless and we don't sleep.'

Prunty and his co-founder at QVG, Tony Waters, had first heard of Afterpay while they were at Ausbil Investment Management, a large fund manager based in Sydney. A young building and materials analyst, Sarah Lau, kept seeing the Afterpay logo when she was searching for clothes online. She tried it and liked it, and bought some shares for her personal account. In Lau's view, there was some sort of powerful network effect at play.

Prunty and Waters had tended to avoid investing in consumer finance companies during their small-cap investing career, and felt it was wrong to define Afterpay in this way. Yes, they were extending finance for a margin. But in one sense Afterpay was the perfect growth stock.

The key to the success of a platform company—of any start-up, for that matter—is to acquire as many customers as quickly and as cost-effectively as possible. In a hypercompetitive world in which businesses are capital-light while finance is cheap, this is what millions of dollars of venture funds are spent on: Google and Facebook adwords, public relations, influencers, adverts—even posters on bus stops.

But Afterpay was hardly spending anything. Its merchants were paying them a fee *and* acquiring their customers for them. Indeed, customers on social media were whipping up the retailers' attention with demands that more merchants add Afterpay. In venture capital land, this outcome seemed too good to be true. Afterpay's margin might not have much room to expand, Prunty and Waters realised, but the absolute quantum of sales had the potential to explode.

The pending merger had stalled the Afterpay share price rally as investors got set. But at noon on 29 June 2017, Afterpay Touch began trading under the new ticker APT. The trading day was uneventful, and the shares closed unchanged at $2.70. The following day, however, the institutions that had backed the merger got a timely performance boost when shares rallied almost 10 per cent. The pop helped the funds rule off the end of the financial year with a strong gain, giving their final performance numbers a boost. Afterpay's share price climbed further, reaching $3.00 the following day.

The merged company's first annual result brought even better news for shareholders. Afterpay's quarterly sales had gone exponential. If the third-quarter figure of $144.9 million had surprised bullish analyst expectations, the fourth-quarter sales—$271.5 million—were nothing short of extraordinary. Afterpay's shares gained 4.8 per cent, and the following day added another 11 per cent to close at $3.60, as analysts came to terms with the impressive numbers.

• • •

Rachel Kelly had agreed to meet Molnar as a favour to Paul Greenberg. She knew the retail sector intimately, having spent six years at Just Group, including two on the board, where she'd worked closely with Solomon Lew, one of Australia's most successful retailers. She had then led T2 Tea as it was taken over, and expanded into new markets, by Unilever.

Cue, and Best Buy, had turned on Afterpay instore, but Molnar was battling to break through with other retailers. While online retail was a growing market, instore retail was ten times larger at $245 billion.

The online teams tended to be small but autonomous divisions, run by IT teams open to new ideas. The networks of physical stores were a different proposition, run by seasoned retailers that were the lifeblood of these organisations.

Kelly wasn't looking forward to the lunch meeting, which Greenberg also attended, at the Winery, a trendy bar on Crown Street in Surry Hills. All she knew was that Molnar was young and hungry and had a private-equity background, which probably meant he had a high opinion of himself.

Molnar arrived and asked if it was okay if he ordered a steak and chips. He had worked through the night and desperately needed iron. That amused Kelly, who was getting the sense this was not the young brash banker she was expecting to meet. He then rattled off everything that wasn't working and exactly where he needed help. Specifically, he was finding it hard to get the retailers to take his instore offering seriously.

Again Kelly's apprehension that she would be pinned to her seat and told how fantastic this start-up kid was turned out to be wrong.

She appreciated Molnar wasn't trying to sell her the dream, but present the problem he desperately needed help solving. Kelly later met the rest of the team, including David Hancock. She thought they were all a little crazy, though. They were ambitious, but unstructured. There were no formal financial plans for each deal they did. When she pointed this out, they told her it was why they needed her. The job description was 'to come in and talk retail'. These were guys she wanted to help, but not bet her career on, at least not yet.

She signed up for a six-month contract. She knew how retailers thought and acted and led the lucrative in-store charge. Kelly also appreciated that Molnar, Eisen and Hancock were doing the right thing by hiring individuals with the experience they needed.

The stakes were higher but the sell was tougher. Kelly pitched the merits of Afterpay to a broader range of managers, from the visual marketing executives to the chief financial officers. The hook was often the digitisation of lay-by, the cost and logistics of which had been a drag.

Across the Pacific Ocean, Afterpay's take-off in Australia had been noticed by a start-up called Sezzle. Charlie Youakim had established Sezzle in Minneapolis in 2016, but the initial idea—payments processing using bank direct debits and customer discounts—was a flop. As the first version of Sezzle was being launched in early 2017, Youakim's wife, Jenn, was scrolling through Instagram and stumbled across Afterpay on the page of Australian retailer White Fox Boutique. It was only available to Australian customers, but she quickly recognised that the instalment payment option made sense. 'You should take a look at this,' she told her husband.

Sezzle pivoted, adopting Afterpay's model and relaunching in August 2017. Youakim knew straightaway he was onto a winner: merchants were telling him it had taken too long for someone to offer digital layaway, and retailers were signing up before they'd even been pitched to. 'I knew we had a rocket and we started to take off,' Youakim recalled.[4]

In late 2017, another start-up, Quadpay, was also preparing to launch in the United States using Afterpay's model. It was founded by two Australians, Brad Lindenberg and Adam Ezra, who had attended the same Sydney school as Nick Molnar and Zip's Larry Diamond, Moriah College. Lindenberg was older than Molnar but their paths had crossed. They were associates before they became competitors. Lindenberg and Ezra had gone to New York to emulate Afterpay's success. But they found the initial going tough: no large US retailers would take them seriously.

Afterpay's market capitalisation was pushing $700 million, and it was in line to be added to the S&P/ASX 300 index. If an IPO marks the birth of a new listed company, then index inclusion is the bar mitzvah—its coming of age.

On 1 September 2017, it was confirmed that Afterpay, along with nine other companies, would be added to the index of the top 300 companies later in the month. The addition typically means that large funds that have been set up to simply track an index and charge a relatively low fee for the passive investment are forced to buy shares in the company being included. The additional demand from the passive funds is assumed to boost the share price. But of equal significance is that investment firms are assessed based on their ability to do better than the index, and their performance fees are tied to doing so.

Now that Afterpay was in the ASX300, small-cap funds who use the Small Ordinaries index (made up of stocks numbered 101 to 300, based on market capitalisation) had to pay attention. Afterpay was a small component of the index, but if it went up, and they owned less than its weight in the index, their performance would suffer. If they owned more than the index, they'd benefit. From that moment, Afterpay mattered. The question was how much.

The index rebalance was forcing Australian shareholders who didn't like Afterpay to buy it. But there was a big world of investors out there who might invest out of choice.

The international investor relations campaign was launched by Phil 'Scoop' Beard, a former journalist who was now Bell Potter's man in London. Beard had initially been posted to London in the mid-1980s as a correspondent for *The Australian*, before he was hired to write for *The Australian Financial Review* by then editor Tony Maiden. When he discovered his contract required him to return home, he switched careers and became a stockbroker.

His job was to introduce Australian companies to London's big funds. Beard had kept an eye on Afterpay after Bell Potter floated the company the previous year. Hugh Robertson, who'd managed the float, was pushing Afterpay, as was the assigned analyst, Lafitani Sotiriou. Beard was prepared to pay more attention to Sotiriou, who had correctly predicted that wealth management platform Hub24 could rapidly eat into the share of incumbent players. But beyond that there wasn't much interest.

Stockbroking firms tend to have the same political topographies as Afghanistan, with feuding warlords protecting their patch, which may explain why the broader firm hadn't thrown its support behind Afterpay. Beard was more intrigued by the lack of interest from Australian institutional investors. He asked a client in Santa Barbara, Tracy Stouffer, who invested in global small companies, what she thought. She had closely followed the rise of Klarna, had invested in a Japanese buy now, pay later player called Golden Wardrobe and was excited by the arrival of a new player.

Robertson had also relayed a story to Beard about how he'd told a sceptical fund manager in Melbourne to ring retail king Solomon Lew. The response had been a glowing testimony about how Afterpay was spurring sales. Impulse had been commercialised, Lew explained.

With the mining boom fizzling out, there was little interest from global managers in Australia's top 50 companies, so Beard began to push the Afterpay story. The problem was that the City traders in London were watching with fascination as reporters at *The Financial Times* battled German listed payments giant Wirecard, alleging the company's profits were fictitious. The appetite among hedge funds to invest in a fast-growing payments company with an air of controversy was low.

To test the waters, Beard set up a meeting with a fund manager who had a reputation as a fintech cynic. The manager was rattling off reasons why he would short Afterpay if he had the chance, before Beard interrupted to tell him that David Hancock and Anthony

Eisen were in town, and he could bring them over for a meeting that afternoon. There the manager put his criticisms to Eisen and Hancock directly while they politely pitched the story. On the way back from the meeting, Beard's mobile rang. 'Start me with 300,000 [shares],' the manager said.

While Beard was trying to sell the Afterpay story to British institutions, the company had another unlikely but effective salesman—celebrity stockbroker Richard Coppleson.

'Coppo' had made his name as a stockbroker at Goldman Sachs. Every day, within minutes of the closing bell, 'The Coppo Report' would be sent to the firm's clients. Often it ran to as many as 20 pages, and was punctuated with highlighted, multicoloured text for emphasis. Past and future prime ministers Kevin Rudd and Malcolm Turnbull made a point of reading The Coppo Report for insights into the market.

In 2014, as the cloud of compliance starved the opinionated and jovial brokers within the big US banks of oxygen, Coppo retired. But in 2016 he was lured back by Colin Bell of Bell Potter.

On the morning of 13 September 2017, he hailed an Uber to take him from his home in Sydney's Eastern Suburbs to the airport. He was heading to Melbourne on a three-day golf tour.

The driver, Ron, showed up and asked Coppleson if he'd heard about Afterpay. He had, but didn't know much about them. Ron told him that his son, Nick, was the founder.

Michele Molnar wanted her husband, Ron, out of the house during the day, since the jewellery store they'd run for 25 years closed as Wynyard Station underwent renovations. So he'd taken to the streets of Sydney as an Uber driver to pass the time and make some extra cash, and when the opportunity arose, sell the Afterpay story. Ron had picked up the chief executive officer of online fashion store The Iconic, as Nick was pitching for its business. He liked to claim a bit of credit for that coup.

Ron Molnar offered to give Coppo the full story, right from the very beginning. He delivered it like the consummate salesman.

Afterpay was now very much on Coppo's radar. That day, it gained a further 10 per cent to close at $4.60 after a deal with budget airline Jetstar was announced. The deal was unusual as it allowed Jetstar to surcharge its customers when they used the service, common practice in the airline industry but something Afterpay insisted could not be done by any other retail partner. Afterpay's bankers were also apprehensive. Airline tickets were of higher value than apparel, and were usually purchased well in advance of being used. The risk of non-payment was too high for them to include these purchases in the loan facility.

The October quarterly numbers were another blowout. Underlying sales reached $367 million and were tracking well in excess of $1.5 billion on an annualised basis. Afterpay had surpassed 1 million customers, and its margins were holding firm. The broader instore rollout would add further sales, while retailers lauded 'Afterpay Day'—30 August 2017—as the best online sales day in history. Afterpay's shares surged a further 10 per cent, passing $5 for the first time. Within a month they touched $6.

Afterpay Day was another Molnar masterstroke. Rachel Kelly had told him that Afterpay's sales weren't tracking well enough to hit his budget expectations. He needed to do something. Molnar headed off to a sales meeting and on returning screamed out at the top of his voice: 'I've got it. We're going to do an Afterpay Day like an Amazon prime day.'

Within two weeks it was ready to go. Kelly rang her friends and told them that maybe Molnar wasn't crazy. He could think through and solve any problem, and had a drive and resilience that she had come to appreciate.

While Afterpay Day was a great idea, it wasn't without its glitches. On 30 August 2017, The Iconic put up a notice on its Facebook page that there was a 20 per cent discount if shoppers entered the code AFTERPAYDAY at the checkout. It didn't work. Shoppers began venting their anger online. Nick and Simon, who were watching the Afterpay Day online from their kitchen, began yanking the offers off their home pages to avoid further fury.

Kelly was soon questioning their sanity. Molnar had just returned from a short trip to the United States, and he and Hancock told her they wanted to take her out for lunch. She didn't want to be fed. She just wanted to know what they wanted: which was to ask her to stay on and head up sales and marketing in Australia full time, as they planned an assault on the US market. Molnar had already told a stunned Afterpay board of his plan. They had no reason to doubt him.

In less than six months since Afterpay Touch shares began trading, they'd tripled in value, while the original shareholders in Afterpay had made six times their money since March 2016. Afterpay was well on the way to becoming a $1 billion company.

The Afterpay story was gathering traction among analysts, who were struggling to keep pace. Julian Mulcahy, an experienced analyst at Melbourne brokerage Evans & Partners, had been dazzled by Afterpay a year earlier at their small-caps conference but had battled to pin down the management team for the meeting he needed to complete his report.

His impression was that Afterpay could be the best business he'd ever seen. It was a simple idea in a big market, with a capable management. Within a day of initiating his coverage of Afterpay on 16 October 2017 with a target price of $4, it had shot up to $5. Mulcahy's clients thought the chance had gone.

Richard Coppleson, too, was falling in love with the stock. At a Bell Potter conference on 26 October 2017, Afterpay presented. What caught his attention was a chart in which they represented themselves as just a tiny little circle in a huge picture of the potential world market. The mission was to take on the rest of the world, with the US first.

For the perennially enthusiastic Coppo, their ambition left an impression. 'It just looked to me as one of the great growth stories if they could pull it off and get into the US,' said Coppleson.

But clouds were gathering on the horizon. The incredible growth of the buy now, pay later sector had been noticed by investors—and now it was impossible for regulators to ignore. On 16 November 2017, *The Australian Financial Review*'s closely read 'Street Talk' column reported that the Australian Securities & Investments Commission, the country's corporate watchdog, would launch an inquiry into the sector. It would examine how buy now, pay later companies—including Afterpay and Zip—made money.

With the emergence of regulatory risk, Afterpay shares fell 5 per cent to $5.50, in a frantic day of trading in which 3.2 million shares exchanged hands, more than any other day in the company's history.

Afterpay sought to calm the nerves of investors with an update to the ASX that was marked non-sensitive. Rather than deny or dismiss the report, it confirmed that ASIC was probing the industry, but stated that it had already been engaging with 'key regulators', and claimed that its product 'clearly fits within the regulatory framework'. But the risk of a legal rule change that would define the product as credit lingered. The possibility that Afterpay's magical business model might be crushed—and, with it, the valuation—was too off-putting for some in the market.

And ASIC wasn't the only government agency Afterpay was having to fend off. In October 2017, Deborah Avery, who operated an online sex shop in Canberra, complained to the ACT's human rights commission that Afterpay and Zip had refused to add her business as a merchant.

'A lot of people go, "Should I buy food for the family, pay my electricity bill or buy a . . . dildo,"' Avery told Fairfax Media.

'Personally, I'd go the dildo but other people for some reason think they have other priorities. I want to be able to offer my customers Afterpay and Zip Pay. It's my customers that are being discriminated against because they're making a [moral] judgement.'

In truth, Afterpay was selective about the segments it was prepared to service. Some purchases were more prone to fraud. The company also had its own reputation to consider. But it had to take the complaint seriously, and endeavoured to investigate. The incident was an unwelcome distraction but was yet another proof point that retailers of all stripes were taking notice of what it had created.

By this time Afterpay had attained the ultimate accolade for a new product: it had become a verb. The young management team would need to deal with the reality that Afterpay wasn't just a business, it was now a phenomenon.

# 8

# MICKEY MOUSE
# AND MARIJUANA

MICHAEL SAADAT WAS a corporate cop with a big beat. The Sydney-born lawyer began his career at ASIC with the best of intentions. He was lured to the private sector to head compliance at the US bank Citigroup, before returning for public duty in a more senior role at Australia's corporate regulator. He saw his role as protecting the consumers of financial services. His rising profile at times put him at loggerheads with other senior staffers at the regulator.

Saadat was already responsible for policing banks and credit card companies, and had been on the warpath over lending duties and excessive fees. An already large remit suddenly expanded to include a sector that had barely existed two years earlier: buy now, pay later.

ASIC is one of the most powerful regulators in Australia, setting and enforcing standards in the banking sector and in markets. So the report in 'Street Talk' on 16 November 2017 that suggested Afterpay might be snared in a regulatory investigation detonated a bomb.

The official probe arrived at a time of peak 'bank bashing' in Australia. Federal opposition leader Bill Shorten had turned one of the nation's favourite pastimes into a political spectacle, relentlessly calling for a royal commission into banks' shocking mistreatment of customers. Transgressions were being reported daily in the national press.

ASIC had taken legal action against banks for allegedly rigging the benchmark interest rates, which set the costs of borrowing across the economy. It was also suing Westpac, Australia's second-largest bank, in the Federal Court for alleged breaches of lending rules. Now 'Street Talk' had made public the fact that ASIC had also opened a file on the buy now, pay later sector. Afterpay remained confident in its offering, but analysts sharpened their pencils.

By November 2017, the hatred of mainstream lenders had reached a crescendo, after a year in which the banks had become a political football. Scandals about banks providing conflicted financial advice and forcing drought-ravaged farmers into bankruptcy when loan repayments were missed were spilling into the public debate, raising concerns among bank shareholders. On the last day of that month, Prime Minister Malcolm Turnbull, having resisted the opposition Labor Party's demands for most of the year, announced the Royal Commission into Misconduct in the Banking, Superannuation and Financial Services Industry at a press conference at Parliament House.

Australia's banks had withstood the ravages of the 2008 global financial crisis, and had emerged stronger and more profitable. But perhaps they were too strong. The misconduct scandals had eroded their public image and made them a convenient target for politicians.

All this made the rumours that ASIC was preparing to investigate buy now, pay later—to 'embark on a deep dive into the niche consumer finance sector' spearheaded by market darlings Afterpay and Zip Money, as 'Street Talk' reported—even more concerning. Uber's experience had shown that governments and regulators were unsure of how to deal with technology disruptors; the outcome of any inquiry into Afterpay was unpredictable.

A former High Court justice, Kenneth Hayne QC, was duly appointed to run the royal commission. He had a reputation for being fearless and an intellectual giant. His inquiry would dominate headlines in Australia and embarrass the banks for most of 2018.

It soon became apparent why the industry had lobbied so hard to avoid the inquiry. The hearings overseen by Hayne were filled with drama, as young barristers Rowena Orr QC and Michael Hodge QC skewered senior bankers, financial planners and officials. The devastating case studies of dead people being charged financial planning fees and lives being ruined by conflicted advice tore apart some of the nation's oldest companies. It did so publicly and in real time.

Ken Henry, the former Treasury secretary and one of the nation's most esteemed public servants, was among those whose reputation was in tatters after the hearings. He had steered the economy through the global financial crisis, and then drafted a review of the nation's tax policies that sparked an epic stoush with the powerful mining industry. In 2015, he had taken up the role of chairman at the National Australia Bank.

Henry, who was often branded as a Labor Party loyalist, was not part of the fee-gouging machine that was being exposed during the commission. In fact, it was hoped his chairmanship would bring about a new era of social responsibility at the big banks. But his gruff and arrogant manner in the witness box in late 2018, when he was confronted by Orr about his evasive answers, took the form of lectures and came across as dismissive. The performance riled Hayne—and served to demonstrate, in the eyes of the public, just how out of touch directors and senior bankers were. Hayne declared in the commission's final report that he was not confident that Henry and NAB's CEO, Andrew Thorburn, had learned the lessons of past misconduct, nor that the bank was 'willing to accept the necessary responsibility for deciding, for itself, what is the right thing to do, and then having its staff act accordingly'.

While big private institutions such as AMP and National Australia Bank were rocked to their core, it was the regulators who were sweating on Hayne's final report. And although it touted its tough stance against misconduct, the evidence was that ASIC had not done enough policing work to stamp out bad behaviour. In one uncomfortable session at the commission, ASIC's Louise Macaulay, who was responsible for overseeing financial planners, was asked to explain why it had taken criminal action just once, and civil action just six times, in ten years.

'It's not an adversarial process,' she responded.

'The basic thing is they haven't got the balls,' Niall Coburn, an ASIC investigator of thirteen years, told Fairfax Media. 'My bosses never had the balls to bring proceedings and if you were outspoken you were basically shut down and isolated.'[1]

ASIC had been exposed as too soft and slow to hold bad actors to account. Hayne had formed the view that the rules in place to protect Australians from financial misconduct were adequate. They simply weren't being enforced. ASIC was on public notice. The accusation stuck that they had been too tame with the big banks, and not bold enough to pursue misconduct for fear of expensive defeat.

The bookish James Shipton was the new chair of ASIC. Recruited from the Securities and Futures Commission of Hong Kong, the former banker at Goldman Sachs—where he had spent five years as head of government relations in the Asia-Pacific region—was little known in Australia. Shipton had been a surprise choice to replace Greg Medcraft, the politically savvy former chair who had as many friends as he did enemies. He assumed his position just as the Hayne Royal Commission was getting started in February 2018. His mission was to re-establish the regulator's reputation as bold and fearless, and restore the public's faith in the corporate cop.

By May, Shipton was championing a 'why not litigate' strategy. Before then, ASIC's overarching philosophy had been one of quick and effective wins—in the form of 'enforceable undertakings', under which the targets of actions agreed to clean up their acts and pay financial settlements, which were typically small. But that had encouraged well-resourced institutions to break the rules and live with the innocuous consequences. Now ASIC would be bolder in using the courts as a weapon, and less fearful of losing if it helped bring clarity to how the law should be applied in practice. Bearded Melbourne barrister Daniel Crennan QC, who brought with him an attitude of aggression, was hired to lead the charge. In the words of then finance minister Kelly O'Dwyer, his mission was to 'send a signal' that the regulator had the intent, ability and the ticker to take on the bad guys.

Saadat, the ASIC executive director whose remit covered the offending financial services firms, was on the front line of a war that was already well underway but getting bloodier.

He was the regulator's point man for the litigation against Westpac, which ASIC was suing in a landmark case for breaching responsible lending rules when it had approved tens of thousands of home loans. The regulator alleged the bank didn't have enough information on customers to determine that they could properly service their loans. In assessing customers' ability to repay, Westpac relied on an index called the Household Expenditure Measure, which provided a benchmark of how much a typical household spends. ASIC said the systematic reliance on the HEM to assess a borrower's spending meant the bank wasn't making sufficient inquiries into their ability to service that mortgage, as required by the statute. ASIC had managed to get a $35 million settlement out of Westpac in 2018. But in a blow to both sides, this had been rejected by the Federal Court, which questioned whether there was enough wrongdoing to underpin the agreement. The case was proving problematic, and the two parties would be forced to slug it out.

Now Saadat was to oversee the first-ever probe of the mush-rooming buy now, pay later sector. ASIC's deputy chairman, Peter Kell, a former chief executive of Choice, Australia's largest consumer advocacy group, would also play an active role.

The seed for the review had been planted directly with Shipton's predecessor by the CEO of the Consumer Action Law Centre, Gerard Brody, in early 2016. Greg Medcraft was coming to the end of his term as chairman of the International Organisation of Securities Commissions and had been hosting global regulators at a hotel meeting in Melbourne, where he bumped into Brody. Consumer Action is an influential advocate and played a key role in agitating for the banking royal commission.

Brody told Medcraft the centre had been receiving a growing number of complaints that minors were getting access to Afterpay and other buy now, pay later services. More and more callers to its National Debt Helpline and legal advice lines were holding buy now, pay later debt alongside other loans. Medcraft said he hadn't given much thought to the space, but reported Brody's comments back to the commission.

Eighteen months later, 'Street Talk' had revealed the regulator wanted to find out about how these companies made money, the credit approval processes, and how late payment fees were levied on customers. Unlike credit cards, Afterpay did not charge interest and did not allow customers to 'revolve' debt from one month to the next—repayments could only be made in the four, equal instalments. Unlike most credit cards, there would be no annual account fees. Missed payment fees would be charged to those who were late to repay: an initial $10 and a further $7 if the payment was still unpaid seven days after the due date. But for customers who paid on time, all they would pay would be the price tag of the item, nothing more.

Consumer Action and other consumer groups had been telling ASIC via the quarterly meetings of its Consumer Advisory Panel that the regulator should be keeping a close eye on the emerging space. Emboldened by their successes in getting various aggrieved customers up before the Hayne Royal Commission to humble the banks, the consumer groups also ramped up pressure in the media, saying Afterpay was exploiting the rules. In the background, the major banks, keen to ensure the new competitors weren't getting a free ride by operating outside the regulations that were applied so stringently to them, were happy to see the upstarts come under scrutiny.

• • •

ASIC's would not be the only investigation Afterpay and the new buy now, pay later sector would face during the course of 2018—the politicians were also circling like sharks.

In the lead-up to the 2019 federal election, Canberra was in a state of flux. The Labor Party, led by Bill Shorten, was well ahead in the polls. Shorten's strategy in opposition was to engage in bank bashing. He had homed in on the misdemeanours of the big banks, and pledged to do more to hold them to account. He had earlier clamoured for a royal commission to stop the rot and protect ordinary Australians from their bad behaviour. As more instances of egregious conduct emerged, from conflicted advice to interest-rate rigging to money-laundering messes, Shorten got his way. The theatre of the commission seemed to validate his position.

The governing Liberal/National Coalition was in disarray. They had dumped their leader, Malcolm Turnbull, in August 2018 amid tensions between him and the more conservative factions within the party. Fearing imminent defeat under the new prime minister, Scott Morrison, senior government figures began to enact their contingency plans.

But until parliament was dissolved, there was work to be done. In October, the Labor-led Senate Economics References Committee called for an inquiry into credit and financial services targeted at Australians at risk of financial hardship.

Much like the Banking Royal Commission, this inquiry was not the idea of the government. Labor, traditionally the party representing the working class, had pushed for the Senate review, and with the support of the Greens and three independent senators the vote was passed. The seven-member committee would be led by Labor senator Jenny McAllister and consisted of three Labor members, two Liberals and two Greens. It would conduct hearings in January 2019 and publish a report in February.

In the crosshairs of the senators were 'payday lenders', which charged usurious rates to Australians who were short of cash, and which operated outside the bounds of regulation. But consumer groups had also pushed for the review to look into the new buy now, pay later sector, and in particular Afterpay, which their intelligence suggested was giving young female shoppers their first credit fix.

There was a strong sense that Labor was preparing for government. Under shadow financial services minister Clare O'Neil, a former McKinsey & Company consultant, Labor was keen to ensure that financial services players that had escaped the Hayne Royal Commission's scrutiny, such as the payday lenders, had the blowtorch applied to them. The consumer groups were telling members of parliament that Afterpay was exploiting a loophole in the lending laws by offering what appeared to be short-term loans without conducting checks of customers' credit histories to make sure they were able to pay back the money.

The *National Consumer Credit Protection Act*, a piece of legislation Labor had introduced in the wake of the global financial crisis, applied to products that charge the customer interest. (Afterpay charged late fees, as a library might do when a book is returned late, but this was not enough to trigger the law.) The legislation also provided exemptions when repayments were made in less than 62 days—and Afterpay's four fortnightly instalments came in under this threshold.

But the Senate review would probe the loophole upon which Afterpay was built. The business model was under threat. Eisen and Molnar would be called to testify in front of the inquiry.

In the days that followed the reports that the inquiry would take place, Afterpay lost almost a fifth of its share-market value, a steeper fall than that of payday lender Cash Converters, which slid 12 per cent, and whose model Afterpay believed should be the real focus of the inquiry, given the costs it imposed on desperate customers. But the market was pricing in the real risk that the Afterpay model would be up-ended if lawmakers decided that, despite their insistence, they really were a lender, and that the loophole needed to be closed. Conducting credit checks as customers signed up on a retailer's checkout page would be a brake on customer growth.

Fund managers who had sat on the sidelines of the Afterpay show were now wondering what all the fuss was about, and whether its model could survive interrogation.

Those in the sector itself were also divided. While Afterpay steadfastly rejected the notion that it was a lender, smaller rival Zip had set itself to comply with the lending rules. Zip's management said nothing about their bigger rival, but the feeling among some of its supporters was that its process for onboarding new customers was more time-consuming than that of Afterpay—and that this was allowing its rival to trample over it in the quest for dominance.

Zip, which offered customers a line of credit and charged them a fee if they had a balance remaining at the end of the month, was rejecting 35 per cent of customers as unsuitable, based on their history repaying other forms of credit, and its brokers theorised that Afterpay's impressive growth would be kneecapped if it, too, was forced to conduct credit checks.

Despite not checking credit histories at the time new customers were onboarded, Afterpay said it rejected 30 per cent of attempted transactions on average, while for first-time customers the rejection rate was up to 50 per cent, as the Afterpay technology system decided which transactions were safe to authorise.

But Afterpay's claim that its technology was more effective than the requirements of the credit act wasn't passing muster in the consumer groups. At the Consumer Action Law Centre's office on Queen Street in downtown Melbourne, and then at Afterpay's base in up-market Collins Street, Brody met with Eisen and other Afterpay executives, including David Hancock, and delivered an unequivocal message: this is consumer credit, and it needs to be regulated as such. As the consumer groups saw it, payment by the customer was being delayed, so it was pretty clear Afterpay was offering credit.

But Eisen dutifully explained, as he had been doing in Canberra, that the product was really a 'budgeting tool'. As well, Eisen told Brody, Touchcorp had gathered data that allowed Afterpay to monitor spending patterns and from these create an algorithm to make credit decisions.

But just because Afterpay was using algorithms, Brody argued in reply, that did not mean it should be able to circumvent the law. The pair agreed to disagree.

As the political pressure mounted, it was clear that Afterpay would have to learn to play the lobbying game—and win.

• • •

While the pending ASIC review continued to cause jitters among investors in the nascent sector, Afterpay's supporters remained confident the company had the situation under control. But a new problem would emerge from left field and introduce a potentially graver threat. It came in the form of a Mickey Mouse.

After the market closed on 3 April 2018, corporate governance research firm Ownership Matters sent a report to its client list of superannuation funds and investment institutions titled 'Afterpay: Compliance, accounting and regulation'.

Ownership Matters was not a typical research outfit. To some, they were among a handful of effective guardians of corporate governance who held the 'old boys' club' of directors and executives to account. But to others, they were activists, almost communists, who were holding back the nation's business leaders from advancing the economy.

The firm was set up in 2011 in Melbourne by Dean Paatsch, Simon Connal and Martin Lawrence to provide advice on how institutions should vote at shareholder meetings. But they had extended their services in recent years and were now providing research on governance and disclosure issues. The firm deliberately steered well clear of valuation assessments, but hunted for instances of 'aggressive accounting, bad incentives and dopey boards'.[2]

Paatsch and Lawrence were both country boys with a social-justice bent who had worked at large international proxy advisory firms—Institutional Shareholder Services and CGI Glass Lewis—before setting up Ownership Matters. They'd built a reputation for spotting the early warning signs of pending corporate disasters, such as the ASX-listed debt bombs Allco and Babcock & Brown, which had detonated in 2008, and more recently Big Un and Blue Sky, which had both collapsed in the wake of disclosure scandals.

But they had also made some enemies among the director class—not the least of which was retail king Gerry Harvey, whose complex accounts had come under intense scrutiny. Harvey branded Ownership Matters 'a dreadful organisation'.[3] Lawrence admitted that their role as professional pessimists often made them unpopular. Their independence, however, was fiercely guarded.

The Afterpay report ranked as one of Ownership Matters' most controversial. It detailed how they had set up an account under the name 'Miguel Laucha'—which is Spanish for Mickey Mouse. Using a fake birthday of 2 January 2000, and a fake address, they had been able to use a prepaid Visa card to transact anonymously using Afterpay. Miguel had spent $260 on wine and other goods, well above the $100 card balance. (His creators later paid the difference.) Ownership Matters had been able to buy goods using Afterpay with no identification, and had not been required to provide any information linking the transactions back to the individual who had carried them out.

'This raises a number of concerns with respect to recoverability and the ability of [Afterpay's] "proprietary transaction integrity technology" to identify suspect customers,' the report stated.

Ownership Matters also explained how the sixteen-year-old daughter of a staff member was about to set up an account and buy $234 of alcohol. 'No age checks were made except for the customer being required to give their age upon joining Afterpay,' the report read. 'This raises concerns about [Afterpay's] ability to conduct checks on its customers, the number of minors with Afterpay accounts, [and] the ability for [Afterpay] to enforce agreements with these minors.'

It didn't take long for the report to circulate within the trading community. The following morning, Afterpay issued a statement to the ASX stating that it was 'committed to responsible customer spending' and that it had 'a strong repayment track record' even as it was growing rapidly. Afterpay said it was upgrading its systems to 'curtail alleged underage usage of its service by dishonest users', adding that customers were legally required to identify their birthdate, and merchants had an obligation not to sell or deliver alcohol to minors. But the Afterpay camp was rattled. They feared the attack could wreck them.

The acrimony between Ownership Matters and Afterpay increased further when Paatsch accepted a request to appear on the Nine Network's *A Current Affair*, a provocative nightly television program. His appearance was prompted by the company's denial that the alcohol was delivered.

'Afterpay is everywhere: 14,000 retailers are spruiking it and 1.8 million of us are using it,' reporter Tineka Everaardt told the cameras. 'But is it growing too quickly? This popular buy now, pay later service is under serious scrutiny.' The segment featured a girl named Noami, a fifteen-year-old who downloaded the Afterpay app and used it to buy a $250 handbag by fudging her birthdate. 'Teenagers are impulsive so it's very easy for them to get $350 worth of credit instantly,' said Paatsch, who was also billed by the show as a concerned dad. Xavier O'Halloran of consumer group Choice also weighed in, labelling the business model of extending funds without undergoing credit checks as a 'legal loophole'.

Afterpay's David Hancock appeared on camera to refute the suggestion that Afterpay was preying on younger consumers. The retailers were paying the fee, he argued, so customers were getting the Afterpay product for free. More than 90 per cent of orders did not attract a late fee. 'We are bringing in additional checks and rolling them out in a quick way,' Hancock said. The show's host, Tracy Grimshaw, signed off ominously, noting that ASIC was looking into the sector.

As publicity, the segment wasn't all bad. Tanya Adamson, a mum, had described Afterpay as a 'godsend' as she walked the film crew through her cluttered apartment. 'You don't pay interest,' she said. 'You get the goods right now and it's really transparent.'

Even so, the Mickey Mouse episode had done more than elevate the battle to evening television. It had raised the threat that another regulator would take an interest—one that would be far harder to negotiate with.

• • •

Australia's financial intelligence agency, AUSTRAC, had operated with relative obscurity until August 2017. That was when it filed a bombshell civil court case against the Commonwealth Bank, alleging

53,700 contraventions of the *Anti-Money Laundering and Counter-Terrorism Financing Act*. A weakness in the bank's 'smart' automatic teller machine network meant that millions of dollars from the proceeds of crimes had washed undetected into the banking system through large deposits made at certain branches. It was an explosive allegation: drug triads were among those using Australia's biggest bank to siphon cash out of the country. As each breach carried a fine of up to $8 million, the Commonwealth Bank was technically facing almost a trillion dollars in penalties. (The case was ultimately settled for $700 million.)

AUSTRAC's case blindsided the bank, but also marked a tipping point for an industry that had until then pushed back aggressively against calls to open a royal commission into its practices. The banks had been embroiled in rolling financial scandals where customers lost money because of poor and conflicted advice, while their trading arms stood accused of manipulating key market rates. Facilitating crime and making it tougher for law-enforcement authorities to nail crooks was too much.

'It is not an angry but disorganised customer base baying for blood,' wrote the ABC's business editor, Ian Verrender, in response to the news of the AUSTRAC case. 'These are issues of national security and the prospect of a concerted legal assault by the Australian Government solicitor.'[4]

Public anger swelled. Commonwealth Bank chief executive Ian Narev would depart, while the case for a royal commission was made stronger.

The environment was hostile to any financial institution that was not doing enough to shut out drug dealers, child traffickers and terrorists from the financial system—no matter how innovative and customer-focused they were. AUSTRAC could come knocking on Afterpay's door, too, and a large fine would hurt. The loss of its social licence to operate would be terminal.

It wasn't only Afterpay's customer onboarding processes that fell under the spotlight in 2018: its marketing also drew fire. To support Afterpay's rollout of a payment functionality in physical shops, which involved using a smartphone to take a picture of a barcode, advertisements had started to appear in big-city department stores.

'Broke AF but strongly support treating yourself?' asked the posters, prominently on show among make-up displays and racks of the latest fashion. ('AF' is millennial shorthand for 'as fuck'.) The Afterpay logo appeared at the bottom, with the words 'is now in store'. The campaign also appeared extensively on social media.

That added fuel to the fires lit by consumer groups as they argued that the product was encouraging irresponsible spending by impressionable youth and vulnerable customers.

But the advertisements were not created by Afterpay, and were not endorsed by the company. Rather, they had been created by the upstart fashion retailer Dish, and were being adopted by retailers to give spending a post-summer kick-along. Afterpay distanced itself from the campaign, but not everyone was convinced.

'A quick scroll through Instagram shows that this poster had been shared multiple times by many Afterpay customers.[5] An oversight? I'll let consumers be the judge,' wrote Debbie O'Connor, creative director of branding studio WRD and CEO of The Creative Fringe, on *Mumbrella*, a widely read online publication covering advertising and media. 'Don't let your brand be negatively affected by the behaviour of others,' O'Connor continued. 'If your logo is on any promotional material, you have a say in whether it gets published or printed. If it doesn't fit into your brand strategy, then you have every right to put your foot down and get it removed.'[6]

Afterpay had given its retail partners carte blanche to advertise on its behalf. After all, its swelling user base was doing its merchant marketing for free. But it quickly killed the campaign, threatening to remove those who didn't comply.

'We were absolutely distressed when we were first made aware of that campaign,' Eisen told the Senate Economics References Committee in January 2019. 'It is not acceptable to Afterpay. We have strict terms and conditions which say that that type of advertising should not occur in any circumstances and it is completely the opposite of our core values. There was nothing whatsoever associated with that campaign that was supported, acquiesced or endorsed by Afterpay in any way.'

Some commentators were starting to appreciate that the Afterpay model was a better alternative to credit cards, but suggested it might still create credit addiction—even if this wasn't with Afterpay.

'I think of Afterpay as the financial equivalent of marijuana,' declared Scott Pape, publisher of *The Barefoot Investor*, in a blog post in December 2018. Pape is a bestselling author of finance guides for investors and families, and his weekly newsletter is read by around 400,000 people. Pape had met with Eisen before he'd written the post but had not reflected the points Eisen had tried to make about why Afterpay was different to credit cards. 'Young people absolutely love it, and old people are doing a lot of finger waving about the dangers of getting hooked on the newest financial drug to hit the streets . . .

'Now, understand there's nothing really revolutionary about Afterpay—men in grey suits have been dreaming up new ways to get people to spend money they don't have since long before Bob Marley rolled his first spliff. This is just the latest incarnation.'

Pape said that in his opinion, the actual terms of Afterpay were not that bad, because so long as users pay their instalments on time, they are not charged any interest or fees. 'So, as far as consumer credit drugs go, it's not too heavy.'

But then came the kicker: '[T]he reason I compare Afterpay to weed is that it acts like a gateway financial drug: it's effectively training young people to rely on the bank's money rather than banking on themselves . . . And, once you get hooked on spending someone else's money, there's every chance you might graduate onto harder stuff—other millennial credit-drug dealers who really rip you off.'[7]

# 9

# BROKER WARS

ACONEX WAS A rare Australian technology success story. The Melbourne company was founded in the middle of the bursting of the dotcom bubble by two friends, Leigh Jasper and Rob Phillpot. They created software that allowed architects and developers to share documents and coordinate activities on large and complex construction projects. By 2017, they'd grown Aconex into a billion-dollar enterprise. But that year it was, technically speaking, also the market's most hated company.

While research analysts at stockbrokers were advising clients to buy shares, hedge funds were shorting Aconex aggressively, more than any other stock on the ASX. Shorting involves borrowing shares from a holder and selling them into the market with the intention of buying them back at a lower price, booking the difference as a profit. Almost a quarter of all Aconex's traded shares had been loaned out by shareholders to hedge funds so they could be sold short.

There were compelling reasons to bet against the company. In January, Aconex cut its revenue targets, triggering a 45 per cent slump in the share price. There was every chance it would miss those already lowered forecasts. Then there were questions about its accounting and the intentions of its founders, who seemed to offload their shares at any opportunity.

But on the morning of 17 December 2017, those shorters had a crisis on their hands. US software firm Oracle announced it would buy the company for $1.6 billion in cash, paying a near 50 per cent premium above the last traded share price. The short-sellers would have to buy shares at that higher price and return them to the owners in order to accept the bid.

On Twitter, Atlassian's Mike Cannon-Brookes baited the luddites in the funds-management community who weren't on the register. 'To local fundies who don't believe in tech, 47 per cent premium will hurt a lot?' he tweeted.

Tim Samway of Brisbane-based fund manager Hyperion, which had made its name backing high-growth companies, told the hedge funds that betting against 'high-quality businesses is a dangerous game in the long term. Businesses with strong value propositions to clients win in the end.'[1]

One fund manager, who remained anonymous, didn't take kindly to insinuations that it was a mistake to pass on investing in Aconex. 'I'd love there to be 20 more Aconexes and for there to be solid, investable tech models. I'd love to see this sector grow in the market,' he told *The Australian Financial Review*'s technology writer Yolanda Redrup. 'It's a shame the banks are the biggest segment and tech is the smallest, but if that does not materialise I'm not going to go squeezing into second-rate models. It has to be driven by economic fundamentals.'[2]

Was Afterpay's tech model solid and investible or second-rate? A modest 6.5 million shares had been loaned out to hedge funds as of 2 January 2018, but every day 100,000 more were taken up. The large presence of Australian institutions in the share market that were willing to loan their shares out for a fee meant there was ample supply for those who wanted to short Afterpay.

But Afterpay began 2018 with a bang. Underlying sales reached over $550 million, a fivefold increase over the previous year, while the number of customers surpassed 1.5 million. In the lead-up to Christmas, Afterpay had been adding 4000 customers a day, and those customers were using Afterpay more. That was only the half of it. The game-changing announcement on 16 January was that Afterpay would expand in the United States, having secured the backing of venture capital fund Matrix Partners.

Matrix would invest US$15 million through the issue of new shares at $6.51 and a $US100,000 convertible note issuance from Afterpay USA Inc—a new company. The notes would give Matrix up to 10 per cent of the future value of Afterpay's US division.

Dana Stalder, a general partner of Matrix, would join the Afterpay board, and become a mentor to Molnar. Stalder is a Silicon Valley native and has worked in technology companies his whole career. He helped to build one of the early internet browsers at Netscape in 1994. After running global customer acquisition at eBay, he joined PayPal in 2004, which eBay had acquired two years earlier, leading product, sales, marketing and technology. He joined Matrix in 2008, which had a 40-year history in the Valley and was an early investor in Apple.

As part of the deal, an employee share-option plan was set up with the intention of luring Silicon Valley's best and brightest to the Afterpay cause. Engineers, sales whizzes and growth hackers would receive options to buy shares in Afterpay's US business at low prices, and cash them in later at an enormous profit. If the US business was a success, they too could end up owning up to 10 per cent of the entire Afterpay Group in 2023, when a conversion date was set.

Although the new structure was slightly complicated, the headline was that Afterpay was heading to the United States—and it had the smarts and capital to make success happen.

Afterpay had been quietly sounding out US retailers since mid-2017, but the official details of its US assault buoyed the market. A record 22 million Afterpay shares traded hands as they gained 16 per cent to close at $7.60. Matrix thus made a cool $2.3 million in paper profit just by announcing it had invested. An offshore expansion sounded like great news for shareholders: the total addressable market in the United States was enormous. In 2017, US$3.8 trillion of retail purchases were made, of which US$450 billion were online—25 times larger than Australia. The US fashion market was twenty times larger than Australia's, while the millennial population of 63 million was ten times larger.

But Australian share-market investors had seen billions destroyed by foreign misadventures before. There remained doubts that Afterpay's model could survive a full credit cycle and a more robust application of the regulation, let alone set up and prosper in the United States, where a large swathe of the population couldn't qualify for a loan. If the valuation was a problem at $500 million, at $1.7 billion it was well into bubble territory.

Fund managers who had been trained by experience to follow the money had one more thing to worry about. The fourth of May in 2018 marked the two-year anniversary of the Afterpay IPO. That anniversary was significant: the escrow period in which Eisen and Molnar pledged not to sell any shares would come to an end. Afterpay's share price rise, from $1 to $7, meant that each was sitting on a $175 million fortune. Surely they would seek to cash in on the wealth they had created?

The so-called smart money would look to sell before the founders dumped their shares onto the market. Ron Molnar was urged by some of his friends in the finance industry to encourage his son to cash in on part of the wealth he'd created so quickly. But Nick wasn't interested: he told his father he was in for the long haul.

• • •

Afterpay's extraordinary share-market success had raised the stakes in the battle over the estate of Adrian Cleeve, contested by his widow, Wendy, and the extended Cleeve family. When he'd passed away, Cleeve and his family owned $20 million worth of Touchcorp shares. Now, after the merger, the ownership was of $100 million of Afterpay stock.

On 13 March 2018, a legal war was declared when a writ was issued to the Victorian Supreme Court in which Cleevecorp claimed that the 13.2 million Afterpay shares in the estate belonged to them, while the estate owed millions of dollars in debt to the family. Of those shares the family claimed, the majority, 9.984 million, were held in ATC Capital, in which Adrian had been the sole shareholder. The Cleeve family argued that these shares were held in a constructive trust on their behalf, and that Adrian owed them money.

The stakes were high and growing by the day as Afterpay's stock price continued to climb. Melbourne's top lawyers were recruited. The family retained James Peters QC as counsel, with Hall & Wilcox acting as solicitors. Wendy Ng and the Cleeve estate were represented by Allan Myers QC, with Mills Oakley retained as solicitors.

Tensions were also simmering in the market. Large shareholders and their brokers were banging the drum. Funds that didn't own Afterpay were being forced to explain why. Hedge funds, meanwhile, were gravitating towards a trade that was ticking all the boxes as the ideal short. On the other side, buying small parcels of shares were suburban hairdressers, compulsive shoppers and savvy store attendants. Also in the mix were the brokers and shareholders of Afterpay's rivals and competitors that had been left behind by its extraordinary surge.

A final element was Afterpay's infiltration into the home. More women were using it, and some of them were the wives, girlfriends and daughters of finance professionals. Afterpay was allowing their wives to mask payments made on joint credit cards by spreading the cost and replacing the name of the retailer, and their daughters to buy stuff without having to beg, borrow or steal.

Jun Bei Liu, one of a small handful of female hedge fund managers, was a believer. She held Afterpay in the Tribeca Alpha Plus fund she was assigned to manage. A key ingredient in Afterpay's success was the early adoption by women, she said.[3]

'Women, especially young women, love to share with their friends what they were wearing, where they got it from, and how much they paid for it,' she said. 'Now they could also spread the word on how they paid for it. That's why Afterpay went viral.'

The mostly male analysts didn't get the appeal. Credit cards were tied to airline loyalty schemes—the more you spend, the more frequent flyer points you accumulate—and this, they figured, should continue to underpin the popularity of cards, which many users paid back on time, before interest was triggered.

Others openly despised Afterpay. Stockbroker Marcus Padley owned the stock. But he was certain it would face regulation. He detailed how his 22-year-old daughter's bank account was 'plagued with Afterpay payments', in his daily newsletter. 'She is an adult, so it's her choice and she won't be told, but she is not experienced with debt and it irritates me that she sees it as allowing her to buy things you can't afford—she'll grow up but it is a bit of cancer for kids in my humble opinion,' he told readers of 'Marcus Today' on 5 July 2018.

Afterpay was extending into new sectors. Under the guidance of Richard Harris, who was now head of business expansion, it was pushing into new retail verticals, including health. Primary Dental Clinics had rolled out Afterpay across its national network; getting the service into other dentists' practices would be made easier by a deal with Software of Excellence, which made practice management software and had agreed to integrate Afterpay.

Harris's banking background had helped Afterpay develop its first credit models. He had spent time, when Afterpay was just getting off the ground, personally calling overdue customers to understand their circumstances, and after negotiating the NAB facility, had created new reporting templates to satisfy the bank's demands for information on the unit economics of each loan. Moving into the health segment would produce different risks such as higher order values, reduced decisioning data for services rather than a physical product, and reputational risk connected to any poor patient outcome.

But the same drivers of demand were there: many younger patients didn't have private health insurance and didn't own a credit card, which made it difficult to pay the doctor in one go.

By now retailers were also facing pressure from their own customers to embrace Afterpay. Molnar devised a plan in which Afterpay would ask its followers which brands they'd like to see on the platform, and then present the results to the most requested brands. He would use Afterpay's social-media channels to encourage its customers to make the sales pitch directly to their favourite retailers.

An example was Lululemon, a Canadian maker of stretchy tights loved by women for yoga and jogging. The Afterpay pitch was: 'Your existing customers are requesting it. Not only will you attract some of our followers as new customers, but you'll also increase brand loyalty, conversion, and order sizes for your existing customers.' It was not a hard sell; the message—this will be beneficial for both of us—was tough to turn down. Afterpay's fans bombarded Lululemon's customer-service line, and soon Lululemon had to ask Afterpay to tell its fans to stop calling.

Finally it relented: 'We've made it official—Afterpay is here, so you can sweat now (and pay later). *AU [denoting Australia] only but not for long,' Lululemon announced on its Facebook page in May 2018.

• • •

The simmering battle of opinions erupted into an all-out war on 14 March 2018, when Credit Suisse desk analyst Sujit Dey sent a note to his hedge fund clients titled 'APT—Don't underestimate ASIC's Review of the Sector'.

Dey's email detailed his disdain for the Afterpay model, which he believed exploited the rules and fed credit to young consumers. But Dey was just as uncomfortable with the $1.7 billion valuation implied by the share price. If Afterpay was worth seventeen times its after-tax profits when it reached a mature phase, that would imply that those profits would be $100 million. Working backwards, he calculated that Afterpay's current share price indicated that the underlying sales it would have to process to generate that profit would need to grow to over $10 billion—a fivefold increase on current levels. That also assumed Afterpay could hold the line on the 4 per cent merchant fee, in the face of inevitable competition. 'I would start selling before then,' Dey told his clients, 'because I'm sure the insiders would want to realise some profits after such a strong share price run (and the potential regulatory events coming up).'

The Dey email, which found its way to *The Australian Financial Review*, rattled Afterpay's management. The buy now, pay later broker wars had been declared. Bell Potter's research analyst Lafitani Sotiriou fired out his own response, branding the desk note misinformation.

Dey had been poached by Credit Suisse from US bank J.P. Morgan as an executive director within hedge fund sales. He was among a small class of brokers who were given free rein to share their unconstrained views on certain stocks to a loyal group of clients, in the hope that they'd ask the bank to broker their trades. Sometimes his ideas were negative, and served to encourage traders to bet against the subject of his note via shorting.

Dey was known for sharing unfiltered opinions in an otherwise compliance-constrained world. And that is exactly what he did with Afterpay, explaining exactly why he thought this local success story was excessively valued at $1.7 billion. The one major risk, he said, was that Afterpay did not do any credit checks on its customers. Customers could sign up within minutes, and were only required to provide their name, date of birth, address and credit or debit card number. Almost immediately they were given a spending allowance of $350. The amount was lifted when initial repayments were made on time. 'This is very surprising to me,' Dey wrote, 'because Afterpay has no idea what the financial situation of its consumers are. It doesn't look like responsible lending to me.'

Dey speculated that Afterpay's stated position—that it did not fall under the jurisdiction of the credit act because it did not charge interest—was wrong. 'Afterpay definitely lends money to consumers and also charges fees,' he noted, 'and therefore it seems clear to me that it needs a credit licence. This means it should be doing credit checks on its customers under the responsible lending laws.'

Dey resurrected a 2014 quote from ASIC's deputy chairman, Peter Kell, shortly after the regulator took on two Queensland-based payday lenders: the action would ensure they 'do not deliberately structure their businesses to circumvent laws that protect consumers'. Afterpay's management had been asked on a recent analysts' teleconference call about whether the late fees charged were excessive. Their line was that late-payment penalties were part of society, like parking fines, which in Sydney could be over $100 for a simple misdemeanour. 'How can you compare this scheme to parking fines?' Dey demanded. 'There is no money being lent when it comes to parking fines and credit card companies are allowed to fine because they have a credit licence and abide by responsible lending standards.'

Dey also took exception to Afterpay's business method of not verifying the age of its customers, which he described as 'irresponsible'. 'There is nothing stopping a 13-year-old from signing up to Afterpay by using a different birth year—the way many young people sign up to Facebook despite being below the required age. You would think many kids that enter high school will have a debit card and therefore I'm not sure what is stopping them from signing up to Afterpay, without really understanding the consequences.'

His conclusion: 'The market needs to take a good hard look at the regulatory risks around this stock. Providing credit to young customers that don't have much money, and then charging huge fees on late payments, is not a moral or ethical business model, in my view. There is strong demand for this product but there is a correct way to do it, in order to protect the consumer.'

Dey's email cut deep in the Afterpay camp. A legal letter was duly dispatched. The freedom of the desk analyst was brought into question. Afterpay said little publicly—Eisen and Molnar were in Israel to celebrate Eisen's daughter's bat mitzvah—leaving the retort to those house brokers who had buy ratings on the stock. Hancock fielded calls from investors until nightfall.

The following Tuesday, Bell Potter's Sotiriou hit back hard, blasting out a note to his clients. He made a point of referring to Dey's comments as the work of 'desk analysts' as distinct from the certified, regulated analysts who produce published work. Sotiriou had been a champion of the Afterpay cause. So far he'd been right, and Bell Potter's clients were both richer and more loyal as a result. He took exception to Afterpay being compared to a payday lender, Dey's focus on late fees and the prospect that ASIC might deem them a credit product.

'Afterpay has been very clear that it has been open and been active with regulators regarding their product,' Sotiriou wrote, 'and at no stage has it been raised that they believe the product should fall under the credit code.' It was a misconception that Afterpay's technology accepted every customer transaction, he argued. And as for the late fees, a High Court ruling had demonstrated that institutions were entitled to levy a fee that is in line with the actual cost incurred. There was nothing excessive or predatory about Afterpay's model, he concluded.

Sotiriou accused the analysts of lacking an understanding of how Afterpay worked in reality. Specifically, he said, users were frozen from buying more stuff until they caught up on their payments. That meant the debts never accumulated. 'We don't see late fees or Afterpay's model as an issue and don't expect anything punitive to come from the regulatory review,' he said.

The gloves were off in the usually cordial analyst community. Afterpay was stirring passions like no company had done before. Short-sellers accumulated their bets against the stock.

The bad press was also dragging down rival Zip, which had lost over 20 per cent of its share-market value as chatter about the ASIC review grew louder. Shaw and Partners senior analyst Danny Younis lamented that Zip's share price had been caught in the cross-fire of the broker wars. The commentary, he said, mostly related to Afterpay, and was based on 'ad hoc innuendo, misinformation and false extrapolation'.

Younis couldn't help but make a specific point to distinguish between Afterpay and Zip. Zip's credit-checking process, he said, was among the tightest in the industry, and it operated with both a financial services licence and a credit licence that allowed it to lend money. Late fees were insignificant to Zip, at 1 to 2 per cent of revenues, compared to 20 per cent for Afterpay. (In fact, Zip earned money from its customers by charging them an account fee to roll an unpaid balance into the next month—something Afterpay did not.) The result was that Zip had nothing to fear from an ASIC review, and perhaps something to gain if its rival's loophole was closed.

Standing behind Bell Potter's Sotiriou was Richard Coppleson. Coppo was a raging bull—and now a raging Afterpay bull. The Copplesons, too, had a large personal holding in Afterpay, and his daily Coppo Report had become so enthusiastic about the company that some readers began to call it the 'Afterpay Report'.

Coppo backed Lafitani as the 'undisputed top financial analyst in the country'. 'When Laf goes hard I suggest you listen,' he said.

The proclamation was not without merit: Sotiriou had indeed made some inspired calls. None more so than advising clients to hop off the burning wealth platforms of AMP and IOOF, which were burdened with conflict, in favour of newer, lighter, digital versions Netwealth and Hub24. Sotiriou, like Coppleson, had bought shares in Afterpay for his personal account.

Sotiriou was prepared to bet his reputation on Afterpay for a number of reasons. The first was it had shown it was capable of delivering a profit so it could finance its growth. He'd also formed the view that Afterpay's ability to attract users would be appreciated by international investors, even if Australian funds regarded it as a financing company. Australian tech companies tended to be software firms that sold products to enterprises. A business fuelled by consumer take-up was rare. He was also encouraged by Afterpay's ability to offer its payment method instore, something that US giant PayPal had struggled to achieve.

Coppleson took aim at what he theorised to be 'short-seller tactics' that were intended to get the bad news into as many business publications as they could. He'd seen it before with A2 Milk, and he told his readers so in a pink font. A2 Milk was another standout performer that had gained over twelve times its value since listing, but sceptics had worried about its reliance on selling infant formula to the Chinese market.

'In this circumstance I strongly believe they will be totally wrong,' Coppo wrote of Afterpay—in green text with yellow highlights. 'Laf does believe the US will be hard to crack but we believe Afterpay will succeed because the formula of why they are succeeding in Australia is more complex than the shorts give credit for, and is exportable.'

If Afterpay felt under siege, the drama escalated on the evening of 3 April 2018, when Ownership Matters circulated its Mickey Mouse report to institutional clients, revealing how underaged users and anonymous purchasers could transact on the Afterpay system. It also raised several other points of concern—the rise in late fees as a percentage of merchant fees charged, and the curiosities of certain accounting treatments relating to earnings.

Afterpay's shares took a battering on the back of the two unrelated reports—by Dey and Ownership Matters. At the end of what Coppleson described as a sixteen-day assault, Afterpay had shed a third of its market value. But he remained bullish. The Mickey Mouse report, Coppleson wrote, had 'only acted to help the [company] iron out a few creases and . . . rather than seeing the stock smashed, has now seen it begin the recovery'. The short-sellers were looking in the wrong direction and missing the big picture, Coppleson said, which was the market in the United States. But, pragmatically, he told his readers to expect an arm wrestle between the bulls and the bears.

Afterpay shares had touched $8 in the days before the broker wars began. They lingered in the mid-$5 range as the market awaited the third-quarter trading update.

Afterpay had always exceeded expectations, and at what was a delicate time for shareholders it could have done with a big beat. Once again, the numbers were impressive, as 300,000 more customers signed up, while total sales for the nine-month period reached $1.45 billion. But the update didn't alter the weaker market, as Afterpay's shares declined 4 per cent.

The company had to demonstrate to investors, regulators and even its board the integrity of its platform, and to the market that it could pull off its plans to enter the United States. Afterpay therefore sought to address the criticisms raised in the Ownership Matters report: new identity checks would be introduced to limit fraud, and late fees capped. For order values under $40, a maximum $10 late fee would apply, while for orders over $40, the cap would be 25 per cent of an item's purchase price and never more than $68.

'We have taken on board the comments and we will continue to learn and grow and evolve the platform,' group head David Hancock told *The Australian Financial Review* on 11 April 2018. 'It has been useful for us to go through this process, and we respect people's different views. It has been difficult, but our merchants and customers are fully engaged and the share price will take care of itself in the longer term.'

In preparation, Afterpay had lined up more financing through National Australia Bank and an 'international bank', the identity of which was not disclosed. But the mystery was short-lived; *The Australian Financial Review*'s 'Street Talk' columnist, Sarah Thompson, had a nose for deal information and soon reported that US bank Citi would front the funds.

Tom Cribb had jumped from Goldman Sachs to Citi, taking several key clients with him: non-bank financier Pepper, and Touchcorp. While Goldman had the cache, Citibank, by virtue of its $1 trillion pool of deposits, had a stable balance sheet and a global presence that could turbocharge a global expansion. That a major global lender, well versed in the ways of credit, was willing to finance Afterpay gave it much-needed legitimacy.

When Cribb read the *AFR* report in his Surry Hills townhouse that morning, he was furious that Citi's involvement had been leaked. He complained to his friend Nick Boudrie, a software entrepreneur who was visiting from Melbourne, and headed to work, texting Hancock on the way. Hancock reassured Cribb that the article was harmless, if not favourable.

When Boudrie ordered an Uber to take him to the airport, he struck up a conversation with the driver. It turned out his son was in software, too, and he proudly told his passenger he'd just got some funding from Citibank. Ron Molnar was once again spreading

David Jones lay-by department, Sydney, December 1941. Lay-by was a method of instalment payment introduced during the frugal era of the Great Depression. Mitchell Library, State Library of New South Wales

Window display of fashion retailer Roxy, in Campsie, Sydney, 1960. The shop was owned and run by Herbert and Ingeborg Nachemstein, who escaped Nazi Germany with their son Peter in 1939 for Shanghai. They migrated to Australia in 1949, and bought the shop with their savings. In the window is a sign advertising a lay-by service. Courtesy Peter Nash and Sydney Jewish Museum

Mike Jefferies, Gary Weiss and Anthony Eisen (left to right) at Guinness Peat in June 2010, shortly after demerger plans were announced. Jefferies was the chair of Touchcorp when it listed and also served on the board of Afterpay, which Eisen chaired. Michele Mossop/*The Age*

Nick Molnar with the ball at a touch rugby tournament at Queens Park, Sydney, November 2014. Noel Kessel/*The Australian Jewish News*

Adrian and Keith Cleeve at the Melbourne listing ceremony of Touchcorp on 31 March 2015. Originally a founding shareholder and technology supplier to Afterpay Group, Touchcorp merged with it in 2017, to form Afterpay Touch. The company was later renamed Afterpay Ltd.
Jesse Marlow/*The Australian Financial Review*

Afterpay's sales head Fabio De Carvalho with General Pants head of ecommerce Paula Mitchell. De Carvalho bet Mitchell that Afterpay would boost online sales. When it did, Mitchell agreed to wear an Afterpay T-shirt at a retail industry event.
Courtesy Fabio De Carvalho

Anthony Eisen and Nick Molnar pose for a photo at the ASX office in Melbourne after ringing the bell to commemorate Afterpay's share–market listing. The company's shares opened for trading at midday on Wednesday, 4 March, 2016, under the ticker AFY. The $1 share price valued Afterpay at $100 million.

David Hancock lights a rocket at Lyne Park, Rose Bay, following Afterpay's staff Christmas Party at nearby Catalina restaurant, December 2016. The party took place 7 months after Afterpay's initial public offering. Courtesy David Hancock

Founder of Cue fashion retailer Rod Levis pictured in November 2008 in the cutting room of their Clarence Street studio. Rod Levis is married to Lynette Eisen, Anthony's aunt.
Anthony Johnson/*The Sydney Morning Herald*

An instore retail advertising poster. The company distanced itself from controversial campaigns that used the term 'broke AF' in May 2018 after a backlash by consumer groups concerned that this sort of advertising was encouraging irresponsible spending by impressionable youth and vulnerable customers.

Signs placed right next to cash registers in stores encourage shoppers to use Afterpay's innovative four-payment system. T. Paskaran/Shutterstock

Nick Molnar, Anthony Eisen, Peter Gray and Larry Diamond appeared at a public hearing for the Senate Economics References Committee in Brisbane on 22 January 2019. Afterpay's public policy head Damian Kassabgi is pictured between Molnar and Eisen. Their appearance was part of an inquiry into credit and financial services targeted at Australians at risk of financial hardship. Attila Csaszar/*The Australian Financial Review*

Michael Saadat, Executive Director, Financial Services and NSW Regional Commissioner of the Australian Securities & Investments Commission, pictured at the regulator's annual forum in May 2019 at the Hilton Hotel in Sydney. Saadat oversaw the buy now, pay later sector, but in August 2019 he was hired by Afterpay. James Alcock/ *The Australian Financial Review*

Commonwealth Bank chief Matt Comyn and Klarna Group founder Sebastian Siemiatkowski, shortly after the companies announced their partnership on 30 January 2020.

Comyn was eager to join forces with Klarna to compete with Afterpay and retain its young customers, who were embracing buy now, pay later.

James D. Morgan/Getty Images

The cover of *The Australian Financial Review Magazine*'s Young Rich edition of December 2020 featured Peter Gray and Larry Diamond of Zip, a buy now, pay later competitor of Afterpay. Louie Douvis/*The Australian Financial Review*

Nick Molnar at Catalina restaurant, presenting the Australian Fashion Laureate award, December 2020. Afterpay solidified its alliance with the fashion industry, which had been early adopters of buy now, pay later. Rhett Wyman/*The Australian Financial Review*

Nick Molnar on the cover of *The Australian Financial Review Magazine*'s fashion edition, April 2021. He is the youngest Australian self-made billionaire. Damian Bennett/*The Australian Financial Review*

the Afterpay gospel on the streets of Sydney as he had to others in the fashion and finance industry including Goldman analyst Ashwini Chandra.

For Cribb, the Citi loan was the culmination of months of perseverance, during which he'd battled with reluctant credit and compliance staffers. They worried that Afterpay's model was unproven, and that it did not rely on credit checks. Citibank was also one of the largest players in the credit card market, and there were concerns the bank was funding a new competitor for itself. But the lending relationship put Citi in the box seat to manage future lucrative capital raisings and other deals. Afterpay had the makings of an ideal client.

Other brokers were jockeying to help the Afterpay founders place some of their stock in the market. And if the market wasn't fully alert to the possibility that Eisen and Molnar would soon be free to sell their shares, Hancock's April 2018 update spelt it out. 'Subject to share price and general market conditions, Anthony and Nick, for asset diversification purposes, may sell up to 10 per cent of their underlying individual shareholdings over the next 12 months,' the statement said.

The trading update was enough to give Ashwini Chandra at Goldman Sachs cold feet as he downgraded the Afterpay share price target to neutral. Once he crunched the numbers, he said, he realised that the company's sales growth had declined over the quarter. 'This may indicate that its usage rates are maturing faster than we previously forecast,' he told his clients as he cut the share price target to $6.30.

The execution of Afterpay's US strategy was now becoming increasingly important for the share price, Chandra said. In his calculation, the nascent US business accounted for about 20 to 25 per cent of the $1.3 billion value he ascribed to the company.

As the 4 May 2018 escrow day approached, after which the founders would be able to sell their shares, the hedge-funds' collective bet against an Afterpay fall increased. An intervention by regulators, the threat of more competition and a looming share dump from the founders made Afterpay the perfect target. The message from hedge fund land was that the buy now, pay later revolution was actually more of an uprising that was about to be crushed.

There was no doubt that Afterpay's future, and any riches for shareholders, rested on 28-year-old Nick Molnar's young shoulders. He'd already been dispatched to the west coast of the United States on an apparently impossible mission: to crack America.

# 10

# SHORT ON TIME

DAYS BEFORE HE boarded QF63 to San Francisco in September 2017, Nick Molnar had taken to the stage at a packed Sydney Town Hall. His uncle had taught him a public-speaking hack to calm the nerves: spread his arms out, like a superhero, to make himself feel really big. It had not failed him yet, and it didn't fail him that evening as he delivered a generational rallying cry to his young audience.

'Hi, my name is Nick, I'm a millennial, 75 per cent of my customers are millennials, and I am here to set the record straight about us,' he told the TEDxYouth@Sydney gathering. 'It's time to stop being the generation that gets written off and start to be the generation that rewrites history.' Molnar probably had the sense he was rewriting Australian corporate history. But could his superhero powers be exported?

Molnar and Eisen were thinking big. But they didn't want to get ahead of themselves. The ever-conservative Eisen wanted to avoid making the mistake other Australian companies had made, by simply assuming that what worked in Australia would work in the larger US market. So they asked around for advice.

The PayPal alumni had brokered a meeting for the Australians with Dana Stalder, the founder of Matrix Partners. If anyone in the United States could tell them whether they had a shot, it would be him. At Matrix's San Francisco office, near Salesforce Park, the home of the Giants baseball team, Eisen and Molnar ran Stalder through the business and the model.

Halfway through, Stalder stopped them to ask why they had come to see him. 'You have positive cash flow and you have made $12 million EBITDA. I do early-stage investments,' he pointed out. Despite this, Stalder was intrigued. He found Molnar and Eisen principled, humble and ambitious. The hour-long meeting stretched to two and a half hours, after which Stalder asked his assistant to clear time in his diary for the next day so they could continue talking. The Afterpay proposition, for both merchants and consumers, was crystal clear to him. And the Afterpay brand had a magic to it that PayPal, which in Stalder's mind was just a utility for making payments, lacked.

Eisen and Molnar, meanwhile, mined Stalder for insights into how the successful tech companies in Silicon Valley had been built. They soon realised Matrix had the connections and corporate know-how to be helpful. The three soon decided to work together and plot the company's US assault.

Eisen headed back to Melbourne, but Molnar called his wife Gabi and asked her to jump on a plane and join him. America was there for the taking, and he wanted to start selling Afterpay as if it was ready to go. For the next three months, Molnar and Stalder worked together to build an engineering team as Molnar crisscrossed the vast nation, working to sign up retailers.

Molnar repeated the trick he used to get a meeting with Shmuel Gniwisch of Ice, telling his contact that he'd be in the area before he'd actually made travel plans. Sometimes he got the meeting out of curiosity. The executive wanted to know what the hell an Australian kid was doing in New Albany, Ohio.

A big win came in Philadelphia, where cult retailer Urban Outfitters was headquartered. The retailer's chief digital officer, David Hayne—the son of the founder, Dick Hayne—was won over instantly. Molnar had landed his first big American catch. Matrix Partners' investment in Afterpay was announced on 16 January 2018. On 1 May, Afterpay officially launched its US offering, announcing that Urban Outfitters would be the first retailer in the country to enable its customers to use Afterpay. The shares responded accordingly, rising 7 per cent. 'We have been impressed with the positive impact Afterpay has brought to their Australian retail partners, and we hope to see a similar response with our US customers,' David Hayne said.[1]

The deal would not only start to open the US retailing sector to Afterpay, but also allow Molnar and Eisen to take some money off the table. Shortly after the share market closed on 21 May, the sales desks at Citi and Bell Potter hit the phones. They'd just emailed their largest clients to ask for bids on 5.5 million Afterpay shares at a minimum of $6.90. If there was any doubt, the buyers were told that the sellers were Eisen, Molnar and Hancock. Within an hour, the trio were $38 million richer. They finally had something tangible to show for the rapid share-market value they had created.

• • •

In Australia, investors were returning to the Afterpay story after the carnage of March and April 2018, as the company fed the exchange with updates on US retailer sign-ups. Afterpay's shares were gaining again, and by 8 June it had graduated to the S&P/ASX 200 index, the market's most followed benchmark. A new cohort of mid-cap investors would be prepared to run the ruler on this high-flying if divisive payments company. The inclusion propelled Afterpay to a new all-time high, with shares within touching distance of $10.

By the end of the financial year on 30 June, Afterpay was a $2 billion company.

The 19 July 2018 business update was another one for the ages, as Afterpay revealed that its US launch was off to a flying start. In just two months it had processed $11 million of sales, a milestone that had taken it sixteen months to achieve in Australia. Urban Outfitters had been joined by Revolve, a distributor of fashion brands with 2.4 million Instagram followers. The update revealed the extent of Molnar's work over the previous nine months: 200 US retailers were already using Afterpay, and 400 more had signed contracts. Overall sales had grown to $2.18 billion, while earnings were forecast to hit $33 million to $34 million. All up, Afterpay had 2.2 million customers and 16,500 retailers signed up, and more users were returning.

The promised land of the United States had been a graveyard for many great Australian companies. National Australia Bank's 1998 acquisition of Homeside Lending, at the time one of the largest mortgage servicers in the United States, had been one of the most spectacular failures, costing its shareholders $3 billion.

An exception was Westfield. Frank Lowy and John Saunders had rolled out their retail model across the United States, starting with a mall in Connecticut in 1976, and had built and managed centres in the biggest cities in the world. In 2016, Westfield had opened a mall at New York's World Trade Center, where the Twin Towers had stood until September 2001, the largest shopping mall in Manhattan. A nine-storey Westfield with 170 stores and a cinema was just two blocks south of Afterpay's makeshift San Francisco office on Geary Street.

The early evidence was that Afterpay's dream of emulating Westfield, albeit with a software play rather than bricks and mortar, was starting to become real. On 19 July, shares surged 24 per cent, adding an astonishing $570 million to its market capitalisation in a single day. If the smart money had sold on 4 May—the day the founders became free to offload their stock—the share price moves since had made them look foolish: the stock had more than doubled, from $6.45 to $13.50.

The performance had Afterpay's US rival Sezzle considering listing in Australia. Charlie Youakim had taken a phone call in May 2018 from Phillip Chippendale, an analyst at Ord Minnett who covered Afterpay and was looking for some intelligence on the US market. The pair spoke for two hours. Youakim explained to Chippendale how US venture capital investors weren't able to wrap their heads around the 'four instalments' model; Chippendale replied that many Australian investors understood it and were believers, and that there would likely be interest in Sezzle. An Australian roadshow was arranged for November.

The Afterpay rally was painful for short-sellers, with half the bets unwound in the face of the surging share price. If a hedge fund had shorted Afterpay shares in May, they would have lost twice their initial investment. 'If you have a company that continues to announce positive news, as Afterpay has done with the pace of their growth in the US continuing to surprise, you have the ingredients for a classic short squeeze,' Darren Letts, a dealer at wealth manager Mason Stevens, told the firm's clients in a morning update.

A short squeeze occurs when a share price rises sharply, forcing those who have borrowed shares to buy them back in a hurry. As they rush to buy, the share price rises further, aggravating their losses. When the short position is crowded and speculators are desperate to get out, the situation can get ugly.

Letts explained that a sell-down by Duncan Saville's ICM Ltd, one of the early Afterpay shareholders, may have made life even more difficult for hedge funds. That's because he believed ICM's shares may have been made available to hedge funds to borrow—and when those shares were sold by the original owner, they had to be returned, forcing the short-sellers to close their position.

Finally, Letts made a comparison to another company that had been involved in a seemingly eternal tussle with hedge funds and had elicited emotions that professional share-market traders are trained to suppress: Elon Musk's Tesla Motors.

Musk, along with Peter Thiel, belonged to the 'PayPal mafia', having founded the groundbreaking payments company to solve the problem of the lack of trust between two strangers transacting online. Musk had taken his fortune and rolled the dice on what his disciples believed were humanity-altering ventures: launching cheap rockets into space, and accelerating the use of electric cars by building models that people actually wanted to drive. Musk was an industrialist of the modern age—the closest thing to Henry Ford the auto industry had seen in decades. But more often than not he was compared to Bruce Wayne, the fictional alter ego of Batman.

Tesla had listed on the stock market in 2010—the first automaker to do so since Ford. Almost immediately, hedge funds showed up to bet that its share price was too high. Within two years, every share that was available to be shorted had been loaned out to speculators who believed the company's $3 billion valuation was close to insane. In a television interview, Musk warned the shorts that a 'tsunami of hurt' was coming: it would be wise for them to fold their bets before they lost all their money. He was right: that would have been wise.

In 2014, short-sellers were taking the view that Tesla's valuation was even more insane at $30 billion. That year Fiat had sold 4.2 million cars, compared to 22,000 Teslas—yet had only a third of the market value. By 2018, not much had changed. Tesla was still struggling to make a profit, or even enough cars to rival the auto majors. But its market capitalisation was now $50 billion.

The short-sellers couldn't help themselves. And Australia's community of global hedge funds was among those taking the other side of the bet against Elon Musk.

'Over-hyped, thematic "disruptors" are increasingly vulnerable to a fight-back from strong incumbent competitors,' Jacob Mitchell, the head of Sydney-based fund Antipodes, told *The Australian Financial Review*.[2]

'Despite the recent share price rally, we believe Tesla's fundamentals remain extremely weak and the company's share price is vulnerable to a large fall, given the persistent huge operating losses, stressed balance sheet and the arrival of dozens of competing electric cars from the world's top manufacturers,' Melbourne-based L1 Capital told investors in a quarterly update.[3]

If Afterpay's brokers were battling, then the war over Tesla was close to a nuclear one as Musk and short-sellers baited each other on social media.

Musk wasn't afraid to cross lines. He tweeted that a takeover bid was on the table; it wasn't true but he somehow got away with it, and then went a step further by baiting the regulators. He insulted analysts on his earnings calls. He wouldn't answer boring questions from short-sellers. But he was building cars that everyone loved, and Tesla's share price was still going up.

The amount of money betting against Musk was staggering, running well into the billions. Two short-sellers who tried to call him out were legends of the hedge fund game—Jim Chanos and David Einhorn. In their opinion, Musk was a huckster who constantly had to sell his vision to raise the money he needed to make it happen. Without constant access to funds, Tesla could not exist. It was an aberration of a world of free money and high share prices built on hype, they believed.

Chanos had helped expose Enron, an energy company built on hubris and hidden trusts that were used to hide losses. Einhorn had warned the public in April 2008 that Lehman Brothers was due to collapse, months before its implosion almost crashed the global financial system. But the world was different in 2018. The information was out there, shared with millions around the world on social media, who believed them and shorted Tesla. But there were millions more who didn't believe them, and they were buying Tesla shares.

What made the battle over Tesla more heated was that it was not clear who was virtuous in the contest. Chanos and Einhorn were mavericks who stood up against the Wall Street money machine, where corporate executives too often played the public for fools. Could the same be said of Musk? He had all the traits of a charlatan, but he was turning his fanciful stories and wild promises into capital, which he was then using to build cars that drivers loved, while his loyal investors—from the big institutions to social-media fans— were getting rich.

The mild-mannered Eisen and Molnar weren't nearly as polarising as Musk. They kept their opinions to themselves and had no desire to antagonise anyone, including short-sellers, and especially the lawmakers and regulators who were working out whether Afterpay was operating within the rules.

The same could not be said about Afterpay's shareholders— some of whom took to social media to champion the company. An alliance of institutions and vocal individual shareholders had formed to fend off an equally vocal army of haters. At stake was not only money, but a vision of how capitalism should work. Tesla and Afterpay were being rewarded by the share market for their potential to disrupt decades-old profitable corporations. Their sky-high share prices implied that they would inevitably succeed well before it was certain that they would.

But these runaway share prices were messing with the minds of a 150,000-strong global army of chartered financial analysts, who had been trained to value companies based on their future cashflows. Then there was the generation of investors who had modelled themselves on the wisdom of Warren Buffett.

Buffet, one of the richest men on the planet, and the most successful share-market investor, had a brand that was defined by patience and discipline. Wonderful companies would be available at the right price, and the schizophrenia of the market would also provide the opportunity to buy when the price was depressed and sell when it was exuberant. But Buffet's approach of 'value investing' in cheap, overlooked companies simply wasn't working in the age of perpetually cheap money—or wasn't working well. The cheap stocks, even if they were making a profit, were getting cheaper, while expensive stocks were getting dearer.

Value investors were facing a crisis of confidence. Was the market telling them the companies they owned were cheap because they were in gradual, inevitable decline? Would they become swallowed up by upstart competitors that had an endless supply of cheap money to attack big markets so long as they could demonstrate they were growing?

It wasn't the first occasion that time had been called on Buffett and the art of value investing. In 1999, moments before the dotcom bubble burst, Buffett had famously stared down his doubters in a speech to media and tech moguls at the vaunted Allen & Co. gathering in Sun Valley, Idaho.

'The key to investing is not assessing how much an industry is going to affect society, or how much it will grow, but rather determining the competitive advantage of any given company and, above all, the durability of that advantage,' Buffett told the audience, which included many of the new internet titans who were adorning the covers of *Fortune* magazine. 'The products or services that have wide, sustainable moats around them are the ones that deliver rewards to investors.'

In 2018 a formal education in finance, which involved sound bases to value companies, was a liability. An imagination was an asset. Value investors clung to that idea and hoped the world would turn in their favour.

What was also different in 2018 was the prevailing level of interest rates. Back in 1999, as dotcom fervour drove stocks such as Amazon, Yahoo!, eBay and America Online, the chair of the US Federal Reserve, Alan Greenspan, was gradually lifting the Fed Funds Rate, which sets the cost of borrowing in the economy. The jobless rate was falling, but that meant prices were rising and inflation was trending up. From June 1999 to May 2000, the rate had been lifted from 5 to 6.5 per cent. The Nasdaq index of tech stocks accelerated even as interest rates were jacked up.

But in 2018, interest rates were much lower. The opportunity cost of moving your money out of a deposit account at a bank was negligible. Any investment that could make a positive return was worth making.

The valuation models used by analysts calculate a business's worth by forecasting the cashflows it would produce in the future, and then discounting them into the present using an appropriate interest rate. If a business will earn $10 ten years into the future but interest rates are 5 per cent, it is only worth $6.50 today. That's because $6.50 invested in a safe investment at 5 per cent a year will be worth $10 in a decade. But if interest rates are zero, future profits become more valuable. And since high-growth companies are expected to make all their profits well into the future, then—all else being equal—their present worth is boosted by low interest rates.

The more valuable these businesses, the more money they can raise from investors, and the more they can then spend, enabling them to grow bigger and at a faster pace. And the bigger they get, the more valuable they are deemed to be by the market.

For old-hat fund managers who made their names by putting their investors' money in reliable companies where profits were protected, this new environment tested their fortitude. Even if they resisted piling into fast-growing stocks, that didn't stop others, and in an industry in which a fund manager's abilities are assessed on a relative basis, ignoring the apparent excess wasn't always possible.

That was the case for celebrity investor Roger Montgomery. He had emulated Hamish Douglass by building a following in the media, appearing regularly on radio and television, and contributing columns to newspapers around Australia. In August, he wrote an article questioning what all the fuss regarding 'Afterpay' was about.[4]

There was nothing new about the company, he argued. It was just engaging in the decades-old practice known as factoring, in which the seller of goods agrees to take payment earlier than otherwise in exchange for a fee. In the case of Afterpay, it provided merchants with the money upfront for a 4 per cent fee, and in return would collect the balance from the shopper. Afterpay would take on the risk of non-payment. Factoring, or invoice financing, is well established and allows even fragile operations to get access to funds, so long as the customers—for instance, a large grocery chain—are of high quality. Afterpay was collecting the money from shoppers who, for whatever reason, could not or did not want to pay for the goods upfront.

'It's easy to lend when the market is going well,' wrote Montgomery. 'But if the economy stalls, and unemployment unexpectedly climbs, then you have a completely different picture. And if Afterpay is successful because it extends credit to some proportion of the population that would not qualify for a credit card (despite smaller transaction values and shorter terms), then it is even possible that such point-of-sale financiers will experience defaults higher than providers of other forms of finance.'

Once again, Afterpay's $2.5 billion market capitalisation was perplexing to a value investor. At that valuation, investors were paying a price that was ten times larger than its revenues, or 50 times its expected $44 million profit forecast for 2020.

Montgomery tried to explain why he thought the market was prepared to ascribe such a high value to Afterpay. Two of Afterpay's early adopters in the United States, Urban Outfitters and Revolve, generated $1 billion of online sales every year. If Afterpay could capture 10 per cent of that, its 2020 profits could double, and therefore its price-to-earnings ratio would halve. 'But that logic fails to acknowledge that the profitability of factoring businesses is not particularly earth shattering and therefore the [price-to-earnings ratio] of 50 times might be exuberant to begin with.'

Was Afterpay a bubble? If so, it was not in isolation. Technology stocks had run hard both globally and in Australia. In the United States, Facebook, Amazon, Apple, Netflix and Google—the so-called FAANG stocks—had run up spectacularly. But investors argued that their share price was only moving in step with their ever-rising revenues. There was no obvious bubble, at least when it came to big tech. But at the smaller end, there were signs that investors were getting carried away.

Australia had its own acronym of tech darlings: the WAAAX stocks. Wisetech, Afterpay, Altium, Appen and Xero. While the FAANGs were global platforms whose reach transcended that of almost any corporation in history, the WAAAX stocks were masters of their niches, providing accounting and logistics software, electronics engineering and artificial intelligence. They were profitable and growing, but the Australian market was willing to pay a far higher price for growth than any other market.

Globally, investors on average were paying about twenty times the following year's profits to own listed companies that were growing profits by more than 20 per cent per annum. In Australia, they were paying twice as much—40 times the following year's profit. There was no single reason for this, but most put it down to Australia's superannuation system, in which 9 per cent of workers' wages were paid into their pension fund each month.

That meant there was always new money coming into the market, of which a fair proportion made its way into the share market, bidding up fast-growing stocks disproportionately.

Another explanation was that fast-growing companies tended to be tightly held by their founders, by index funds and by a small cohort of funds that specifically targeted growth companies. The rest of the market had to clamour for a small float of available shares. Unusually, the most expensive shares, measured by the highest price-to-earnings ratios, were the ones that were going up in price, while the cheapest stocks fell further. This was a value investor's nightmare.

L1 Capital, a Melbourne hedge fund, told its clients that the share prices of Big Tech stocks may be grounded in reality, but there were still two parallels with the tech bubble of 2000. The first was that 80 per cent of companies listed on the market were losing money. The second was that they were, on average, doubling within six months.

Afterpay's extraordinary growth was very real. The question in investors' minds was whether the asking price for a share of its future profits had become unhinged in reality. Afterpay was not making a profit. But in 2018, that was a badge of honour. A dollar of profit was a dollar that was not being invested in growing the company further. In the United States, and increasingly at the smaller end of the Australian market, investors were encouraging companies not to show a profit, as that might be taken as a signal that a company was nearing maturity far sooner than its optimistic investors had hoped.

Afterpay became a unicorn in October 2017, almost a year and a half after going public. Eight months later, on 28 June 2018, it had doubled in value again, to $2 billion. Less than two months after that, on 23 August, it doubled in value again, to $4 billion.

Some shareholders took the opportunity to bank some profits. Alex Waislitz was one of them. The valuation had got ahead of itself, he felt, so he trimmed his position.

• • •

On the day Afterpay reached that $4 billion milestone, it presented its annual results. Sales were up strongly enough, and Afterpay had actually increased its net transaction margin to 2.6 per cent. Its customers were 'using the platform responsibly', resulting in a decline in net transaction losses from 0.6 per cent to 0.4 per cent of sales. If the doubters were right and customers were struggling, it wasn't with their debts to Afterpay. The company's US sales were growing fast—clocking in at $20 million in July, up from $12 million in June—its first full month.

The bigger news was Afterpay's request for trading in its shares to be halted. The company announced it would raise $108 million by selling new shares. The surging share price meant it would have to give up less ownership to raise those funds, issuing half the number of shares than would have been required two months earlier. Citi would oversee the placement to institutions, while Wilson HTM and Bell Potter were assigned a supporting role.

Cribb had got the call from Eisen as he was about to board a flight to Turkey. It was a planned vacation, but he had waited years to reel in a deal of this size. So from taxicabs in Istanbul and calls in the dead of the night, he worked to get approval for Citibank to underwrite the share sale. The funds would replenish Afterpay's cash balance, bankrolling its international expansion.

Afterpay also revealed it was expanding into the United Kingdom, which it had identified as the third-largest ecommerce market in the world. To do this, it purchased a buy now, pay later operation called Clearpay by issuing 1 million Afterpay shares to the vendor, ThinkSmart Limited.

There was a snag: AfterPay—with a capital P—already existed in Europe. Dutch entrepreneur Stefan van den Berg's company had developed a 'pay after delivery' solution, similar to Klarna, which was also rolling out in Europe. AfterPay allowed online shoppers to try products and return them before paying for them, or to postpone or split payments. Now owned by powerful media group Bertelsmann's financial solutions division, Arvato, it was in no hurry to give up the naming rights. There was no alternative: Afterpay's expansion into the United Kingdom would have to take place under a different banner.

Afterpay's capital raising went off without a hitch. On 27 August 2018, its shares topped $20 for the first time as its valuation exceeded $4.5 billion. The turn in market sentiment had been both spectacular and rapid: Afterpay shares had now tripled since 8 May, when short-sellers were amassing a $100 million bet against the company.

By 5 September, short-sellers had returned 10 million shares as they scrambled to recover what had been a losing bet. It had been a tough year for some of Australia's hedge funds. The stocks they owned went down, while the ones they bet against ripped.

One of Australia's top traders took to the stage at a gathering of investors in September to offer his thoughts. By the numbers, there were few better than Phil King of Regal Funds Management. King had worked out better than most how to trade in the Australian share market, and was not afraid to take big bets in turbulent markets. Whether he had shorted Afterpay was a fact he'd neither confirm nor deny. Parts of the Australian market, he told the audience, were in a bubble, and it was caused by low interest rates.

'There's very little time cost of money,' he said. 'If you miss earnings this year, investors are happy to be patient and hold their stocks for maybe another year or so. You take the extreme example of zero interest rates and you can almost justify any sort of multiple you want. This is one of the reasons that it has been hard shorting in Australia over the last few years and few months.'

King's comments were prescient. Interest rates had been low for a long time. In the United States, low interest rates had aided the long, slow recovery from the depths of the 2008 financial crisis. But just like in 1999, they were moving higher as Federal Reserve chairman Jerome Powell tried to get ahead of an economy that might yet run hot. As for the proverbial boiling frog, the heat was being turned up so gradually it was hard to perceive. But at any minute investors could leap out of the market.

In October 2018, global stock markets began to buckle as bond rates edged higher. Tech stocks that had been bid higher in an environment of low rates were dumped. Australian stocks, which this time did not exclude Afterpay, were caught in the selling.

For Afterpay, the effects of this turn in the market were compounded by an escalation in its battle to keep the lawmakers at bay. On 17 October, reports of the looming Senate committee inquiry sent the stock plunging. The ever-more-real prospect that Afterpay would be deemed a credit provider and be forced to undertake credit checks on customers posed a potentially devastating blow to its model. Almost 20 per cent of Afterpay's value vanished on the news. That was now $600 million. Short-sellers ramped up their position, steadily amassing a 10 million share position.

The Australian market had a reputation for being small and clubby, which meant hedge fund aggression, either in the form of shorting shares or buying them and agitating on their behalf, would invariably see toes trodden on. Short-sellers kept their views to themselves, in order to maintain cordial relationships with boards, management and investors who disagreed with them.

But short-sellers often need catalysts. VGI Partners, a fund that mainly managed money for wealthy families, had become known for its take-no-prisoners approach to investing. In 2015, it had been public about its short position in law firm Slater & Gordon. The trade worked out spectacularly: VGI made money for its existing clients and attracted more funds from impressed observers.

That October, it picked a new target, Brisbane-based travel agent Corporate Travel Management. VGI had dispatched analysts around the world to visit Corporate Travel's offices, even one in Alaska. They found that many either didn't exist or were unstaffed. The explosive report had divided the market as it entertained it. Now investment analysts had to be on the alert for fake offices.

That's why the hearts of David Allingham and Tim Serjeant, the Eley Griffiths analysts, and Wilson HTM's broker Duncan Gamble skipped a beat when the elevator door opened on the fifth floor of 77 Geary Street, near San Francisco's Union Square, at 5 pm on Thursday, 22 November 2018. The trio were about to fly back to Sydney after a research trip to the United States, but were keen to drop in on the Afterpay offices to discuss its progress in the United States.

Afterpay had just told the market that in just six months it had already signed up 900 merchants and attracted 300,000 users. Nick Molnar had been difficult to pin down all week, but he had finally carved out 45 minutes to meet with them in the late afternoon before they headed to the airport. But when they arrived, there were no signs of Molnar, or of Afterpay. Half-jokingly, they feared that they might be writing up a VGI-style report of their own.

Eventually they navigated the serviced office and found Molnar and the small Afterpay team. To Allingham, it seemed like Molnar hadn't slept but 'was jumping out his skin'. It was clear that the US launch was going well, and the traction Afterpay was getting was already exceeding its Australian experience—in a market ten times the size. They headed back to Sydney suspecting that Afterpay's shares, which closed that day a touch above $11, were probably too cheap.

In fact, it was by design that Afterpay's extraordinary traction was going largely unnoticed. Stalder's biggest worry was competition—the possibility that some other Silicon Valley venture capitalist would realise the power of the Afterpay model and rip it off. Sezzle had already adopted the 'pay in four' construct. Quadpay had been established in New York the previous year, with a similar offering. It would only be a matter of time before Klarna, Affirm and PayPal would do the same. Molnar and Stalder made a conscious decision to keep their story out of tech-industry publications, which had become a medium for venture funds to promote themselves and their start-ups.

But they desperately wanted to get their story out to the retail industry. Instead of *TechCrunch*, Molnar courted the women's fashion trade press and attended events hosted by the WWD Digital Forum in New York and Los Angeles. The retail and fashion influencers were exactly who he needed to win over.

Brian Sugar, who was deeply connected with the millennial zeitgeist after setting up the popular culture blog *PopSugar* with his wife, Lisa, came on board as an Afterpay investor and adviser. *PopSugar* reported on beauty trends, fitness and diet for the same female audience that Afterpay was targeting, and had acquired a shopping search engine called ShopStyle. Brian helped to open many retailing doors for Molnar, just as Paul Greenberg had done in Australia through his NORA network.

Afterpay was also coming to the attention of the world's largest social-media influencers. Shortly after arriving in the United States, Molnar had been told by a young member of his new team that Afterpay's growth in the world's biggest retailing market would be turbocharged if he could get the Kardashian sisters on board. After rising to fame from a reality television series, the omnipresent Kardashians had created a vast online retail network that included selling beauty products to millennials—an Afterpay sweet spot. Molnar tried for months to get a meeting, but the doors didn't open. But then, just before the Thanksgiving holiday in November, one of the Kardashians' crew made contact—via the Afterpay website.

'We tried every single angle to get in the door there, and one morning they filled out our contact form. They came inbound to us. And we were like, "The world is lovely,"' Molnar told *The Australian Financial Review* for a profile for the 2019 Rich List.[5]

The Kardashians were demanding. Molnar received a phone call from a member of the digital team over Thanksgiving, when no one was at work in Afterpay's San Francisco office. They wanted Afterpay live that same day, so they could take full advantage of 'Black Friday'—the day after Thanksgiving, and the biggest day for retail sales in the United States. The Kardashians knew their customers would be attracted to splitting payments into instalments, and this could help them sell more make-up.

Molnar swung his team into action, and Afterpay was live on the Kardashians' site in two hours. The frenetic work on a public holiday paid back in spades when Kim Kardashian uploaded an Instagram post to her 120 million followers; she also endorsed Afterpay to her 60 million followers on Twitter, via a post on 28 November:

> We added #AfterPay to our sites to make purchasing easier! Choose AfterPay at checkout to purchase your #BlackFriday favs and the Must Have #GlamBible in 4 easy payments. Our 30–50% off site wide #KKWBeauty sale and 30% off site wide #KKWFragrance sale ends tonight at 11:59 pm PST

It was just what the young business needed to kickstart further growth. By the end of March, Afterpay hit 1 million customers in the United States, just ten months after its launch—an impressive growth rate even by Silicon Valley's lofty standards.

The Kardashian camp intuitively understood the product, and the fortuitous connection helped put Afterpay on the radar of America's millennial generation, those aged between 22 and 37 in 2018—of whom there were 63 million. 'Some of the best millennial brands in the world are being developed out of the US and they didn't exist three years ago,' Molnar said. 'They have built amazing brands and are speaking to the consumer how they want to be spoken to. It is amazing to watch retail change.'[6]

• • •

The success of Afterpay's US launch was turning heads at Klarna, one of the original point-of-sale fintechs seeking to disrupt credit cards. Klarna had been founded five years before Eisen and Molnar met, by Sebastian Siemiatkowski, Niklas Adalberth and Victor Jacobsson, all students at the Stockholm School of Economics.

In front of the King of Sweden, Carl XVI Gustaf, at a 'shark tank'–style event at their business school, their initial pitch describing an online buy now, pay later service ended up coming last. But they persevered, and on 10 April 2005 Klarna's first transaction took place at a Swedish bookshop called Pocketklubben. In Sweden, debit cards have always been more popular than credit cards, but Swedes didn't like the idea of using a debit card to pay for something online before it had been received, so Klarna built a 'try before you buy' offering. It wasn't initially high-tech: invoices were sent out in the mail.

Klarna launched in the United States in 2015, signing up online retailer Overstock.com as its first major merchant, but got its initial product wrong. The checkout offering required retailers to change their payments infrastructure: a hard sell. Klarna was forced to lay off half its US staff at the start of 2017, according to a report in *Forbes*.[7]

It then shifted to a model like that of Affirm, which had been founded by one of PayPal's founders, Max Levchin, in 2012, offering digital versions of traditional finance products that charged interest, with a focus on higher-cost items. But Affirm hadn't been setting the payments world on fire either.

Then Klarna saw the success of Afterpay and it pivoted again, creating an interest-free 'Pay in 4' instalment offering in 2018, and a new consumer app. Its US customer traction began to improve. Just three years earlier, Afterpay had modelled itself on Klarna and Affirm to its earliest backers. Afterpay was now forcing these major players to change their models and come onto its turf.

Along with the Kardashians, Skechers and Kylie Cosmetics, footwear retailer Steve Madden also came on board with Afterpay. 'We're very excited to launch Afterpay in the US market after seeing its success in Australia,' the Steve Madden Group said in Afterpay's 8 November 2018 update.

According to Steve Madden, in its first week after going live Afterpay was the second-most popular payment method after credit cards, and was also encouraging customers to spend more than they otherwise would have. 'We saw a 25 per cent uplift in average order value,' the company noted.

Steve Madden was a retailer with its own fascinating stock-market backstory. The company had listed on the Nasdaq stock exchange in 1993, with the help of the most notorious brokerage firm in history, Stratton Oakmont. That was the firm run by Jordan Belfort, the 'Wolf of Wall Street'. Madden had turned to Stratton Oakmont because a childhood friend, Danny Porush, worked there. For Madden, that was unfortunate: Stratton Oakmont engaged in a so-called 'pump and dump scheme', whereby they manipulated the share price higher so that insiders could offload the shares and profit. Madden himself was charged as a result.

But the incredible irony, as Sydney hedge fund manager John Hempton pointed out, was that Steve Madden made great shoes that people loved. Unlike every other company Stratton Oakmont touched, this one turned out to be a winner. 'Every company I short I have to ask myself—even if I am sure this is dodgy—how do I know I do not have the next Steve Madden? To me that is the stuff of nightmares,' Hempton wrote on his blog.[8]

Hempton and his fund, Bronte Capital—named after the pictur-esque beach in Sydney's Eastern Suburbs—had a cult-like following for colourfully exposing corporate frauds, and sometimes profiting from their downfall. He'd been following the Afterpay story closely and, as he often did, weighed into the debate on social media. On 28 November 2018, when ASIC released its report into the buy now, pay later sector, he read it with interest (the report is covered in more detail in a later chapter).

For the market, the most important piece of news was that ASIC was not recommending that the apparent loophole in the rules allowing Afterpay to extend funds without conducting a credit check should be closed. That position lifted Afterpay's shares by almost 9 per cent.

But Hempton told his followers he saw enough to be concerned about. In his eyes, Afterpay was a 'cult stock and cult product among millennials', he wrote as he tried to make sense of the positive market reaction to what he felt was an otherwise troubling report. It was not at all shocking to him that ASIC, which 'does not have a reputation as an aggressive regulator', would take a wait-and-see approach. 'All I can say is that ASIC has helped out with researching a controversial stock,' he signed off ominously.

Stockbroker Marcus Padley had invested in Afterpay, but was forced to trim his position as its share price run meant his investment was too large compared to other holdings. In September 2018, still worried about the rise of buy now, pay later, he'd published a note about the trappings of debt after paying off his daughter's $345 bills to Afterpay and Zip. 'Generation after generation has indoctrinated the next generation into believing consumption funded by debt is acceptable,' he said. 'But it isn't if your dad has to pay for it.'[9]

In a later commentary he signed off the year by recounting that the day of reckoning had arrived for the high-growth darlings of the market. 'It was worse among the concept stocks, the stocks with no earnings, the stocks with price to earnings of infinity, the bandwagon stocks that have no obvious fundamental value bit which have been given the benefit of the doubt.'[10] The short-sellers were scaling up their bet against Afterpay amid the sell-off. By Christmas, more than 17 million shares were on loan to the shorts, representing a $200 million collective financial bet that Afterpay's share-market rise would reverse.

As Afterpay's share price plunged, Coppleson sought to reassure his readers to hold their nerve. On Thursday, 22 November, he wrote that the stock had been battered 'by the press and others who are trying to tear down their great success story.'

When it comes to tech or growth businesses, 'you either love it and believe or think it's all hot air. Most value people I know can't understand it or want to understand it—it's just too expensive for them . . . But . . . this one is real, management (and this is so important in a company like this) are competent, honest and realistic. It's a future ASX 100 company and it's a BUY here . . .'

Since August, Afterpay had slid 40 per cent and shed $1 billion in market value. But, in what was an extraordinarily volatile year, investors had still doubled their money. The S&P/ASX 200 had fallen 2.8 per cent in 2018, its worst year since 2011. But Afterpay was the second-best stock to own.

# 11

# HOUSE OF CARDS

'WHEN YOU ARE growing so fast, it is very hard to get caught up in that stuff,' Nick Molnar told *The Weekend Australian*'s Damon Kitney, who had asked about his $400 million paper fortune. 'You are trying to hold on when the snowball is rolling down the mountain.'[1]

The interview for the paper, published in January 2019, recapped a tumultuous year in which Afterpay had fended off regulators, short-sellers and critical governance reports—yet had still emerged with a business that had doubled in value.

For Molnar and Eisen, 2018 had been a roller-coaster both personally and professionally. In San Francisco in late December, Nick's wife, Gabi, had given birth to Ella. The month before, Anthony Eisen had splashed out $7.6 million on a holiday home: the White House on Wategos Beach, near Byron Bay. The iconic five-bedroom hilltop mansion overlooking the Pacific Ocean had been rented to supermodels Kate Moss and Elle Macpherson; Eisen bought it from Charlie Arnott of the Arnott's biscuit company.

In the newspaper profile, Molnar spoke about how he'd been warned that fatherhood would change his life, while the intensely private Eisen spoke of the 'cringe-worthiness' of wealth and unwanted attention.

Afterpay was now a big team, with a staff of around 400, split between Sydney and Melbourne. The Sydney crew had moved from its initial digs in the inner-city suburb of Surry Hills and was now based in a larger warehouse space up the hill. The area that had housed the city's rag trade was now a hub for tech firms and creative types. The digs had the start-up feel: the stairwell up to the office was adorned with graffiti, while a set of Technics vinyl decks sat on a table in the centre of the open-plan space. (Eisen is a decent DJ.) But there were also signs the business was getting more professional: motivational values about the importance of hard work and customer centrism had been fixed to the main wall. 'Do things differently', 'Hustle every day' and 'Borrow less and live more' were written in coloured chalk on a blackboard near the entrance. The glass surrounding the conference room was adorned with the logos of hundreds of the biggest retail brands in Australia.

Eisen, based in Melbourne, had also come to appreciate that a presence in the nation's capital, Canberra, was crucial to Afterpay's long-term prosperity: they would need to bolster their lobbying efforts. He and David Hancock took meetings with whoever would accept them. The networking was relentless. The logic was that when issues arose, people would know of Afterpay, and know who to call to explain what was going on. Early encounters with the banks had alerted them to the fact that the carpet wasn't always rolled out to new players. Quite the opposite. Lobbying was a dark art, but Afterpay wasn't above it.

The banking industry was being represented in Canberra by Anna Bligh, a former premier of Queensland, who had performed with distinction as the Banking Royal Commission hearings unfolded during 2018, and as banks repaired their relationships with officials while the inquiry's recommendations were put into action.

In September 2018, Afterpay hired Damian Kassabgi, a former adviser to Labor prime ministers Julia Gillard and Kevin Rudd. He had been in Rudd's office the day the *National Consumer Credit Protection Act* had been passed by the federal parliament in 2009. Kassabgi had also spent three years at Uber, the fast-growing ride-sharing platform, as a director of public policy in Singapore, before moving to San Francisco.

It was there that he had received an email from Andrew Charlton, who had also worked for Rudd, as an economic adviser. The Oxford-educated Rhodes Scholar had a wealth of policy experience and had represented the government at various global economic forums. Charlton told Kassabgi his new economic advisory firm, Alpha-Beta, had been working for this company called Afterpay, whose co-founder Nick had just arrived in San Francisco and was looking for Australians to hang out with.

Over a ramen soup for lunch at Ippudo, in the artsy Yerba Buena quarter, Molnar expressed to Kassabgi his shock at the Afterpay share price falling 20 per cent merely on reports of a Senate inquiry. Kassabgi quickly realised public policy mattered a lot to this young company, which was being battered around on the market by investors that might not understand the strange machinations in Canberra.

Uber had grown from a start-up to a $120 billion company in just five years, not by playing by the rules but by breaking them— and by forcing lawmakers to change them. Kassabgi brought that regulatory arbitrage mentality to Afterpay, which needed to remain out of reach of the credit act.

As part of his employee share plan, Kassabgi was granted 300,000 share options at an exercise price of $10.40. Options are contracts that allow the holder to buy shares at a specified price. If the share price rises above the exercise price, the holder stands to make a windfall gain.

Afterpay's management had come to appreciate the incredible power of incentives that could be harnessed through stock options. In some respects, it was the secret fairy dust that motivated those with little interest in Afterpay's cause to publicly fight hard for its future, or to privately tug strings. Employee stock options were also extended to external consultants. At no upfront cost, lobbyists would embrace the Afterpay cause, and get stinking rich doing so, if they helped it succeed. The payout would come in the form of new shares being issued, but if the share price was materially higher in the future, everyone would win.

With Afterpay's shares having the demonstrated potential to double, triple or better, the stock option was a powerful currency. The same could not be said of the stock of Australia's lumbering big four banks, which paid a healthy dividend but lacked the allure of rapid, life-altering wealth creation.

Among those granted share options was Sharon McCrohan. McCrohan had little public profile, but she had a reputation in elite circles as an indispensable image consultant. In 2018 she had signed up for two repair jobs of iconic proportions—advising both Australia's former cricket captain, and the man many believed would be a future prime minister.

In late March 2018, Australia's boy wonder cricket captain Steve Smith had found himself in a potentially career-ending scandal. In an acrimonious Test match against archrival South Africa in Cape Town, a junior player, Cameron Bancroft, had been caught by the broadcast cameras scratching the ball with sandpaper.

Scuffs on a cricket ball can make it move through the air more erratically, and so it's harder for batsmen to hit. Ball tampering is against the rules, and the blatant real-time evidence of the Australian player's cheating was an instant national scandal. Prime Minister Malcolm Turnbull branded the event a 'shocking disappointment'.

Shortly after the incident, Cricket Australia found that Smith, who had turned a blind eye to the ball tampering that Bancroft and senior player David Warner were planning, had brought the game into disrepute, in what was now being referred to as 'Sandpapergate'. All three players were sent home in disgrace and battled a media throng as they left the tour.

Sharon McCrohan worked her magic. She insisted that Smith's father be there at Sydney Airport when he landed and faced the Australian media. His dad Peter's positioning—over Smith's left shoulder, upon which he rested his hand—was carefully choreographed. Smith cried and begged Australia for forgiveness. He'd not only let Mum and Dad down, but the whole nation.

'I know I will regret this for the rest of my life,' Smith said through tears. 'I'm absolutely gutted. I hope in time I can earn back respect and forgiveness.' Like disappointed parents, of course Australia still loved its cricket captain, and he was welcomed back into the national side a year later, having served his suspension period.

McCrohan's other task was harder: to get Bill Shorten elected. Having advised some of the country's most powerful unions, she was hired to advise on the Labor Party campaign for the federal election in May 2019, when it appeared to be in pole position. Although the Coalition seemed to be doing everything possible to lose the election—such as deposing their own leader, Malcolm Turnbull, during the year before the election—the Australian public had a deep distrust of Bill Shorten. A former union boss who was thought by some voters to be among the party's 'faceless men', Shorten had little public affection. The strategy McCrohan was advising was for him to say as little as possible.

In April 2019, only a month before the federal election, McCrohan was brought into the Afterpay tent. The connection was made by Leon Zwier, a partner at top-end law firm Arnold Bloch Leibler, whose ability to solve any problem had earned him the nickname 'Mr Fixit'. Zwier had acted as Shorten's legal adviser during the gruelling Royal Commission into Trade Union Governance and

Corruption, and was close to the would-be prime minister, given the Coalition was widely tipped to lose power. McCrohan received 100,000 Afterpay options with a strike price of $5.66. Her talents would be called on as and when they were needed.

Afterpay also recruited top-end public relations firm Cato & Clegg—the newly formed partnership between Sue Cato and former newspaper journalist, investment banker and media executive Brett Clegg.

Clegg was the ultimate man about town. He'd made his name as a star journalist at *The Australian Financial Review* before moving to Macquarie Bank, when the so-called Millionaires' Factory was in its heyday. When he returned to journalism, he became a deal newsbreaker extraordinaire, getting wind of some of the era's biggest corporate mergers and snaring newspaper exclusives from his corner desk overlooking Sydney's Darling Harbour. He'd also cemented his relationship with Australia's most important bankers. Clegg eventually snared his dream role of running the business media division of *The Australian Financial Review*, before entering the world of public relations.

Sue Cato was a force of nature. She was a master of the art of corporate spin, working long hours and using all her powers of persuasion to shape stories in favour of her high-paying clients. Among them was Fairfax chief executive Greg Hywood, himself a former journalist. That year she'd taken on embattled AMP chairman Catherine Brenner as a client. Brenner had faced a barrage of criticism as the Banking Royal Commission exposed how she'd been aware of efforts by the firm's in-house lawyers to seek changes to an independent report into the firm's compliance ordered by the regulator.

While Cato & Clegg was paid a retainer by Afterpay, stock options were also on the table. A total of 40,000 were accepted by Clegg—but not by Cato, who privately claimed to have refused the offer, and that she was under the impression Clegg had as well. Corporate spinners are paid tens of thousands of dollars to advise companies, boards and chief executives on how to deal with the media, especially in a crisis. But payment in the form of shares and options presented an ethical dilemma. While small PR firms were known to take payment in shares to help speculative mining prospectors win over the punters, it was a highly unusual practice in Australia and risked raising the suspicions of journalists, who to some degree trust the consultant to play a straight bat.

Another stock-option benefactor was David Gazard, a close confidant of the new prime minister, Scott Morrison, and now a crack lobbyist. Gazard had set up a Canberra advisory firm called ECG Financial in 2011 with former treasurer Peter Costello. The one-time Liberal Party staffer could navigate the corridors of power and access key decision-makers, which would prove invaluable to Afterpay.

One external adviser who would not accept stock options was Andrew Charlton. Afterpay was one of the anchor clients of Alpha-Beta, which had been commissioned to conduct research into the spending and payments habits of millennials. It was hoped the report might counter the findings of ASIC, which had begun sourcing data from the biggest players in the nascent industry. But for producing it, Charlton insisted AlphaBeta be paid its fee in cash.

The stakes for Afterpay's team of lobbyists were taken up a notch in October 2018. As the Banking Royal Commission hearings drew to a close, the Senate had voted for its Economics References Committee to conduct a review into 'financial services targeted at Australians at risk of financial hardship'. The seven-member committee was instructed to look into the impact of payday lenders and consumer lenders, but the buy now, pay later sector was also tacked on to the inquiry's remit.

Part of that remit was to examine whether the rules in place needed to change to meet community expectations, and whether reform was needed. For Afterpay, there was now a clear and present danger. Lawmakers were being explicitly asked to determine whether the rules that applied to providing credit needed to be changed to include its model.

The Consumer Action Law Centre, the powerful advocacy group run by Gerard Brody in Melbourne, had been fielding reports from community case workers that more and more clients were presenting with buy now, pay later debts. Its concerns went beyond Afterpay: buy now, pay later products were proliferating, and included not just a pair of jeans or shoes but also solar installations costing more than $10,000. Providers included Certegy and Brighte, in which Atlassian's Mike Cannon-Brookes was an investor. Brody had also been supporting the Australian Competition & Consumer Commission's investigations into high-pressure door-to-door sales tactics being used by solar-panel retailers offering the instalment products.

'The explosion of BNPL services such as Certegy, Afterpay and Zip Pay comes at a time when Australians hold record levels of household debt. As the popularity of these products has grown, so too have calls to the National Debt Helpline from individuals with debts owed to BNPL providers,' the CALC told the Senate inquiry in its November 2018 submission.

Good Shepherd Microfinance, a not-for-profit organisation that offered vulnerable borrowers no-interest loans, also expressed its concerns to the senators. Buy now, pay later providers were taking advantage of 'legal loopholes to avoid having to comply with responsible lending obligations', it said. It estimated 30 per cent of applicants for its program were repaying a buy now, pay later purchase, and noted that 'it is rare that buy now, pay later is the only form of credit that appears on an applicant's bank statement'. One loan applicant had provided a 90-day bank statement containing 288 buy now, pay later transactions with various providers totalling $5600.

Rising regulatory scrutiny came as Afterpay's growth continued to go gangbusters. On 8 November 2018, it had filed a business update with the ASX, showing that in less than six months after launching in the United States, it had attracted 300,000 customers and 900 retailers, and it had a strong pipeline of retailers preparing to come on board. Meanwhile, in Australia, more of its 2.5 million-strong customer base were using the service more often.

Then ASIC finally broke its silence. A full year after the 'Street Talk' report had flagged the inquiry and excited the short-sellers, on 28 November 2018 ASIC finally unveiled its landmark report into the sector. The review had been meticulously overseen by ASIC's Michael Saadat, in his role as executive director, and Peter Kell, ASIC's deputy chairman. It detailed how the buy now, pay later sector was encouraging more millennials to spend. In just three years, the number of users had increased fivefold to 2 million, while transactions were up 40 times since April 2016 to 2 million.

ASIC Commissioner Danielle Press said that while many consumers enjoyed the arrangements, there were potential risks. The sector was mainly attracting young spenders, and some were becoming 'financially over-committed and liable to paying late fees'. One in six users was late on payments or had overdrawn as a result of the plans.

ASIC found that the buy now, pay later services allowed shoppers to spend more than they otherwise normally would, while some providers used behavioural techniques to influence consumers. By displaying prices that emphasise the amount of each instalment, for instance, rather than the full price, 'this can make a purchase seem more affordable', Press reported.

ASIC had conducted a consumer survey as part of its research. One female shopper, aged between 30 and 35, told the researchers: 'I often find myself considering (and buying) things that I don't necessarily think are a good price or good value just because I am not paying the full amount upfront, it kind of seems like it actually costs less than it does.' Meanwhile, an 18- to 24-year-old male also explained the consumer psychology: 'Before I used to see that price as $400. Now, when you buy using buy now pay later, I see it as just $100 per instalment. I think it just makes me feel less guilty about spending on some expensive things.'

ASIC's survey results also suggested that many users were over-spending: 81 per cent said splitting the payment into four allowed them to 'buy more expensive items that I couldn't afford to buy in one payment'; 70 per cent said they had been 'more spontaneous when . . . buying goods and services'; while 64 per cent said the products allowed them to 'spend more than [they] normally would'.

The talk was tough—but there was little action. ASIC said it would continue to monitor the sector, and could use its newly granted product intervention powers to stamp out any problems if required.

Crucially, ASIC's report said it had not identified any reason for the *National Consumer Credit Protection Act* to be extended to the buy now, pay later sector. Internally, ASIC considered such a decision to be a matter for parliament, and not for it as the regulator, but the consumer groups hoped it would nonetheless lob a recommendation in support of an extension for parliament to consider. For now, though, Afterpay would remain outside the definition of a lender and avoid having to conduct customer credit checks as stipulated by the act. The company's share price rose 27 per cent in the days that followed. The relief was real.

But ASIC's report only seemed to deepen the divisions both in the market and in regulatory circles. Some of the data seemed to contradict Afterpay's claims that more than 90 per cent of trans-actions didn't attract a late fee, or at least told a different story when the numbers were presented differently. An ASIC chart showed that, in an average month, 18 per cent of Afterpay's active users were charged a missed payment fee.

ASIC also included case studies to demonstrate how vulnerable consumers were being lured to use Afterpay, piling debts on top of debts, so they could buy goods they didn't need and be granted loans without any inquiries being made into their financial position.

'Vicki', an unemployed mother of three who was relying on welfare payments, already had $15,000 of debts and was late paying her bills. But Afterpay allowed her to 'buy goods at a butcher and several clothing stores', incurring $740 of debt. 'John' said he started using Afterpay in early 2018, and now owed $960. 'He said he doesn't recall being asked about his expenses when he signed up for this arrangement.'

'Ben', meanwhile, was unemployed, received a disability support pension and lived with his father, who assisted him as a carer. He had told ASIC he had a shopping addiction and felt overwhelmed by debt. 'He had a $5,000 credit card debt, and he was able to accrue a $1,500 debt with Afterpay, and a $1,000 debt with Zip Money,' the report noted.

Despite these concerning case studies, the report was an unambiguous win for Afterpay, and for the sector. But it only served to galvanise a growing army of sceptics. Unbeknown to Afterpay, the governor of the Reserve Bank of Australia appeared to be among them.

• • •

The headquarters of the Reserve Bank of Australia sit at the top of Martin Place, a plaza closed to vehicles in the heart of Sydney's CBD. The office of the Reserve Bank's governor, Philip Lowe, is now showing its age: there are a few cracks in the walls alongside the windows looking out to Sydney Harbour. The office goes back to the days of the first governor of the RBA, H.C. 'Nugget' Coombs, installed in 1960. It still has the same, modernist furniture designed by Frederick Ward.

In November 2018, Lowe hosted a meeting with Peter McNamara, the then CEO of the not-for-profit organisation Good

Shepherd Microfinance, who was there to brief Lowe on the shadow credit system. Reserve Bank officials kept a close eye on the money the banking system was extending to households and businesses, but they had a limited view at best of the expanding pool of unregulated lending.

Lowe understood deeply the politics that had triggered the Banking Royal Commission, which had shamed the nation's big four banks throughout 2018. The very public grilling of the stalwarts of the Australian economy had propelled groups such as Good Shepherd Microfinance into the national consciousness.

Lowe, who has run the Reserve Bank since 2016, has an inquisitive and gentle demeanour. He was keen to hear from Good Shepherd, which had been established in 2012 to grow a program that provided no-interest loans to the downtrodden. It is backed by the federal government's Department of Social Services (DSS), and by various governments in Australia's states. NAB, Afterpay's key banker, is also a supporter.

McNamara saw it as his mission to make sure leaders at the top of the Australian economy understood the impacts that excessive credit could have on borrowers unable to handle it. During the global financial crisis, consumer groups had worked with the Labor government of Prime Minister Kevin Rudd to introduce the *National Consumer Credit Protection Act*, which came into force in 2009. It required lenders to conduct detailed checks on customers using bank statements, and to verify applicants' income and expenses to ensure that they were able to repay loans. Despite the legislation, many of the most vulnerable members of the community were still getting into trouble because of products with high interest rates.

As CEO of Good Shepherd since July 2018, McNamara managed over 100 full-time staff and 1300 volunteers in 600 sites nationwide, with a $25 million budget. He was also serving as president of the Australian Council of Social Service, the peak body for the community sector, set up in 1956 to provide a voice for people affected by poverty, disadvantage and inequality in Australia.

He'd taken the former NAB chairman Ken Henry, who was forced to stand down from the bank after that disastrous appearance in the royal commission's witness box, to the Good Shepherd Microfinance Money Store on Smith Street, in the Melbourne suburb of Collingwood, showing him firsthand the damaging impact lenders could have when customers didn't have the discipline to borrow within their means.

In the governor's office, the conversation soon turned to the buy now, pay later sector, which was under increased scrutiny in Canberra. McNamara pointed to an 'emerging cliff' of buy now, pay later providers engaging in predatory lending. He quickly realised the sector had arrived on the radar of the Reserve Bank, the peak regulator of the Australian payments system. The central bank regarded keeping payment costs across the economy as low as possible a core role.

In Lowe, McNamara's words found a sympathetic ear. The governor, who had a daughter aged seventeen at the time, told him he'd experimented with Afterpay, having downloaded the app to see how it worked—and it seemed like credit. McNamara explained his concerns that Afterpay was a gendered offering, preying on 18- to 24-year-old females. He suggested it was probably the first credit product specifically targeted at impressionable young women. 'I'm concerned lobbying is winning the debate, and we are not thinking about protecting vulnerable people,' McNamara said. He asked the governor what he could do about it.

Lowe replied that the central bank did have mechanisms it could use to regulate the sector, and he would look into it further. McNamara left the meeting hopeful that the RBA would use its immense power to intervene and curb the fast-growing sector. It would take almost a year for those hopes to materialise.

In the background, Afterpay was bolstering its ranks. Senior ranking ASIC commissioner Peter Kell, who had led the charge against the payday lenders for decades, was finishing up at the regulator. He had initially intended to serve at ASIC until May 2019. But it had been decided that it was in everyone's interest that he finish at the end of 2018.

Kell had been forced to front the Hayne Royal Commission himself, and he'd faced tough questioning over the $1 billion of compensation owed to bank customers who had been charged for financial advice they never received. Damian Kassabgi thought it would be a good idea for Afterpay to swoop on Kell. Those advances were rejected.

• • •

While the regulatory scrutiny was rising, at the start of 2019 global stock-market sentiment had turned for the better. Federal Reserve chairman Jerome Powell calmed anxious markets after a harrowing 20 per cent fall in 2018, putting the market officially into correction territory.

Powell had communicated in late December 2018 that there was no reason for the Federal Reserve to reverse the path to restoring interest rates to a level that was considered normal. On 4 January that message changed; he was paying close attention to what was being relayed to him by the financial markets.

The Federal Reserve's change of course was a pivotal moment. The financial markets had become so central to the economy that central banks had no choice but to underwrite them. By late January, global share markets were running hard again, recovering the sharp falls of November and December in a V-shaped turnaround. Afterpay was on the rise once more. Short-sellers were caught out, and began unwinding their positions in a hurry.

The rally was helped by yet another wildly positive market update on 18 January. Afterpay's half-year sales had reached $2.2 billion—a 240 per cent increase on the first half of 2018. More than 3.1 million customers had signed up, along with 23,000 merchants, while late fees had declined to make up less than 20 per cent of revenues. Afterpay's shares ran up 13 per cent to $16.

Afterpay's summer battle, however, was not with a volatile share market but with lawmakers as they considered whether the rules needed to change to keep up with the sector. Andrew Charlton was working away in the background on his own report, which was ready to be released to the media by mid-January. His findings into how Australian millennials manage money were pitched to journalists as 'commissioned by Afterpay but not about Afterpay': 'It's about millennials and has some great new stats which dispel the smashed avo on toast clique [sic].' Before its public release, Eisen had taken the AlphaBeta report to Canberra to use as a talking point in meetings with politicians, as he attempted to soften the hostile forces that had included buy now, pay later in the Senate inquiry.

The smashed avo cliché had become a millennial meme after demographer Bernard Salt wrote a column in *The Weekend Australian* expressing his astonishment at the millennials in his local cafe who were spending $22 on 'avocado with crumbled feta on five-grain toasted bread' when they could have been saving for a house. The tongue-in-cheek column proved a flashpoint in an intergenerational war as young Australians lamented their inability to save amid a barnstorming property market—so they chose instead to savour their breakfasts.

Charlton's report aimed to bust those myths. It detailed how millennials were rejecting credit cards because they were too risky and costly. Afterpay was preferred because they could avoid interest costs and debt traps. Millennials were savvier spenders, too, and prioritised education, health and lifestyle over buying a house, the report said. They smoked and drank less, and spent more on health insurance and public transport. They were also better savers than their parents, the researchers said. While 67 per cent of older Australians said they budgeted, 80 per cent of millennials had a budgeting plan. Afterpay had actually helped millennials to budget—it was essentially a budgeting tool.

The message of Charlton's research was that millennials were not frivolous smashed avo munchers who wanted things before they'd earned them. Afterpay was a product built around the virtues of the generation, not its vices.

'Afterpay is one of the ways that millennials are managing their expenses in a way that maybe reduces the risks and the costs of other approaches like credit cards. I think that's one of the reasons why so many young people are using Afterpay,' Charlton told business journalist Alan Kohler.[2]

The consumer groups were not buying this argument, but they were beginning to appreciate the effectiveness of Afterpay's lobbying efforts. The company was playing both sides of the political fence ruthlessly, all but neutralising their adversaries.

On 8 January 2019, a day before the Senate hearings were due to commence, Afterpay rolled out their new economic adviser—none other than former senior Labor politician Craig Emerson. The former trade minister took to the airwaves to warn the public that the big banks were running a scare campaign to arrest the declining use of credit cards.

The Australian Banking Association had made their own submission to the Senate committee on the behalf of the country's banks. It said the elderly, the mentally ill and those who couldn't speak English were vulnerable targets of payday lenders and what it called 'deferred payment scheme operators', such as Afterpay and Zip.

'I don't think any Australian would be relying on the banking industry for advice on dodgy practices. We have seen enough in the royal commission,' said 2GB radio host Luke Grant, before asking Emerson what the hell the problem was with Afterpay, as he couldn't see it.

There wasn't any problem, Emerson confirmed. 'Do we really want the banks designing regulation for their rivals who are having a go and engaging in responsible lending practices? You can't get into a debt trap if the maximum amount that can be loaned is $2000, but you can with credit cards,' Emerson said. 'This is a group of young people who came up with this idea. Let's call them disruptors to the traditional credit model. It's no surprise the disrupted don't see the funny side. That is what is going on here.'

But the big banks, too, had a foot in both camps. Westpac was a large shareholder in Zip, while NAB was Afterpay's key financier. Commonwealth Bank was also sniffing around the sector.

Emerson himself was yet to register as a lobbyist, which he later explained was because he had not yet engaged with government officials. Either way, Afterpay had well and truly established itself as a force, not only in the payments world but also in politics.

• • •

For Molnar, the jobs of handling a baby and lobbying politicians had all arrived at once. Just a month after his wife gave birth, he was summoned home from the United States to searing hot Brisbane to front the Senate inquiry. He naively asked Kassabgi if his appearance could be delayed on account of his new parental responsibilities. But he had a job to do: convince the senators that Afterpay was a force for good as an alternative to credit cards, and that it was not lending money.

Afterpay's lobbyists, led by David Gazard, were also working the Canberra circuit, allaying fears that the ASIC report would dent the company's prospects. So it was with some cover that Eisen and Hancock also headed to Brisbane to face the committee. Brett Clegg had been working closely with the Afterpay team to prepare speeches to the committee and rehearse answers to potential questions. The Afterpay team was joined in Brisbane by Zip co-founder Larry Diamond.

Molnar soon grasped the gravity of the situation: he was seated before elected politicians who were seeking his input as they considered whether to recommend a rewriting of the federal credit rules. What was a moment of nerves and discomfort was also one of immense pride. Molnar was not yet 30, and Afterpay not yet five years old, but it had well and truly shaken up the banking industry.

Molnar said Afterpay's loans were small, with an average consumer's balance being just $208, compared to $4200 for a credit card. Unlike credit cards, customers who were late to pay were cut off from the Afterpay system. Eisen was asked about credit checks; he replied that this was 'sensitive information', but assured the senators that a high number of consumers were rejected. Molnar again said that just 5 per cent of transactions incurred a late fee in 2018, even though ASIC's data showed that 18 per cent of users were late in an average month.

Although Molnar and Diamond were appearing together, they weren't always singing from the same song sheet. Zip had set itself up as a lender, and any move by regulators to ping Afterpay as a credit provider could dull its edge. 'We wholeheartedly support ASIC's position that buy now, pay later is a form of credit,' Diamond said. That, Molnar retorted, would be a 'blunt and simple solution to a more complex issue, and one that risks stifling innovation'. After his day in Brisbane and a quick, one-day stopover in Sydney, he flew back to the US west coast.

The Senate Economics References Committee hearings moved to Canberra on 24 January for the final session, which would be chaired by Liberal senator Jane Hume in the magnificent parliamentary building. The hearing would provide the inquiry with a chance to probe the regulators—including Saadat, who would be questioned on ASIC's report and its view of the sector.

Hume had worked in the finance industry herself, in both sales and research at NAB, and she remained close to the industry that had been torn to shreds by the Banking Royal Commission. She was a rising star in her own right, even though it was anticipated that she would be spending the next three years on the opposition benches.

The payday lending sector was the focus of much of the morning session, until Hume turned her attention to buy now, pay later. She directed the billion-dollar question at Saadat: is buy now, pay later providing credit?

'I guess there are a few answers to that question,' Saadat said. He explained that because of the way the *National Consumer Credit Protection Act* defines credit, operators fall within the exemptions in the law. But under the *ASIC Act of 2001*, 'buy now, pay later products are credit', he said.

The *ASIC Act*, which governs the regulator, contains general consumer protection provisions to prevent misleading, deceptive or unconscionable conduct. It includes provisions enforced by the competition regulator to protect the public from offerings that are not financial services and products.

'If you're thinking of credit in the ordinary, everyday understanding of what credit is, then we would say it is a form of credit because it enables consumers to pay for goods over time, and by postponing the payment of goods, you're effectively being given a form of credit in the ordinary sense of the word,' Saadat elaborated.

Saadat, who has a quiet, polite disposition and was motivated to act for the customers' best interests, said that ASIC was prepared to monitor the sector. He hoped that the granting of broader product intervention powers would allow it to step in and shut down or modify a company's offerings, if things got out of hand.

If Saadat and ASIC wanted to lobby the senators about anything, it was to urge them to grant ASIC the powers for which its leaders had been calling for years, and which the financial system inquiry conducted by David Murray had called for in 2014. Under what would be known as the product intervention power, ASIC would be able to take action against any financial products that were clearly harmful—from usurious loans rigged against the borrower to high-risk derivatives marketed aggressively on the internet—and force changes to their design. ASIC would also police a new duty, known as the design and distribution obligation, that would require issuers of financial products to ensure they are suitable for customers.

Hume later turned her attention specifically to Afterpay. Out came the i-word—'innovation'—which had been a rod for the government's back when Malcolm Turnbull was prime minister. 'One of the concerns, particularly with Afterpay, is that overregulation in this space will stifle the innovation of what seems to be a very successful and quite encouraging business model,' she said.

Hume was also worried that the ASIC report had lumped all the bad stuff under one heading, with its statistic that one in six users was being harmed. 'There wouldn't be too many 23- or 24-year-olds out there who haven't at some stage gone, "Whoops, I might have spent on something or other and I've had to move a bit of money about or change the priority of the bills that I pay." It's not the government's responsibility to protect people from the mistakes of life; it's just to protect us from predatory behaviour. My concern is that when we hear evidence—and there has been some pretty appalling evidence of bad behaviour in this inquiry—our knee-jerk reaction is to overregulate.'

Hume asked Saadat what the cost of overregulating would be.

This was 'a broad question', he said. 'It will depend on what that overregulation does and how firms respond to it. One potential risk is that the amount of credit available to consumers might be constrained. People might find it more difficult to get a loan. But it's hard to anticipate all of the potential knock-on effects.'

The hearings concluded. The seven-member committee had a month to draft and deliver their report. In the vacuum, the lobbyists went to work. David Gazard went about meeting the media and politicians, and had some important points to make about Afterpay. It does not charge interest, he explained, but is similar to lay-by; and unlike with credit cards, users are started on small amounts and shut out of the platform if they're late on payments. His job was to convince as many as he could in Canberra that Afterpay was a force for good.

# 12

# TAKING CREDIT

MATT COMYN, THE chief executive of the Commonwealth Bank of Australia, had a lot on his mind. It was the evening of Thursday, 7 February 2019, and the final report of Kenneth Hayne's Banking Royal Commission had been released three days earlier. Across the sector, bankers had been criticised for their greed, while CBA, Australia's largest bank by loans and market capitalisation, had been referred to the corporate regulator for mistreating superannuation customers.

The day before, on 6 February, CBA had delivered a half-yearly result to the market showing some Hayne-inflicted pressures. On the back of the excoriating inquiry, CBA had reported a surge in risk and compliance investment spending, while its net interest margin had been hit by higher funding costs. Cash profit for the half-year was strong, at $4.68 billion, but lower than the previous first half.

Despite the whirlwind week, Comyn and his senior executive team still found time to have dinner with senior finance journalists in an upstairs room at the Centennial pub in Woollahra, a posh suburb a short Uber ride from the Sydney CBD. In fact, it was the city's banking writers who were struggling to make the dinner on time.

At 5.15 pm, NAB published a release to the stock exchange to announce that chairman Ken Henry and chief executive Andrew Thorburn had resigned. A media teleconference was hastily scheduled for 6 pm.

Hayne's report had been scathing of the duo, suggesting their performance at the inquiry showed past lessons had not been learned, while reporters on the call were asking what they knew about an escalating expenses scandal that had led to the arrest of Thorburn's chief of staff, Rosemary Rogers. Dan Ziffer, who had covered the royal commission for the ABC, asked Henry if he'd lost his job because he got out on the wrong side of the bed—a reference to his uncharacteristically combative appearance at the hearings.

'Maybe I did hop out of bed on the wrong side,' Henry admitted. 'I've relived that performance . . . I've even re-read the transcript.'

Henry, who was without doubt the biggest casualty of the commission, then headed to the ABC for a live television interview on its current affairs program, *7.30*.

Another casualty of the dramas at NAB was a closer relationship with Afterpay. A deeper partnership may have involved the bank making a direct investment via its newly created NAB Ventures fund, which had a mandate to invest equity into start-ups that could help NAB develop its relationships with customers. Separate to the warehouse funding, a tie-up had been under consideration during 2018 by NAB chief operating officer Antony Cahill, and was awaiting input from the bank's board. But in the wake of the royal commission, Cahill had left to join Visa as its European managing director, and now the leadership turmoil meant that the plan to take the partnership to the next level died there and then.

The late-breaking news gave the assembling banking journalists more to chew over with their peers and Commonwealth Bank's senior executives as they gathered for the dinner. The diversion of attention suited CBA's corporate affairs team, exhausted by years of scathing coverage.

Over plates of slow-cooked lamb shoulder, dips, bread and vegetables, the discussion shifted from NAB's travails to Commissioner Hayne's report, to CBA's earnings pressures, and then to Afterpay. During the summer, the Australian Banking Association, the lobby group run by Anna Bligh, had urged the Morrison government to bring the rapidly expanding buy now, pay later players under the regulatory umbrella of the broader financial services sector. CBA and ANZ Bank were pushing the anti-BNPL arguments harder than NAB or Westpac.

But similar arguments from consumer groups during the 2018 inquiries had not found a receptive ear, and it didn't seem likely that the banks, having been humiliated by Hayne, had sufficient currency to influence the government on what regulatory standards should apply to others. Comyn understood that the rise of buy now, pay later would require a more strategic response.

Studying transactional and card data from different age cohorts of CBA customers, Comyn saw the same trend Molnar had identified back in 2015: millennials were shifting away from credit cards. CBA had the most to lose, given it had the largest proportion of millennial customers in the country—the product of its Dollarmites school banking program, which lured primary-school–aged kids into CBA deposit accounts.

Comyn was keen to get CBA back on track, especially when it came to technology. This had been a key asset during much of the 1990s and early 2000s, when the bank had invested in a new core banking IT system and reaped the rewards in terms of customer intelligence. But the royal commission, and claims by AUSTRAC that CBA's automated teller machines had aided organised criminals to siphon drug money out of the country, had sucked precious resources into risk mitigation, legal and compliance.

Comyn had shown the royal commission he was more attuned to customer service than his predecessor, Ian Narev, had been, whom Comyn had replaced in April 2018 in the wake of the AUSTRAC scandal. Narev had famously told Comyn to 'temper your sense of justice' as Comyn advocated for the bank's customers; Comyn had kept a note of the meeting and used it to defend his leadership of the retail bank.

Now he told the small group at dinner that while banks had been fighting over the pennies and dimes of interchange fees, they had missed the dollars that retailers would be willing to pay for help in driving sales. 'It has been one of the biggest misses for us,' he said. 'We missed that retailers would be willing to pay so much.'

That off-the-cuff comment summed up how Afterpay had built a multibillion-dollar business under the nose of the big banks. It also pointed to the frustrations of almost two decades of regulatory pressure on bank-issued credit cards, which had depressed returns and imposed stricter duties around issuing plastic to customers.

As the banks locked horns with the Reserve Bank during the late 2000s, battling to drive down payment costs by tens of basis points, they had been blinded to the fact that retailers could be convinced to hand over 400 basis points—as they had for Afterpay—by connecting their shops to millions of budding customers. Banks had become so big they had failed to see the wood for the trees. Organised in silos, retail bankers, who issue cards and make loans, don't engage much with business bankers, who manage merchants.

Banks have also had a testy relationship with retailers over decades, triggered by the introduction of credit cards.

For Australian department stores such as David Jones, Myer and Grace Bros, the arrival of the Bankcard, launched by Prime Minister Gough Whitlam in 1974 under a joint venture known as The Bankcard Association of Australia, created tensions. It challenged the retailers' profitable store card businesses, which allowed customers to revolve debt and pay retailers an interest rate.

The history of credit cards in Australia shows how the banks struggled with innovation, and often failed to respond to changing social and technological trends. In the decade to the mid-1980s, the major Australian banks resisted issuing Visa and Mastercard credit cards, preferring the Bankcard. But ultimately it failed to keep up with customer demands because it could not be used overseas, and more Australians had started to travel more frequently. This forced the banks' hand and they began issuing Visa cards and Mastercards from 1984.

Australia's major banks were slow to shift debit payments onto the networks run by the global payments giants Visa and Mastercard, seeking to protect their own fee income—and when they did in the early 2000s, they were also motivated by new revenue streams. The large banks had been earning big money by charging smaller banks for using the domestic EFTPOS network. But big retailing groups, including the Australian supermarket duopoly Coles and Woolworths, had insisted on a slice of the fees, given that cards were being used in their stores. With banks bleeding EFTPOS transaction revenue to the retailers, the major banks were enticed by Visa and Mastercard's offer to pay 'interchange fees' to the banks that issued their cards. The interchange fee, set by the credit card networks, charged merchants per transaction and this was used to pay the banks that issued cards to customers, incentivising them to issue more cards. The fees would come under intense regulatory scrutiny and eventually be capped.

The arrival of credit cards was driven, too, by new technology: paper cheques were falling out of favour, and by the early 1980s new plastic cards could be read by machines that had started to replace the manual 'zip-zap' readers to authorise transactions.

The opportunity for Afterpay—and for the buy now, pay later sector more broadly—has also been driven by fundamental structural shifts in technology, to which the banks have been slow to respond: cards and machine readers, which banks charge retailers for, have been replaced by smartphones and cheaper point-of-sale hardware powered by the internet.

Afterpay has also benefited from decades of intense regulatory pressure on credit cards, which has made them less attractive to banks and customers. This kicked off in April 2001, when the Reserve Bank officially designated Bankcard, Mastercard and Visa credit card schemes as payments systems. The decision came out of the 1996 financial system inquiry chaired by Stan Wallis, the former boss of industrial powerhouse Amcor.

The number of credit card accounts in Australia rose from 6.5 million in 1994 to more than 10 million by the end of the decade. But Wallis found that card payments systems were characterised by opaque fees and restrictions on entry. He also found that interchange fees were ultimately paid by consumers in the form of higher prices. The government accepted Wallis's recommendations, which included setting up a Payments System Board inside the Reserve Bank with powers to set rules and standards when it was in the public interest to do so.

The RBA used its new powers to issue limits on merchant pricing and interchange fees, and an access regime in August 2002. Visa and Mastercard challenged their designation as payments systems in the Federal Court, but the judge rejected their arguments, saying the mandate of the Wallis inquiry supported 'a broad construction of the expression "standard"'. It was a decision that laid the foundations for more than a decade of pressure on credit card pricing by the Reserve Bank. This ultimately forced down the revenue that major banks earn by issuing cards—part of the reason that Matt Comyn was thinking about new ways to attack the market.

Credit cards also faced scrutiny in the United States, culminating in the 2009 *Credit Card Accountability, Responsibility, and Disclosure Act*, which was signed into law by President Barack Obama. The legislation was saving US consumers US$20 billion a year, according to research quoted by *The New York Times* in 2013. Australian scrutiny on credit cards intensified in 2015, with an inquiry by the

Senate Economics References Committee that found $33.1 billion of $51.5 billion in credit card debt was accruing interest, and much of it was paid by people who were less capable of servicing the debts.[1]

ASIC was forced to swing into action. Reviewing five years of data, it found that one in five credit card holders was struggling to make repayments, while banks used 'honeymoon rates' to lure customers to new cards only to ensnare them in a 'debt trap'. Meanwhile, 11 per cent of credit card consumers repeatedly exceeded their credit limit, while nine of twelve providers did not prompt customers making repayments near the minimum amount for extended periods to repay more. 'Consumers who are in persistent debt, or repeatedly making low repayments, are profitable for credit providers,' the regulator warned. 'However, providers have obligations to conduct themselves efficiently, honestly and fairly.'[2]

ASIC's regulation was slowing down approval times for getting a credit card—making the buy now, pay later onboarding processes, which took minutes on a smartphone and did not require credit-checking, much more appealing. In contrast, banks were being required to assess borrowers' ability to repay their entire credit card debt within three years, and to take proactive steps to help customers reduce problem debt. Banks would also have to minimise credit extended to customers who frequently exceeded their limit and make it easier for them to cancel cards.

'People who are just keeping their head above water are very profitable for a bank as they are paying a lot of interest and fees, but are not in delinquency,' said ASIC's Michael Saadat after ASIC released a critical report on credit cards in July 2018. 'But we don't think it's good enough to allow consumers to continue to struggle when the bank knows they would be better off with a lower-rate card.'

As the Reserve Bank and ASIC action reduced the profitability of credit cards, millennials were also getting savvier about the dangers of revolving debt, and were increasingly keen to avoid high interest and fees. The regulatory pressures were hitting both the demand and supply side, observed Lance Blockley, a payments industry veteran at Sydney-based The Initiatives Group. 'Credit cards may become the new "senior's card", as youth stick with debit,' Blockley told clients in 2019.

Millennials were voting with their feet. The proportion of young people with a credit card had fallen from 58 per cent to 41 per cent over the preceding fourteen years, while millennials are 37 per cent less likely to own a credit card than older Australians 'because they see credit cards as being costly and risky', AlphaBeta found in 2019.[3]

Comyn realised he had to get CBA into the buy now, pay later game; it was just a matter of when—and how.

• • •

The AlphaBeta research was commissioned to accentuate the positives of Afterpay as the Senate Economics References Committee mulled over its decision. But the day before its report was due to be released, 21 February, the share market was in a jumpy mood. Afterpay's shares fell as much as 11.5 per cent as speculators bet on what the report contained. There were unsubstantiated rumours that officials in possession of the report had leaked it, and that it was harmful to Afterpay's cause.

'Sources close to the company insisted it did not have the contents of the secret report but the firm was being proactive to explain to a jittery market how the Senate standing committee on economics process worked,' *The Australian Financial Review* reported. 'The Labor-led Senate references committee is not a government-led legislation body and has relatively little influence on changes to policies or laws, a fact not well understood by investors who are on edge about the pending report. The Liberal minority on the committee will publish a dissenting report.'[4]

Afterpay's investor relations and management team rang brokers and analysts to let them know they were ready for whatever the report contained. If that was meant to reassure them, though, the courtesy calls had the opposite effect.

When the report was finally made public late on Friday, 22 February 2019—after traders had ruled off for the week—it came as a huge relief to all the shareholders who had held tight. The Senate committee was recommending that the government consider what sort of framework could regulate the buy now, pay later sector that would require providers to assess consumers' financial situations. But, crucially for Afterpay, it stopped short of calling for Afterpay to be regulated under the *National Consumer Credit Protection Act*, which would have required it to conduct 'responsible lending' checks on consumers. Indeed, the report suggested that the providers themselves develop a code of practice for the new industry: self-regulation would be preferred over proscriptive law. The findings from the Labor-led inquiry aligned with ASIC's report in November and delivered a blow to the consumer groups.

'It is a very benign report with only cursory comments around more industry scrutiny,' wrote Wilson analyst Mark Bryan, who had cut his recommendation from buy to hold in November 2018, in part because of concerns that regulators might change the rules. 'The potential spectre of inclusion in the National Credit Code has not been flagged as a recommendation. The review should stimulate a relief rally in Afterpay.'

Bryan faced some heat at Wilson for cutting the recommendation on a stock that had been widely held by clients, but the binary nature of the looming Senate recommendation had spooked him. 'This risk has been clearly removed post a benign Senate publication,' he observed. (His lingering concern for the stock was the company's future in the United States, where he worried it would be too expensive and less profitable than the current consensus held.)

A material risk that could have mortally wounded Afterpay had been removed. And when trading opened on Monday, 25 February, buyers rushed to snap up Afterpay shares. The stock surged 20 per cent—the same amount it had fallen when news of the inquiry had first been reported—adding $800 million to its market capitalisation. The share price topped $20 for the first time since August 2018. In a statement to the stock exchange, Afterpay said it did not expect 'any material impact on our business or business model' from the recommendations, which it described as a 'sensible, appropriate and a proportionate policy'.

In April, ASIC got what it wanted, too. A bill was passed granting it the product intervention powers it had asked for. The regulator could now intervene if it felt that customers were being harmed by buy now, pay later products. The committee was 'alive to the risks' that vulnerable Australians could fall prey to these offerings, and said there was no guarantee that future entrants would take the same principled approach as the sector's leaders—which made an industry code of practice important as a form of self-regulation.

The charm of Diamond and Molnar, and masterful lobbying behind the scenes, had won over the senators.

Afterpay had triumphed in another crucial regulatory battle, and emphatically so. The following day it handed down its half-year financial report, which showed earnings before interest, tax, depreciation and amortisation doubling from $17 million to $35 million. The company earmarked a further $10 million to invest in its UK expansion, with a launch slated for the second half of 2019.

Bell Potter analyst Lafitani Sotiriou called the result one of Afterpay's most important. 'It has shown that it can expand overseas while maintaining a lid on bad debts, and a stable overall net-margin,' he noted. 'It was able to absorb late-fee caps, and invest heavily into establishing the US business.'

The market's near-term enthusiasm had been exhausted as Afterpay's shares dipped on results day. Richard Coppleson told his readers that the stock was taking a breather after going on a big run since January.

Still, Afterpay's incredible performance meant the share market regarded it as more valuable than the 53-year-old empire of Australia's best-known retailer—and the master of 'interest-free' financing offers at the checkout—Gerry Harvey. 'I think we all got the shock of our lives when we saw that,' Harvey told *The Sydney Morning Herald*. 'It seems so simple, and suddenly you've got a business that's worth $4 billion or $5 billion. It was worth nothing five minutes ago.'[5]

• • •

Early on the morning of 11 April 2019, Prime Minister Scott Morrison's motorcade drove to Government House, the home of the Queen's representative in Canberra. He was there to request the Governor-General call a general election for 18 May and dissolve the parliament. It would be a long and gruelling campaign, and Bill Shorten and the Labor Party were odds-on favourites to claim the Lodge. The civil war within the Liberal Party, which had culminated in Prime Minister Malcolm Turnbull's ousting, was widely considered to have consigned the Coalition to at least three years in the political wilderness.

But Labor proceeded to snatch defeat from the jaws of victory. To fund its spending plans, Labor had proposed to wind back the generous dividend imputation scheme that many retirees relied on. Fund manager Geoff Wilson galvanised his grey army of investors to vent their disapproval, egged on by a young MP—and a distant relative—Tim Wilson. Labor's climate change pitch, too, was interpreted as degrading the value of jobs in the coal sector. The other problem was that Shorten was unelectable in the eyes of many voters. Perhaps he'd said too much.

Even so, on the eve of the election, Shorten was expected to win, and he shared a drink with journalists at Melbourne's John Curtin Hotel, a favourite watering hole of former prime minister Bob Hawke, who had passed away days earlier. The Liberals, meanwhile, made one last push in the battleground electorates. But as the results trickled in on the evening of Saturday, 18 May, it became clear that a shock result was on the cards.

The Coalition's surprise victory was branded the 'Morrison Miracle'. Scott Morrison had been expected to spend the next three years restoring his party's battered brand; now he found himself in a position of power and authority not held by an Australian politician since Kevin Rudd in 2007. The crucial role young Liberal politicians had played in the victory meant that they would have increased influence over the party and the nation.

When the opening bell rang on the following Monday morning, share-market traders celebrated the victory: battered and bruised after years of bad press and the threat of ever greater regulation, the election result was a rare good-news moment for the big banks. Shares in Sydney-based Westpac leapt an extraordinary 9 per cent, part of a broad-based rally in the financial services sector.

An era of looser regulation could only be welcome for Afterpay, which had prepared for life under a Labor government.

Not that the Afterpay business needed any help. On 5 June 2019, Nick Molnar crossed the United States to present at a fashion industry event, Women's Wear Daily, at the Conrad Hotel in New York. He preached the virtues of Afterpay's instalments model to the world's biggest brands. He told the audience of 200 fashionistas that Afterpay was taking off. The service had been used by 1.5 million customers, and iconic brands Levi's and Ray-Ban were two of some 3300 merchants who had signed up.

The problem was that Afterpay hadn't officially informed the ASX of this positive news. Its shares jumped 10 per cent, a sure sign of the materiality of the information, which raised eyebrows. 'As is usual, if we have concerns about a company's disclosure we may consider issuing a query to help keep the market informed,' a spokesman for the exchange told *The Sydney Morning Herald.*[6]

A day later, Afterpay issued the overdue official update. Underlying sales reached $47.7 billion in the eleven months to May, a 143 per cent increase, and in total 4.3 million customers and over 30,000 retailers had now signed up, it noted. On the final page, the company provided a regulatory update.

Afterpay had decided to cancel its credit licence, as it was now clear that it had dodged any reclassification as a credit provider. 'The licence was acquired some time ago, prior to the report being released by ASIC into the BNPL sector, the recent Senate inquiry, and the passage of PIP [product intervention power] legislation through the Parliament,' the company said. 'The licence has not been used and its cancellation will have no impact on the Afterpay business or service.' This was nothing short of a declaration of victory: Afterpay would never be considered a provider of credit.

Afterpay's regulatory battles no longer revolved around its status as a lender. The focus had shifted to its compliance with anti-money–laundering laws. In July 2018, in response to the Mickey Mouse scandal, Afterpay had updated its systems to include identity checks. Encouragingly, it said it had not found any evidence of money laundering in its system. But Afterpay did flag one item of concern: AUSTRAC had raised some issues with its compliance with anti-money–laundering and counter-terrorism–finance rules. The matter had not been resolved.

AUSTRAC made its own statement in response to media questions, confirming it was working with Afterpay, while still talking tough: 'Stopping the movement of money to criminals and terrorists is a vital part of our national security defences and it is critical for regulated businesses in Australia to comply with the AML/CTF regime.'

The market had become accustomed to regulatory risks, but Afterpay's growth was showing no signs of slowing down, and that was converting sceptical investors. The rising share price presented an opportunity for the company to raise more funds, and for the management trio of Eisen, Molnar and Hancock to cash in on its success to date.

On 11 June, Afterpay announced it would issue 13.8 million new shares to raise $300 million of new equity capital. The shares would be sold to institutions and current investors. Eisen and Molnar would sell 2.05 million shares each to US hedge funds Tiger Management and Woodson Capital, while Hancock would dispose of 400,000 shares. The raising was completed the following day. Afterpay had the funds it needed. The US hedge funds were set on the register, and the trio of founders were $100 million richer.

But on the morning of 13 June, AUSTRAC dropped a bombshell. In a harshly worded statement, the financial intelligence agency said it had identified concerns with Afterpay's compliance, ordering it to appoint an external auditor. Afterpay had fourteen days to comply, and the auditor in turn had 60 days to file a preliminary report, and 120 days to deliver a final report.

Nicole Rose, AUSTRAC's chief executive, who had taken on some of the biggest names in finance including a high-profile action against Commonwealth Bank, reminded the fast-growing buy now, pay later sector that it had 'serious obligations' to the law. 'These laws are in place to protect businesses, the financial system and the Australian community from criminal threats,' she said.

AUSTRAC's escalation could not have come at a worse time, and the Afterpay camp felt they had been blindsided. In the lead-up to the deal, Afterpay, its bankers, its lawyers and its bankers' lawyers had engaged with AUSTRAC to inform them that they would be conducting a significant transaction. They wanted assurances that there was no imminent action, otherwise they would delay the raising. Afterpay felt comfortable enough to proceed, while Citi signed off on an underwriting agreement.

But they'd either miscalculated or misunderstood, and now Afterpay had a reputational scandal on its hands. It not only had to be subjected to a potentially devastating probe, but the founders and the board faced an interrogation of what they knew and when they knew it. Shares in Afterpay plunged as much as 12 per cent just as the offer for smaller investors was opening up. The share price fall and the AUSTRAC revelation led Afterpay to defer the final leg of the share offer, and Molnar and Eisen pledged not to sell any more shares for another twelve months.

The episode was a major embarrassment, and Afterpay's governance was called into question. Anthony Eisen had chaired the board through a period of incredible growth, but a shake-up was on the cards.

On 2 July 2019, the second day of the new financial year, Afterpay unveiled a suite of board changes intended to increase its independence. Elana Rubin would step up as the interim chair, replacing Eisen as the company embarked on a global search.

There would also be a major departure. David Hancock, one of Afterpay's earliest investors, and until now group head, exited the business. Hancock, who had spent the last two years putting out fires at Afterpay and Freedom Insurance, where he chaired the board, was ready to call time on his management career.

Before he left, however, he received a surprise phone call. It was from Michael Saadat. His wife had seen a posting on social-media site LinkedIn about a regulatory affairs role Afterpay was seeking to fill, and he wanted Hancock to know he was interested.

The irony of the call was not lost on Hancock. Saadat had spent the last eighteen months trying to work out how to police Afterpay, and the credit card industry that it was competing against. Now he wanted to switch teams.

'Michael, I cannot be having this conversation,' Hancock told Saadat as he stepped out of the boardroom.

The unexpected and unsolicited approach caught Hancock off guard. There was a risk that hiring Saadat would not play well with lawmakers, policy-makers and the consumer advocate groups that had been in Saadat's ear, trying to convince him that Afterpay was a credit product with the potential to harm its customers. But Saadat was capable, ambitious and knew better than anyone how Afterpay could sidestep and shape the rules to work in its favour.

Hancock called his contacts at ASIC to discuss the development. He wanted to know what protocols Afterpay should follow to undertake the highly sensitive hiring of their own direct enforcer.

# 13

# THE CUB CLUB

ALFRED WINSLOW JONES was born in Melbourne on the ninth day of the ninth month of 1900. His father had been posted to the city to run the Australian operations of General Electric, and within four years the family returned home to the east coast of the United States. Almost half a century later, in 1949, A.W. Jones pioneered what we know today as a 'hedge fund'.

The concept was an alternative to a traditional mutual fund, which simply bought shares in companies in the hope their price would appreciate. Jones felt this left investors too exposed to the violent whims of the broader market, so he devised a strategy that would hedge against those uncontrollable forces. Jones would borrow money to buy shares he thought would go up, and borrow shares to sell if he thought they would go down. With the shares he owned offset against the shares he was betting against, the market's broader machinations were neutralised. The returns he generated were a pure reflection of his insights, intellect and trading prowess. The fee for Jones's services was 20 per cent of the profits, in keeping with the tradition of ancient Phoenician sea merchants, who retained one-fifth of the spoils of a successful voyage.

Jones inspired a generation of hedge fund investors who backed their abilities to deliver stellar returns in all markets. In the 1990s, a duo of hedge fund titans shouldered above the rest: George Soros and Julian Robertson. These larger-than-life personalities charged high fees but delivered high performance, outsmarting the conversative mutual funds of the day.

Soros, a Hungarian Jew whose family had fled to New York during World War II, was a trader with an almost telepathic sense. His billion-dollar profit from betting against the British pound in 1992 added to the mystique of high-octane speculators who took on and beat first-world governments.

Julian Robertson, a burly Southerner, was cut from a different cloth, but his trading skills were equally remarkable. Robertson's fund, Tiger Management, which operated out of Park Avenue, New York, returned over 30 per cent a year for close to twenty years. But there was no apparent magic in how he generated one of the greatest performance runs in investing history.

In a letter to a staffer, Robertson explained that Tiger should manage money aggressively, removing good companies for better ones; limit any bet to 5 per cent of capital; and keep swinging through the bad times until the good times returned.[1] Robertson later said he looked for companies that had decent and honest managers with competitive streaks.

At the peak of Tiger Management in 1998, Robertson had amassed US$22 billion of assets. But the mania of the Nasdaq bubble of 1999 proved his undoing. While dotcom stocks were doubling and tripling on debut and the tech index was surging, Robertson was trapped in old-world stocks, such as auto parts makers and airlines. 'We're going through a most unusual market where in many instances fundamentals are being ignored,' he told investors in April 1999, as the market defied his trading book.

As his positions soured, day traders and mutual funds made millions from the inflating tech bubble. But the market masters were dazed and confused. Soros and his lieutenant, Stan Druckenmiller, had attempted to short technology stocks, only to post hundred-million-dollar trading losses. The pair swallowed their pride and reversed their strategy to bet on the bubble, only to lose money again.

Robertson grew increasingly frustrated by the 'irrational public' that drove the Nasdaq index—of mostly unprofitable companies—up by almost 40 per cent in December 1999 alone. His investors, however, were cashing out, forcing him to sell down holdings, further pressuring their price. Robertson had never seen such a frenzy, fed by 'mouseclicks and momentum'. The day of reckoning, he said, would come.

Come it did. First for the Nasdaq, which, unbeknown to Robertson, peaked on 10 March 2000 and then duly collapsed as speculative fervour turned to panic. Then for Tiger Management itself. On 30 March Robertson made the call to effectively shutter his fund, returning capital to those investors who had not already redeemed their money.

Robertson was among the first great trading titans to fall. But, counterintuitively, that set him on a path to hedge fund immortality.

In the aftermath of the Tiger Management closure, Robertson's former analysts left to start their own funds, which he backed with capital. They soon became known as the Tiger Cubs, and over the twenty years since they have eclipsed the influence and reach of their patriarch.

Biographer Daniel Strachman told *The Australian Financial Review* that an estimated 20 to 30 per cent of all the money allocated to the hedge funds was handled by a Cub, or the cub of a Cub. That, Strachman said, made Robertson an investing legend whose legacy would outlive all the greats. 'When Soros dies there'll be his

Open Society Foundations,' Strachman said. 'When Buffett dies, Berkshire Hathaway will probably die with him. When Julian dies, he doesn't really die.'[2]

Robertson made his presence felt when he encountered the Tiger Cubs, who craved his approval. The Cub culture was that no one should know more about a company than the assigned analyst. There were no budgets. Whatever it cost to do the work was worth it. That meant analysts could travel anywhere and stay as long as they needed. But they had better get the call right.

The Tiger Cubs were also known to hunt in packs, appearing on the same registers and betting against the same stocks, and they shared the same overriding strategy of betting on good companies and shorting bad ones. And, whether instructed by Robertson's downfall or not, they were determined to find themselves riding, not fighting, the tech parabolas.

The Cubs were the modern-day hedge fund managers the public imagined them to be. Robertson's favourite was 25-year-old Charles Payson Chase Coleman III. Robertson handed his former US tech analyst US$25 million to start Tiger Global. A natural-born winner, Coleman married a wealthy heiress to a chemical fortune, befriended world champion surfer Kelly Slater, co-invested with Snoop Dog and was a scratch golfer. He took a helicopter to work from the Hamptons.[3]

By 2019, the 44-year-old Coleman managed US$30 billion from the 35th floor of the Solow Building, behind Manhattan's Park Plaza. Tiger Global had made money in recent years by backing ecommerce winners in both public and private markets, and had an impressive track record.

Ten floors below him in the most coveted office building in Manhattan, Philippe Laffont's Coatue Management ran US$16 billion of assets in his specialist technology hedge fund. While most hedge fund reception halls were decorated with expensive art, Coatue's paid homage to tech nostalgia. A white cabinet displayed relics that were precursors to the dawning computer age: early Nintendo consoles, the first-ever Apple computer, and the Apple Newton, a clunky handheld device that was discontinued in 1998.

Laffont had been an analyst around the same time as Coleman, but Robertson had passed him over for funds, instead backing Coleman, Lee Ainslie's Maverick and Ole Andreas Halvorsen's Viking Global. The Belgian-born Frenchman was a graduate of the temple of nerd-dom that was the Massachusetts Institute of Technology, and in the mid-1990s was hired by Robertson to cover European tech stocks. In 1999, he left the original Tiger Management to start Coatue, which he named after a beach on Nantucket island. Laffont navigated the looming tech-stock crash, and by 2019 he, too, had grown in both assets under management and stature.

Coatue was a tough place to work, as Laffont was both brilliant and volatile. He burnt through analysts almost by design. The unwritten rule was that they used Coatue to bolster their résumés before departing for more money and more responsibility elsewhere. One-third of analysts left each year. Like Robertson, Laffont favoured competitive types and a cut-throat environment. That meant the office was populated with tech nerds in jock bodies. But they had a fanatical dedication to research, and made it a mission to hunt for anything new. They were trained to suspend their suspicion until a fad could be proven as such. Cynicism was consensus. Adaptation was contrarian.

According to Coatue folklore, on the day the first iPhone was released, 29 June 2007, Laffont's analysts pulled it apart. They bought shares in every company that supplied parts and shorted every one that didn't—which included Nokia and Blackberry. This all-out bet on the iPhone was one of Coatue's most profitable trades ever.

Tiger Global and Coatue were among the most fabled of the Tiger Cubs. But there were at least 50 others, spanning four generations, which controlled at least US$155 billion. In Greenwich, Steve Mandel operated the US$30 billion Lone Pine, while Ainslie's

Maverick managed US$15 billion from Dallas. And among the Tiger Cubs and beyond, a view was forming that the present-day boom in technology stocks was very different to the bubble of 2000.

Back in February 2014, Bill Ackman, a high-profile New York hedge fund manager, had told students at Columbia University to look out for 'white swans'. Unlike in 2000, founders could now create businesses with the potential to up-end industries at very low cost. They could rent servers through the cloud, work out of serviced offices, and scour the world for developers. The age of disruption was upon us. And the Tiger Cubs got that memo.

In his 2019 quarterly letter, Lone Pine's Steve Mandel told his investors the fund was investing in the shares of the companies that are disrupting 'large swathes of the economy' and betting against, or shorting, the shares of companies that are being disrupted. Lone Pine, he said, invests in 'established businesses with known growth algorithms and long runways for expansion'. He gave some examples: credit card networks, data analytics companies, internet platforms and vertical software leaders.

Afterpay had landed on the radar of the Tiger Cubs long before it knew it. In early March 2019, David Hancock and chief financial officer Luke Bortoli went on a whirlwind tour of the world's financial capitals to introduce Afterpay to more international investors. Goldman Sachs brokered a week of meetings between Australian corporations and institutional investors, split between London and New York.

In London they met the likes of M&G, Invesco, West Yorkshire Pensions and Baillie Gifford. Baillie Gifford, the 110-year-old Edinburgh-based firm, had managed the pensions of monks and friars, and provided the loans required to set up plantations in Ceylon and Malaya. Baillie Gifford's Scottish Mortgage Trust was an early investor in Tesla, and its analysts were on the lookout for opportunities to make further big bets on disruption.

The show then shifted to New York for two days of meetings at the JW Marriott Essex House. With a stunning view looking north over Central Park, Hancock and Bortoli held court alongside executives from ASX titans BHP, Westpac and Star Group. To their surprise, Afterpay was the only company that any of the US investors had any interest in meeting.

From Chicago, Oberweis and CastleArk Management checked in. So, too, did secretive low-profile funds that managed billions of dollars. Rip Road Capital, Garelick, Whale Rock and mega fund Wellington Capital made the trip south from a frosty Boston. Soros Capital and Indus, founded by former Soros traders, attended from their nearby offices. Dragoneer Investment Group, an early investor in Alibaba, Uber, Spotify and Atlassian, travelled the furthest, from San Francisco.

Hancock and Bortoli were struck by how enthused US hedge funds were about Afterpay, whose growth they'd been carefully tracking. They were following the regulatory debate in Australian politics, the difficulty investors had in justifying the valuation, and the cultish following Afterpay had attracted. They'd also become aware, from talking to US retailers, of how popular Afterpay now was.

Afterpay had tapped the millennial zeitgeist like few other brands had. It had created a cool shopping aesthetic. Hancock and Bortoli were told how comparable their business was to Juul Labs, the e-cigarette company that Tiger Global had backed with private capital. After tobacco giant Altria bought a third of the company in December 2018, Juul Labs was valued at US$40 billion. Its success had as much to do with the technology, which was a healthier version of smoking, as it did with its branding and marketing. Juul sold tobacco the Apple way, in pods inserted into sleekly designed devices. And it brought the glamour of 1980s cigarette advertisements into the modern era, hiring influencers and models to deploy hashtags on Instagram. The virality of an effective campaign and an already addictive substance turned vaping into a craze among teenagers, disturbing health experts, who feared their decades-long battle to beat Big Tobacco was rapidly unwinding.

Juul's apparent attempts to target teenagers made an enemy of outgoing Food and Drug Administration chief Scott Gottlieb, who openly blamed Juul for a surge in vaping. Eventually Juul was pulled into line. As Juul moderated its marketing to position its e-cigarettes as a healthier alternative to old-school cancer sticks, its growth slowed and its valuation was slashed by half. The experience showed that in the new age of consumerism, products that tapped the wants and needs of customers could win big and win fast. Virality and influence could be unleashed in new markets, forcing lawmakers to respond in real time.

If New York hedge funds could find another Juul—and preferably one that would stay on the right side of the regulators—they stood to make millions. For Hancock and Bortoli, the takeaway was that Wall Street's and Silicon Valley's shrewdest investors thought Afterpay could be the one.

Their standout meeting was with Woodson Capital. The fund's 38-year-old founder, Jim Woodson Davis, and three analysts had made the short journey from their midtown office on the 48th floor of 101 Park Avenue. Davis was a young Tiger Cub who'd spent almost two years as an analyst at Chase Coleman's Tiger Global before setting up his own fund in 2010. He had attended college in North Carolina, Robertson's home state, and made an impression on the Tiger patriarch. The Woodson analysts knew Afterpay inside and out and had already bought some shares. They had rung customers and retailers, and searched the world for any piece of data that could add to their understanding of the business.

As part of their research, Woodson conducted a survey of Afterpay's target demographic—young college-age women. They asked if they'd heard of Afterpay. The result was a staggering 86 per cent in the affirmative. Only ubiquitous social-media network Facebook had registered such a high hit rate that early on in its existence. Woodson's conviction levels went through the roof.

That meeting was Afterpay's first encounter with Tiger Cubs who were hungry for a bite. And it was timely. Afterpay's bankers were planning a big-bang capital raising, while Eisen, Molnar and Hancock had $100 million of shares to sell. Woodson Capital and Tiger Global wanted to invest aggressively, and stood ready to take those shares off their hands.

If the objective was to demonstrate that Afterpay insiders weren't dumping stock onto uninformed mum and dad investors, it would have been hard to find more sophisticated buyers than the New York hedge funds—and Tiger Cubs to boot. But the AUSTRAC announcement that dropped a day after the June capital raising now made these masters of the universe appear like the suckers, at least in the short term.

Molnar and Eisen, stunned by the development, contemplated handing the funds back to the Tiger Cubs, and scheduled a call with Davis. The usually unflappable Molnar was on edge as he dialled in from San Francisco, while Eisen was in Melbourne. But Davis said they had his full support. He didn't want his money back. In fact, the softly spoken Davis later confessed that he felt bad buying the shares off the founders, given how cheap he thought they were.

• • •

The AUSTRAC incident was another manifestation of a recurring theme for Afterpay. The underlying business was growing at an accelerating rate, but the threat of regulation and sanction consistently undermined investor confidence.

That had been the case in Australia. But Afterpay was now drawing the attention of more offshore funds, and some Australian investors were banking on the shareholder register gaining a more international flavour. Eley Griffiths' David Allingham wrote on investment insight website *Livewire* in March 2019 that Afterpay's US volume had grown five times faster than in Australia, in a market ten times the size. It was only a matter of time, he argued, before more US investors emerged as marginal buyers of Afterpay shares, and set the share price valuation. Allingham pointed to Australian companies Altium, which made software for engineers to make printed circuit boards, and NextDC, a data-storage centre operator, which had increased in value as US investors accumulated up to 40 per cent of the registers. US investors, by contrast, owned only 15 per cent of Afterpay shares.

But many investors in Australia were still grappling with the question of whether Afterpay was a platform business or a more traditional lender. Among them was Investors Mutual's Marc Whittaker. As he saw it, digital platform companies such as eBay and Google were attractive to investors because of their strong economies of scale: once these platforms are built, the cost of adding a new user to the platform is near zero, which means that its operating margins are very high.

'This network effect gives these platforms real barriers to entry,' Whittaker said. 'In contrast, Afterpay is a consumer finance company that requires capital to grow. In the past 14 months alone, Afterpay has raised more than $450 million in a mixture of debt and equity. This has been done in part to fund the company's entry into the US and UK markets. However, it is apparent that growth for Afterpay comes at a cost to both its earnings per share and returns.'[4]

Afterpay's already low returns, he argued, would decline in the future as the privilege of light-touch regulation was whittled away, and as more competition moved in to erode its margins.

Those fund managers who didn't own Afterpay shares may have been comfortable with their logic, but the rising share price remained a source of considerable discomfort.

In the second quarter of 2019, NovaPort Capital, which ran a $100 million micro-cap stock fund from Sydney, told investors that not owning Afterpay shares was the second-biggest drag on its quarterly investment return relative to the market. The small-companies fund of another Sydney manager, Ellerston, also had a lacklustre start to the year. Its 6 per cent return lagged the Small Ordinaries index return of 11 per cent. Ellerston had been a substantial shareholder of Touchcorp before it merged with Afterpay. Again, not owning Afterpay shares was its second-most costly decision. Some investors simply could not buy Afterpay shares without overwriting their formal rules, which limited them to buying shares in companies that generated a certain amount of free cashflow, or that traded within an acceptable valuation.

Afterpay's governance was still a matter of interest for Ownership Matters. In March, the firm's analyst James Samson titled a twelve-page presentation '5 Things to Watch for Afterpay Investors', shortly after the company released its half-year results. The looming end of the founders' self-imposed escrow period was on the list.

Samson also called out 'changing metrics'. Afterpay was not consistent in how it reported measures of profits and bad debts from one period to the next, muddying attempts at comparison. The company was also paying a growing portion of its expenses with shares and option grants, which masked the true operational cost of running Afterpay.

'Options issued to external advisors are valued on the basis of the fair value of the services provided,' Samson wrote. 'Employing external consultants or service providers with options has the potential to understate the true cost of "normal" expenses, particularly during the start-up phase. It seems particularly incongruous to value options issued to external advisors on the basis of the "fair value of the services" provided, then to exclude those expenses from "normalised EBITDA [earnings before interest, tax, depreciation and amortisation]".'

Ownership Matters described Afterpay's use of options as 'opaque'. After inspecting the issue of Australian share options to staff, it found that 'a small number of options had been issued to external advisors in fields such as communications, political lobbying, industry consultants and web "influencers" for services rendered'.

Later in the year, *The Australian Financial Review*'s Joe Aston revealed that former media executive Brett Clegg had been granted Afterpay options that netted him a gain of $800,000. The revelation forced the break-up of the Cato & Clegg public relations firm, which Afterpay had hired to help it navigate the fallout from the first Ownership Matters report and Senate inquiry. Afterpay had also sprinkled the options love in the United States beyond the staff in its San Francisco office: hip-hop star Jay-Z's manager and the CEO of music label Roc Nation, Jay Brown, was granted 75,000 options to buy shares at $25.

A related matter was Afterpay USA's use of options to lure staff and to recruit consultants and other aides to Afterpay's cause. Dana Stalder had impressed upon Eisen and Molnar that to win in Silicon Valley, they had to attract the right talent. But that wasn't going to be easy. The top engineers at the likes of Uber and Airbnb had millions of unvested shares and options, and if they were going to walk away from these it had to be worth their while. Working in Afterpay's favour was that many engineers desired to build stuff from the ground up, and Afterpay offered them that opportunity.

After its investment in January 2018, Matrix had sent dozens of staff, from its extensive start-up venture capital networks, into Afterpay USA as Molnar and Stalder spent four months bedding down a team. These included two of the most senior members of Uber's technical staff, Xin Ge and Akash Garg.

The courtship of Xin Ge, who was the global chief risk analytics officer at Uber, involved multiple sessions before he was convinced to join in May. It was a year before Uber would float, and head backwards on the share market. Stalder knew Xin from eBay and PayPal, where he'd spent fourteen years. Stalder considered him one of the smartest people he'd ever worked with in the Valley.

Garg joined Afterpay USA as chief technology officer and vice president of product, having been director of engineering at Uber. Before that, he was senior director of engineering at Twitter. Afterpay also announced in May that Melissa Davis was joining as US chief revenue officer from ShopStyle, one of the largest fashion websites in the United States, which had been part of PopSugar.

Afterpay had issued almost all the options in the US company that it was allowed to under an agreed plan. But exactly who had these options remained a closely guarded secret.

The options had been granted to holders at an attractive price of US$0.19—even as the shares traded above $20—putting them in line to reap a bonanza when they converted. The catch was the dilution. Afterpay was effectively giving away ownership in the company for free. As *The Australian Financial Review*'s columnist Aston later wrote, cheap options were 'no magic beans'.[5]

Molnar told *The Australian Financial Review* the structure was the brainchild of Dana Stalder. 'It's not traditional for a US venture capital fund to put money into an Australian-listed business at a $1 billion-plus market cap,' he said, 'and it wasn't that we needed access to the money, because we were public and could have done a raise. It was all about, how do we set up the right structure to bring the best talent in the world into our business?'

There was a lot of negative sentiment among Australian investors who had seen companies fail in their efforts to expand offshore, Molnar explained. So Afterpay had set up a separate US company. 'We want people to feel heavily invested in our business. So we set up a structure with Dana that let us bring people in out of Google, Airbnb, Harvard and Stanford MBA students,' Molnar said.[6]

What the future conversion of US option holders meant for the future value of Afterpay was too detailed for most analysts, who largely chose to ignore it. The general view was that the conversion would be limited to less than 20 per cent of the shares on issue, and the enormous growth of the US business would mean everyone got rich.

But the US structure posed a conundrum for Afterpay. In 2023, Afterpay USA shares would be converted into Afterpay shares, once an independent expert determined the value of the company. In the interim, they'd have to sit and wait—while Australian staff were able to cash in tens of millions of dollars of life-changing wealth.

As Afterpay was courting Stanford MBAs with stock options, Molnar was dazzling Harvard MBA professors: Donald Ngwe and Antonio Moreno had flown to San Francisco to spend two days studying the start-up. Ngwe told *The Australian* that Molnar was 'a great guy and a true visionary', and in April Molnar travelled to Harvard's intimate classroom theatres on the east coast to talk about Afterpay.[7]

Molnar and the team in the United States were making inroads attracting the attention of investors, but more importantly they were signing up retailers and customers at an extraordinary rate. That was fuelling the interest and the share price rise. The Ivy League business schools had become seminaries of winner-takes-all capitalism, but each had its own emphasis. Harvard Business School looked at case studies and real-world examples of entrepreneurship.

Molnar's HBS paper was titled 'Afterpay US: The Omnichannel Dilemma' and explored the challenge of making Afterpay available in stores. Molnar recounted how he had paced up and down in his San Francisco headquarters, trying to come up with ways to grow the business faster. 'Our shoppers are going into stores and asking if they can use Afterpay,' he told the students. 'When they hear they can't, they say okay, I will buy online instead. Nothing gets retailers moving faster than missed sales opportunities.' The decision, the paper concluded, was that Afterpay would move instore once it had a critical mass of 2.3 million users. 'There's no science behind it,' Molnar said.

His competitors Klarna and Affirm were nipping at his heels, but the moment to go instore was when they'd built up a portfolio of merchants and competitors that could exert 'collective pressure'. 'If you wait enough for the right point of inflection, the opportunity offline can become so much bigger than online,' he noted.

Not long after, Eisen joined Molnar in New York, where they had an audience with the patriarch himself, Julian Robertson. The pair had shown up soaked after a Manhattan downpour, and a concerned Robertson made sure they were dry before the hour-and-a-half meeting began. Seated around the table in the Park Avenue boardroom were Cubs controlling upwards of US$100 billion of capital. Robertson asked a couple of questions but let the others do the talking.

When the Australians left in a car, arranged for them by Robertson, Eisen was still pinching himself. He'd been a junior banker in New York at the height of the tech boom, back when Robertson was at the peak of his powers. The office they'd just been in was almost sacred on Wall Street. 'There would be a million people in this city who would give their right arm to have an hour in that room,' he told Molnar.

'He was a lovely guy,' Nick replied. 'That was a great meeting.'

• • •

The middle of 2019 was also marked by a flurry of competitive responses, including from one of the world's largest payment giants,

Visa, and from the Commonwealth Bank, Australia's largest. After-pay's growth had awoken the giants.

Visa was the first to move. It said on 27 June that it would offer banks that issued its cards, and merchants that accepted them, the ability to offer buy now, pay later instalments via a suite of 'instalment solutions APIs'.[8] The market was spooked and Afterpay's shares fell 15 per cent. But the history of Visa suggested it was a facilitator of activity over its network, not a direct competitor to the companies that used it. The Afterpay bulls saw its desire to help banks enter the space as an endorsement that short-term instalments represented the future of payments.

Visa's release detailed how instalment payments were growing twice as fast as credit cards, and pointed to its research showing that 74 per cent of cardholders thought instalments were helpful for budgeting, while 70 per cent said they alleviated the stress of making large purchases. It also highlighted the global nature of the product: in Brazil, around 50 per cent of all credit payment volume is made on short-term repayment plans, while in Canada, 41 per cent of cardholders told Visa they would consider using instalment payments on purchases of US$500 or more.

A month later, one of the US-based start-ups that adopted Afterpay's model in the United States, Sezzle, listed on the ASX to take advantage of fattening trading multiples. The roadshow in Sydney and Melbourne in late 2018 had gone well, giving Charlie Youakim the confidence to pull the trigger. Stockbroker Ord Minnett's Phil Chippendale shepherded Sezzle onto the ASX, which was desperate to attract new technology listings from abroad to reorientate the market towards software industries.

Youakim had been given confidence by another buy now, pay later player, Splitit, which had listed on the ASX in January 2019. The Israel-based company had been founded ten years earlier by Alon Feit and Gil Don, and had operations in 27 countries. It let merchants create repayment plans from six to 24 months for customers using existing credit cards, also helping to increase average order value and reduce cart abandonment. Youakim had watched as its share price multiplied by five times in its first four months of trade on the ASX. Sezzle hit the boards on 29 July, doubling to $2.20 on its first day. Investors now had another avenue for exposure to the US market.

Next it was the Commonwealth Bank's turn to make a move. CEO Matt Comyn and his strategy team had been searching for a way to use point-of-sale lending to recapture the fickle youth market. In August, CBA announced it had found a match in Sweden's Klarna.

Partnering with start-ups was uncomfortable territory for CBA. It had taken tentative steps with an offshore player, South Africa's TymeDigital, in 2015, but those efforts had been abandoned as CBA retreated from international markets. Tyme was ultimately sold to minority shareholder African Rainbow Capital in November 2018.

The prevailing attitude in CBA's self-assured management ranks under Ian Narev had been that 'we are big enough to build it ourselves', but Comyn was open to forming partnerships. Westpac had already made a $40 million investment in Zip back in 2017, backing this up with another $9 million in 2019. Comyn realised that the top-quality buy now, pay later trailblazers had become too big to acquire, and it would take too long to attempt to replicate one. So on 7 August 2019 CBA announced that it would invest US$100 million in Klarna. A few months later, it put in another US$200 million.

The move was controversial. The Australian government was supporting local start-ups and encouraging them to expand offshore, and here was Australia's largest bank—one that had resisted backing local fintechs with venture capital equity investments, as Westpac, ANZ and NAB had done—investing in one of Afterpay's and Zip's biggest global competitors. Not only that, the acquisition would bring Klarna into Australia to compete with Afterpay and Zip in the local market.

Klarna was not a pure buy now, pay later provider: it offered a suite of products, including financing for larger purchases for up to three years, for which it charged interest. Indeed, Klarna is a bank: the Swedish Financial Supervisory Authority awarded it a full banking licence in 2017. But it was its 'Pay in 4' instalment product, launched in 2018, that had turbocharged Klarna's customer growth in 2019.

Comyn would use the Klarna investment to provoke Afterpay, telling reporters one of the bank's intentions 'would be to lift standards' in the sector.[9]

Afterpay was unimpressed. Eisen hit back, saying CBA should concentrate on getting its own house in order before criticising the behaviour of others. 'As the royal commission has proven, the banks do not set the standard for best practice,' he said. 'The bulk of the way [Klarna] makes its money is applying a new skin to a traditional credit lending model. They are retro-fitting a customer-centric approach into an old model, which is in a lot of ways broken. We are transparent about value and we don't try to make it up in another way like a Klarna credit model charging customers in bank ways.'

That same month Afterpay unveiled its new recruit via the 'Chanticleer' column in *The Australian Financial Review*. Michael Saadat, the head regulator in charge of overseeing the sector, had agreed to head up regulatory affairs at Afterpay.[10]

Afterpay's spinners had anticipated that the news would be taken as a sign the business was serious about lifting its game with regulators, and navigating the gauntlet of lawmakers and enforcers it would need to pass through. But as some within Afterpay had anticipated, the move came as a shock to the consumer groups that had leaned heavily on Saadat when airing their concerns about Afterpay and the explosion of the sector.

'It is ludicrous that they are sitting in this nebulous space outside of regulation,' said Karen Cox of the Financial Rights Legal Centre, after expressing surprise at the appointment.

There was another high-profile hire in October. Former US treasury secretary Larry Summers, who had been an economic adviser to President Barack Obama, had been convinced by Andrew Charlton to join an Afterpay advisory board to help connect it with key influencers in the United States. 'I think people are afraid of credit card addiction and looking for healthier ways to pay over time for what they want,' Summers said. He had received options to buy Afterpay shares from September 2020 at a price of $32.[11]

Afterpay had proved itself adept in Canberra, and the re-elected Coalition government was planning to review its technology policy settings to help reignite innovation policy, which had been a hard sell to the electorate and hardly featured at all during Morrison's campaign. On 11 September 2019, a young Liberal senator, Andrew Bragg, moved a motion to establish an inquiry with a long-winded name—the Select Committee on Financial Technology and Regulatory Technology—that would start to shift the regulatory sands. This inquiry had far more positive connotations than the Labor-led inquiry, which had explored the possibility that unregulated credit was putting borrowers under pressure and Afterpay on the back foot.

For Afterpay, the timing of Bragg's inquiry could not have been better. From the outset, the select committee would be pro-fintech, intending to report on 'the progress of fintech facilitation reform and the benchmarking of comparable global regimes' and the 'effectiveness of current initiatives in promoting a positive environment for fintech and regtech start-ups'.[12]

After failing to win preselection for the Senate and the lower house before the 2016 federal election—which saw Liberal prime minister Malcolm Turnbull sneak home to victory over Labor's

Bill Shorten—Bragg had joined the Menzies Research Centre, the policy think tank for the Liberal Party, as policy director, before shifting to the Business Council of Australia, the peak lobby group for Australia's largest corporations. He considered the consumer groups activists.

Armed with a Masters degree in financial regulation from Macquarie University, Bragg had won preselection to run on the Coalition ticket for the Senate at the 2019 election. He now saw an opportunity to make his mark on policy development in Canberra. His run for parliament had been supported by Turnbull, but now he could align himself with Morrison, who as treasurer had given a high priority to developing Australia's fintech policy.

Morrison and members of his staff had privately referred to fintech as their 'happy place'. It combined technology policy with competition that could exert pressure on the major banks. Bank bashing had been a big vote winner for Labor, and the anti-bank politics had forced Turnbull to set up the Hayne Royal Commission. But Turnbull's innovation push had failed to cut through in the 2016 election campaign—which he'd won with a one-seat majority, the closest result since 1961. Many Australians feared new technology would see them lose their jobs. Morrison realised he would need a new way to frame the inevitable march of progress for a sceptical electorate.

After visiting the United Kingdom in early 2017, Morrison had been influenced by the pro-fintech policies of the UK government under Conservative chancellor of the exchequer George Osborne. At a speech to a high-level conference of G20 leaders in January 2017, Morrison said Australia would support fintech to boost banking competition and help facilitate access to new forms of finance. Australia wanted fintechs to 'grow big, to thrive and deliver benefits for consumers and the economy', he told heads of governments in Wiesbaden, Germany.

Now the Senate's powerful committee process would be used to quiz regulators, incumbents and start-ups—including Afterpay and Zip—on how the government's policy settings could be improved. Bragg was confident that any recommendations his committee made would be well received by the prime minister, who was keen to safeguard his fintech legacy, and by treasurer Josh Frydenberg.

• • •

If Afterpay's June capital raising had proved anything to Australia's bankers and brokers, it was the money-making opportunities this client presented. The ties to Bell Potter, which got the company off the ground, were deep, while NAB and Citi had backed Afterpay early. Highbury Partners—the former J.P. Morgan duo of Matt Roberts and Allan Young—were also trusted independent advisers and helped to manage the June transaction, which involved a placement, capital raising and an acquisition.

Australia's so-called retail brokers—such as Bell Potter, Shaw, Morgans, Ord Minnett and Wilsons—were alive to the potential to service not just Afterpay but also its competitors. Openpay, another provider targeting higher-value items such as sporting club memberships, was lining up an ASX listing for December. Now the big brokers wanted in on the act.

The buy now, pay later sector was a match made in heaven for financiers. These companies were growing and hungry for debt and equity capital. Meanwhile, the founders and staff had large blocks of shares that would require selling, while more institutions would be forced to establish themselves on the share register. Their sky-high valuations also made acquisitions and tie-ups more compelling as a means of fast-tracking growth and expanding into new markets.

The research analysts who covered Afterpay were predictably enthusiastic. Goldman Sachs had momentarily lost faith a year earlier, but had been won over by the company's fast growth in the United States. In October 2019, seven analysts were listed by Bloomberg as covering Afterpay; all but Wilson had a buy rating, and all had lifted their price targets.

The cynics may have concluded that the analysts, who are technically independent, were doing their masters' bidding by setting bullish price targets. But Afterpay was delivering the revenue growth, and the share price was following. Everyone involved in Afterpay was making money.

Well, almost everyone. In October 2019, UBS, the country's top equity house, weighed in on Afterpay with a splash. Jonathan Mott, one of the country's leading banking analysts, initiated coverage on Afterpay alongside Tom Beadle, a young and sharp analyst who was not afraid to ruffle a few feathers. The call was to sell Afterpay, as they predicted the share price would halve from $36.56 to $17.25.

Afterpay's momentum was 'undeniable', and it would smash its two-year growth forecasts, they acknowledged. But there were three risks the share market was not factoring in, even if they were spoken about. The first was regulation: the threat of surcharge regulation and reclassification as a lender would weigh on the stock. The second was competition, given the low barriers to entry. The third was the risk that Afterpay would fail to deliver on its aspirations. By UBS's calculations, Afterpay would have to process eight times more transactions within five years to justify even the lower end of its share price range.

The market's price implied that Afterpay would be used to pay for $100 billion of goods within five years and $175 billion within ten years, compared to around $5 billion at present. In the analysts' view, that was wildly optimistic. The UBS brokers shared their research with clients, reminding them that it was easy to source shares to borrow, and short, or to price derivatives to bet against Afterpay shares.

In the days that followed, Afterpay's share price took a hammering. After four days of relentless selling, almost 20 per cent, or $1.3 billion of value, had been wiped off the stock.

The episode was a reminder of the influence of research analysts: even in an era where there were reduced commissions and onerous laws about how the service was paid for by clients, they could move the market more than ever. A growing pool of capital was being managed by quantitative funds that traded based on algorithms, and many of those algorithms relied on the forecasts and recommendations of analysts. Adjustments had the potential to trigger significant share price moves.

The UBS research, however, offered a glimpse of what the world might look like if Afterpay's growth led to some form of domination. The analysts had raised yet another regulatory risk that had the potential to kneecap the company: the potential for Reserve Bank intervention on 'no surcharge' rules. Their maths suggested that the fees merchants were paying to facilitate a sale were becoming a large impost on commerce.

Afterpay's merchant agreements meant retailers could not pass on the cost to customers. (Credit cards originally had the same restrictions, until the RBA outlawed them in the early 2000s.) Making the service free for customers to use, with the cost funded by the merchant, 'arguably creates a distortion which could significantly influence consumers' choice of payment method', UBS said. In other words, buyers who could easily afford to purchase an item without Afterpay's instalment method would use it because it was free, imposing costs onto the merchant.

UBS calculated the cost to the system if Afterpay was used to pay for $173.8 billion of retail consumer goods purchases in 2019. After the cost of goods, wages, rent and other expenses, the collective earnings before interest and tax for all retailers was $8.5 billion.

But the Afterpay surcharge would cut that by $5.2 billion, or 60 per cent, to just $3.3 billion.

An Afterpay future was one in which white-collar workers were given a revolving loan to fund discretionary purchases, paid for by those who could least afford it—the merchants.

Afterpay's success was also due in part to what is known in economics as 'the fallacy of composition'—which simply means it is wrong to infer that because something is true in one instant, it is true in every instant. In the case of Afterpay, some merchants were deriving incremental sales from Afterpay. But others were forced to adopt Afterpay or risk losing existing customers. And the more merchants that signed on, the less incrementality there would be. That was something Afterpay was only too well aware of.

For the large retailers, the decision about whether or not to use Afterpay, which was once a matter for the marketing departments, was now handled by the chief financial officers. For some retailers, after paying rent and wages, Afterpay's merchant fees had grown to become the business's third-largest expense.

The Reserve Bank of Australia had its eye on the same issue. Two days after the UBS report, on 18 October 2019, the RBA published the annual report of its payments system board. It struck Afterpay like a thunderbolt.

While not referring to providers by name, it asked whether there were 'policy implications' from the 'no-surcharge' rules imposed by buy now, pay later contracts. The euphemism was not lost: the RBA was set to probe the sector's opaque pricing.

Any move to stop Afterpay preventing merchants from sur-charging could be catastrophic, striking its central claim that customers only pay more than the price tag on the goods if they are late making repayments. Consumers had signed up in droves, trusting the sim-plicity of Afterpay's offer and that there were no hidden fees. Adding transaction costs now could fatally destroy that trust.

To the payments wonks sitting in the RBA's headquarters at the top of Martin Place, no-surcharge rules always rang alarm bells: the ability for merchants to pass on payments costs is the core mechanism by which downward pressure can be exerted on those costs. The RBA sees keeping payments costs as low as possible as a key part of its mandate. Now it was considering whether buy now, pay later players should be held to the same price-regulation standards as credit cards. Visa and Mastercard had fought their designation, which led to their no-surcharge rules being banned, in the Federal Court, but lost.

For investors, the questions raised by UBS and the RBA may have highlighted further risks, but they also clarified the size of the prize for Afterpay. While early investors had feared credit losses from millennial and underage buyers who couldn't afford to pay for what they were buying, now the hedge funds were concerned about customers of high credit quality ramping up their use of Afterpay to the point where regulators viewed it as a burdensome cost on commercial activity.

Exactly what line of business Afterpay was in remained a matter of contention. Was Afterpay a provider of consumer finance, or was it a marketing company that drove retail sales? Mott and Beadle strongly believed Afterpay was a 'financial services business'.

To fund purchases, Afterpay had a loan book, and the interest it paid on the loans was a 'raw material' rather than a source of capital. As Afterpay processed more sales, it would need more equity and debt capital to fund that growth, and that would come at a cost. Afterpay borrowed money, advanced it to merchants on behalf of customers, and charged a fee. The value of the business should be measured by the future excess returns it would generate after funding those loans and meeting its other expenses.

A further issue UBS had with Afterpay was how it reported the extent to which customers never paid their debt. The favoured metric of Afterpay was gross losses—which calculated the ratio of impairments against the sales it processed. That was a modest 1.1 per cent, which looked favourable when compared to the credit impairment charges of the major bank credit cards of 2.6 per cent of average gross loans.[13] UBS argued that the true performance of Afterpay's book would be shown by calculating the losses relative to loans extended, not sales processed—which would be consistent with decades-long industry standards.

Afterpay had argued that those age-old ways of measuring losses didn't work when it was lending out the same dollar twelve to thirteen times a year. But UBS said credit cards turned six to seven times a year, and they still reported losses relative to loans. To account for Afterpay's faster turnover, UBS used an average loans figure of $396 million. The near $60 million of impairments was just shy of 15 per cent of average loans. That implied that if Afterpay standardised the way it reported losses, they would be almost three times more than those of Zip, which were estimated at 4.6 per cent, and more than five times worse than major bank credit card losses. That figure was worse than the peak US credit card charge-off rate of 10.5 per cent, experienced towards the end of the recession that accompanied the global financial crisis.

Even before the UBS intervention, sentiment on the sector was souring, hitting Latitude Financial particularly hard. On 15 October, the day before UBS's report, Latitude was forced to abandon an initial public offering for the second time in two years.

A fortnight earlier it had been touting a pivot into buy now, pay later via a new product called LatitudePay, which allowed shoppers to pay for purchases in ten weekly instalments without paying interest. Potential investors in the IPO, which was seeking $1 billion, were being told that some of the biggest names in jewellery had agreed to join Harvey Norman and The Good Guys, whitegoods and electronics retailers, in offering the service.

Latitude's boss, Ahmed Fahour, had been a senior executive at NAB and then CEO of Australia Post for seven years to mid-2017. He'd lifted the proportion of revenue Australia Post earned from ecommerce from 45 per cent to 70 per cent, but tough decisions he'd taken—including job cuts, price hikes on stamps and reductions in service—made him unpopular, and he'd quit in 2017 after a dispute with the federal government about his remuneration package.

Latitude made most of its money from issuing credit cards and interest-bearing loans, and there was a feeling among its sceptics that it was making a belated shift into the popular interest-free space to support its valuation. But the free-instalment offering was a potentially powerful tool to acquire new customers.

Comparisons to old-world companies were not convincing to new-world investors, who were being rewarded by a share market that salivated over top-line growth.

As Australian brokers headed off to the United States to meet with its most powerful hedge funds, the same debate that had been had on Macquarie Street was playing out in Manhattan skyscrapers and Connecticut office campuses. The grizzled banking analysts, who thought they'd seen it all before, could not look beyond credit loss rates and capital intensity. They'd seen enough lower-case fintech start-ups that had fooled investors into thinking they were cutting-edge, only to be exposed as new twists on centuries-old lending models. But tech analysts had a vision of explosive growth, the self-reinforcing network effect and the enormous total addressable market for payments.

The doubters that believed Afterpay was more akin to a lender and would have to constantly tap the share market for funds soon felt justified.

On 13 November, the day of its annual general meeting, Afterpay announced it had placed $200 million of shares to one of the most elusive of the Tiger Cubs: Philippe Laffont's Coatue Management.

The Tiger Cub way was to spare no expense, and Coatue had a US$30 million budget to buy data for its algorithms. Those algorithms, Molnar revealed, had unearthed Afterpay. 'They found us in their data and they went, "What is this?" And then they dug into it and started asking retailers,' Molnar said at the firm's annual general meeting.

Stephen Mayne, a shareholder activist and serial agitator at annual general meetings, called it 'almost the biggest credibility-building capital raising' that Afterpay had ever done.

Eisen explained: 'When somebody can independently see the difference that you're making in the retail and consumer landscape, and has also had experience investing in platform companies that can scale, that's the basis upon which the conversation started.'

Coatue and Afterpay said they would work together to share data to develop products that would help retailers develop offers for customers. Eisen said there was a difference between using data to manage risk and using it to entice consumers to transact. 'That's the bridge that we're trying to build.'

Four days before the Coatue deal settled, AUSTRAC would again intervene—but this time with good news. The powerful financial crime regulator had issued Afterpay a clean bill of health. The investigation by an external auditor, Neil Jeans, had found some 'matters of historic non-compliance'—which had been addressed or were being fixed—but confirmed that Afterpay's current program met the requirements of the strict legislation. Jeans said Afterpay had got the wrong legal advice from law firm Dentons, which determined it was providing finance to merchants rather than loans to customers, resulting in insufficient compliance.

He also found that Afterpay was 'a low-risk business in regards to its vulnerability to be used for money laundering or terrorist financing'.

The relief at Afterpay was in stark contrast to the mood at Westpac, which had been hit with a bombshell case from AUSTRAC the previous week alleging 23 million breaches of anti-money–laundering laws, some concerning suspicious transactions that were possibly related to child sex exploitation. It led to the premature departure of the bank's chairman, Lindsay Maxsted, and the exit of CEO Brian Hartzer; Westpac would later settle the claim for $1.3 billion, the largest fine in Australian corporate history.

There was another shock in store for Anthony Eisen and some of Afterpay's longest-standing investors. On the morning of 18 December 2019, the 82-year-old Ron Brierley left his home in the harbourside suburb of Point Piper for Sydney Airport. Before he boarded a flight to Fiji, he was stopped by police, who had received an anonymous tip-off. After examining the contents of several USB thumb drives, he was arrested on child pornography possession charges, to which he pleaded guilty. The stunning allegations shocked the Guinness Peat fraternity. It left the reputation of the famed corporate investor and one of Afterpay's first meaningful investors in tatters.

# 14

# GOING VIRAL

ON 5 FEBRUARY 2020, Governor Philip Lowe of the Reserve Bank of Australia made his first public appearance of the year at Doltone House, a function hall on Sydney's Pyrmont wharf, which juts out into the harbour on the western side of the Harbour Bridge.

That summer, Australia was burning. For weeks bushfires had ravaged all parts of the country, devastating regional communities, wiping out fauna and flora, and smoking up the big cities. The natural disaster made global headlines, and relief donations flooded in from around the world.

Prime Minister Scott Morrison, who had carved out an image as a knockabout dad, faced the first reputational crisis of his leadership. Morrison and his family had left the country for a holiday in Hawaii, while at home exhausted volunteer firefighters continued battling the raging blazes. When confronted about his absence, he snapped that he didn't 'hold the hose, mate'.

Lowe had also holidayed in the United States with his family, in California—and in his prepared remarks to the National Press Club, he mentioned the risks posed by the bushfire and a new coronavirus that had locked down the city of Wuhan, in China. The bushfires were a tragedy, he said, but there would be no enduring hit to the economy. As for the virus designated by the World Health Organization as COVID-19, the experience of the SARS virus in 2002 was instructive: activity would be depressed but would snap back sharply once the health authorities brought the virus under control. Australia's economic fortunes were more tied to China than before, so this time the virus may bring a greater cost.

In the back of the room, Ben McGarry, of hedge fund Totus Capital, listened intently. He'd been openly betting that Tesla shares would fall; as they ripped higher, even his family were ribbing him. But he, like other hedge fund managers, had been paying close attention to the virus. The market was too complacent, he believed.

If Lowe was alert but not alarmed by the coronavirus in early February, by the end of the month he had a greater sense that he, along with the entire public service, was about to face his greatest test.

Lowe and treasurer Josh Frydenberg had flown to Riyadh, Saudi Arabia, for a G20 meeting held over two days from 22 February. There, International Monetary Fund officials informed them that the virus had spread to Iran, South Korea and Italy, and the following day those countries had gone into lockdown. That three geographically distinct countries could be quickly infected left Lowe in little doubt that the world was on the cusp of a major episode for which it was not well prepared. That evening, he told Frydenberg that the virus was 'coming to Australia, and was going to be a very big deal'.[1]

If hedge funds and large institutions were growing deeply concerned, the broader share market wasn't showing it. That day, Afterpay shares touched $40, before closing slightly lower. November 2019 had been the company's best-ever month, as it processed $1 billion of sales. In addition, the Black Friday and Cyber Monday sales days had recorded the largest sales volumes Afterpay had ever seen, up 160 per cent on the previous year. It had gained 140,000 new customers over those two days alone. The business was preparing to deliver its half-year results, and investors had no cause to expect anything other than a stellar outcome.

But before that, some burning regulatory fires needed to be put out. In a submission to the Reserve Bank, the Australian Retailers' Association was calling for buy now, pay later to be 'brought into line' with major credit card schemes, which weren't allowed to stop merchants passing costs to customers. Few merchants would actually impose surcharges, but the power to pass on costs 'will become a bargaining tool and give retailers strength to be able to negotiate to reduce the fee', said the association's executive director, Russell Zimmerman.[2]

The Council of Small Business Organisations Australia was also on the attack, arguing that SMEs accepting buy now, pay later schemes would be forced to recover costs by lifting prices. 'There is no free lunch here,' said its chairman, Mark McKenzie. 'Why should buy now, pay later be treated any differently? It needs to be treated in the same way as other payment systems. That small business should cop the additional costs is an assertion we reject.'[3]

Australia's peak consumer groups were using the Reserve Bank's inquiry to re-prosecute concerns that Afterpay was facilitating easy credit that was being paid for by all consumers. 'BNPL providers are thriving in a regulatory black hole, and the inability for merchants to allow surcharging for this payment option is distorting the market,' the Consumer Action Law Centre, CHOICE, Financial Counselling Australia and the Financial Rights Legal Centre told the RBA in a January submission.[4]

With the RBA on their back, Eisen and Elana Rubin, in her first public appearance as chair of Afterpay, presented to the Senate's Select Committee on Financial Technology and Regulatory Technology. It was 20 February 2020, the week before the full-year results would be released, and they made a plea for more regulatory support.

In a dingy basement room in a commercial office building to the north of the city, just alongside the road leading to the Sydney

Harbour Bridge, Eisen, dressed in his customary dark suit and a white shirt, sat at a table facing the half-dozen committee members.

Afterpay, he explained, wasn't seeking to operate outside the law. 'What we have been talking about is not to skirt anything in terms of responsibility,' he said. The problem was the laws. They were outdated and they were holding back tech start-ups. Regulation, Eisen said, should be 'fit for purpose for what we do'.

Afterpay had found it 'very difficult' to grow because of the regulatory uncertainty, he continued. 'Some of the biggest retailers in the world don't understand how we are perceived back here in Australia—is it positive? Is it negative? If there is no regulatory definition, even though we don't fit in a box, that creates lots of ramifications in the way we are perceived.' The committee took the complaints on board.[5]

In the face of the renewed pressure from consumer groups, small businesses and retailers, Afterpay argued in its own submission to the Reserve Bank that the fundamental way it was being viewed was wrong: it should not be considered as a payments system at all, but rather as a 'platform'. In Afterpay's mind at least, it was more like Uber or Amazon than like Visa or Mastercard. While its 4 per cent fee might look large compared to, say, the 1 per cent charged by credit cards, it was low compared to the fees of the big US technology platforms: merchant charges of 10 per cent at Google and Facebook, 11 per cent at eBay, 15 per cent at Amazon, and 30 per cent at Uber Eats. 'As a customer acquisition channel for merchants, Afterpay competes with large players such as Google and Facebook and provides leads to merchants at a much lower cost,' the company said.[6]

Afterpay was also providing the RBA with a very different narrative when it came to describing its own performance. Pointing to the 'nascency' of the sector, it said buy now, pay later had processed $6.2 billion of transactions in 2019, less than 1 per cent of total payments in the Australian economy. This compared to 17 per cent for cash, 40 per cent for debit cards and 42 per cent for credit cards. 'Overall retail transaction data confirms the BNPL sector remains in its early stages and constitutes a tiny proportion of the overall retail payment economy,' the company argued. The smaller it was, the less likely the Reserve Bank was to intervene.

It might be small, but it was still growing. On 27 February, Afterpay delivered its half-year numbers. Eisen and Molnar were joined by chief financial officer Luke Bortoli to present another 'pleasing' result, which saw sales and customers more than double, while losses reduced. US sales had grown by five times over the year, and it was on track to process $11 billion of sales. The UK operations were tracking well, too, from a standing start, as retailers ASOS, Boohoo, Marks & Spencer and JD Sports jumped on board to offer Afterpay to their customers.

Afterpay was also benefiting from an uptick in repeat business. Existing customers were using it more frequently: early adopters who had signed up between 2015 and 2017 were making an average of 23 purchases a year, higher than the fifteen purchases for 2018 customers, eight for 2019 customers and three purchases by customers who'd joined in 2020. This was increasing sales and improving loss rates as good customers used the platform more frequently.

Meanwhile, customers were flocking to the 'shop directory' that Afterpay had set up in its app to point users to the retailers that accepted it as a form of payment. Customers were coming to Afterpay to decide where to shop, and it was referring them to retailers, like a search engine does.

Afterpay was also targeting older, cashed-up professionals and, after extensive research, had rolled out its first brand advertising campaign. 'We're incredibly strong in the millennial cohort, but how do we start to expand and grow the demographics that use Afterpay?' Molnar asked.

The results briefing touched on regulatory risks: Afterpay's growth in the United States was naturally drawing attention, which meant it would need to introduce and explain itself to those who mattered, but Eisen admitted that 'you cannot basically get around to all of those particular stakeholders as a very young company to explain the differences and the dynamics'. The hour-long conference call ended without a single mention of the coronavirus.

But the virus was about to consume Afterpay, the nation and the planet.

• • •

The following day, 28 February 2020, Morrison activated the health sector's emergency response plan. On 1 March, Australia experienced its first death from COVID-19. As cases escalated, panic set in among Australians who feared catching the disease or—what was apparently worse—running out of toilet paper, as they were placed in lockdown.

The anxiety was infiltrating global share markets. In the last week of February, all the year's gains were wiped out as the selling accelerated. Afterpay shares had come under selling pressure, too, but faithful investors who had experienced white-knuckle rides in the past were willing to hold on. By the end of the month, the shares held above $30 and were still positive for the year.

But the selling accelerated into March. The panic of lost investments, the economic devastation from a prolonged lockdown and the nightmare scenario of hospitals overwhelmed by patients requiring ventilators spooked investors. The spectrum of outcomes seemed to range from benign to apocalyptic.

Fear set in. On 9 March, the Australian market shed a harrowing 7 per cent. By the end of the week, Afterpay's share price had slid by a whopping 29 per cent. On Friday, 13 March, after another bloodbath on Wall Street, Australia's top financial regulators held calls on how to deal with what was the biggest crisis since 2008, if not in the post–World War II era.

The Australian Securities Exchange had been overwhelmed with orders. At the Reserve Bank, Lowe and his deputy, Guy Debelle, who had been juggling calls while setting up his eight-year-old's birthday party, readied to enact the emergency playbook. Of immediate concern was an unruly bond market. At times of crisis, anxious investors rush to buy government bonds, driving prices up and yields down.

But what hedge funds, pension funds and corporations needed was cash, and as they rushed to sell bonds, dealers were clogged. Worryingly, broken markets were forcing bond rates up, not down. That meant borrowing costs across the global economy were rising, threatening mass bankruptcies in the future.

On Monday, 16 March, the Reserve Bank told the market it would hold an emergency board meeting that Thursday, and would intervene in the bond market. Lowe and Debelle had learned from previous crises to 'go fast and go hard and don't die wondering'.[7]

While the market waited, the selling accelerated. Bond rates jumped around erratically, while share markets dropped like a stone. Investors had initially been forced to sell what they could, which meant shares in large global companies, and government bonds. But as they scrambled to raise cash, they were having to sell everything. That meant liquidating holdings in smaller companies. Afterpay was hit by a wave of selling.

Was the selling justified? Afterpay's business model was to extend financing to shoppers. If those shoppers suddenly lost their income, that could lead to a sharp rise in non-payments, which would wipe out a large share of Afterpay's revenues. Consumers might also choose not to spend money, which could reduce the volume of transactions Afterpay processed. And Afterpay relied to some extent on capital, in the form of new equity from investors and debt provided to it by its bankers via warehouse financing arrangements. Previous crises showed that when bankers observe a rise in bad debts or face their own capital squeeze, warehouse lines can be cut or yanked entirely, creating a vicious and sometimes terminal wind-down.

On 17 March, the market was spooked about new regulatory risks in the United States. Afterpay's shares fell by 10 per cent when it said it would refund $905,000 in late fees to about 640,000 customers in California for loans made before it was granted a licence in the state the previous November. These had been deemed illegal by the state's financial regulator.

The California Department of Business Oversight had also hit Sezzle for a similar gripe in January, triggering a share slump, but it had recovered when the licence in California was announced a few weeks later. 'While Afterpay does not believe such an arrangement required a license from the DBO or was illegal, Afterpay has agreed to conduct its operations under the DBO license as a part of this settlement,' Afterpay told Reuters in an email, calming the market's nerves.

Amid the chaos, another settlement was reached. On 11 March 2020, Melbourne Supreme Court Justice Peter Almond ruled that 6.6 million shares held in ATC Capital belonged to the Cleeve trust, and ordered that they be transferred by the estate within 60 days. Adrian Cleeve's extended family had managed to secure half the shares held in his name. Wendy Ng and the estate owed the Cleeve trust a sum of $6.5 million, but retained the 6.6 million share balance.

The combined wealth accrued to Adrian Cleeve was $375 million when Afterpay's shares reached $30. It would now be shared equally between his widow and his relatives. Their fortunes were larger than they could ever have imagined, but the market was swinging its worth by tens of millions a day. Shareholders of all sizes were beginning to wonder whether it might all evaporate.

Ben McGarry added a short position of Afterpay to Tesla. Totus had previously owned Afterpay shares as his team sought out platform businesses that had the ability to grow and attract customers. But both Tesla and Afterpay, he figured, would be reliant on external funding, which would now be harder to source, and on customers who were increasingly vulnerable. The market seemed to agree: Totus was making double-digit trading profits in March as the market was in freefall.

Afterpay's management did its best to calm nerves even as its board of directors watched events with unease. On 19 March, Anthony Eisen wrote a letter to shareholders to reassure them that fears about Afterpay's ability to withstand the emerging crisis were unfounded, at least for the time being. The business model, balance sheet and customer base provided protection in times of uncertainty, he said. Afterpay had $400 million in cash, ample access to funding via its warehouse, and enough capital to operate and grow. They had not experienced a hit to business activity or a rise in losses.

Afterpay's users, whose average age was 33, had enough income to make their instalment payments, which at an average of $150 were modest in size. Afterpay would adjust its risk settings in Australia so that the first of its four 25 per cent instalments was paid at the time of the purchase, leaving users to make just three more repayments.

Retailers, however, were staring into the abyss, and urged Afterpay to go ahead with its annual Afterpay Day sales event, which was to take place over two days, to help stir up sales amid the nail-biting volatility.

'We believe it's important that we continue to support our merchants who are rapidly looking to increase their online exposure in the current environment and will redirect a portion of our existing budget's marketing spend for this purpose,' Eisen wrote in the letter, and he reminded shareholders that 75 per cent of Afterpay's sales were from online purchases. As it turned out, COVID-19 meant ecommerce was about to get a jab in the arm.

• • •

Anthony Eisen's letter was lost in one of the most eventful days in Australian finance history. In a few short hours, the Reserve Bank had crossed a Rubicon, dropping official interest rates to their lowest level possible while embarking on a bond-buying program. It opened up a $90 billion funding line, known as a Term Funding Facility, which would be made available to the banks.

The Australian dollar had plunged below 60 US cents only to recover, while banking shares fell 7 per cent to post–global financial crisis lows. Treasury, meanwhile, announced a $15 billion emergency fund for non-bank financiers of households and small businesses. Australia and New Zealand had shut their borders to prevent the virus from entering. Qantas, Australia's national airline, stood down two-thirds of its workforce.

The response from policy-makers was bold and dramatic. It was hailed as a 'Team Australia' moment where the collective wisdom, fortitude and planning of the nation's leadership had stepped up to manage the escalating crisis.

COVID-19 had unsettled the nation, but in late March a large crowd gathered undeterred at Bondi Beach to enjoy an unseasonably hot Sunday afternoon. The authorities had initially feared there was too much panic, but now they worried there wasn't enough. Were people taking the health crisis seriously?

The following Monday, long lines snaked outside the unemployment offices of Australia's inner-city suburbs. A nation that prides itself on its high prosperity was seeing baristas, gym instructors, chefs and other part-time workers in the service economy put their hands out for support. The images of Australians of all ages lining up for welfare benefits elicited comparisons to the lines that had formed along the 'Hungry Mile' near Sydney's CBD during the Great Depression.

The selling continued through the week, stress-testing Australia's multibillion-dollar super funds. For almost 30 years, a cut of workers' wages had flown to them, and been allocated to local and international investments, including shares, bonds and property. Now those flows were in danger of slowing, if not reversing. The sharp fall in the Australian dollar meant the funds were scrambling to find the cash required to appease their derivative counterparties.

Among the most dramatic policy responses of the federal government was to allow Australians to raid their superannuation funds, whose mandated savings were supposed to be locked up until retirement. But those in strife could now draw $10,000 of their pension savings, on either side of 30 June. Money was going to be sucked from the market so that Australians could pay their rent, feed themselves and meet their everyday expenses.

The situation was alarming for lending businesses, and that included the buy now, pay later operators. Zip co-founder Larry Diamond had cut short a holiday in Bali, returning to Sydney to implement 'Operation Blowfish', named after a creature that could lie on the bottom of the ocean for a long time to conserve its energy. He had endured the ravages of the financial crisis as a young banker at Macquarie, and was prepared to cut costs and jobs to save the company. The sector prepared to use its goodwill to lobby for support and access to government programs. They were certain they'd need it. In the United States, the Australian founders of Quadpay contemplated mothballing their start-up and heading home.

In another remarkable week, a tense stand-off was brewing between the nation's largest retailers and their all-powerful landlords. On 26 March, Solomon Lew, the battle-hardened head of Premier Investments, which owned a range of brands including Just Jeans and kids' stationery store Smiggle, took the 'nuclear option', declaring he would shut all the company's stores for a month and stand down its 9000-strong workforce.

That night, Lew phoned Treasurer Frydenberg in tears, and recounted how the lay-offs had been passed down the chain of command. Premier would not pay rent to its landlords, the largest being Scentre Group, which operated the Westfield shopping centres. An all-out battle for survival had begun.

Pressure was mounting on the Coalition government to follow the lead of other countries, such as the United Kingdom, to announce a wage subsidy program. The long Centrelink lines had revealed the agency could not cope with the task of getting money into the hands of those who needed it. But Morrison and Frydenberg were reluctant to spend big. It was simply not in their party's DNA.

But the following Monday, the $130 billion JobKeeper program was announced. Frydenberg had consulted the government's debt agency, the Australian Office of Financial Management, and the Reserve Bank and was confident the global bond market would stump up the funding it needed. The program provided companies with $1500 a fortnight to be passed on to each staff member who had been stood down as a result of the lockdowns. The Coalition, which had long pitched itself as more fiscally responsible than its Labor opposition while preaching about the dangers of government debt and budget deficits, had crossed its own Rubicon.

The policy was a major turning point in the crisis. Confidence was instantaneously lifted. Economists overloaded with information surmised that household incomes would be materially higher even than before the crisis. For Afterpay and other buy now, pay later businesses, that was undeniably good news.

Although Afterpay Day in 2020 was meant to mark a moment of solidarity among retailers, it actually helped birth an online retail boom. Stuck at home and in need of retail therapy, many Australians tried buying things online for the first time.

In the big investment firms, risk-averse bank analysts who doubted the viability of Afterpay's model were finally gaining the upper hand in their long-running intellectual stoush with their tech peers. This was the crisis that would test Afterpay.

At boutique funds-management firm Firetrail, 29-year-old Eleanor Swanson had tried for months to convince the firm's investment committee to buy into Afterpay, with some success. Swanson had been a junior analyst at Macquarie's high-conviction investment unit, which had defected in 2018 under Patrick Hodgens to create their own fund.

Swanson used Afterpay for her own online shopping—not because she needed the credit, but because it was simpler to use than a credit card. But she faced obstacles in winning over the investment committee. The retail analysts weren't convinced that merchants were willing to give up 4 per cent of their already thin margins. The banking analysts, meanwhile, worried about rising loan losses eating into Afterpay's capital base, forcing it to raise more money at the worst time. Afterpay was also fending off a growing army of competitors, which they believed would inevitably erode that margin.

Swanson, however, stood her ground on all fronts. Afterpay's dominance was growing, and she believed it had a better and more dynamic handle on credit risk than the banks. In early 2019, she'd convinced one of Firetrail's funds to buy into Afterpay at around $20. Her pitch at the time was that it was a $56 stock. Her models had suggested it was worth even more, but she was wary of startling her colleagues, who already thought it was too expensive.

When the pandemic hit, Afterpay shares got a lot cheaper. On 20 March, Swanson arranged a call with Eisen and Molnar, who detailed how much cash Afterpay had to withstand a crisis. Afterpay had an additional $400 million of cash in its balance sheet, they said, while $270 million was posted with the banks as part of their loan agreements. All up, Afterpay had about $800 million of equity.

Swanson felt that the fears about Afterpay's desperate need to raise capital were exaggerated. She convinced the Firetrail team to buy more in one of the funds at $11.85.

There was, however, apprehension about adding to the position amid such anxiety about what a pandemic would do to the income of Afterpay's customers. The market's message was that this model was facing an existential threat, and not everyone was willing to ignore it.

On 23 March, Afterpay shares dropped further, to below $9. In six harrowing weeks, they had fallen 76 per cent. Eisen, speaking to global investors, felt their widespread panic. For some of Afterpay's early investors, the plunge was too much to bear. It was on that day that Troy Harry, whose shareholdings predated the creation of Afterpay, decided to sell his shares. He loved the company, but was fearful of where the world was headed. Harry had made 40 times his initial investment. The risk of losing it all was too much.

But that evening the markets turned. The US Federal Reserve rolled out a series of measures to pump the financial market and the real economy with funds, pledging to begin buying corporate bonds via several programs. Buying private-sector debt was a line the central bank had been reluctant to cross, but drastic times called for drastic measures. The signal was that the authorities would backstop, to the extent they could, the cost and quantum of debt provided to private enterprise. The system was liquid, if not solvent.

As the selling was exhausted, share markets mounted a recovery. First, pension funds bought shares as they sought to rebalance their portfolios. And then, slowly, bored bargain hunters who had been confined to their homes nibbled at the market via online trading.

The fears that Afterpay was about to unravel appeared unfounded, or at the very least premature. If anything, the lockdown was fuelling a rise in online shopping, and the income boom from wage subsidies was accelerating its growth. Afterpay would not be asphyxiated by the crisis; on the contrary, it had been pumped full of oxygen.

On 14 April, the company confirmed as much, reporting that sales over the three months had topped $2.6 billion, almost double the previous period. 'We have not experienced a material deterioration in loss performance indicators—year to date—however it is still early,' Afterpay said. Relief was palpable: its shares surged 30 per cent, one of the biggest ever one-day gains for the stock. The result was encouraging, even if Afterpay and analysts alike were reserving judgement, given the extraordinary environment.

'We're in a period unlike any other,' Eisen told an analysts' briefing. 'We're managing through this period so we emerge with the firepower to continue our accelerated growth plan. I feel good about the way we've been able to continue operating.'

Some old shareholders bulked up their positions. Alex Waislitz began snapping up Afterpay shares at prices of around $10 to $11. He had every faith in the company that he said had 'withstood all sorts of challenges' to expand internationally.[8]

The share price was now on a sounder footing. But there was a hidden force propping it up: traders at Goldman Sachs had been given instructions to buy Afterpay shares for a large client. By Friday, 1 May, Goldman had bought $300 million of Afterpay shares at an average purchase price of $22.63.

In New South Wales, the health authorities felt they had got a handle on the crisis after nearly six weeks of hard lockdowns, and restrictions were being eased. That Friday, for the first time, families could venture into other homes. For Jewish families, like Eisen's and Molnar's, which had broken thousands of years of tradition by not gathering for the Passover feast, the relaxed restrictions meant they could celebrate the Sabbath with their extended family.

But at 7 pm, the moment they were saying the prayers over bread and wine, big news was breaking. Chinese internet giant Tencent had just gone 'substantial' in Afterpay. That meant it had acquired more than 5 per cent of the company's outstanding shares; under Australian share-market rules, a disclosure was required.

A 'substantial shareholder' notice was published, followed by an Afterpay press release 23 minutes later. Eisen and Molnar said the investment would provide an 'opportunity to learn from one of the world's most successful digital platform businesses', and they pointed to the 'potential to collaborate', including in technology and future payment options.

Tencent provided a comment via chief strategy officer James Mitchell, a former Goldman Sachs banker, who complimented Afterpay's 'customer centric, interest-free approach as well as its integrated retail presence and ability to add significant value for its merchant base'.

There was speculation that Tencent's arrival had been opportunistic and made by stealth. But the coordinated press release suggested an alliance of sorts. Afterpay's success had not gone unnoticed by Big Tech. The company had been in dialogue with the likes of Tencent and Japan's Softbank, which had invested aggressively in promising tech plays.

But it was no coincidence that Tencent had found itself investing alongside the Tiger Cubs. The Chinese tech giant also became a savvy investor in both private and public technology companies, and had a stake in Epic Games, the maker of the smash hit video game *Fortnite*. In 2017, it took a 5 per cent stake in Tesla. The man overseeing Tencent's portfolio was Mitchell, who was close to the Tiger Cubs from his Goldman Sachs days. He often shared information and ideas about trends, start-ups and investment opportunities with the various Tiger Cub founders.

Tencent also had an astronomical advantage: access to 1.2 billion users through its Chinese communications and payments platform WeChat. It operated Tenpay, which allowed users to transfer funds through WeChat, as well as WeBank, which connected individuals and SMEs to banks and other financial institutions. It had also been developing an instalment product called Fenfu. WeChat allowed Tencent to run experiments on what worked and what didn't—

it was an immensely powerful real-world laboratory in which new ideas could be validated.

Analysts salivated over the prospect of Afterpay expanding into China. While the chances that China's giant payment platforms, including Alipay and JD, would integrate with a foreign buy now, pay later provider were slim, *Stocks Down Under* said there were 'opportunities for foreign BNPL players to partner with some of the other Chinese online malls, such as Pinduoduo, Vipshop, and Little Red Book, where we think that the BNPL service is less adopted by shoppers. Given the size and continuing expansion of the Chinese e-Commerce market, even just scratching the surface of the smaller Chinese online marketplaces will bring material upsides to a BNPL provider.'[9]

Afterpay holders tipped out some extra wine in celebration. But the announcement was nothing short of a nightmare for the short-sellers who had borrowed and sold 9 million Afterpay shares in the hope they could buy them back at a lower price. They were in need of a stiffer drink. The timing of the release, after Friday's market close, left them stranded. They spent the weekend certain they'd book large losses, but uncertain just how big they would be. Collectively, over $350 million of Afterpay shares had been shorted. A bloodbath was inevitable as they scrambled for cover.

And scramble they did. Afterpay popped almost 25 per cent on the Monday, as it edged back toward $40. By the end of the week, hedge funds had bought back some 2 million shares. By the end of May, Afterpay had hit $50 for the first time, and a month later it had hit $60. It was now a $15 billion business.

Afterpay's staff and management switched to working from home. Anthony Eisen was occasionally sighted in his Mercedes doing the morning coffee run near his house in Brighton, a bayside suburb south of Melbourne's CBD. The lockdown allowed him to spend more time with his wife, Samantha, and his three daughters after five frenetic years.

Nick and Gabi Molnar were expecting their second child in August, so they had returned from the United States, which was being ravaged by the virus, to be closer to family. This made it tougher for Nick to manage Afterpay's US staff, who were becoming restless as COVID-19 spread like wildfire. Then the country erupted after the killing by police of George Floyd, which had triggered massive Black Lives Matter protests. In mid-June, Molnar, Eisen and the Afterpay board dialled in to a briefing, where staff in San Francisco demanded that Afterpay support the movement by ensuring its US workforce become more diverse.

'The US is obviously going through a difficult time at the moment,' Molnar said. 'We have people in the business who are vocal about what they expect . . . It became very clear our team in the US wanted to have a conversation. They want to know who [we] are appointing for diversity and inclusion.'[10]

• • •

Afterpay's share price recovery had been extraordinary, and was predicated on the online boom. In just six months the company's value had doubled—but only after it had stared into the abyss after falling 75 per cent. In June alone, Afterpay gained 40 per cent. Molnar and Eisen had amassed fortunes larger than their wildest dreams could have allowed, but it had been a white-knuckle ride. In mid-February their individual stakes topped out at $800 million but within a month $600 million of that was wiped off. On 3 June 2020, the Afterpay share price topped $50. That meant Molnar and Eisen each owned shares worth $1 billion. The 30-year-old Nick Molnar became Australia's youngest self-made billionaire. When Atlassian's Cannon-Brookes hit the billionaire club in 2014, he was 34 years old, and co-founder Scott Farquhar was 33. Afterpay's run was not an isolated event. Share markets had mounted a recovery as 'new economy' and work-from-home stocks surged well beyond their pre-COVID levels. Australian Bureau of Statistics retail data showed e-commerce sales were 60 per cent higher in April compared to the same month a year earlier. A similar dynamic was playing out in the United States, where PayPal shares were also on a tear, up 50 per cent by the end of June from their lows in March.

The pandemic had also unleashed a new force into the stock market that had been missing since the last tech boom: the day trader. In all past episodes of market crashes, generations of traders nursing crushing losses swore off the stock market. But for the 'corona generation', it was their siren. Stuck at home, idle and with stimulus cash to play with, millennials were dabbling in the market. In the United States, the Robinhood mobile trading app, which allowed users to trade commission-free, made it cheap to speculate on stocks. The rise of social media allowed day traders with limited capital to amalgamate and form vigilante mobs akin to decentralised hedge funds.

As the market boomed, the retail army gathered on Facebook and Reddit to share tips. They'd anointed their own antiheroes, such as 'Davey Day Trader'. Dave Portnoy had switched from offering sports betting tips to trading on the market. He'd exploded in the mainstream when he called trading 'the easiest game there is' and he mocked Warren Buffet: 'I'm the new breed. I'm the new generation. There's nobody who can argue that Warren Buffett is better at the stock market than I am right now. I'm better than he is. That's a fact.'[11]

In Australia, the same ingredients were in place. Millennials and Gen Xers of both sexes gravitated towards online forums on Reddit and Facebook. A new counterculture of self-assured trading was being fostered online. They had no interest in Boomer stocks or Boomer wisdom.

The sector of the most unbridled speculation was buy now, pay later. The day traders thought they'd missed the Afterpay ride. So the rocket to board was Zip, which had become the most traded stock on CommSec, the dominant retail trading platform, owned by the Commonwealth Bank.

'Z1p your f\*\*cking spacesuits up and give your wife's boyfriend one more kiss on the lips because we're going to the MOON today boys,' one poster on Reddit told his followers.

While day traders were attempting to ramp up Zip's stock price, its co-founder Larry Diamond tapped Sydney connections in New York to announce a transformative deal. On 2 June, Zip said it would acquire the rest of Quadpay by issuing scrip representing 23 per cent of Zip, in a deal worth $403 million. Zip already had a 14 per cent stake in Quadpay after buying New Zealand–based PartPay in 2019, which had a strategic holding in Quadpay after supplying its technology platform.

Diamond knew the Quadpay founders well: Brad Lindenberg and Adam Ezra had also attended Moriah College and, as he drew up the initial plans for Zip in late 2012, Diamond had worked in a Double Bay office on the same floor as Lindenberg, and had worked with Ezra at Macquarie.

Quadpay had surged to 1.5 million customers, 3500 merchants and $1 billion annualised transaction volumes—and those numbers were accelerating. Its virtual card technology allowed it to be used at any retailer that accepted a Visa card, giving it wider acceptance than Afterpay, which had to sign up individual merchants. Klarna had been the first to adopt virtual cards and was seeing its US numbers soar on the back of it, while Affirm was also pushing for ubiquity via an open system that allowed customers to 'shop anywhere'.

When Zip shares resumed trading, they surged 39 per cent. 'Afterpay has enjoyed a significant re-rating and growth uplift from USA and overseas expansion, and this is the playbook for investors with Quadpay and the US now coming into the envelope,' said Shaw and Partners analyst Jonathon Higgins.

Afterpay was also seeing renewed enthusiasm among research analysts. In early July, analysts at Citi more than doubled its share price target from $27.10 to $64.25 after considering the Tencent investment and rapid growth in the United States and the United Kingdom, where customers of its Clearpay subsidiary had hit 1 million. Soon, Royal Bank of Canada analysts doubled their target from $29 to $60. There was a whiff of a deal in the air. Afterpay's bankers encouraged the company to hit up the market for funds while it was running hot.

The share price recovery did provide a window of opportunity for Afterpay and its founders. On 7 July, the company announced a $1 billion deal. Afterpay would issue $650 million of shares to institutions and a further $150 million to smaller shareholders via a share purchase plan. Molnar and Eisen would each sell 2.05 million shares, the same amount they disposed of in June 2019. This time the proceeds were three times larger, at $94 million each.

In the depths of March, Afterpay had said it didn't need the money. But even its harshest critics agreed this deal made sense. As a marker of how unusual it was, UBS upgraded its stubbornly low price target of $25 to $27, because the new equity was, unusually, 'accretive to shareholders'.

The unwritten law of corporate finance is that it is always cheaper for a company to raise debt—that is, to borrow money—than it is to raise equity, which means giving up future profits by sharing ownership. Equity is riskier than debt, and therefore should cost more. But the market had become so optimistic about Afterpay's future that it was prepared to provide funds at a cheaper cost than debt-holders. The mere act of issuing new equity at the price it was available to them made the company more valuable in their models.

The founder's sell-down also made sense after the harrowing velocity with which their paper wealth had dropped and then recovered. Even if they had the fortitude to endure that again, their families might not. Molnar and Eisen had attained billionaire status on paper. The sell-down meant they banked an enormous fortune.

The headlines shouted that 'Afterpay founders run for the exit'. But to follow the money didn't apply to Afterpay, whose shares marched higher even as the founders cut their stakes. The pair still retained just under 7 per cent (worth $1.1 billion) each in the company.

While Molnar and Eisen's share sales tended to attract negative attention, other tech CEOs had lobbied for rule changes to make it easier for them to sell shares. Disclosure requirements for insider buy and sell transactions had been introduced so that smaller shareholders could be informed by the actions of those who had a grasp on the inner workings of a listed company, even if all required information had already been disclosed.

Atlassian's Cannon-Brookes and Farquhar didn't have the same problem, as they operated under US rules. These allowed founders and insiders to inform the market of how many shares they would sell and over what period, rather than selling via large blocks that had to be carefully negotiated and disclosed at a point in time. Each year, in May, they disclose that they'll sell 2 million of their shares. The trades are handled by broker algorithms that net them each about US$8 million a week. And given the amount of shares they own, they can keep selling at that pace for the next 30 or so years.

Richard White, the founder and CEO of WiseTech Global, one of the ASX's other large tech companies, called on the ASX to adopt a similar rule. He was joined by other venture investors, who argued that adopting the US rule would encourage more founders to list in Australia. The debate was highly controversial. Australia's share market was a source of abundant and cheap capital even with its apparently draconian laws—and perhaps because of them.

It wasn't just Afterpay's founders who were selling stock. On 6 August 2020, a substantial shareholder notice was filed by Lone Pine Capital, the US$8 billion Tiger Cub hedge fund. Lone Pine, alongside three other Tiger Cubs—Coatue, Woodson and Tiger Global—had amassed a large position in Afterpay. In the depths of March's sell-down, Lone Pine had invested $27 million in Afterpay. That had halved in value in a matter of days, but Lone Pine had held on, and sold out now for around $70 a share, netting a quickfire $56 million profit.

While some of the smart money was selling out, the animal spirits were stirring among brokers as tech stocks entered melt-up territory. The race was on among the brokers to come up with the most bullish forecasts for Afterpay. Morgan Stanley's Andrei Stadnik was the first to slap a three-figure price tag on the stock. His upgrade to a $101 price target represented a near tripling of his previous $36 level. 'While [the] valuation seems challenging, we think it is warranted by the global buy now pay later platform that Afterpay is building out,' he wrote.

The $101 price target required Morgan Stanley's usually conservative analyst to look at the stock through a bullish lens. Stadnik estimated Afterpay would generate $520 million of revenue, which would grow to $885 million. The $100 price tag was more than 30 times his forecast revenue, and valued Afterpay at almost $30 billion. But he said that was reasonable compared to other ecommerce peers, such as Canada's Shopify, which developed software for retailers to sell online, and payments-processing firm Adyen in the Netherlands, which were priced at 38 to 45 times next year's revenues.

Morgan Stanley didn't expect Afterpay to make a profit until 2022, when its revenues were forecast to double to over $1 billion. Either way, Australian investors would have to come to the party. 'We think APT is under-owned by Australian institutional investors, and we have seen other Australian businesses, successfully expanding offshore, sustain premium multiples,' Stadnik wrote.[12]

But stockbroker Marcus Padley wasn't impressed by the feverish broker reports, which he said were all about winning business rather than analysing businesses. '"Get in the game" would be the instruction from the corporate department to the analyst, from the CEO to the analyst, from the dealers to the analyst,' he wrote in a *Livewire* post. 'Print that click bait research! If they don't they will miss out on some of the best money-making opportunities brokers have had in years. Making trades in a high-volume frenzy, and raising capital on the back of flying share prices.

'This is not about getting it right, it's about having research that attracts attention. It's about attracting trades and it's about endearing yourself to companies that are almost certainly going to be doing further capital raisings at these extraordinary share prices. The reports were about being at the table to pitch deals to management,' Padley argued. 'It's worth millions in corporate fees. But you won't get the deal with a $36 target price. You won't get the deal saying it's expensive. You won't get the deal saying sell. It's a game.'

Padley was speaking on behalf of a large class of bewildered investors, attempting to explain how the market had got so far ahead of itself. 'A Porsche is a great car, just as Afterpay is a great company, but you wouldn't pay $1,000,000 for a Porsche. You also don't pay the eventual price for a house that is going to be built, upfront. Until it is finished and inspected there are risks.' Padley compared After-pay's share price surge to the run-up in miner BHP as the China-led resource boom took its share price from $7 to $43. The difference is that journey took five years as its prospects were validated. The market wasn't waiting with Afterpay. 'Sometimes it "Trusteth too much" and too soon,' he concluded.[13]

The Afterpay bears may have baulked at the increasingly bullish take of brokers, but the share price rise had the potential to be a self-fulfilling prophecy. The higher it went, the more access to capital Afterpay had, which would enable it to realise and accelerate its growth ambitions. And the faster it grew, the greater its chances of becoming an entrenched and indispensable player in payments.

In fact, the share market had shown a willingness to ascribe more value to Afterpay revenues the bigger it got, as its model was validated by more investors. As a report by *Stocks Down Under* pointed out, when Afterpay generated $100 million of sales in 2018, the market was only prepared to pay less than eight times that amount. The following year its sales increased to $250 million and the market paid close to fifteen times. In 2020, sales of $500 million were worth 30 times that. The combination of rising sales and expanding multiples put a proverbial rocket under the share price.[14]

But supporters would have to stomach another round of volatility, driven by the emergence of new competition in the United States, while consumer groups were again raising their heads above the parapet.

Max Levchin, who co-founded PayPal alongside Peter Thiel and Elon Musk, had created Affirm in 2012 out of his incubator, HVF. In early 2014, he decided to make Affirm his full-time job. It had partnered with more than a thousand US retailers by July 2017, the company said. But its product was built on charging customers interest; its pitch centred on better transparency on charges, and the fact that it didn't charge late fees. Rates could be high, between 10 per cent and 30 per cent annual interest rates, but customers were told exactly how much extra they would pay to buy a product today, instead of saving up for several months and buying it later.

'Our goal is to be the app on your home screen for all of your financial needs,' Levchin had told a profile in *Racked* magazine in November 2017. 'We are starting by reinventing credit because we believe it is fundamentally broken. You need not look any further than the fact that credit card companies made more profit in fees last year than in interest income.'[15]

After Klarna had copied Afterpay's 'Pay in 4' construct in 2018, leading to a surge in customers in 2019, Affirm belatedly decided it would offer the same product. On 22 July 2020, it announced it was moving into the short-term, interest-free lending game. It had struck an exclusive deal with Shopify, the Canadian ecommerce giant that had more than US$1.5 billion in annual revenue, to power its Shop

Pay instalments program in the United States, which is set to launch in 2021. Affirm had experimented with 'zero-interest loans' with some of its merchants in 2017 and 2018, but this deal was belated recognition that it was Afterpay's product construct that customers were flocking to.

The next month, on 31 August, PayPal revealed its own four-instalments offering. That prompted more concerns that Afterpay would be forced to cut its merchant fees, given that PayPal, which had 190 million active accounts in the United States alone, was offering instalments within its standard pricing of 2.9 per cent of sales. PayPal had already offered an interest-free product for purchases up to six months called PayPal Credit, originally known as Bill Me Later, which Eisen and Molnar had studied as they were putting together the original plan for Afterpay. Like Affirm, it was now morphing its design to home in on the desire for short-term repayments. The market response was vicious: Afterpay shares fell almost 20 per cent in two trading days, while Sezzle and Zip, which Citi downgraded to a 'sell', sank almost 30 per cent.

Molnar was asked about the rising competition a few months later by New York University professor Scott Galloway. He told him that fintech companies that had started with a traditional finance offering and that made money from revolving credit books that charged customers interest would struggle to win trust despite new interest-free offerings.

'You have this hybrid world where you have competitors who are trying to produce an Afterpay-like product as a customer-acquisition channel to cross-sell them credit because that is the higher-margin solution,' Molnar said on Galloway's podcast. 'That is where people who did start life doing credit checks, hitting people's credit files—they just create a very different relationship with the customer and their existing business models [that] makes it difficult, in a pure way, to come into our market.'[16]

Afterpay was also facing mounting criticism about its late fees. On 27 August, the week before the PayPal bombshell, Afterpay released its full-year financial results for 2020, showing underlying sales more than doubling over the year to more than $11 billion, delivering total income of $503 million. Of this, just under $70 million, or 14 per cent of its income, came from customer late fees, which were up 49 per cent in dollar terms over the year. Afterpay had successfully shifted arguments away from late fees—which were falling as a proportion of overall revenue, to 14 per cent from almost 19 per cent a year earlier—but there was now no denying that it was a material source of revenue.

Consumer groups jumped on the late fees the day after the results. The Consumer Action Law Centre's Gerard Brody said ASIC needed to take a position on how buy now, pay later providers should be regulated in its report on the sector, which was expected to be released before the end of the year. Afterpay's low default rates 'don't tell us about the broader outcomes for consumers', he said. 'Some people tend to prioritise repayments to Afterpay over other costs, even housing and utilities—because they get denied access to the app if they do not. The business model severely influences consumer behaviour in this harmful way and low default rates hide this impact.'[17]

Amid the market carnage, Afterpay put its foot down on its global expansion, announcing on 24 August, three days before releasing its full-year results, that it had bought Spanish credit provider Pagantis in a deal worth €50 million ($82.4 million). Pagantis, which had 1400 active merchants and about 150,000 active customers, offered buy now, pay later services in Spain, Italy and France, with plans to operate in Portugal.

But there was even better news for investors at home, as Senator Andrew Bragg tabled his committee's interim report. For Afterpay, it was a godsend: the report backed self-regulation, under an industry code of conduct that was being developed by the Australian Finance

Industry Association. Michael Saadat was leading Afterpay's engagement on the document.

Even more encouragingly, it also put regulators on notice not to put start-ups such as Afterpay into a straitjacket. 'Although it is appropriate that ASIC and the RBA undertake reviews into various regulatory issues, the policy in this space must be set by the parliament,' the report said.[18]

The Hayne Royal Commission had criticised regulators for being too meek; now policy-makers were concerned they would overcompensate. The desire in Canberra for regulators to stick to enforcing the law rather than creating policy on the run would provide a strong tailwind that propelled Afterpay into 2021. As the economy began to recover from COVID-19, Bragg had left the regulators in no doubt that he wanted politicians and government departments, and not 'independent' regulators, to take responsibility for industry policy.

Soon that would become the official position of the government, but not everybody was on board with the Bragg committee's direction. Consumer groups argued that ongoing scrutiny of Afterpay remained crucial, especially given its unrelenting growth. Even some members of the Liberal Party were raising red flags. At a hearing of the House of Representatives Economics Committee on 4 September, two days after the interim report was released, Queensland Liberal MP Julian Simmonds said Afterpay was popular in his household, but 'it does scare the bejesus out of me, in terms of the unsecured nature of the credit and how much people are looking into people's actual capacity to pay'.[19]

A week later, the deputy chair of the economics committee, Andrew Leigh, a member of the Labor Party, said findings that large numbers of buy now, pay later customers were going into overdraft could be due to fears they would be cut off from fintech services. 'It's critical we look at the whole picture, and account for any negative spill-overs these services might have on other aspects of their customers' lives. With household budgets squeezed, lenders have a responsibility to ensure that they're not putting customers into financial jeopardy,' Leigh said.[20]

He also raised concerns about merchant fees. Technology should be driving transaction costs down, and Leigh, an economist, said it was not optimal for society if 5 per cent of the costs of goods was being spent to facilitate the transactions. 'The wedge between retailers and consumers should be as low as it can be, and new technology should be reducing transaction costs. I get worried when I see technology is increasing them,' he said.[21]

In the United Kingdom, consumer advocates were also getting on Afterpay's back. As the coronavirus and prolonged lockdowns amid Brexit confusion crippled the British economy, the Financial Conduct Authority said in September 2020 that its interim chief executive, Christopher Woolard—who had taken over from Andrew Bailey when he became governor of the Bank of England, replacing Mark Carney—would review the regulation of consumer credit. A UK consumer group said it had found that 24 per cent of buy now, pay later users were spending more than they had planned to—a similar finding to ASIC's a few years before.

Afterpay shareholders had by now become accustomed to regulatory scrutiny and extensive musings about the business's apparently exorbitant valuation. But in every instant, a decision to sell was marked with regret. If insider selling was a busted signal to get out, another tried-and-tested warning sign had also proved premature: chief financial officer departures.

Steven Johnson, the head of Australian value fund Forager, had declared on social media that he would always sell if a CFO resigned unexpectedly—whatever the reason. He'd been caught out too many times by revelations of bad news from the replacement. And so when Afterpay's Luke Bortoli resigned as CFO on 24 September, having cashed in $60 million of shares, some investors got anxious. His replacement was Rebecca Lowde, an unfamiliar name. Departures had become commonplace at Afterpay: earlier in the year, company secretary Chris Stevens had resigned, while chief technology officer Jon Donoghue left in April to join NAB's digital bank UBank as chief information officer.

The perpetual exodus of senior staff was a lingering red flag as many doubters turned into believers. The rapid run-up in the share price made mid-ranking staffers millionaires, and more senior executives richer than they'd ever dreamed possible. Early retirement was an enticing option. Afterpay's huge growth, from a small start-up into a major payments player that the market believed was worth ten times more than centuries-old conglomerates, meant roles changed too rapidly.

On his way out, Bortoli defended Afterpay's sky-high share price, which he said was justified by the large gross merchant value the business generated. It was the growth in these metrics that had allowed US tech investors to successfully bet on Uber, Facebook, Google and Amazon well before they generated a profit.

Scott Galloway, who a year earlier had questioned whether Afterpay could survive an onslaught of competition, was also changing his tune. 'I thought Afterpay was a good company, I didn't think it was strategically weak, I just thought it was overvalued,' he told Australian media on a call to promote the Sohn Hearts & Minds charity conference. 'With a company like that I thought that other players, whether it's Amazon or Square, would get into that business and it would face well-funded, deep-pocketed competitors. To their credit, [Afterpay] have executed really well. Good for them. We need more companies like them to innovate and maintain that momentum . . . I was wrong on Afterpay, and time will tell.'[22]

Short-sellers squeezed by the Tencent trade and the relentless march higher threw in the towel. 'We learnt a lesson,' Ben McGarry said. 'It doesn't matter what the cash flows are or whether there are corporate governance [issues], red flags or regulatory uncertainty. If the product is amazing and there's a fan club in the user base and the shareholder base, you want to be very careful.'[23]

The performance table said Australian institutional investors that didn't own Afterpay were wrong, too. Top-ranked Australian share funds Solaris, Alphinity and Pendal included an all-too-familiar line: that not owning Afterpay was its single costliest decision in August. It would become even more costly in the fourth quarter of calendar 2020, as the share price resumed its march higher.

• • •

On 20 October 2020, Afterpay hit a milestone that even its biggest believers never thought they would see—a $100 share price. While analyst calls predicting this had appeared fanciful, now Afterpay was there.

In its most important strategic announcement in a frantic year, Afterpay provided its first indication that it would expand into banking services by offering deposits and budgeting tools in a separate app through an innovative deal with Westpac.

At 8.31 am, Westpac put a release over the ASX platform that sent waves through the banking establishment: Australia's second-largest bank said Afterpay would become its first client for a new 'banking-as-a-service' platform. Afterpay issued its own ASX release eleven minutes later, confirming it would be offering deposit and transaction accounts to its more than 3 million Australian customers, using Westpac's licence—and might look to do something similar for customers in its global markets. Afterpay Money would be the business's first foray beyond the simple instalments plan.

'In deepening our relationship with our customers, we will gather greater insights into how they prefer to manage their finances and better understand their savings goals,' Eisen said. 'This will allow us to assist them to budget more effectively and avoid debt traps. This is clearly just the beginning as we explore this opportunity globally.'

The news that Afterpay would team up with Westpac lifted the stock on a day the broader market was down. Earlier that week, Westpac had dumped its stake in Zip for a tidy profit. It was changing horses. The deal was the start of Afterpay's 'march into receiving fees and revenues outside of merchants and late fees' as it 'looks to build engagement with consumers outside of pay in four, and potentially different revenue models', Shaw's analyst Jonathon Higgins told clients. After Klarna and Affirm had adopted Afterpay's product, now Afterpay was shifting towards the model of Klarna, which took deposits in Europe and said it was open to becoming a bank in the United States, although in Afterpay's case, it would leave the regulated parts of banking to Westpac.

Investors Mutual marked Afterpay's $100 moment with a note questioning whether the market had become detached from fundamentals. The company now had a higher value than industrial companies Investors Mutual favoured, such as global logistics giant Brambles, which rented pallets for goods to be transported to and from warehouses, and explosives manufacturer Orica. 'Afterpay has become a poster child for the momentum-type growth-obsessed phenomena currently driving share markets,' the fund manager said.

Afterpay, according to Investors Mutual's Anton Tagliaferro and Daniel Moore, was not profitable. And even the modest $25 million profit forecast in 2021 was likely to be pushed out as it invested to grow. But Afterpay's $29 billion price tag, they said, suggested the company's future profits would need to reach $1 billion—as 29 to 30 times profits was a reasonable valuation for a growing company. By their maths, Afterpay would need more than 40 million customers and a market share of a third of all payments. 'This is a big leap of faith, given the credit, competition, and regulatory risks involved in getting to that scale,' they wrote. As far as Investors Mutual was concerned, we were back in 1999. 'Many investors appear less concerned about the underlying fundamentals or valuations of many companies, instead focusing on anything with "blue sky" potential, particularly in the technology sector.'

Simon Mawhinney of Allan Gray, another Australian-based value investing fund, offered a similar perspective on investment website *Livewire*. For Afterpay to justify a $30 billion valuation, it would need to generate $3 billion of profits in a mature state. Given it earned 2.5 per cent per sale, Afterpay would have to process $264 billion of sales. That, Mawhinney explained, was a pretty ambitious number. If the addressable market for consumer purchases was 5 per cent of GDP, and the combined GDP of the countries Afterpay operated in was US$33.7 trillion, its universe of opportunity was between US$1.7 trillion and US$2.4 trillion. A $264 billion figure was 11 per cent of that addressable market. To hit that target, Afterpay would have to process three times as many sales as Amex and as many as Mastercard, the number-two player to Visa.

Mawhinney concluded that it 'would take world domination and the toppling of massive incumbents who are unlikely to watch from the sidelines. And even then a long-term investment in Afterpay today might just be okay and nowhere near as high returning as investors have enjoyed over recent years.'

But as the run continued, a decision not to own shares in Afterpay proved difficult to maintain. One of the few Australian institutional investors with a meaningful presence on the register was First Sentier, the rebranded Colonial First State. The fund manager, one of Australia's oldest and largest, had accumulated a large position after its analysts determined that the Afterpay model was more scalable and capital-efficient than the stock market appreciated.

At Firetrail, Eleanor Swanson's success in adding Afterpay to the portfolio had helped lift the company's numbers, and demonstrated the importance of diversity of thought in investment firms.

Afterpay's march higher also forced the hand of one its longest-standing shareholders. The company's institutional fund managers, constrained by portfolio limits to ensure they're not overexposed to a single company, had constantly been forced to sell their shares as they rose relative to others. And as Afterpay graduated from a micro cap to a small cap to a mid cap to a large cap, specialist fund managers were prohibited from buying.

Eley Griffiths and David Allingham had gone as far as they could on the journey. In June 2020, they sold out of their last remaining stock, as their mandate prevented them from investing in a company of Afterpay's size. Allingham sent an email to tell Molnar and Eisen, and to wish them the best. He would have to recycle the funds in search of the next Afterpay, but he didn't fancy his chances of ever seeing a company like it again. Within moments, both Molnar and Eisen replied to thank him for his support.

The company had a far less emotional connection with its newer shareholders, which were large, passive, index-tracking funds that simply owned whatever stocks comprised the market. Afterpay was on track for inclusion into the ASX index of the twenty largest companies, and that meant multitrillion-dollar funds such as Blackrock and Vanguard had to accumulate Afterpay shares.

So-called passive funds had grown in popularity as investors—from self-directed investors to enormous sovereign wealth funds—lost faith that the professionals who charged high fees could consistently beat the market. A better option was to pay lower fees and accept the returns of the market indices via the index funds. The net result was a global increase in passively managed funds from US$2.4 trillion a decade ago to US$12 trillion.

But the speed of Afterpay's acceleration up the market capitalisation rankings caught these funds off guard. The sheer size of Afterpay, and its ability to swing, left the likes of Blackrock scrambling to buy shares.

Traders at the big firms had rung the big investment banks to put them on notice that they would buy any large blocks of Afterpay that were up for sale. Vanguard, the multitrillion-dollar index fund giant, had owned 2.1 million Afterpay shares at the end of 2018, and had increased its holding to 7 million shares a year later. By mid-2020, Vanguard owned 9.7 million shares. By the end of the year, it had upped this to 15.7 million. Blackrock, the other index fund titan, had to scramble harder. In the fourth quarter alone it had upped its stake in Afterpay from 4.5 million shares to 14.5 million, spending about $1 billion in the process.

Afterpay's rapid ascent had transformed the share-market index. In doing so, it had confronted Australian investors of all sizes who had been accustomed to buying steady, monopolistic businesses that were compelled by their shareholders to distribute a high share of their profits in the form of tax-advantageous dividends. That had led to years of underinvestment, as favoured blue-chip companies creaked and crumbled.

Had Afterpay's success exposed the conservatism of Australia's institutional investors? Some old market heads compared it to Fortescue Metals Group, led by a divisive founder, Andrew Forrest, which found an ore deposit under the noses of giants BHP and Rio. Forrest's pitch was that he could get the ore to port more cheaply, through rail transport that he would construct. The financing came from a maverick New York investment firm, Leucadia, and the US high-yield bond market. Few Australian institutions gave Forrest a chance in 2006; one analyst even pledged to tie himself to the tracks on the day the first train left the ore site, because it wouldn't happen. But it did happen, and by 2020 Fortescue was a top twenty company, paying out north of $5 billion in dividends to shareholders. Afterpay's rise, rare in the oligopolistic Australian corporate landscape, might once again expose a lack of imagination among Australian institutions.

• • •

The year had been a chaotic and stressful one for the world's stock-pickers, but one in which they could prove their worth. Reputations had been made—and broken.

In late December, *The Wall Street Journal*'s Juliet Chung profiled the hedge funds that had 'earned billions' during the COVID-19 chaos. Among them was a little-known 40-year-old hedge fund manager named Jim Davis. His bets 'against bricks-and-mortar retailers and on e-commerce firms hit pay dirt', helping him to a near 100 per cent return as his fund, Woodson Capital Management, doubled its assets from $675 million to $1.7 billion.[24] Woodson and fellow Tiger Cub Lone Pine had bet on Australia's top stock of the year, as Afterpay tripled in value—and had bet against one of its worst, mall operator Unibail Rodamco Westfield, which had halved. Also profiled was Chase Coleman of Tiger Global, who cautioned investors that it was 'too early to sell the best growth companies'.

The *Financial Times*, meanwhile, reported that Philippe Laffont's Coatue Management had gained 52 per cent, due largely to a bet on Tesla, and another against German payments company Wirecard, which had collapsed as fraudulent activities were exposed by the paper.[25] In just over a year, Coatue's $200 million placement with Afterpay had become worth four times as much.

When Bloomberg[26] compiled its list of top hedge fund earners of 2020, Chase Coleman topped it, raking in US$3 billion in the form of management fees and gains on his investments. Lone Pine's Steve Mandel was the fourth-biggest money earner, growing his personal fortune by US$1.8 billion, while Coatue's Laffont was US$1.7 billion richer, ranking him at sixth. Julian Robertson's Tiger Cubs were roaring on the right side of the market euphoria, thanks in part to Afterpay.

'A bad year for humanity was a wonderful year for the hedge fund elite,' wrote Stephen Taub of *The Institutional Investor*.[27]

# 15

# STANDING DOWN

IF THE INTERIM report of Senator Andrew Bragg's committee didn't send a strong enough message to ASIC and the Reserve Bank about the government's desire to see the buy now, pay later sector supported, then speeches from the treasurer and prime minister as 2020 came to a close made it crystal clear.

And if the speeches weren't enough, another government inquiry—to review the regulatory architecture of the entire payments system, including whether the Reserve Bank should continue to be the primary regulator—would hammer home Canberra's wishes.

As the Reserve Bank probed whether buy now, pay later providers should be able to keep stopping merchants from passing their costs on to customers, Treasury said on 21 October that it wanted to ensure the payments system 'remains fit for purpose and is capable of supporting continued innovation for the benefit of both businesses and consumers'.[1] A new review, which would run alongside the Reserve Bank's own review of payments regulation, was designed to put the RBA back into its box, and it ruffled a few feathers at the top of Martin Place. For Afterpay, it provided an insurance policy in case the payments wonks sided against them.

The Bragg committee's interim report—the first attempt to create a fintech plan for Australia—had been blunt in its assessment that regulators were stepping too far into policy-making. Now Treasury was backing that view up.

'To ensure Australia is well placed to safely leverage the benefits of new technologies, our regulatory architecture must be agile, responsive to technological advances and capable of setting a long-term direction for payments policy in Australia,' an issues paper said. 'It needs to create an environment in which businesses—particularly new entrants—are able to meet regulatory requirements in a straight-forward and streamlined manner, and have the confidence and certainty to invest and develop new forms of payments technologies that are tailored to the needs of end-users.'[2]

Anthony Eisen's testimony to the committee back in February had been heard. 'Fit for purpose' was the mantra.

During the second week of November, word began to circulate that ASIC's second report into the sector, delayed due to COVID-19, had been completed and was ready for public release. Bragg decided to get on the front foot. In a Twitter post on 12 November, he described the report as 'an important test for ASIC which must not stray into policymaking or extensive public commentary'. Bragg's message wasn't subtle. 'I want to see ASIC enforce the law, not pontificate on policy. Certainly I do not want to see ASIC inflict damage on the market which risks undermining innovation and choice.'

The following day, a Friday, ASIC commissioner Sean Hughes, a former banker and lawyer who had also run the financial markets regulator in New Zealand, was a keynote speaker at the annual conference of the Australian Retail Credit Association, which represents the credit card industry. He confirmed the report was indeed ready to be released, and would 'cover some of the harms that we continue to see' with buy now, pay later services.

But he made it clear that the message from the Bragg report had been heard. 'Of course, what government wishes to do in terms of future regulation, if any, of the buy now, pay later sector is a matter for government,' Hughes said. ASIC's job was merely to put forward the facts and provide data to support good policy decisions in future.[3]

On 16 November 2020, ASIC released its long-awaited report. It was three years to the day since 'Street Talk' first reported that Afterpay would come under regulatory scrutiny. The headline findings were, again, alarming: similar to its report of two years earlier, ASIC found that one in five buy now, pay later users was struggling with repayments, while more than 1.1 million transactions in Australia in 2019 had incurred multiple missed payment fees. More sensationally, one in five users had 'cut back on or went without essentials, for example, meals', and half of this group were aged between eighteen and 29.

'Buy now pay later arrangements are clearly popular as a payment method,' ASIC found. 'While working for the majority of users, some consumers are suffering harm.' Despite this, the report contained no recommendations for additional customer protections.[4]

ASIC agreed with the Bragg report's suggestion that it should not be the primary enforcer of standards in the buy now, pay later industry—rather, these should be defined by the industry itself.

The Australian Finance Industry Association was working on a code of conduct, but was finding it tough to get the buy now, pay later operators, who had quite different business models, to agree on proper standards. The date for the code had already been delayed twice. ASIC had criticised a draft version of the code back in June for being too vague in attempts to define the upfront customer assessment process.

Despite its concerns, and the early signs that the industry was struggling to agree on standards, ASIC was now saying that defending consumers from harm was best done via self-regulation. In other words, the industry would be allowed to write its own rules and police itself. ASIC would only get involved if it identified specific problems using its new regulatory tools, the design and distribution obligation and product intervention power. It remained to be seen whether these would be effective.

Afterpay's shares had dropped slightly in the wake of the ASIC report, before the ASX suffered a rare outage when defective Nasdaq software began using incorrect order identification numbers and trading was halted. That afternoon, Afterpay's head of public policy, Damian Kassabgi, was a guest at the UBS Australasia Conference, which was being delivered virtually to the investment bank's clients all over the world. He was interviewed by Tom Beadle, the analyst who had slapped the sell recommendation on Afterpay back in October 2019, and had followed that report up with a series of critical analyses highlighting regulatory and credit risk.

Beadle asked Kassabgi for his views on the ASIC report. Kassabgi described it as 'insightful', given it pointed to the different business models within the sector, and its comparison of outcomes for Afterpay customers compared to traditional credit cards. 'What we are also seeing from this ASIC report is there is increasing alignment between ASIC, the parliament and government in relation to the way the industry should be regulated,' he said. 'They have clearly stated it is not like traditional credit—there is clear acknowledgement of that in the report.'

Concerns that some users were struggling to repay debt were probably related to other buy now, pay later services and not Afterpay, he argued, given its low average order values, and given that some other providers allowed users to revolve debt for a fee, which Afterpay did not. He said the history of the regulation of innovative industries suggested consumer demand for new services could change the regulatory framework. He pointed to Uber, and suggested the same would happen with Afterpay.

'For us, as we go down the path of countries and regulators and governments understanding Afterpay and its innovation in the economy, the question becomes, how do traditional industries actually keep up with the standards new technology is bringing? And the question becomes less about how Afterpay should be regulated, and more how can credit cards meet the standards that some of the buy now, pay later providers are bringing to the market, especially as it comes to consumer fees.'

Afterpay's lobbying had gone to the next level. The pitch was no longer that its offerings should be regulated more actively, but that the industries it aimed to disrupt were the ones who needed stricter policing.

Two days after the ASIC report was released, treasurer Josh Frydenberg kicked off *The Australian Financial Review* Banking & Wealth Summit. Even though Sydney had largely eradicated the coronavirus, the event was being staged in a vast empty room in the International Convention Centre in Darling Harbour, which had lain dormant for most of the year, and broadcast to subscribers. The Treasurer dialled in for a video presentation from his office in Melbourne.

Frydenberg's speech confirmed that the warnings from Andrew Bragg's committee—that regulators should not drift into the domain of the parliament—also reflected the views of the executive government. The public expected regulators to pursue enforcement activities independently of the government, he said, but 'regulators do not carry out their mandates in a vacuum . . . They must pursue their mandates in a manner that is consistent with the will of the parliament. There need to be mechanisms to hold them to account . . . It is the parliament who determines who and what should be regulated. It's the role of regulators to deliver on that intent, not to supplement, circumvent or frustrate it.'

Frydenberg pointed to the COVID-19 recovery, during which the Reserve Bank and other financial regulators had been recognised as being members of 'Team Australia', coming together with the banks to formulate the economy's response plan, which included deferrals of loan repayments for mortgagees and small-business borrowers. Now Frydenberg wanted to ensure that regulators were 'conscious of the environment they are operating in and have the flexibility to respond in a way that simultaneously fulfils their mandate, enhances consumer outcomes and supports rather than hinders the recovery'.

While Phil Lowe may not have been influenced by a Senate committee report, or indeed by a Treasury issues paper, it would be hard for him to ignore such a clear message from the Treasurer, even though the RBA guarded its independence fiercely. Lowe could read the tea leaves.

Two weeks later, on 7 December, Lowe gave a speech to an online forum hosted by the Australian Payments Network, which represented 130 organisations in the crowded payments space. Lowe had spoken to the same event the previous year at the Four Seasons Hotel near Circular Quay, but this year he was speaking to dispersed listeners from his Martin Place office. For Afterpay investors, his message brought early Christmas cheer: buy now, pay later providers would not have to remove their no-surcharge rules, at least in the near term. They could continue to insist that merchants not pass their costs on to customers. It was a tactic he acknowledged could help the upstarts grow against the incumbent card networks, which weren't allowed to stop surcharging.

The buy now, pay later sector had grown fast, Lowe said, but even the largest providers accounted for a small proportion of overall total consumer payments, while new competitors could still put downward pressure on merchant costs. The central bank had there-fore formed a 'preliminary view that the BNPL operators in Australia have not yet reached the point where it is clear that the costs arising from the no-surcharge rule outweigh the potential benefits in terms of innovation'.

The Reserve Bank was leaving the door open to some form of pricing regulation down the track. A case to remove the rules could still be made, if buy now, pay later got bigger—but by how much would depend on the outcome of discussions with industry participants. Lowe said he'd prefer to reach a voluntary agreement, as the bank had done with American Express and PayPal, which had agreed to remove their no-surcharge rules even though they were not formally required to, as Visa and Mastercard had been. The RBA would also 'discuss with the Australian government the best way to address the issue' before making a final call.

At least in the medium term, Afterpay's regulatory battles were finally over. ASIC, AUSTRAC and now the RBA had retreated. The national government had Afterpay's back. And the next day, 8 December, that official support was confirmed by the prime minister himself.

In a speech to the Singapore Fintech Festival, a large talkfest organised by the Monetary Authority of Singapore, which had hosted 60,000 people the previous year and in 2020 was holding the event virtually, Morrison joined a heavy-hitting line-up of speakers, including Microsoft founder Bill Gates, Microsoft boss Satya Nadella, Google CEO Sundar Pichai, Blackrock head Larry Fink and former US treasury secretary Hank Paulson. While Gates and Pichai addressed financial inclusion, Morrison spoke about 'what I believe is the compelling Australian fintech story'. He referred to the 'great work' done by Andrew Bragg and his committee.

Morrison had appointed one of his mentors and close advisers, Peter Verwer, who was based in Singapore, as special envoy to attract talent to Australia, and had included fintech in his mandate. The prime minister told the audience Australia wanted to attract more 'highly skilled people to develop and commercialise the next wave of cutting-edge innovations', and fintech entrepreneurs should consider Australia a place to build their businesses. Fintech was still his happy place. Afterpay was specifically mentioned by Morrison in his speech. Buy now, pay later was 'an Australian innovation', he proclaimed.

• • •

After the COVID-19 roller-coaster, Afterpay finished a tumultuous 2020 triumphantly. With the regulatory risks that had been looming since late 2017 finally removed, Eisen and Molnar enjoyed a more relaxing break than they'd had in years—although Australia's state border closures, following a short-lived re-emergence of the coronavirus in Sydney just before Christmas, forced Eisen to end his Byron Bay holiday early to get back to Victoria so he could avoid a mandatory period of hotel quarantine. Molnar also holidayed in Byron Bay, a fashionable beachside village on the far north coast of New South Wales, with his wife, young daughter and new son, contemplating a return to the United States in 2021.

Eisen was a guest at *The Australian Financial Review*'s Banking & Wealth Summit on 18 November, which Frydenberg had opened with that warning to the regulators. Asked for his views on Canberra's support, Eisen said policy-makers had 'done an excellent job to become informed about the reality of the opportunity, and the reality of talent that exists in this country, and the reasons why technology can be an export industry'.

'It's never been about avoiding regulation or not having it,' he continued. 'One hundred per cent, consumer harms need to be protected. But that's the basis upon which we invented Afterpay in the first place. It was to respond to a customer that wasn't getting what [they] wanted and did not have a trust relationship with incumbent players.'

Eisen and his head of public affairs, Damian Kassabgi, had met with Bragg around half a dozen times during the course of his inquiry, both in Sydney and in Canberra, and Kassabgi had kept in regular contact with Bragg's office as the inquiry determined what issues it would tackle. During one of his conversations with Eisen, Bragg asked whether Afterpay could support a not-for-profit organisation, Uphold & Recognise, whose work was of interest to him. Uphold & Recognise was co-founded by one of Bragg's Liberal Party colleagues and a member of parliament, Julian Leeser, and was working to recognise Indigenous Australians within the principles of the Australian Constitution. Eisen dutifully made a cash donation.

'I really admire the work that Senator Bragg and others have done to really understand what the landscape is,' Eisen said at the Banking & Wealth summit. 'I think there's a way to go, but I've been very impressed with the way that the conversation has developed, and is gaining momentum.'[5]

Australian regulators were moving with the times. In a symbolic move just before Christmas, the government said the Reserve Bank headquarters at 65 Martin Place, which had been built in the 1960s, would receive a $260 million makeover. The cracks in Governor Lowe's office would be fixed, and new windows and lifts would be installed as part of the facelift.

# 16

# TRENDING

ON A SUNNY midweek December day in 2020, Nick Molnar slipped a navy blazer over his white T-shirt. He made his way to Catalina restaurant in Rose Bay to attend the Australian Fashion Laureate awards. Afterpay had sponsored a new category, the People's Choice Award, and Molnar was to present the prize to the winner, macgraw, an edgy brand created by Sydney sisters Beth and Tessa MacGraw. He sat next to the editor of *Vogue*, Edwina McCann, and chatted with Carla Zampatti, a fashion industry icon who had invested in Afterpay in its early days and was keen to see pictures of Molnar's newborn son on his phone.

At Catalina, Molnar was on home ground. A favoured lunch spot for Sydney's Eastern Suburbs socialites, the upmarket restaurant sits at the edge of the harbour. It is a short walk from the Molnar family home, and is separated from Lyne Park by a narrow footpath.

Catalina was also the venue of Afterpay's first corporate Christmas party, held four years earlier, almost to the day. The table of sixteen had eaten and drunk their way through a long lunch, and toasted the progress they'd made in their first year as a listed company. After the meal, the team walked across to the damp field at Lyne Park and, in a moment of intended symbolism, gathered around David Hancock, who prepared to launch a toy rocket. He lit the fuse, it sizzled—but then the little rocket tipped over and lay still. As a metaphor for Afterpay, it could not have been less apt: ever since that gathering, the company had soared.

Molnar also felt at home at Catalina because of who he was hanging out with. Afterpay and the fashion industry went together like a hand and a glove. The high margins on fashion items—the mark-up on a luxury handbag could be 50 per cent or more—meant there was plenty left for the retailer to pay Afterpay's fee as the platform delivered customers and incremental sales. Molnar got fashion, but he also got the business of fashion. It was part science and part art.

'Fashion holds a far larger share of mind than it does of your wallet. So how do you get people to spend more on the things that occupy their mind?' Molnar told *The Australian Financial Review*'s fashion editor, Lauren Sams.[1]

Molnar noted that fashion brands accounted for 70 per cent of the physical space at a shopping centre, but only a fraction of the overall dollars spent in the retail sector. In the time after the pandemic, fashion could move online to occupy a larger share of both mind and wallet—and less space in the malls.

While this presented a concern for commercial property empires such as Westfield, which rely on rent from tenants occupying bricks-and-mortar stores, in many respects Afterpay was turning into the online equivalent of Westfield, with its digital fashion retailing super-market. Many big brands—not to mention the share market—had come to appreciate that.

By the end of 2020, the combined share-market value of Scentre Group, which operates the Westfield shopping centres in Australia and New Zealand, and Unibail Westfield, which owns its US and UK malls, was roughly equal to that of Afterpay at $30 billion. The coronavirus pandemic had moved the scales: at the start of the year, the malls had been worth $50 billion, while Afterpay was valued at $8 billion.

With the virus receding, Sydney was opening up for business and events, and Australian fashion was getting the spring back in its step. It had survived the worst of the pandemic, and before that the hordes of foreign, 'fast fashion' invaders such as Zara, H&M and Uniqlo, which had opened stores in iconic locations in a challenge to local brands.

Afterpay had consummated its alliance with fashion in October 2020, when it was unveiled as the lead sponsor of Australian Fashion Week. That ended the almost uninterrupted patronage of Mercedes-Benz since the event's inception in 1996. Natalie Xenita, of IMG Events, which runs the week, had known Molnar from her days editing the teen magazine *Girlfriend*; back in the day, he had made offers for Ice Online to sponsor fashion editorials.[2]

'After the washout of 2020 there was a palpable sense of hope, relief and renewal as Molnar spoke of his commitment to the Australian fashion industry,' Sams wrote in her *AFR* profile.

Afterpay was also following its customers onto new social-media platforms, including TikTok, which hosted short, user-made videos. Afterpay conducted a week-long campaign engaging young Australian musicians to create sounds that, as Natasha Gillezeau wrote in *The Australian Financial Review*, 'alludes to Afterpay's payment mechanism that splits payments into four instalments through the lyrics "Pose . . . two, three, four, strut".'[3]

And Afterpay was endearing itself to the industry by embracing philanthropic causes. On a February afternoon in 2021, Molnar headed to the industrial suburb of Banksmeadow, near Sydney International Airport. Thread Together, a charity that gathers unsold clothes and distributes them to those in need, was opening a new warehouse.

Molnar rubbed shoulders with luminaries of the industry, all of whom he'd come to know during his rapid ascent. 'Millennials and Gen Z are now leading the charge because they're earning enough disposable income that their trends can become *the* trends,' he told them. 'So that's where we should all be looking. Don't underestimate their power.'

• • •

That power was on full display the time of the Thread Together event. That same week, a stock-market episode of epic proportions was captivating the world's attention as traders had gathered online and orchestrated a short squeeze in struggling video-game retailer GameStop.

GameStop, which sold everything from Monopoly to the latest video consoles, had over 5000 stores across the United States. But the business was in decline as a new generation of gamers simply downloaded releases over the internet instead of buying them in boxes at its physical locations. The lockdowns saw a slump in foot traffic, while the slow demise of the mall weighed further on its sales. Over the last three years it had accumulated US$1.4 billion of accounting losses.

That made the ailing bricks-and-mortar business the perfect stock for hedge funds, such as the Tiger Cubs, to short. Among the elite hedge funds betting on its demise was $12.5 billion New York–based fund Melvin Capital. Melvin had been one of the top-performing hedge funds in 2020, returning 52 per cent. That made its founder, Gabe Plotkin, US$850 million wealthier. Melvin had shorted GameStop since the fund was founded in 2015, and the pandemic made it even more confident. The gaming industry boomed, but GameStop still lost money. The trade went to plan, until the unpredictable virality of the digital age made GameStop shares the currency of a social uprising.

Melvin's bet had become an obsession for Keith Gill, a 34-year-old out-of-work financial planner from Massachusetts. From his home, he wrote about GameStop on social-media platform Reddit's sub-group Wallstreetbets, under the pseudonym 'Deep Fucking Value', a homage to stock pickers who searched for undervalued companies. On YouTube he used another alias, Roaring Kitty, to urge his followers to get behind his trade.

The crux of his thesis was that short-selling hedge funds—and in particular Melvin—were destroying the company that had sold people like Gill video games in their youth. Since Melvin had actually shorted more shares in GameStop than there were on issue, Gill surmised that if enough of the Reddit mob united to buy shares and drive the price higher, eventually Melvin would be squeezed out of its position. He would have to close his shorts by buying back shares from every holder. They just needed 'diamond hands'—that is, to hold firm.

It sounded crazy. But it worked. The reach of social media and low-cost trading firms that democratised the market combined with devastating effect. The allure of life-changing financial gains and the revolutionary zeitgeist lured thousands to the cause.

In several short sessions during the last week of January 2021, GameStop's share price surged ten times to a value of over US$30 billion. Melvin Capital's positions were crushed, while social-media mavens Elon Musk and day trader Dave Portnoy egged on the retail revolution. The suits of Wall Street were about to be toppled by people power.

'This is the regular Joes versus Wall Street,' a young Texan, Colin McLelland, told news reporters. 'Even if I lose everything, I like being part of it.'[4]

The GameStop trade was David and Goliath meets *Revenge of the Nerds*. The company itself became a meme stock. GameStop shares were hot because a critical mass of people had determined it to be so.

The underlying business and the price didn't matter as much as the fact that the digital collective had decided they wanted it to go up.

Then reality collided with the market's plumbing. Robinhood, the brokerage that processed most of the buy-orders, had to stump up hundreds of millions of dollars in cash to assure sellers that their customers were good for the money. It was forced to draw emergency loans from the banks and then raise billions from its investors. It also blocked investors from buying more GameStop shares. To ease its cash requirements, Robinhood halted buying of GameStop shares on its platform.

The buying halt then caused a rapid crash in the GameStop share price. And the Reddit army cried conspiracy. The suits had rigged the system in their favour. The digital mob got angry. 'Too big to fail, too small to win,' read one protest placard.

Dave Portnoy lost $700,000 and called for Robinhood's founders to be jailed. Democrat politicians Elizabeth Warren and Alexandria Ocasio-Cortez leapt to the defence of the day traders and demanded Wall Street be called to account for rigging the system against the little guy.

'And then now as technology advances it starts to actually "small d" democratize some of these systems and people are starting to figure out all these little ways in which the game was rigged,' Ocasio-Cortez said in an interview.[5]

The GameStop episode hit Plotkin hard. But it had also forced some of Wall Street's most illustrious hedge funds into a rapid retreat, and they closed out their bets. They'd made millions mastering the trade-off between risk and reward, but a new, unquantifiable but existential risk had emerged: that one of their many positions could go against them by an inconceivable magnitude.

As hedge funds scrambled to close their positions, heavily shorted 'old economy' stocks briefly rallied. Among them were Unibail Westfield, which soared 10 per cent in the days that followed the GameStop surge. Tiger Cubs such as Lone Pine, Woodson and Tiger Global all had existing bets against the mall operator.[6]

GameStop was more than a stock-market event. It was a cultural awakening. A generational moment. Molnar, who had become a billionaire by understanding the millennial mindset, was about as informed as anyone to comment on what had just happened.

'Consumer people power is reaching a point and a moment in time where things are really, really changing,' he told the *AFR*'s Lauren Sams at the not-for-profit event in Banksmeadow. Millennials and Gen Z were cashed-up, leading the charge and setting the trends. 'It is not like this wasn't happening or coming, it's just now at a significant enough point that they can truly make change.'

The smart money wasn't underestimating this new trend. Millennials and Gen Zs were uniting not to make money, but to have fun and make a point. Some GameStop traders used their profits to buy giant billboards on freeways, marking their moment of triumph.

Social media was primed for the next meme trade. It didn't have to be a stock. In fact, most millennials and Gen Zs preferred trading cryptocurrencies. Elon Musk, rapper Snoop Dogg and former porn star Mia Khalifa encouraged their followers to buy one called Dogecoin, which was created not to be taken too seriously. The price went up 800 per cent. There was a lot of money to be made.

Serious investors could make money by latching themselves onto millennial trends, and the most lucrative was cryptocurrencies. Increasingly, institutional investors became converts, and pitched the asset class to their clients. Mark Carnegie, who had spent the pandemic in a bolthole in New Zealand, told the *AFR* that investors should allocate 1 to 2 per cent of their net worth to crypto as a hedge against inflation risk.

Carnegie had never invested in Afterpay, even though the 22-year-old Molnar had sat in his office and developed Ice Online and its payments plan right under his nose. When Sams asked Carnegie, as she researched her profile of Molnar, whether he regretted not putting money in, his response was: 'What do you fucking think?' He was not going to miss out on the crypto revolution, which was part mind-blowing futurism, part unhinged speculation.

Now the share market, too, had been well and truly gamified. It wasn't a venue in which capital was allocated to those who needed it the most. Valuations based on what something was actually worth were a very Boomer approach. Now the market was a place to get very rich, very fast—or have fun trying.

And everyone was cool with that.

• • •

While Wall Street was in the throes of a revolution, the buy now, pay later sector, which had been rocketing on the ASX, had just made its US stock-exchange debut.

Affirm, the company Max Levchin founded in 2012, two years before Afterpay, was putting the final touches on its initial public offering on the Nasdaq, the venue of choice for high-growth technology companies. Its reception was a big test for the sector, as ownership passed from private venture investors to the larger and at times more discerning public market.

The intellectual divide that was evident among analysts in Melbourne and Sydney for five years as Afterpay rose through the ranks of the ASX was now appearing in New York. Was Affirm a payments platform that became more valuable to both merchants and retailers as it scaled by powerful network effects? Or was it just a glorified lender, which borrowed money and loaned it out at a rate high enough to cover expected losses?

'Pessimists may imagine a world in which Affirm's unique value proposition disintegrates, becoming a commodity. Banks and other capital providers with low cost of capital deposits build similar products,' wrote fintech blogger Mario Gabriele. 'As a result, consumers do not repeat purchases on Affirm, Affirm's pricing power with merchants erodes, and acquisition costs grow. Affirm's revenue becomes consumer funded, growth becomes difficult, and the business resembles a tech-enabled personal loans provider.'[7]

That was the bear case. Wall Street had been fooled before into thinking old-school lenders were newfangled fintechs. Lending Club, a peer-to-peer lender that matched borrowers to individual investors seeking a higher rate of interest, had lost 90 per cent of its value as loans went sour and senior management were tripped up in ethical scandals. OnDeck was another fintech flop that had been exposed as an old-world business dressed up for new-economy investors. It had seen its shares surge after a late 2014 IPO, but was hit by rising competition and the high cost of acquiring customers. The problems were exacerbated when COVID-19 struck; in mid-2020, OnDeck was sold for just US$90 million, compared to a valuation at the time of its IPO of US$1.3 billion.[8]

But Gabriele and others argued that Affirm and the buy now, pay laters were different to these overrated lenders. The new breed did not have to spend large amounts of current and future revenues to attract customers, or lend at non-competitive rates to achieve scale. Their models were built to grow on their own.

Affirm, however, had a few twists. One was its partnership with Shopify, the Canadian retail giant that had emerged as a real competitor to Amazon. Shopify allowed small merchants to easily set up a website to sell whatever they wanted, providing order, payments and distribution functionality. Afterpay and many other buy now, pay later providers can be used on Shopify. But under Levchin's deal, Affirm would be the exclusive provider of instalment finance to its US merchants.[9] For Afterpay, it was a sign that the competition was heating up.

Another twist with Affirm was Peloton. During the 2020 lock-downs, exercise bikes had become wildly popular, and Peloton had created virtual exercise experiences with personal trainers. Sales soared to the point that fees from Peloton made up 30 per cent of Affirm's revenue.

There was no doubt the sector had become highly competitive. Several new and established players, including PayPal and Klarna, were offering instalment payment plans. It seemed inevitable that the fees charged to merchants would be whittled down.

PayPal launched its 'Pay in Four' product in September 2020 and was blown away by the take-up. In the final quarter of 2020, it processed US$750 million of merchant sales, a figure that took Afterpay more than a year to achieve. CEO Daniel Schulman said the rollout in France had produced an 'up-tick . . . well beyond any of our expectations. We just rolled out in the US and the demand is tremendous.'[10] Goldman Sachs analysts wrote that the rapid take-up of the buy now, pay later option was 'the biggest positive surprise to management in the result' for the company's fourth quarter, as its shares went on another tear.[11] But PayPal's fees undercut those of other providers: they were the standard PayPal rates of around 2.9 per cent of the cost of the goods.

PayPal's extraordinary traction raised questions as to whether Afterpay could demonstrate it could withstand the eventual onslaught of low-cost competitors. PayPal's entry and the Affirm deal with Shopify 'could lead to significant competitive pressures over coming years', according to UBS's Tom Beadle, who ran scenarios to look at the consequences if the Afterpay merchant fee was squeezed.[12] But those in the Afterpay camp thought Affirm and PayPal would be unlikely to re-create the network effects that Afterpay had via its shop directory, which was driving tens of millions of retailing referrals each month. 'At a high level, PayPal is coming into the space from a payment processing perspective, while BNPL providers have positioned themselves as valuable marketing lead channels, data insight providers and conversion drivers for their merchant partners,' Tim

Piper, a Sydney-based analyst at RBC Capital Markets, said when PayPal's entry was announced in the United States.[13]

For the time being, there was plenty of land available to be grabbed. All the providers could grow without having to compete on price. The buy now, pay later industry was just getting started.

When Affirm listed in the middle of January 2021, the market enthusiastically backed the growth story. It hit the Nasdaq at a price of US$49 on 14 January, implying a US$12 billion valuation. By the end of the session, this had doubled. The listing price suggested it was worth only half as much as Afterpay, and therefore appeared to be great value. So investors snapped it up until it was worth as much as Afterpay.

When the Australian session opened, the market surmised that Afterpay should have been more valuable, given its growth numbers, so it, too, went up, as did the entire sector. It was a very different story to 2019, when Visa's announcement of an instalment API for banks, and PayPal's announcement that it was entering the sector, had sent Afterpay into freefall.

Affirm's IPO was yet another validation of the sector and its prospects. Afterpay, Zip and others were all immediately deemed more valuable in the share market's eyes. But that still left Peter Gray, the co-founder of Zip, frustrated.

A week after the Affirm float, Zip reported what Gray described as a 'cracking' quarter, as its US arm, Quadpay, helped Zip double its customer numbers to 5.7 million. That, in turn, had lifted its quarterly revenue growth by 88 per cent to over $100 million. Quadpay was riding the US growth wave and was charging a much higher fee to merchants than Afterpay, at 7 per cent of sales compared to 4 per cent. Zip's share price on the ASX had been trading through 2020 on a lower valuation compared to Afterpay and Sezzle. Gray thought its numbers simply weren't being appreciated. Zip had processed $1.6 billion of transactions in the quarter, compared to Afterpay's

$4.1 billion, which was 2.6 times more. Yet the market considered Afterpay eleven times more valuable than Zip, which was valued at $4.1 billion.

'Our view would be that on the revenue multiples we are significantly undervalued when directly compared to Afterpay and obviously Affirm,' Gray told *The Australian Financial Review*'s Tom Richardson after the Affirm listing.[14]

Meanwhile, 'Street Talk' reported that Zip was exploring a secondary listing on the Nasdaq or New York Stock Exchange.[15] Over the next two days, Zip's share price surged by 12 per cent.

The Affirm listing, Gray suggested, supported the argument that Zip was undervalued and underappreciated. While Afterpay was a pure buy now, pay later business that only offered a short-term instalment product, entirely paid for by merchants, Affirm, Klarna and Zip offered other, longer-term credit products and charged customers like banks did.

These products closely resembled consumer loans, and were regulated as such. Klarna is a bank in Europe, while Affirm has a relationship with Cross River Bank, which holds its deposits and writes its loans. These companies essentially digitised a credit card application process for the smartphone age. They made better use of data than banks, and provided faster approvals based on application processes that involved no paper. But still, their loans products charged interest and the companies earned a good, old-fashioned net interest margin, the difference between what they received in interest from customers and what they paid in funding costs. On these products, interest rates could be high—similar to those for credit cards. Klarna had been profitable since its inception in 2005, until it started to spend big to chase Afterpay's growth in the United States. This sent it into its first year of financial loss in 2019.

As more analysts cast their eyes over the sector, they began to pay attention to the varied business models, even if they remained divided. Credit analysts had often mulled over the 'book turn', or the pace at which money is loaned out and returned, or recycled. The faster the loan turns, the more fees or interest earned by the lender. But a fast-turning book can also accumulate write-offs, and can shrink in size if demand slows.

A pure buy now, pay later model that charges a merchant a 4 per cent fee can turn $1000 twelve times a year, earning $480. But the write-offs are high, too. If 2 per cent of that $1000 isn't repaid, that's $240 of losses. The gross profit is the $240 difference, or 50 per cent.

But a consumer lender might lend $1000 and charge interest of 9 per cent over six months, or 18 per cent annualised, with 2 per cent set-up fees. The $1000 will only turn twice, to earn $180 of interest, plus $40 of fees over a year. The write-offs are similar at 2 per cent, but since the book turns slowly, that only occurs twice. Write-offs tally only $40. That model makes a lower profit of $180, as the fees net off against the write-offs. But the ratio of revenues to write-offs is much higher.

Some investors deemed that the pure buy now, pay later companies such as Afterpay and Sezzle were better businesses. Their value was in providing free finance for customers and leads for merchants, in an apparent win-win arrangement. To them, these companies were true disrupters, while the likes of Zip, Klarna and Affirm were simply repackaged credit products, with the same pitfalls as the financing model they'd sought to disrupt.

But others believed that Zip, Klarna and Affirm were more sustainable businesses, and that buy now, pay later was in itself not particularly profitable without the prospect of selling more credit or banking-like products to customers who would pay interest rates for longer-term financing. This would allow customers attracted to the 'pay in four' instalment construct to be 'monetised' later, via a banking-like cross-sell of more profitable products.

The divergent models played out in a public-relations war. The proponents of the consumer finance model complained that the buy now, pay later players were lending money with no responsibility. The buy now, pay later advocates said the consumer finance companies were just repackaged credit cards. It was responsible spenders versus responsible lenders all over again.

The strategy of Affirm, Klarna and Zip/Quadpay also differed from Afterpay's in another key respect: a lot of their growth was being driven by 'virtual cards', also known as 'ghost cards', which could be issued digitally for individual transactions at any retailer that accepted a Visa or Mastercard. For the merchant, the sale was processed as a regular card transaction. In contrast, Afterpay could only be used at retailers that had integrated with its service. But this allowed Afterpay to secure its merchant fee in a bilateral contract, whereas the 'shop anywhere' virtual card model required the providers to seek revenue by more complex affiliate referral fees or payment fees charged to users, which Afterpay could avoid.

● ● ●

Peter Gray's comments about Zip's share price deviated from the executive playbook. Company executives tended to steer clear of openly debating their valuations, leaving it to the investor-relations departments or countenancing it only in private briefings with analysts. But Zip had a large cohort of retail traders, and Gray's argument seemed to resonate with them. Remarkably, Zip was often the most traded share on the CommSec retail stockbroking platform, owned by Commonwealth Bank, even though it was not among the 100 largest companies in Australia by market capitalisation.

Indeed, Zip had become something of a meme stock in the Australian market. While the strong trading update on 21 January 2021 had led to a near 25 per cent share price pop, Zip's stock kept rising until 16 February, when its valuation reached $7.7 billion. In three weeks, buyers added $3.6 billion to Zip's market value, more than it had created in the six years since its backdoor listing.

The hype wasn't anywhere near the scale of that for GameStop. But buy now, pay later featured a lot on Reddit. Meanwhile, the enthusiasm for Afterpay showed no signs of easing. On 10 February, its share price topped $160, valuing it at $45 billion.

Afterpay had risen to become Australia's twelfth-most valuable company. The larger companies were the big four banks CBA, Westpac, NAB and ANZ, plus Macquarie; the three mining giants BHP, Rio Tinto and Fortescue; blood plasma firm CSL; grocer Woolworths; and retailing conglomerate Wesfarmers.

The investment bank Macquarie, the eleventh-largest at $51 billion, was forecast to generate a $2.5 billion profit in 2021. The estimate for Afterpay, Australia's best-known tech stock, was $31 million. But within weeks it would tell the market to wait a little longer for its maiden profit, reporting a first-half net loss of $76.5 million.

• • •

British fashion vlogger Oghosa Ovienrioba embodies the new digital economy. On the strength of her style and sassiness, she has built an online following of over 45,000 fans, whom she entertains and informs on YouTube and Instagram. Oghosa is a modern-day influencer. And that means she's courted by fashion brands to help them market their products and reach their target audience. But on 11 February 2021, she turned on one of her partners—Klarna— which had sponsored some of her Instagram story posts.

'I read about how some young shoppers who bought items with Klarna had gone into debt and were struggling to get their credit score back under control,' she wrote. 'I was horrified at what

I learnt and I felt this incredible pang of guilt at what I'd done, and what I'd supported and promoted. I knew I had a lot of younger viewers who looked to me for advice and I couldn't believe my ignorance had meant I'd potentially encouraged them to make bad financial choices.'

The United Kingdom was having its buy now, pay later awakening. The sector had grown so quickly and marketed itself so well that questions were being asked as to whether it was in danger of getting out of hand.

Klarna had attracted Calvin Broadus, an American rapper better known as Snoop Dogg, as an investor and star of its 'Get Smoooth' marketing campaigns, which featured him as Smoooth Dogg. 'Of course the colours, the language, the celebrities it uses in campaigns, will make it seem quite benign and obviously cool,' wrote Iona Bain, creator of the Young Money Blog.[16]

Oghosa's confession ran on the BBC as the Financial Conduct Authority lobbed the eagerly awaited 'Review of Change and Innovation in the Unsecured Credit Market' report, written by Christopher Woolard, who was departing the FCA. It didn't make for favourable reading.

The rapid growth of the buy now, pay later segment was colliding with a relatively new regulatory regime in the United Kingdom, which had been redesigned after the global financial crisis. A decade later powers and authority were still being established. Moreover, there was a troubled history of payday lending in Great Britain, which had spurred consumer groups to publicise the dangers of easy debt for vulnerable people.

The Financial Conduct Authority was created after the global financial crisis exposed holes in Britain's model of financial regulation under the Financial Services Authority, which was dissolved in 2013 following public outrage about misconduct by banks that had been missed by regulators. Bank prudential regulation was handed to the Bank of England, while the FCA was created as a new conduct regulator for financial services, under legislation passed in 2012.

However, this law was not as broad as the act governing the Australian Securities & Investments Commission. Even though buy now, pay later was not captured by Australia's consumer credit laws, ASIC had been closely monitoring the sector and could act against misleading conduct. Furthermore, the FCA had product intervention powers similar to those that Australia created for ASIC, but in the United Kingdom these powers were drafted too narrowly to capture buy now, pay later.

Amid growing pressure from British consumer groups—who, as in Australia, play a powerful role in policy development—the FCA board called for a review in September 2020. Woolard's report, released on 2 February 2021, recognised that buy now, pay later sat outside the scope of consumer credit regulation and needed to be brought in. Once the necessary powers had been obtained, Woolard wrote, the FCA should develop a 'proportionate regulatory framework'.

The United Kingdom also flagged a potentially more aggressive approach than Australia's. New laws should require buy now, pay later providers to conduct 'affordability checks' before lending to customers. Depending on the sort of information that would be required in an assessment, there was a risk this could slow down the pace of customer onboarding. The rate of merchant sign-ups could also be impacted if the UK government classified them as 'credit brokers', as Woolard recommended.

'Many consumers do not view interest-free "buy now, pay later" as a form of credit, so do not apply the same level of scrutiny,' the UK Treasury said. 'Checks undertaken by providers tend to focus on the risk for the firm rather than how affordable it is for the customer.'[17]

The UK press was also turning hostile. The *Evening Standard* reported that vulnerable people were being exploited. 'They include young people in particular who some say are targeted on social media by firms such as Klarna, Clearpay and LayBuy and are at risk of running up big debts during the pandemic. With unemployment rising among the young especially, those debts could be a major problem later. Some see parallels with the Wonga pay-day loan scandal.'[18]

Wonga, which collapsed in 2018, had become a symbol of the household debt crisis in the United Kingdom, and more than 70 cross-party MPs had warned the government that buy now, pay later could be 'the next Wonga waiting to happen'. Labour MP Stella Creasy declared 'regulation cannot come soon enough', while John Glen, economic secretary to the Treasury, told *The Guardian*: 'The review found it would be relatively easy to accrue around £1,000 of debt that credit reference agencies and mainstream lenders cannot see. With several buy now, pay later providers planning to expand to higher-value retailers, or offer their products in store, the risk that consumers could take on unaffordable levels of debt is increasing.'[19]

The connection with payday lending had been made by the Australian Senate in 2018 during its inquiry into financial services targeted at Australians at risk of financial hardship. That inquiry had provided an opportunity for Afterpay to explain how its product differed to payday loans because it didn't charge customers any interest, let alone the extortionate rates levied by predatory payday lenders. Now the Woolard report made clear that Afterpay would need to go through the same process of educating policy-makers in Britain, where payday lending had become a major problem in the wake of the financial crisis.

Back in Australia, Damian Kassabgi said the Woolard review had 'recognised the diverse nature of the industry'. As in Australia, there was a broad church with different models operating under the buy now, pay later umbrella, and Afterpay's UK subsidiary Clearpay would work with the British authorities to 'create the right regulation for the sector'.[20]

Afterpay had mastered the art of lobbying in Australia. It was confident it could convince British rule-makers that its product did more good than harm. Investors had come to appreciate that Afterpay tended to find a way to navigate regulatory landmines, and would likely do so again. The day after the Woolard report appeared, buy now, pay later stocks slipped on the ASX: Afterpay finished 1.3 per cent lower at $144.70. But the falls were nothing like those shareholders had experienced during the regulatory turmoil of 2018.

The timing of the report did take some of the shine off another big partnership: Clearpay had secured the principal sponsorship of London Fashion Week in a two-year deal. The British Fashion Council touted Clearpay's support as a 'new way to support the industry and help jumpstart retail and make fashion more inclusive and accessible to the British public'.[21]

But now the fashion trade media wanted to know what the industry body thought about the FCA's concerns. The British Fashion Council said, in an emailed response to trade website *FashionUnited*, that the FCA had 'acknowledged the benefits of products like Clearpay in the UK and by regulating the industry, there is more certainty for the customers and merchant partners. It is important that consumer protection is recognised through regulation. Clearpay has always supported fit for purpose regulation that recognises the diversity of the industry and desire from consumers for flexible payment options that don't trap them in long term debt.'[22] But within a fortnight, a cross-party selection of 60 members of parliament signed a letter to the council to express concerns about the sponsorship deal, urging the event organisers to provide warnings about the 'risk this form of lending presents'.[23]

Meanwhile, on social media, users were documenting their love–hate relationship with buy now, pay later as it exploded across America.

'Someone send me to afterpay rehab I need help,' wrote one TikTok user, showing her bank account cleared out. Another appeared on her laptop, looking defiant: 'Me using afterpay to order cloths [sic] with only 10.49 in my bank account'.

To Canadian rocker Alanis Morissette's lyrics 'I'm broke but I'm happy', one TikTok user displayed a list of Klarna, Quadpay and Afterpay debits on her bank account, and a Christmas tree surrounded by wrapped gifts, while a girl in another TikTok video shrieked in panic like she'd seen a cockroach, before breathing a sigh of relief: 'When you almost submit payment with your default debit card instead of clicking the Quadpay button.'

In the videos, the influencers coached their followers on how to use 'ghost cards' to split just about anything—from groceries to metro cards, to fake eyelashes—into four easy payments.

• • •

When Michael Saadat began work at Afterpay's Surry Hills office on 1 November 2019, the project at the top of his to-do list was the new buy now, pay later code of conduct. The loose alliance of buy now, pay later providers in Australia was turning the threat of regulation into an opportunity to write the new industry's own rules. It was a mission-critical piece of work that, if deployed properly, would ensure regulators took a light-touch approach to the sector as it continued to scale.

At ASIC, Saadat was familiar with the banking industry's code of conduct, which had come under intense pressure during the Hayne Royal Commission for not having sharp enough teeth. Despite it being the primary mechanism for bank customers to enforce their rights against banks, it had been buried deep on bank websites; few customers knew the code existed, let alone took any action based on its provisions. Saadat and Damian Kassabgi knew it would be important to get the buy now, pay later code of conduct right.

While there had been some talk within Afterpay about developing an industry code during 2018, it wasn't until the Senate inquiry recommended one be developed, in its report in February 2019, that Afterpay, Zip and other players—including FlexiGroup (which rebranded as Humm in 2020) and Brighte—swung into action. After the Senate report, a code of conduct was not just a good idea, it was an imperative, an instruction from the national parliament that a genuine attempt at self-regulation could keep the regulators at bay and ensure customers could transact in the knowledge their rights would be protected if something went wrong. Moreover, ASIC's November 2018 'Review of Buy Now Pay Later Arrangements' had identified specific harms that required the industry's attention.

In the months after the Senate report, Afterpay, Zip and another five providers approached the Australian Finance Industry Association to determine if it could oversee the code's development. AFIA had helped to develop a similar set of principles to govern conduct in the emerging small business fintech lending space, and its ability to build a self-regulation document for buy now, pay later was boosted in November 2019, when it hired a new CEO, Diane Tate, from the Australian Banking Association.

Tate had spent fourteen years at the ABA, the peak body for the nation's powerful banks, including oversight of the banking code of practice. She had led the redrafting efforts after the Hayne Royal Commission to ensure that banking products became easier for customers to understand. Before the ABA, Tate had worked at both ASIC and AUSTRAC.

Tate and Saadat worked together closely to write the new buy now, pay later code with the rest of the industry, and both relished the opportunity to build something from the ground up that was genuinely focused on customers while also reflecting the arrival of new technology. Hayne had expressed a dim view of self-regulation that it was weak, and his critique had left its mark. But Tate and Saadat recognised that the royal commission had also endorsed self-regulation if it was done properly. They knew it would continue to play an important role in setting standards, and believed it could be more effective than prescriptive laws, especially in an emerging industry.

As Tate, Saadat and other representatives from seven providers met regularly over the summer to draw up the code, they came to appreciate that oversight and checks on customers would need to be ratcheted up as loan amounts got larger. It didn't make sense that checks on a customer buying a $10,000 set of solar panels would be the same as for someone buying a $100 pair of jeans.

The consumer groups were brought in for consultation, and the buy now, pay later providers funded a joint submission and remained open to incorporating their views.[24] When COVID-19 struck, they were overwhelmed and AFIA decided to push the initial launch date back from 1 July 2020 to 1 January 2021, to allow the consumer groups enough time to prepare their feedback.

The consumer groups remained wary of self-regulation and were consistent in their demands for formal credit checking, as set out in the *National Consumer Credit Protection Act*. ASIC also made its concerns about the code known in documents filed in a legal case in which FlexiGroup was opposing attempts by the ACCC to incorporate 'responsible lending' style duties from the credit act into a separate code of conduct for the new energy industry. ASIC told the Australian Competition Tribunal it was concerned about a 'vague' upfront assessment process in the draft code, which 'might conceivably give rise to adverse consumer outcomes'.[25]

But in Canberra, there were extraordinary moves afoot. By late September 2020, Treasurer Josh Frydenberg was preparing to scrap the 'responsible lending' laws that former prime minister Kevin Rudd had introduced after the financial crisis. They would ensure banks were not tripped up by ASIC when making decisions on whether to lend to support the economic recovery.[26] Westpac had fought ASIC over its interpretation of the laws in the Federal Court and ultimately won its case, which examined a relatively narrow issue of whether the bank could rely on a benchmark index of household spending when assessing loans. But the banks' concerns about conflicting lending rules being policed by two different regulators—ASIC and APRA—had taken on new meaning during the pandemic crisis, and the government was preparing to free them from the ASIC shackles that had slowed down the loan application process.

For the consumer groups, the government's proposals were devastating. The provisions in the *National Consumer Credit Protection Act* had been hard-won, and the onus on lenders to ensure a loan was 'not unsuitable' for a borrower had become a fundamental principle that allowed individual customers to take action against their bank if too much credit had been provided. But with the government now seeking to shift the onus back towards 'buyer beware', and arguing that the laws shouldn't even apply to banks, the consumer groups' demand that strict duties apply to buy now, pay later would not have an impact on the drafting of the code.

Nevertheless, the buy now, pay later providers decided that there should be some process for checking customers' ability to take on interest-free loans, and that this should be codified. Tate advised there should be three buckets. After analysing data and surveys on how customers saw the products, thresholds were set at $2000 and $15,000.

After another two-month delay, this time to ensure ASIC's views could be incorporated after the regulator delayed a second review into the sector, AFIA settled on a system that would require the largest providers—those offering limits above $15,000—to use both customer income and expense data and an external credit file before approving a loan. For transactions under this level but above $2000, one of those data sources would be required. But for providers offering less than $2000—and Afterpay's average transaction size is around $150—there would be no requirement to conduct credit checks using any external credit file or customer income data. Providers could continue to rely on their own systems to assess whether to approve a transaction and take on the risk that the customer would not pay what they owed.

Crucially for Afterpay, Saadat had landed a document that would not slow down its onboarding process by requiring it to do anything different to what it was doing already.

The code included other consumer protections. Power would be given to an independent committee to 'name and shame' contraveners of the code, and it could order compensation to be paid to customers. The players committed to never initiating bankruptcy proceedings against a customer. Furthermore, the Afterpay protection—whereby a customer who is late in repaying just one instalment cannot make further purchases on the service until their repayments are up to date—was set as the standard for all signatories to the code. Caps on late fees and a commitment not to allow the products to be used by minors or for gambling were also included.

These were improvements on credit cards but were not enough to satisfy the consumer groups. As the code was released, the Consumers' Federation of Australia dispatched an angry media release. In it, Financial Counselling Australia chief executive Fiona Guthrie identified an apparent inconsistency: buy now, pay later providers 'run a mile at the mention of the word "credit", telling their customers the service is all about better budgeting', she said. But 'what they tell retailers, however, is much closer to the truth—that [buy now, pay later] encourages people to spend more. What BNPL providers are really doing is turning a loophole in the law into a gaping hole.'[27]

Like the advocacy groups in the United Kingdom, Australia's consumer groups had also picked up on the marketing tactics. 'BNPL companies use a simple but seductive psychological trick to attract customers,' said Financial Rights Legal Centre CEO Karen Cox. 'Spreading out the cost of an item makes it feel less expensive, but that doesn't mean you can afford it.'[28]

The industry hit the airwaves to defend its efforts at creating standardised consumer protections that went beyond the requirements of the law in several respects. The day before the code was set to start, 1 March 2021, Diane Tate and Consumer Action Law Centre CEO Gerard Brody sparred on Channel Seven's *Weekend Sunrise* television program. 'The code is a useful thing to have in place but it is no replacement for consumer protection at law,' Brody said. 'A code is a positive step. But we also know from the Financial Services Royal Commission only a few years ago that there are a number of limitations with self-regulation: there can be weak standards, there can be inadequate compliance, and the consequences of a breach cannot be there.'

Within the corridors of power, however, the industry's efforts to draft a code with teeth was well received—by both sides of politics. Labor's shadow assistant treasurer, Stephen Jones, issued a media release welcoming the code as a 'genuine attempt by the industry to set sensible and fair rules around conduct in an emerging sector'. Labor's Senator Jenny McAllister, who had chaired the Senate inquiry that called for the code, told Tate that she, too, supported the initiative, and Labor would be watching to ensure the independent code compliance committee vigorously enforced it.

Senior members of the governing Liberal Party also gave the code the thumbs-up. The Minister for Superannuation, Financial Services and the Digital Economy, Senator Jane Hume, told Tate the document had the government's support. Senator Andrew Bragg, who had firsthand experience drafting industry codes at the Financial Services Council before he entered parliament, and knew how much effort went into finding consensus, welcomed the self-regulation efforts. Politically, Afterpay had once again prevailed.

# 17

# ONCE IN A LIFETIME

THE WORD 'AMPLIFY' was chosen for the cover page of Afterpay's half-yearly results, released on 25 February 2021, alongside the corporate logo elevated in a slick 3D design. The numbers showed how the online shopping boom of 2020 had turbocharged its growth in the latter part of the year. The gross merchant value of goods bought on Afterpay had more than doubled to $9.8 billion, while the business's income had increased by 89 per cent to $420 million.

Numbers for Afterpay's shop directory, which pointed users to the retailers in particular categories that accepted Afterpay, were also surging as customers came to its app to decide where to shop. The growing use of Afterpay as a directory, a tool to manage discretionary lifestyle spending, strengthened the arguments made to the Reserve Bank's review of payments system regulation. In defence of preventing merchant surcharging, Afterpay argued it should be compared to internet referral platforms such as Google rather than payments processors such as Visa or Mastercard. In December alone, Afterpay had delivered 45 million referrals to its merchant partners; the monthly average was 35 million over the second half of calendar 2020. For many retailers, Afterpay was the second-highest referrer of traffic after the giant search engine.

All the trends were favouring Afterpay. The shift to online shopping was real and significant. Millennials and Gen Xers were spending more in the economy, while more mature users had begun embracing Afterpay and were transacting with greater frequency. Active customers were using Afterpay fifteen times each year on average, a number that had risen by 30 per cent over the year. Afterpay's earliest customers, who had begun using it in 2017, were now transacting 29 times per year. This was also helping to depress bad debts: gross losses had fallen to 0.7 per cent of underlying sales, down from 1 per cent a year earlier, as risky customers who didn't repay were fettered from the platform, while regular users, whose credit limits were increased over time, became more loyal.

'Afterpay was built for this generation,' Molnar told analysts. 'We were founded on trust and transparency.'

But the incredible growth was coming at a cost. Afterpay's net cash outflows had topped $587 million. Molnar told analysts this was the cost of establishing new and lucrative partnerships with large merchants 'with tens of billions of addressable gross merchant value'.

The shares, however, didn't trade that day as a halt was called. Once more, Afterpay was in the market for new funds, while Molnar and Eisen declared they were planning to sell more shares.

The reason for the $1.5 billion of new capital in the form of a convertible note was intriguing. Matrix Partners, Afterpay's US venture partner, was due to inherit 10 per cent of the Afterpay USA business in 2023, but had agreed to cash out of 35 per cent of that stake ahead of time. Afterpay was also offering to cash out staff, consultants and other US option holders, whose identities remained a secret. Matrix and the US option holders weren't due to realise their stakes for another two years, and some analysts had flagged the complex US ownership structure as an expensive problem that would have to be dealt with.

The agreed price to buy out Matrix's 35 per cent of the 10 per cent holding (or 3.5 per cent of Afterpay USA) was $373 million. That price implied Afterpay's US business was worth $10.06 billion. But this valuation was at odds with the share market, which valued Afterpay in its entirety at US$30 billion, or $38 billion.

The United States was by far Afterpay's largest market, and the one in which it had the best prospects. Most analysts suggested it was worth 40 per cent of Afterpay's total value, at a minimum. If Matrix was getting a fair price, then Afterpay was only worth $90 a share at best, not the $130 the market had assigned it.

But Afterpay's logic was that this was precisely why it was a good deal. The company was buying a share of the US business it didn't own at an attractive price, so it was 'accretive' for shareholders.

Eisen told analysts that it was 'fortuitous' that the sale had arrived, but to those who hadn't studied its disclosures, the fact that Afterpay had to pay so much to buy back part of its own business may have come as a surprise. 'We think the opportunity for the US to become more of a substantial proportion of our business and our value is absolutely there. But if we could combine increasing our ownership of that entity . . . with having the team aligned on that global structural basis, we think it's a win-win.'

That was just the half of it. The Employee Share Option plan meant that a secretive list of staff, consultants and influencers were entitled to the share of the company they had been promised. Afterpay had agreed to spend $225 million to buy out any holders who wanted to cash in early, at the same valuation as for Matrix. So Afterpay had accrued at least $1 billion in staff and consulting expenses to turbocharge its US expansion. That came in the form of options gifted to staff, which had been expensed in the company's accounts at a neglible amount.

The true costs of the business's breakneck US expansion never really showed up in the financial accounts when they were being incurred. They would be paid for by shareholders in the future, through a dilution of their ownership as the options converted to shares, or through the early cash payouts running into the billions of dollars.

To finance the initial phase of the buyout, Afterpay launched a $1.5 billion sale of convertible notes, rather than a share issue. A convertible note typically involves a buyer accepting a low interest rate for the life of the note, and then having the right to convert the investment into shares at an agreed price. For Afterpay, the convertible notes paid zero interest for five years and gave investors the right to convert the investment to shares at $194.80, a 45 per cent premium to the price that day.

Some of the buyers of the convertible bonds engaged in a common practice of 'delta-hedging', where the bond investors protect themselves from a potential fall in the share price by shorting the shares. The investment bankers managing the deal helped to find buyers of the shares that were sold, or shorted, by building an order book of investors who wanted to buy shares. Eisen and Molnar, who had flagged that day that they would reduce their Afterpay holdings, each added 450,000 of their shares to that order book. As a result, they cashed in an additional $46.5 million. Eisen and Molnar had each sold 7.5 million shares since June 2018 for proceeds of $185 million. The sum was enormous, but relatively modest compared to the $2.6 billion worth of shares each still owned.

The half-year result, corporate transactions, product launches and sell-downs were all executed with precision by Afterpay's advisers. But the company had also revealed the cost of its historic US growth, of which the lion's share was yet to be paid.

What the market made of Afterpay's flood of releases was hard to decipher. That's because the bond market was once again transmitting powerful signals that were overwhelming any new information about Afterpay. Long-term bond rates were rising, not falling, and the pace at which they headed higher was accelerating. The US ten-year bond rate—the discount rate for almost every asset—lingered at around 0.8 per cent at the start of 2021. It gradually drifted north, but in February it accelerated to 1.7 per cent. The reason was that the rollout of vaccines to tackle the coronavirus pandemic meant it was only a matter of time before economies reopened at full capacity. Already the data pointed towards a better-than-expected recovery. The consequence of that was that workers' wages across the economy would eventually rise, and prices for goods and services would begin to rise. Inflation—all but absent over the past decade—was going to return. That meant central banks would have to act to prevent economies overheating by increasing interest rates sooner than initially expected.

The threat was not imminent, but over the next ten years the market was betting that interest rates would have to rise sharply. For fast-growing companies that delayed delivering profits in pursuit of growing revenues and market share, higher bond rates meant the cost of waiting for those profits went up.

Tech-stock valuations had become incredibly sensitive to those changes in long-term bond rates. A seemingly modest quarter per cent rise in the ten-year bond rate from mid-February to mid-March wiped 10 per cent, or $1.5 trillion, of share-market value from the Nasdaq 100 index. By the end of March, Afterpay had lost more than one-third of its value from its February peak. The ASX All Tech benchmark index lost nearly a fifth of its value over the same period.

In the United States, Affirm had touched US$147 in early February—but had crumbled to US$77 by the middle of March, wiping out the spectacular early gains after the float in January, and imposing losses on any investor who bought in after the first day's doubling. The air had quickly come out of the fast-growing payments space. Even PayPal got hit hard, falling by 25 per cent in late February and early March.

But Klarna bucked the trend. The private company was yet to be subjected to the whims of the share market, and had raised US$1 billion of new funds at a valuation of US$31 billion, it said on 1 March, triple its valuation from six months before.

While the tech winners of 2020 were getting sold, old-economy stocks, by contrast, got a fillip. And that meant value investors, who had been made to look foolish in 2020, had a spring in their step again. Banking and energy stocks started to lift as a rotation from new-world growth stocks into old-world value stocks took hold.

'What we think is sensible right now is avoiding the parts of the market that are priced as though inflation can never come back. That's obviously a portion of this high price to earnings/growth sector, as well as this loss-making tech stock dynamic,' Emma Fisher, an analyst at Australian share fund Airlie Funds Management, told investors on a webcast. Afterpay fitted the latter description, she said. The buy now, pay later company should be considered a financial business, but was priced as a fast-growing tech company. 'It's a lending business—you borrow at a rate, and lend out at a higher rate,' Fisher said. 'I view it as a mispriced asset. It's priced off the wrong multiple, in my view.'[1]

Was the market in the middle of a dramatic rotation out of growth stocks and into value stocks?

'Growth is about predicting the future, value is usually about fixing the past,' Coatue's reclusive founder, Philippe Laffont, told his Twitter followers. He'd sporadically imparted his wisdom on the social-media platform since the start of the year.

But rising bond rates had made the future more expensive, and investors turned back to look at what stocks they'd left behind in the rampage. For the time being at least, sentiment had swung.

• • •

Matthew Wilson was a banking analyst with decades of experience. He knew the big four banks and their storied histories inside out. He had strong views on where they'd gone right and where they'd gone wrong. And he wasn't afraid to share them with his clients and discuss them with banking executives.

As Afterpay and Zip had grown into large listed titans, small-companies analyst Julian Mulcahy passed coverage to Wilson, who'd joined stockbroking firm Evans & Partners eighteen months earlier from Deutsche Bank. Wilson viewed the rise of Afterpay as a problem partly of the big banks' own making. For decades they had focused their efforts on squeezing as much as they could by pushing one main product—the standard home loan—on their customers.

A home loan is a highly commoditised product. There are six million of them in Australia, and after all costs, the big banks made an annual profit in 2020 of about 1 per cent on the $1.5 trillion loaned out, around $15 billion. But global banking rules considered mortgages ultra-safe, and the big banks were large and sophisticated enough not to lose money by writing them. A typical bank is required to hold 10 per cent of shareholder capital against any loan, but a mortgage written by a big bank is allowed to be 'risk weighted' to 16 per cent of its value. A $500,000 loan, for instance, can be treated as a $70,000 loan, which means only $7000 (10 per cent) of equity had to be put up. The 0.5 per cent lending profit, or $2500, represents a 35 per cent return on equity. That attractive return meant the winning strategy was simply to flog more home loans. Little else mattered.

Afterpay, Wilson said, had been allowed to prosper at the expense of the blinkered banks. 'The major banks focused on harvesting excessive returns from one product ([approximately] 35% RoE [return on equity] home loan), under-invested and behaved poorly, because shareholders demanded dividends and executives, big salaries—short-termism,' he wrote. 'Afterpay seized the opportunity, its shareholders content with growth—the true allure of equity. The major banks are now relegated to low margin disenfranchised factories. Meanwhile, Afterpay has morphed from a once quaint payments app to lifestyle tool—much like the "old bank manager"— trusted and fair. Ah, the irony.'[2]

The irony was not lost on Commonwealth Bank chief Matt Comyn. He had headed up the retail banking division that sold home loans and was the engine of the bank's profit machine before rising to the top job. But CBA had come unstuck in the process, and bore the brunt of the public's ire before and during the Banking Royal Commission.

CBA also knew that, as a regulated bank, and one that had only just recovered from the intense spotlight of the Hayne inquiry, it would not be able to launch a buy now, pay later product with anything lighter than the existing checks it applied to other credit products. It was an issue of frustration for Comyn as he watched Afterpay accumulate customers without applying extensive customer checks. Comyn had endeared himself to Canberra as the bank moved swiftly to support customers through the pandemic by deferring loan repayments. But it was not able to onboard young customers as quickly as Afterpay, which did not screen customers by examining income or expenditure when it accepted them onto its platform. CBA had also done better than its rivals in catering to the next generation of customers through banking, savings and investing apps. And it was prepared to take on Afterpay head on.

Commonwealth Bank had pumped US$350 million into Klarna, including a pro-rata allocation in the capital raising that Klarna announced at the start of March. As Klarna's valuation soared, CBA had made a $1.5 billion return on its investment. But it wasn't in it for the venture capital gains. CBA had to stay at the cutting edge of customer engagement—and it wasn't satisfied as it lost customers in their early to mid-20s. While Klarna was surging in the United States, merchant and customer numbers in Australia were low, and CBA feared Afterpay would lure away its own customers, especially its younger ones. It was turf CBA was intent on defending.

The battle had taken on added significance as Afterpay was preparing to launch transaction and deposit accounts with the help of CBA's biggest rival, Westpac. This would inevitably see millennials park their regular pay with Afterpay.

So, on 17 March 2021, CBA dropped its bombshell. It would create its own buy now, pay later product. Customers could create an instalment payment plan when they purchased something by choosing a new buy now, pay later card in their digital wallet as an alternative to the traditional debit or credit card. Similar to PayPal's addition of a 'Pay in Four' button for online shopping, CBA would allow up to 4 million of its retail customers to pay in four instalments, and it would not charge merchants any more than the normal payment fees.

The move was stunning, because the bank had already partnered with Klarna to compete with Afterpay. Now it was raising the stakes. While the move was billed as a beefed-up attack, in reality it was a defensive move, prompted in part by the Afterpay tie-up with Westpac.

Commonwealth Bank also sent a message to regulators: it would conduct credit bureau checks to ensure deferred payments plans were suitable for its customers, and said some of its customers were struggling with multiple buy now, pay later debts during COVID-19. 'We are going to treat it like it is credit,' CBA's group executive for retail banking services, Angus Sullivan, told journalists on a conference call.

Sullivan had met consumer-group representatives, including Fiona Guthrie, CEO of Financial Counselling Australia, through the bank's consumer advisory group as the product was being prepared, and knew that the more detailed credit checking would win their support. After being at war during the royal commission, CBA and the consumer groups now found themselves in an unlikely alliance.

It was one that irked those in the Afterpay camp, who felt their common ground was a misguided devotion to the status quo, to existing frameworks and structures that were ill-equipped to handle new models such as Afterpay's.

But analysts now recognised another key difference: Afterpay had created a platform that was driving retail sales, a feat a new digital card in a CBA wallet was unlikely to replicate. Because CBA would not create a referral service to merchants or undertake any marketing services to help drive incremental sales like Afterpay had done, 'there is still a strong case for merchants to continue to accept Afterpay as a payments option', Credit Suisse analyst James Cordukes said.[3]

Afterpay had a comeback of its own. It had hired a seasoned banking executive, Lee Hatton, from Suncorp, and before that NAB, who provided the latest thinking on Afterpay Money, which would use Westpac's 'banking-as-a-service' offering to create new banking experiences using customer data.

'Anything the banks are thinking about is not on our horizon,' Hatton explained. 'We are not building another "me too" . . . The user experience is more like a shopping experience than it is a banking experience.'[4]

There was another benefit of the banking plan: the potential to reduce the costs of transacting on the card networks. Processing fees paid to the card companies represented around 26 per cent of Afterpay's revenue in 2020; using direct bank account transfers could lower Afterpay's costs by reducing its reliance on the Visa and Mastercard networks.

'Afterpay may have the potential to offer transactions between their own platform and the banks' directory without having to transact through Visa or Mastercard's payments network which would essentially cut out the middleman for the transaction fee whereby BNPL would effectively supplement the credit card,' Macquarie analysts said in a report on 24 March.[5]

The deal with Westpac showed that Afterpay was thinking about how to diversify its income from merchant fees and late fees. While it wasn't planning on charging customers for the transaction and deposit accounts, it would gather data on customers' spending beyond the buy now, pay later product, helping Afterpay understand its customers' needs. In the future, it could act as a broker, referring customers to various products, in or beyond financial services, potentially earning a referral fee from the product provider. There were also options around loyalty programs, which could diversify its revenue base.

But a shot across Afterpay's bow came in the form of a report by lobbying group C/T. Political strategists Lynton Crosby and Mark Textor had run successful election campaigns and their reports were read closely in Canberra. The C/T report, featured in the 'Chanticleer' column in *The Australian Financial Review*, found that 75 per cent of Australians thought buy now, pay later had led them to buy things they couldn't afford, while one in three users said it had pushed their debt to 'uncomfortable' levels. Buy now, pay later users took advantage of the scheme that allowed them to tap their superannuation funds during the COVID-19 pandemic, and spent more than they saved during that period, the report said.[6]

To date, ASIC and the RBA had been subtly discouraged from tampering with an Aussie success story, but transmitted reminders that they were still very much watching the space. 'On the whole, buy now, pay later is awesome for most consumers, but unfortunately for one in five it is a very expensive form of credit,' ASIC deputy chair Karen Chester told *The Australian Financial Review* Business Summit in March.[7]

A week later, on 18 March 2021, the Reserve Bank's researchers published a sober but highly insightful paper as they continued to mull over how to regulate the sector. 'While the development of these new payment services is evidence of Australia's innovative and evolving payments system, it may also raise issues for policymakers,' RBA staffers Chay Fisher, Cara Holland and Tim West wrote.[8]

For all the hype, buy now, pay later accounted for only 1 per cent of all transaction volumes, and 3 per cent of online transaction volumes, in the Australian economy just prior to the pandemic. It hadn't become large enough to warrant the Reserve Bank's intervention.

But the RBA's justification that the sector was too small to worry about just yet was branded 'twisted logic' by an unnamed bank chairman. 'Normally you try and address a problem before it gets too big,' that person told *AFR* columnist Karen Maley. 'That's because once it gets bigger, it is more difficult and disruptive to stop things, because business has organised itself around a certain model.'[9]

As the banks fought to defend their turf, there was a genuine dilemma for the Reserve Bank, which had made it a mission to reduce the costs and frictions in the financial system that payment fees create. The no-surcharge rules Afterpay had forced on its merchants, requiring them to not pass on its fee to customers, ran directly counter to that. But the RBA had to consider that other sprawling, low-cost payments networks had also been small once.

Repeating RBA governor Philip Lowe's observations in his speech before Christmas, the paper said that, over time, a public policy case might emerge where the no-surcharge rules would have to go. But when? And how? The Reserve Bank said it was talking to providers to determine specific thresholds on exactly when buy now, pay later would become too much of a systemic force for it to ignore.

• • •

Anthony Eisen's colleagues had always marvelled at both his intellect and his work ethic. By applying both, he'd helped to create a company that had grown to be Australia's twelfth-largest by value in just five years before its share price began to fall in March and April.

One mid-November evening in 2018, in the Toorak mansion of Alex Waislitz, Eisen had admitted to a fund manager seated next to him at a charity dinner that he was exhausted. The frequent trips to Canberra to meet lawmakers and face committees to defend Afterpay from more regulation had worn him down. But on 11 February 2021, Eisen had the luxury of fronting politicians in his home town of Sydney. The Senate committee he was appearing before didn't want to grill him about the virtues and vices of buy now, pay later, but on what Australia could do to foster its own vibrant technology industry.

As always, Eisen prepared meticulously and spoke deliberately, repeatedly referring to businesses such as Afterpay that 'didn't fit in a box'. He told the MPs that in the aftermath of the pandemic, Afterpay staffers in Silicon Valley were clamouring to come to Australia. With Australia's 'incredible lifestyle, fairness and government opportunities, what we've seen is a real interest in staff, employees, from overseas and employees from other companies that would consider coming to live in Australia'. Australia had a 'once in a lifetime, once in a generation opportunity to become a world leader' in technology, he offered.

Australia had the skills. But it lacked the mindset to scale-up ideas and export them around the world. Now, the Australian health authorities' stellar management of the COVID-19 pandemic provided Australia with a chance to compete with Texas, Canada and Tel Aviv in luring money and talent away from Silicon Valley.

Whether Australia's edge was a fleeting pandemic aberration or a dispersion of money, power and control to new outposts was an open question. And despite Afterpay's extraordinary growth, there was still a widely held view that its high valuation would itself be fleeting.

Afterpay had been listed on the ASX for nearly five years. In that time, its active customers had increased by 344 times, from 38,000 to 13.1 million, and the number of merchants was up by 747 times, from 100 to 74,700. Monthly transaction volumes had grown from 2.8 million to 1.6 billion, or nearly 570 times. The company's valuation had increased from $100 million to $30 billion, creating an extraordinary amount of wealth, a large share of which resided not with venture capital funds and large institutions, but in the hands of individual investors and Afterpay's staff.

Afterpay had made ordinary people rich beyond their dreams, and haunted those who had passed on the investment, or sold too early.

Among the winners were Eastern Suburbs real estate agents, as Afterpay staffers bought multi-million-dollar mansions in exclusive suburbs such as Bellevue Hill, Dover Heights and Bondi—and still had tens of millions left over. On 20 March, Domain's real estate reporter Lucy Macken revealed that Molnar had paid $18 million for an unattractive block of six apartments in Ben Buckler, the rocky outcrop at the northern end of Bondi Beach. In August 2019, the Molnars had bought the penthouse of the adjacent triplex for $10 million, and they'd since purchased the two apartments below for $8 million each.

Nick Molnar had become Moriah College's most famous alumnus. Earlier that week, on 18 March, he'd returned to his alma mater to speak at a cocktail party hosted by the school's foundation. It had been fourteen years since he sat in Stephanie Schwarz's computing class and wandered the playground amid the buildings branded with the names of Jewish benefactors who had achieved so much in Australian business. The enduring gift the school gave him, he said, was the friendships he formed with his classmates.

A week later, on 25 March, Molnar was at the Westfield in Bondi Junction, whose signage he'd seen countless times from the Moriah playground as he was growing up. He was there to launch Afterpay's latest offering, a digital card for its customers' mobile phones that would allow them to tap on payment terminals to make instore purchases, replacing the system of taking a picture of a barcode. Molnar had grown up in the shadow of this Westfield shopping centre; now he was helping its retail tenants connect with new customers and sell more stuff.

It had been a tumultuous twelve months. It was almost exactly a year since Afterpay's share price had plunged below $10, as Molnar was stuck in San Francisco. At the launch, he was asked about the latest threat from the banks coming onto his turf. He wasn't worried. Afterpay users didn't trust the banks, he said. That banks were getting more aggressive was further validation that the world was shifting from credit to debit—the fundamental shift in millennial behaviour after the global financial crisis that he'd identified while selling jewellery from his bedroom.

On the day of the Westfield digital card launch, *The Australian Financial Review Magazine* published its cover interview with Molnar. Most subscribers read the article online. But those who ventured into a newsagent's to buy their scratch cards or lotto tickets and picked up the glossy edition inside the printed newspaper would have seen his face on the cover, under a headline that read 'So Hot Right Now'.

There was also a quote from Molnar on the cover that pointed to the strain of building a start-up, and the inevitable pressure of being in the spotlight at such a young age. Although he'd become spectacularly successful, and created more wealth than he could ever have dreamed of, Molnar wasn't sleeping any easier.

'This has happened really fast,' he said. 'So you feel like you're on a knife's edge. And you feel like that every day. I wake up in the morning with the same level of anxiety that I woke up with on day one.'

# EPILOGUE

On Tuesday, 20 April 2021, as this book was being edited for publication, Afterpay released a trading update to the Australian Securities Exchange that pointed to another strong quarter of growth. Buried near the end of the four-page release was a statement of intent: the company had advanced plans to list its shares in the United States. Goldman Sachs was appointed to manage the process. Afterpay's investors were largely US institutions, and as the US market was larger and its business was growing more rapidly there, Afterpay was morphing into an American business. The logical next step was to relist either on the Nasdaq or the New York Stock Exchange. As for the numbers themselves, they once again showed that Afterpay was growing at an impressive rate in the United States and expanding its presence in new European markets. In Australia, the growth was slowing.

Afterpay said it would remain headquartered in Australia, but the move was rich in symbolism. If it occurs, it would cap off a turbulent and spectacular five years on the Australian Securities Exchange. Afterpay had outgrown its roots; it was moving into adolescence. The announcement provided an appropriate moment with which to conclude this book.

Writing a book about such a rapidly evolving subject was always going to leave us exposed to the risk that we'd be caught out by a dramatic plot twist. But regardless of what happens next for Afterpay, the developments won't change the context of the extraordinary events that led to the creation, growth and coming of age of Afterpay and the buy now, pay later sector around it. It was a story that took place amid a backdrop of significant change in banking, financial markets, politics and society, change that has influenced Afterpay's path. The shape and substance of our version of events was a function of those who were willing to engage with us, and to what extent.

Nick Molnar and Anthony Eisen provided assistance, as did others close to Afterpay. But this was an independent book, and we approached it as we do our day-to-day reporting. Over a six-month period of research and writing, we found it fascinating that highly intelligent people reached completely opposed conclusions about Afterpay's value and its merits: this is a company that polarises opinion on many issues, from how it should be regulated and valued to how long it should be allowed to operate without producing profits. On these matters, we took no position. The future will settle these debates.

Amid all the nay-sayers and the doubters, one question kept niggling: why has Afterpay succeeded so spectacularly? Over the course of our reporting, we were offered many thoughts on why it had achieved so much so quickly. Many of those insights are captured in the book.

One reason is undoubtedly the partnership between Nick Molnar and Anthony Eisen. The founders' blend of entrepreneurialism and experience was perhaps the most important factor. Both are fiercely competitive and hardworking. There was plenty of admiration—if begrudging at times—for the way they have executed their vision. A common comment was that all their success had not changed them as people.

A second reason Afterpay succeeded was because it hired well, recruiting experienced people in key roles. The company was prepared to pay for talent—and, as some have legitimately argued, at too great a cost—but quality staff has undoubtedly been instrumental in Afterpay's success.

Like all young companies, Afterpay made many mistakes and survived some near-death experiences. But Eisen and Molnar acted quickly to rectify them, and learned how to turn unrelenting scrutiny and looming disaster into an opportunity. If they hadn't, the journey would have ended far sooner.

They maintained their focus on a product that worked for young customers who viewed credit differently to their parents. It became clear that the product was more than a mechanism for paying for things: it was a whole new way to experience shopping.

Afterpay was also able to remove the shackles that have restrained many Australian companies operating in a relatively small market of 20 million people: how to conjure up new products to sell to the same customers. Instead, Afterpay was prepared to venture into new markets to achieve the growth its investors had come to demand. In that respect, Afterpay will encourage more Australian entrepreneurs to export their ideas, rather than import the ideas of others.

Afterpay proved to be the ultimate networking company. It was built on relationships established over decades in the trenches of bank dealing rooms and during twenty-minute drives to the airport. The interconnections fed on each other, to build a business that itself grew stronger through the same powerful network effect.

Above all else, Afterpay has come to embody an era of capitalism when new ideas were given more time and more money than ever before to reshape industries and the rules that govern them. Afterpay unearthed that unsuspected secret and created untold wealth well before it delivered the profits the market had valued. Only when it does will the purists embrace buy, now pay later as not only disruptive, but enduring.

# ACKNOWLEDGEMENTS

THE IDEA THAT 'success has many fathers' came up a lot in our interviews about Afterpay. That is unequivocally the case for this book, which would not have been possible without the goodwill of many individuals, who all believed that the story of Afterpay had to be told, and told well.

Whether we achieved that or not is for others to decide, but we are immensely grateful for their extensive assistance. They took the time to speak to us, often in detail, about their role in the Afterpay story, and trusted us to relay their experiences fairly and accurately. The nature of our work requires us to operate with some degree of discretion. That makes it difficult for us to name certain individuals whose help was integral in the writing of this book. They know who they are, and without their participation the story we have told would be inferior. The anecdotes, tip-offs large and small, clues and introductions were individually and collectively invaluable.

We would also like to acknowledge all those involved in the Afterpay story that we never got to speak to or didn't mention in the book. We were constrained by several factors, mainly time, and concede that key contributions have no doubt gone unrecognised in these pages.

At Afterpay, Anthony Eisen and Nick Molnar were great sports. They made it clear from the beginning that our book was not desirable to them, but still they took the time to help us where possible, answering our questions. While Afterpay divided many in Australian finance, there was unanimous respect for what Eisen and Molnar had built and how they'd built it.

A special thanks to Marie Festa at Afterpay for helping us arrange internal Afterpay interviews, and for helping us during the fact-checking process.

The book would not have been possible without the support of *The Australian Financial Review*, where we both work. Editor-in-chief Michael Stutchbury, editor Paul Bailey and managing editor Joanne Gray gave the project their blessing. The companies and markets editors Ben Potter and James Daggar-Nickson dealt with our absence when we took time off to write the book. The help, support and encouragement of our colleagues, too, many of whose reporting we relied upon, was much appreciated.

At Allen & Unwin, Elizabeth Weiss embraced the idea for this book almost immediately, and held us to a deadline that we privately thought was impossible but always appreciated was essential. Samantha Kent and Julian Welch meticulously edited our book with patience and skilfully identified weak spots in our storytelling before others did. Special thanks to Philip Campbell for the cover, which went through a few iterations before landing on fonts, colours and images that we hope have captured readers' attention. Also, special thanks to a very good friend for the introduction to Elizabeth long before we actually had a half-decent book idea.

We are immensely grateful to David Gonski, Malcolm Turnbull, Jane Lu and Greg Zuckerman, who all kindly agreed to read our book—a tremendous support for first-time authors.

Tinny Lenthen and the team at the Sydney Jewish Museum's library were accommodative, warm and insightful. The early chapters would not have been possible without their help. More generally, the museum's effort to document the lives of immigrants and Holocaust survivors was a huge help to us, and will be to future generations.

We would also like to pay our respects to the family of the late Carla Zampatti, whom we mention in the book. She was an avid reader of books, and a champion of immigrants paving their way in Australia and of Afterpay.

On a personal level, the writing of the book coincided with a difficult period for the Shapiro family, as the co-author's uncle Ian passed away from COVID-19 in South Africa. The pandemic has separated the family for longer than we could bear, but the support and encouragement of family around the world is greatly appreciated.

Without doubt, the heroes of the book are our partners, Anya and Jenny, who carried the extra burden with our young families, while we slaved away late into the evenings and on weekends to deliver this book. And of course our kids, Archie and Elijah, and Sam and Hannah, who spent less time with their fathers over the past six months than they would have liked as we were chained to our desks, heads buried in our laptops. Theirs is the first debt we have to pay back!

# NOTES

**Chapter 1**

1 Susie Wise, *The Brighter Side of Darkness,* Darlinghurst: Sydney Jewish Museum, 2013.

2 Hungarian Jewish men were not conscripted to the armed forces so were instead forced to work in camps.

3 Wise, *The Brighter Side of Darkness.*

4 Jill Margo, *Frank Lowy: A Second Life,* Sydney: HarperCollins, 2015.

5 Margo, *Frank Lowy.*

6 Suzanne D. Rutland, *Edge of the Diaspora: Two Centuries of Jewish Settlement in Australia,* New York: Holmes & Meier, 2001.

7 Simon Lipski, 'Partisan', *Australian Jewish Times,* 21 August 1986 (referenced in Rutland).

8 Roslyn Sugarman & Peter McNeil, *Dressing Sydney: The Jewish Fashion Story,* Darlinghurst: Sydney Jewish Museum, 2013.

9 Rutland, *Edge of the Diaspora.*

10 Rutland, *Edge of the Diaspora.*

11 Roslyn Sugarman, Peter McNeil, *Dressing Sydney.*

12 Roslyn Sugarman, Peter McNeil, *Dressing Sydney.*

13 Roslyn Sugarman, Peter McNeil, *Dressing Sydney.*

14 Roslyn Sugarman, Peter McNeil, *Dressing Sydney.*

15 Roslyn Sugarman, Peter McNeil, *Dressing Sydney.*

16 Cara Waters, 'Afterpay "brain bubble" came from jeweller Ice Online', *The Sydney Morning Herald,* 3 November 2019.

17 Nick Molnar, Speech to graduating class at Sydney University Business School, 2018, <www.sydney.edu.au/content/dam/corporate/documents/business-school/industry-and-community/alumni/nicholas-molnar-graduation-speech-2018.pdf>.

18 Joshua Hyatt, 'Brothers from another planet: Four rabbis. One internet incubator. So, who won?', *CNN Money,* 1 February 2002.

19 Hyatt, 'Brothers from another planet'.

20 Hyatt, 'Brothers from another planet'.

## Chapter 2

1 Anthony Hughes, Geoff Wilson & Matthew Kidman, *Masters of the Market: Secrets of Australia's Leading Sharemarket Investors*, Milton: John Wiley & Sons, 2005.
2 Jennifer Hewett, 'The Ron and Gary Show, 20 years on', *The Age*, 9 November 2002.
3 Yvonne van Dongen, 'Sir Ron Brierley: The old warrior', *The New Zealand Herald*, 3 June 2011.
4 Trevor Sykes, 'Sir Ron runs a tight ship at GPG', *The Australian Financial Review*, 2 October 2000.
5 Sykes, 'Sir Ron runs a tight ship'.
6 Anthony Hughes, Geoff Wilson, Matthew Kidman, *Masters of the Market*.
7 Eli Greenblat, 'No rest for this merry band of raiders', *The Australian Financial Review*, 3 January 2006.
8 Tony Boyd, 'Exit Sir Ron, scourge of lazy boards', *The Australian Financial Review*, 12 February 2011.
9 Yvonne van Dongen, 'Once a Warrior', *The Australian Financial Review Magazine*, 27 May 2011.
10 George Liondis, 'GPG has Clearview on offer', *The Australian Financial Review*, 13 July 2012.

## Chapter 3

1 Lauren Sams, 'In Vogue', *The Australian Financial Review Magazine*, April 2021.
2 Cara Waters, 'Afterpay "brain bubble" came from jeweller Ice Online'.
3 Caitlin E. Anderson (curator), 'Buy now, pay later: A history of personal credit', Harvard Business School Historical Collections, <www.library. hbs.edu/hc/credit/credit4b.html>.
4 Beverley Kingston, *Basket, Bag and Trolley: A History of Shopping in Australia*, Melbourne: Oxford University Press, 1994.
5 Beverley Kingston, *Basket, Bag and Trolley*.
6 James Surowiecki, 'Delayed Gratification', *The New Yorker,* 25 December 2011.
7 Cara Waters, 'Afterpay "brain bubble" came from jeweller Ice Online'.

## Chapter 4

1 XTCL was shorthand for ex-Touch Corp Limited, the remnants of the original Touchcorp.

## Chapter 5

1 'Crutching' refers to the removal of wool from around the tail and between the rear legs of a sheep for hygiene purposes.
2 Damon Kitney, 'Broker says small best in hard times', *The Australian*, 13 March 2012.
3 Kitney, 'Broker says small best in hard times'.
4 Jessica Gardner, 'Inside the booming baby business', *The Australian Financial Review*, 6 September 2014.

5 'Tips from a (newly engaged) jeweller on choosing the perfect engagement ring', *Easy Weddings*, <www.easyweddings.com.au/articles/tips-newly-engaged-jeweller-choosing-perfect-engagement-ring/>.

## Chapter 6

1 Philippa Coates, 'Showpo's Jane Lu debuts on Young Rich List after leaving accountancy for fashion', *The Australian Financial Review*, 20 October 2017.
2 Interview with Dean Fergie, January 2021.
3 Shaun Drummond, 'ZipMoney attacks FlexiGroup, GE through $5m backdoor listing', *The Australian Financial Review*, 30 June 2015.
4 Shaun Drummond, 'Afterpay fintech float closes up 25pc', *The Australian Financial Review*, 4 May 2016.
5 Vesna Poljak, 'Why Dean Fergie likes Skydive the Beach, Freelancer, and Afterpay', *The Australian Financial Review*, 22 August 2016.
6 Vesna Poljak, 'Best small cap longs and shorts for 2017', *The Australian Financial Review*, 28 December 2016.

## Chapter 7

1 Strictly speaking, a unicorn is a private company with a valuation of more than a billion dollars, but fund managers have increasingly used the term for listed companies as well.
2 'Dissecting Afterpay', *Find the Moat*, 13 April 2017, <http://findthemoat.com/2017/04/13/dissecting-afterpay>.
3 Pamela Williams, *Killing Fairfax: Packer, Murdoch & the Ultimate Revenge*, Sydney: HarperCollins, 2013.
4 Tom Richardson, 'How Sezzle seized on Afterpay model to go from flop to unicorn', *The Australian Financial Review*, 19 July 2020.

## Chapter 8

1 Mark Solomons, 'ASIC lacks courage on enforcement says former investigator', *The Sydney Morning Herald*, 27 April 2018, <www.smh.com.au/business/banking-and-finance/asic-lacks-courage-on-enforcement-says-former-investigator-20180425-p4zbn0.html>.
2 Sarah Danckert, 'The "two strike" rulers playing and winning the shame game', *The Sydney Morning Herald*, 18 May 2019.
3 Danckert, 'The "two strike" rulers playing and winning the shame game'.
4 Ian Verrender, 'How the Commonwealth Bank laid the groundwork for a royal commission', ABC News, 7 August 2017, <www.abc.net.au/news/2017-08-07/commonwealth-bank-laid-the-groundwork-for-royal-commission/8779598>.
5 O'Connor most likely is referring to Afterpay merchants as distinct from customers of merchants.
6 Debbie O'Connor, 'Why retailers' ads targeting millennials with Afterpay loans is a brand risk', *Mumbrella*, 23 March 2018, <https://mumbrella.com.au/afterpay-ads-encouraging-millennials-to-get-into-debt-must-stop-506810>.

7 'Why Afterpay is the marijuana of credit', *Barefoot Investor*, 4 December 2018, <www.barefootinvestor.com/articles/why-afterpay-is-the-marijuana-of-credit>.

## Chapter 9

1 Yolanda Redrup, 'Aconex deal shows investors ignore Aussie tech at their peril: Mike Cannon Brookes', *The Australian Financial Review*, 18 December 2017, <www.afr.com/technology/shareholders-back-aconex-deal-as-short-sellers-weep-20171218-h06bmn>.

2 Redrup, 'Aconex deal shows investors ignore Aussie tech at their peril: Mike Cannon Brookes'.

3 Interview with Jun Bei Liu, January 2021.

## Chapter 10

1 Clancy Yeates, 'Afterpay shares surge on US launch', *The Sydney Morning Herald*, 15 May 2018.

2 Jonathan Shapiro & Vesna Poljak, 'Fundies' best long and short ideas', *The Australian Financial Review*, 6–7 January 2018.

3 L1 Capital, June 2018 quarterly investor letter, 30 July 2018.

4 Roger Montgomery, 'The market loves Afterpay, but how long will the euphoria last?', 1 August 2018, <https://rogermontgomery.com/the-market-loves-afterpay-but-how-long-will-the-euphoria-last>.

5 James Eyers, 'How the Kardashians helped Nick Molnar launch Afterpay in the US', *The Australian Financial Review*, 31 May 2019.

6 James Eyers, 'How the Kardashians helped Nick Molnar launch Afterpay in the US'.

7 Sam Shead, 'Klarna becomes Europe's most valuable fintech firm with new $5.5 billion valuation', *Forbes*, 6 August 2019.

8 John Hempton, 'Afterpay, a regulator view', Bronte Capital, 28 November 2018.

9 Marcus Padley, 'Imagine a world where debt doesn't exist', *The Sydney Morning Herald*, 18 September 2018.

10 Marcus Padley, 'Glory and pain—the hazards of being a fund manager', *The Australian Jewish News*, 10 December 2018.

## Chapter 11

1 Damon Kitney, 'Afterpay, pays the price', *The Australian*, 12 January 2019.

2 Alan Kohler, 'How millennials are spending their money', *Eureka Report*, 29 January 2019.

## Chapter 12

1 Senate Economics References Committee, *Interest Rates and Informed Choice in the Australian Credit Card Market*, Commonwealth of Australia, 16 December 2015.

2 Australian Securities & Investments Commission, *Report 580: Credit Card Lending in Australia*, July 2018.

3 AlphaBeta, *How Millennials Manage Money: Facts on the Spending Habits of Young Australians*, Report commissioned by Afterpay, 2019.

4 John Kehoe, Misa Han & Jonathan Shapiro, 'Afterpay share plunge probe explores Chinese whispers', *The Australian Financial Review*, 21 February 2019.

5 Colin Kruger & Patrick Hatch, 'Millennial masterstroke: All credit to Afterpay in generation grab', *The Sydney Morning Herald*, 2 March 2019.

6 Colin Kruger, 'Afterpay spikes after big growth in the US', *The Sydney Morning Herald*, 5 June 2019.

## Chapter 13

1 Sebastian Mallaby, *More Money than God: Hedge Funds and the Making of a New Elite*, New York: The Penguin Press, 2010, p. 113.

2 Brook Turner, 'Lunch with the AFR: Julian Robertson', *The Australian Financial Review*, 19 July 2013.

3 Hema Parmar, Melissa Karsh & Sophie Alexander, 'Quiet achiever: The 44-year-old investing genius with a $6.6 billion fortune', *The Sydney Morning Herald*, 28 June 2019.

4 Marc Whittaker, 'How different is it this time?', Investors Mutual Ltd., 18 July 2019, <https://iml.com.au/news-and-views/insights/how-different-it-time>.

5 Joe Aston, 'Former Afterpay CFO in $48 million options haul', *The Australian Financial Review*, 2 February 2021.

6 Jonathan Shapiro & James Eyers, 'Disclosure cloud over Afterpay's US growth push', *The Australian Financial Review*, 17 April 2019.

7 Adam Creighton, 'Afterpay goes to top of class at Harvard', *The Australian*, 1 June 2019.

8 An API, or application programming interface, is a piece of software that connects computer systems.

9 James Eyers, 'Afterpay CEO dismisses threat from CBA's big investment', *The Australian Financial Review*, 12 August 2019.

10 Tony Boyd, 'Afterpay snares ASIC's buy now, pay later guru', *The Australian Financial Review*, 1 August 2019.

11 James Eyers, 'Larry Summers: Why I joined Afterpay', *The Australian Financial Review*, 17 October 2019.

12 Parliament of Australia, *Journals of the Senate*, no. 14, 11 September 2019, p. 441.

13 In fact, Afterpay's net transaction loss was 0.7 per cent, but the gross losses, excluding the addition of late fees, was 1.1 per cent.

## Chapter 14

1 CEDA annual dinner, Transcript of Q&A, published in *The Australian Financial Review*, 17 November 2020.

2 James Eyers, 'Consumers join retailers in war on Afterpay', *The Australian Financial Review*, 5 February 2020.

3 James Eyers, 'Consumers join retailers in war on Afterpay'.

4 Reserve Bank of Australia, 'Submissions on Review of Retail Payments Regulation', 3 February 2020, <www.rba.gov.au/payments-and-infrastructure/submissions/review-of-retail-payments-regulation/index.html>.

5 Senate Select Committee on Financial Technology and Regulatory Technology, *Committee Hansard*, Sydney, 20 February 2020, p. 24.

6 James Eyers, 'Afterpay tells RBA it's "not a payments system"', *The Australian Financial Review*, 6 February 2020.

7 Guy Debelle, 'The Global Financial Crisis', 13 March 2019, <www.rba.gov.au/education/resources/videos.html>.

8 Julie-anne Sprague, 'Why a walk in the park beats Zoom, says Alex Waislitz', *The Australian Financial Review*, 9 June 2020.

9 Marc Kennis & Chen Ge, *The Buy Now, Pay Later Revolution*, Stocks Down Under research report, 25 August 2020.

10 James Daggar-Nickson, 'Why global expansion makes most sense now for Afterpay', *The Australian Financial Review*, 30 June 2020.

11 Chris Farrell, 'You can have fun in the stock market, but keep sums small', *Star Tribune*, 20 June 2020.

12 Andrei Stadnik, Jenny Hau, Richard Wiles, Sona Fernandes, 'Afterpay upgrade to OW: Building a global BNPL platform', Morgan Stanley, 8 July 2020.

13 Marcus Padley, 'The Afterpay bubble', *Livewire*, 11 July 2020, <www.livewiremarkets.com/wires/the-afterpay-bubble>.

14 Marc Kennis, Chen Ge, *The Buy Now, Pay Later Revolution*.

15 Susie Cagle, 'Would you take out a loan for a pair of jeans?', *Racked*, 29 November 2017.

16 Scott Galloway, *The Prof G Show* (podcast), 3 December 2020.

17 James Eyers, 'Afterpay urges ASIC to focus on its low bad debts', *The Australian Financial Review*, 28 August 2020.

18 Senate Select Committee on Financial Technology and Regulatory Technology, *Interim Report*, Commonwealth of Australia, September 2020, p. 216.

19 House of Representatives Economics Committee, 'Review of the Four Major Banks', *Committee Hansard*, Sydney, 4 September 2020.

20 James Eyers, 'Reserve Bank, ASIC urged to keep pressure on Afterpay', *The Australian Financial Review*, 14 September 2020.

21 James Eyers, 'Reserve Bank, ASIC urged to keep pressure on Afterpay'.

22 Supratim Adhikari, 'I was wrong on Afterpay: Big tech's fiercest critic lauds buy now, pay later darling', *The Sydney Morning Herald*, 28 October 2020.

23 Interview with Ben McGarry, February 2021.

24 Juliet Chung, 'Covid-19 caused chaos for investors in 2020. These hedge funds earned billions', *The Wall Street Journal*, 25 December 2020.

25 Robin Wigglesworth, '"Tiger cub" hedge fund Coatue surges to 52% gain', *The Financial Times*, 2 December 2020.

26 Tom Maloney & Hema Parmar, 'Coleman leads $23 billion payday for 15 hedge fund earners', *Bloomberg*, 15 February 2021.

27 Stephen Taub, 'The 20th annual Rich List, the definitive ranking of what hedge fund managers earned in 2020', *Institutional Investor*, 22 February 2021.

# NOTES

## Chapter 15

1 The Treasury, *Review of the Australian Payments System*, 21 October 2020.
2 The Treasury, *Payments System Review: Issues Paper*, November 2020.
3 James Eyers, 'ASIC to call out buy now, pay later "harms that we continue to see"', *The Australian Financial Review*, 13 November 2020.
4 Australian Securities & Investments Commission, *REP 672: Buy Now Pay Later: An Industry Update*, 16 November 2020.
5 The Australian Financial Review Banking & Wealth Summit, transcript, 18 November 2020.

## Chapter 16

1 Lauren Sams, 'In Vogue'.
2 Lauren Sams, 'In Vogue'.
3 Natasha Gillezeau, 'Afterpay underscores fashion links in TikTok campaign', *The Australian Financial Review*, 2 November 2020.
4 'Robinhood trader "sticking it to the man"'. *Reuters Now*, 30 January 2021, <www.reuters.com/video/watch/idPWzc?now=true>.
5 Nicholas Reimann, 'AOC calls Reddit-fueled GameStop frenzy similar to movement that put her in Congress', *Forbes*, 30 January 2021.
6 Dutch Authority for the Financial Markets (AFM), net short positions archive, <www.afm.nl>.
7 'Affirm: The morality of money', *The Generalist*, 10 December 2020, <https://thegeneralist.substack.com/p/affirm-the-morality-of-money>.
8 Donna Fuscaldo, 'Struggling online lender OnDeck sold to Enova International', *Forbes*, 29 July 2020.
9 Jeff Kaufli, 'Inside the billion-dollar plan to kill credit cards', *Forbes*, 8 February 2021.
10 Tom Richardson, 'PayPal flags extraordinary demand in buy now, pay later space', *The Australian Financial Review*, 3 November 2020.
11 Ashwini Chandra, *Some observations on US BNPL from PYPL's 4Q20*, Goldman Sachs research report, 4 February 2021.
12 Tom Beadle, 'PayPal's entry into "Pay in 4": Running the scenarios', UBS Global Research, 10 September 2020.
13 Tim Piper, *BNPL: Payments giant PayPal enters 'Pay in 4'*, RBC Capital Markets report, 6 September 2020.
14 Tom Richardson, 'Zip valuation frustrates boss after "absolutely cracking" quarter', *The Australian Financial Review*, 21 January 2021.
15 Sarah Thompson, Anthony Macdonald & Tim Boyd, 'Zip Co goes shopping for US investors, mulls second listing', *The Australian Financial Review*, 7 February 2021.
16 Thea de Gallier, Harvey Day & Hannah Price, 'Influencer: "Why I stopped working with Klarna"', BBC, 11 February 2021.
17 HM Treasury, 'Buy-now-pay-later products to be regulated', 2 February 2021, <www.gov.uk/government/news/buy-now-pay-later-products-to-be-regulated>.

18 Simon English, 'City watchdog launches clampdown on buy-now-pay-later loans', *Evening Standard*, 2 February 2021.

19 Julia Kollewe & Kalyeena Makortoff, 'Buy now pay later firms such as Klarna to face FCA regulation', *The Guardian*, 3 February 2021.

20 Hans van Leeuwen & James Eyers, 'Britain wields regulator's rod on buy now, pay later firms', *The Australian Financial Review*, 3 February 2021.

21 Danielle Wightman-Stone, 'London Fashion Week names Clearpay as principal partner', *FashionUnited*, 10 February 2021.

22 Danielle Wightman-Stone, 'London Fashion Week names Clearpay as principal partner'.

23 Danielle Wightman-Stone, 'MPs criticise London Fashion Week sponsorship deal with Clearpay', *FashionUnited*, 22 February 2021.

24 Consumers' Federation of Australia, 'Joint consumer submission: Australian Finance Industry Association (AFIA) Buy Now Pay Later Code of Practice', 6 May 2020, <http://consumersfederation.org.au/wp-content/uploads/2020/05/20200506-FINAL-Submission.pdf>.

25 James Eyers, 'ASIC lashes buy now, pay later code of conduct', *The Australian Financial Review*, 10 June 2020.

26 John Kehoe, 'Responsible lending laws to be axed', *The Australian Financial Review*, 24 September 2020.

27 James Eyers, 'Consumer groups attack the new buy now, pay later code of conduct', *The Australian Financial Review*, 24 February 2021.

28 James Eyers, 'Consumer groups attack the new buy now, pay later code of conduct'.

## Chapter 17

1 Richard Henderson, 'Nowhere to hide from market's growth traps', *The Australian Financial Review*, 9 March 2021.

2 Matthew Wilson & Nikolai Dale, 'Afterpay: Launched by Gen Y, embraced by Gen Z, positioning for Gen Alpha', E&P Financial, 25 February 2021.

3 Credit Suisse, 'Research Bulletin', 17 March 2021.

4 James Eyers, 'Afterpay readies for battle with CBA', *The Australian Financial Review*, 18 March 2021.

5 Macquarie Research, 'Afterpay: Buy Now Pay 2030', 24 March 2021.

6 Tony Boyd, 'Buy now, pay later has an image problem', *The Australian Financial Review*, 16 March 2021.

7 Michael Roddan & Jonathan Shapiro, 'ASIC will test new powers on buy now, pay later', *The Australian Financial Review*, 10 March 2021.

8 Chay Fisher, Cara Holland & Tim West, 'Developments in the buy now, pay later market', *RBA Bulletin*, March 2021.

9 Karen Maley, 'Bringing an end to the buy now, pay later lunacy', *The Australian Financial Review*, 22 March 2021.

# BIBLIOGRAPHY

THE BOOK RELIED on dozens of background interviews with Afterpay staff, past and present, and with investors, analysts, consultants, consumer advocate groups and regulators. They were conducted between December 2020 and April 2021.

For market data, pricing, share sales and stock-exchange filings, we relied on Bloomberg and Refinitiv Eikon, in addition to transcripts and recordings of various briefings over the period 2014–21. We relied on the Australian Securities Exchange website (www2.asx.com.au) for public disclosures, and we sourced corporate filings from the Australian Securities & Investments Commission (https://asic.gov.au). The resources to access these information sources were made available through our roles at *The Australian Financial Review*, which is owned by the Nine Entertainment Corporation. We used many research reports published by Australian brokerage firms and global investment banks, most of which were produced by knowledgeable analysts based in Sydney or Melbourne, and we thank them for their insights on the nuts and bolts of Afterpay's business model. These analysts were also integral to the story itself. In addition, the independent analysis of investors, consultants and other researchers was critical to our having an objective understanding of the sector.

The book relies extensively on tireless news coverage from our colleagues at *The Australian Financial Review* and other newspapers now owned by Nine but previously part of Fairfax Media, in particular *The Age* and *The Sydney Morning Herald*. In addition, we have made references to helpful articles in *The Australian*, and to global news publications such as *The Wall Street Journal*, *Bloomberg*, *The Financial Times* and especially *Forbes*' coverage of fintech in the United States. We also drew upon specialised retailing publications such as *FashionUnited* in the United Kingdom.

Several books uncovered during our reporting process were immensely helpful. We are most grateful to the Sydney Jewish Museum, which maintains a confronting yet inspiring collection of material in Darlinghurst, where we spent several hours in early 2021 reading about the horrors of the Holocaust, the history of Australian immigration and the foundations of the fashion industry in this country.

Our special thanks to Tinny Lenthen, librarian at the Sydney Jewish Museum, who found a collection of books for us that were invaluable. These included Susie Wise's *The Brighter Side of Darkness*. Susie is the grandmother of Nick Molnar. Her account and others provide a detailed insight into the lives of immigrants arriving in Australia after World War II. There was also a fascinating history of the rag trade in Sydney, *Dressing Sydney: The Jewish Fashion Story*, a catalogue for an exhibition of the same name, which provided an amazing account of the contribution of Jewish immigrants, who mostly gathered in Surry Hills and put skills often learned in European concentration camps to work to create the retailing industry in Australia. Lenthen also uncovered a special book documenting the creation of Moriah College, the Jewish school in Sydney that Nick Molnar attended from kindergarten, which bears a beautiful title: *If You Will It, It Is No Dream*.

Outside the Sydney Jewish Museum collection, there were some other classics that informed our thinking, including *Basket, Bag and Trolley*, Beverley Kingston's intriguing history of shopping in Australia, which detailed the rise of department stores and the influence of advertising and the consumer movement.

Sebastian Mallaby's *More Money than God: Hedge Funds and the Making of a New Elite* was helpful in retelling the rise and fall, and the enduring legacy, of hedge fund manager Julian Robertson. As we explored the history of credit and its close connections to retail, Joseph Nocera's *A Piece of the Action: How the Middle Class Joined the Money Class*, which details the creation and arrival of credit cards in the United States via the Bank of America, was an insightful guide. We would also like to thank Lanie Tindale, who helped us with our researching of retailers.

A comprehensive list of references follows below.

## Chapter 1

Susie Wise, *The Brighter Side of Darkness,* Darlinghurst: Sydney Jewish Museum, 2013

Jill Margo, *Frank Lowy: A Second Life,* Sydney: HarperCollins, 2015

Suzanne D. Rutland, *Edge of the Diaspora: Two Centuries of Jewish Settlement in Australia*, New York: Holmes & Meier, 2001

Simon Lipski, 'Partisan', *Australian Jewish Times,* 21 August 1986 [referenced in Suzanne D. Rutland's *Edge of the Diaspora*]

Roslyn Sugarman & Peter McNeil, *Dressing Sydney: The Jewish Fashion Story*, Darlinghurst: Sydney Jewish Museum, 2013

Suzanne D. Rutland, '*If You Will It, It Is No Dream: The Moriah Story, 1943–2003*', Caringbah: Playright Publishing, 2003

Cara Waters, 'Afterpay "brain bubble" came from jeweller Ice Online', *The Sydney Morning Herald*, 3 November 2019

Nick Molnar, Speech to graduating class at Sydney University Business School, 2018, <www.sydney.edu.au/content/dam/corporate/documents/business-school/industry-and-community/alumni/nicholas-molnar-graduation-speech-2018.pdf>

Joshua Hyatt, 'Brothers from another planet: Four rabbis. One internet incubator. So, who won?', *CNN Money*, 1 February 2002

**Chapter 2**
Anthony Hughes, Geoff Wilson & Matthew Kidman, *Masters of the Market: Secrets of Australia's Leading Sharemarket Investors*, Milton: John Wiley & Sons, 2005
Trevor Sykes, 'Sir Ron runs a tight ship at GPG', *The Australian Financial Review*, 2 October 2000
David Walker, 'At front line of Telstra battle', *The Age*, 19 November 1997
David Walker, '$35 billion man', *The Age*, 22 November 1997
Nick Tabakoff, 'Chris Tyler's secret past', *The Australian Financial Review*, 20 April 2000
Jennifer Hewett, 'The Ron and Gary show, 20 years on', *The Age*, 9 November 2002
Yvonne van Dongen, 'Ron Brierley: The old warrior', *The New Zealand Herald*, 3 June 2011
'Tony Ryan: wizard of the skies', *Royal Irish Academy*, 15 July 2016, <www.ria.ie/news/tony-ryan-wizard-skies>
Eli Greenblat, 'No rest for this merry band of raiders', *The Australian Financial Review*, 3 January 2006
Tony Boyd, 'Exit Sir Ron, scourge of lazy boards', *The Australian Financial Review*, 12 February 2011
Yvonne van Dongen, 'Once a Warrior', *The Australian Financial Review Magazine*, 27 May 2011
George Liondis, 'GPG has Clearview on offer', *The Australian Financial Review*, 13 July 2012

**Chapter 3**
Lauren Sams, 'In Vogue', *The Australian Financial Review Magazine*, 26 March 2021
Cara Waters, 'Afterpay "brain bubble" came from jeweller Ice Online', *The Sydney Morning Herald*, 3 November 2019
Caitlin E. Anderson (curator), 'Buy now, pay later: A history of personal credit', *Harvard Business School Historical Collections*, <www.library.hbs.edu/hc/credit/credit4b.html>

Beverley Kingston, *Basket, Bag and Trolley: A History of Shopping in Australia*, Melbourne: Oxford University Press, 1994

James Surowiecki, 'Delayed gratification', *The New Yorker,* 25 December 2011

Live Differently Productions, 'Afterpay commercial—Try before you pay—Master', <https://vimeo.com/136589621>

**Chapter 4**

Court documents filed in the Supreme Court of Victoria, Cleevecorp Pty Cleeve Group v Wendy Sze Teng Ng, S CI 2018 00897. Writ filed (13 March 2018), Amended Statement of Claim (21 June 2019), Defence (9 July 2019), Summons (1 November 2019), Affidavit (10 March 2020), Judge Signed Order (11 March 2020)

Takeovers Panel, 'Reasons for Decision: Touch Holdings Limited [2013] ATP 3', Australian Government, 15 May 2013

Touchcorp Limited, *Prospectus: Initial Public Offering*, 2015

Jonathan Shapiro, 'The secret battle for a billion-dollar Afterpay fortune', *The Australian Financial Review,* 23 December 2020

**Chapter 5**

Damon Kitney, 'Broker says small best in hard times', *The Australian,* 13 March 2012

Afterpay fundraising presentation, June 2015

'Tips from a (newly engaged) jeweller on choosing the perfect engagement ring', *Easy Weddings,* <www.easyweddings.com.au/articles/tips-newly-engaged-jeweller-choosing-perfect-engagement-ring>

Gabby Leibovich & Hezi Leibovich, *Catch of the Decade: How to Launch, Build and Sell a Digital Business,* Milton: Wiley, 2020

Jessica Gardner, 'Inside the booming baby business', *The Australian Financial Review,* 6 September 2014

**Chapter 6**

Glennon Capital, Quarterly webinar slide presentation, 2018

Philippa Coates, 'Showpo's Jane Lu debuts on Young Rich List after leaving accountancy for fashion', *The Australian Financial Review,* 20 October 2017

David Winton Harding & James William Holmes, *The Pit & The Pendulum: A Menagerie of Speculative Follies,* London: Winton Capital Management, 2012

Nick Molnar, Speech to graduating class at Sydney University Business School, 2018, <www.sydney.edu.au/content/dam/corporate/documents/business-school/industry-and-community/alumni/nicholas-molnar-graduation-speech-2018.pdf>

James Eyers, 'To $3b and beyond. What's the Zip Co special sauce?', *The Australian Financial Review Magazine*, 27 November 2020

Shaun Drummond, 'ZipMoney attacks FlexiGroup, GE through $5m backdoor listing', *The Australian Financial Review*, 30 June 2015

John McDuling, 'Atlassian IPO: Dual class shares and the case for founder control', *The Australian Financial Review*, 11 November 2015

Shaun Drummond, 'Afterpay fintech float closes up 25pc', *The Australian Financial Review*, 4 May 2016

Mark Bryant & Wilson Wong, 'Afterpay Another day, another deal', Wilson HTM Research, 29 November 2016

Vesna Poljak, 'Why Dean Fergie likes Skydive the Beach, Freelancer, and Afterpay', *The Australian Financial Review*, 22 August 2016

Vesna Poljak, 'Best small cap longs and shorts for 2017', *The Australian Financial Review*, 28 December 2016

**Chapter 7**

Court documents filed in the Supreme Court of Victoria, Cleevecorp Pty Cleeve Group v Wendy Sze Teng Ng S CI 2018 00897. Writ filed (13 March 2018), Amended Statement of Claim (21 June 2019), Defence (9 July 2019), Summons (1 November 2019), Affidavit (10 March 2020), Judge Signed Order (11 March 2020)

Arowana Australasian Value Opportunities Fund, Afterpay lunch presentation slides, April 2017

'Dissecting Afterpay', *Find the Moat*, 13 April 2017, <http://findthemoat.com/2017/04/13/dissecting-afterpay>

Vesna Poljak, 'The top stock ideas from Future Generation fundies', *The Australian Financial Review*, 16 May 2017

Jonathan Shapiro, 'Australian hedge fund Caledonia bets big on US property portal', *The Australian Financial Review*, 26 November 2014

Pamela Williams, *Killing Fairfax: Packer, Murdoch & the Ultimate Revenge*, Sydney: HarperCollins, 2013

Richard Coppleson, 'The Coppo Report', 27 November 2017

Tom Richardson, 'How Sezzle seized on Afterpay model to go from flop to unicorn', *The Australian Financial Review*, 19 July 2020

Emily Baker, 'Canberra sex toy business takes Afterpay, ZipPay to ACT Human Rights Commission', *The Canberra Times*, 10 October 2017

Marc Whittaker, 'How different is it this time?', *Investors Mutual Ltd*, 18 July 2019, <https://iml.com.au/news-and-views/insights/how-different-it-time>

## Chapter 8

Mark Solomons, 'ASIC lacks courage on enforcement says former investigator', *The Sydney Morning Herald*, 27 April 2018, <www.smh.com.au/business/banking-and-finance/asic-lacks-courage-on-enforcement-says-former-investigator-20180425-p4zbn0.html>

Sarah Danckert, 'One prosecution in 10 years: ASIC's track record under fire', *The Sydney Morning Herald*, 27 April 2018

Sarah Danckert, 'The "two strike" rulers playing and winning the shame game', *The Sydney Morning Herald*, 18 May 2019

James Samson & Nikitha Kariyawasam, 'Afterpay Touch Bespoke Analysis', Ownership Matters, 3 April 2018

Sujit Dey, Email to clients, 'Sales Commentary: APT Don't Underestimate ASIC's review of the sector', 14 March 2018

'Afterpay alert', *A Current Affair*, Nine Network, 16 April 2018

Debbie O'Connor, 'Why retailers' ads targeting millennials with Afterpay loans is a brand risk', *Mumbrella*, 23 March 2018, <https://mumbrella.com.au/afterpay-ads-encouraging-millennials-to-get-into-debt-must-stop-506810>

Ian Verrender, 'How the Commonwealth Bank laid the groundwork for a royal commission', *ABC News*, 7 August 2017, <www.abc.net.au/news/2017-08-07/commonwealth-bank-laid-the-groundwork-for-royal-commission/8779598>

'Why Afterpay is the marijuana of credit', *Barefoot Investor*, 4 December 2018, <www.barefootinvestor.com/articles/why-afterpay-is-the-marijuana-of-credit>

Senate Economics References Committee, 'Credit and financial services targeted at Australians at risk of financial hardship', *Committee Hansard*, Brisbane, 22 January 2019

**Chapter 9**
Vivek Shankar, 'Australia's most shorted stock has only one analyst saying sell', *Bloomberg*, 30 March 2017
Yolanda Redrup, 'Aconex deal shows investors ignore Aussie tech at their peril: Mike Cannon Brookes', *The Australian Financial Review*, 18 December 2017, <www.afr.com/technology/shareholders-back-aconex-deal-as-short-sellers-weep-20171218-h06bmn>
Court documents filed in the Supreme Court of Victoria, Cleevecorp Pty Cleeve Group v Wendy Sze Teng Ng S CI 2018 00897. Writ filed (13 March 2018), Amended Statement of Claim (21 June 2019), Defence (9 July 2019), Summons (1 November 2019), Affidavit (10 March 2020), Judge Signed Order (11 March 2020)
Marcus Padley, *Marcus Today*, 5 July 2018
Email comments from Lafitani Sotiriou, forwarded by Adam White, 20 March 2018
Richard Coppleson, 'The Coppo Report', 3 March 2018
Sarah Thompson, Anthony Macdonald & Joyce Moullakis, 'Citi prepares to put $200 million on the line for Afterpay Touch Group', *The Australian Financial Review*, 12 April 2018
James Eyers, 'Afterpay to cap late fees, bolster fraud checks', *The Australian Financial Review*, 11 April 2018
Ashwini Chandra & Grace Fulton, 'Afterpay Touch: Domestic momentum slowing', Goldman Sachs, 12 April 2018

**Chapter 10**
Jocelyn Prasad, 'A breakthrough business that's changing how we shop', *The University of Sydney*, 26 March 2018, <www.sydney.edu.au/news-opinion/news/2018/03/26/a-breakthrough-business-thats-changing-how-we-shop.html>
Nick Molnar, 'Why the stereotypes about millennials are holding us back', *TEDxYouth@Sydney 2017*, 6 September 2017, <https://tedxsydney.com/talk/why-the-stereotypes-about-millennials-are-holding-us-back-nick-molnar>
Clancy Yeates, 'Afterpay shares surge on US launch', *The Sydney Morning Herald*, 15 May 2018
'Short Stories', *Mason Stevens Daily*, 30 July 2018

Sarah Thompson, Anthony Macdonald & Julie-anne Sprague, 'Citi, Bells seeking bidders for Afterpay', *The Australian Financial Review*, 21 May 2018

Jonathan Shapiro & Vesna Poljak, 'Fundies' best long and short ideas', *The Australian Financial Review*, 6–7 January 2018

L1 Capital, June 2018 quarterly investor letter, 30 July 2018

Warren Buffett & Carol Loomis, 'Mr. Buffett on the stock market', *Fortune Magazine*, 22 November 1999

Roger Montgomery, 'The market loves Afterpay, but how long will the euphoria last?', 1 August 2018, <https://rogermontgomery.com/the-market-loves-afterpay-but-how-long-will-the-euphoria-last>

Sarah Turner & Jonathan Shapiro, 'Regal's Phil King says growth stock valuations could move a lot higher', *The Australian Financial Review*, 13 September 2018

James Eyers, 'How the Kardashians helped Nick Molnar launch Afterpay in the US', *The Australian Financial Review*, 31 May 2019

Sam Shead, 'Klarna becomes Europe's most valuable fintech firm with new $5.5 billion valuation', *Forbes*, 6 August 2019

John Hempton, 'Afterpay, a regulator view', Bronte Capital, 28 November 2018

Marcus Padley, 'Imagine a world where debt doesn't exist', *The Sydney Morning Herald*, 18 September 2018

Marcus Padley, 'Glory and pain—the hazards of being a fund manager', *The Australian Jewish News*, 10 December 2018

Richard Coppleson, 'The Coppo Report', 22 November 2018

## Chapter 11

Damon Kitney, 'Afterpay pays the price', *The Australian*, 12 January 2019

Staff reporter, 'Afterpay boss Anthony Eisen buys Arnotts family heir Byron Bay trophy home The White House', *Urban.com.au*, 3 December 2018, <www.urban.com.au/news/93176-arnotts-family-heir-sells-byron-bay-trophy-home-the-white-house>

Colin Kruger, 'Afterpay tried to hire top ASIC exec Peter Kell', *The Sydney Morning Herald*, 5 August 2019

AlphaBeta, *How Millennials Manage Money: Facts on the Spending Habits of Young Australians*, Report commissioned by Afterpay, 2019

Alan Kohler, 'How millennials are spending their money', *Eureka Report*, 29 January 2019

Luke Grant, 'Big banks launch attack on Afterpay and buy now, pay later rival', 2GB radio broadcast, 9 January 2019, <www.2gb.com/big-banks-launch-attack-on-afterpay-and-buy-now-pay-later-rivals>

Senate Economics References Committee, 'Credit and financial services targeted at Australians at risk of financial hardship', *Committee Hansard*, Brisbane, 24 January 2019

Australian Securities & Investments Commission, *Report 600: Review of Buy Now Pay Later Arrangements*, November 2018

**Chapter 12**

Dan Ziffer, Twitter, <https://twitter.com/danziffer/status/1093416570137636865>

Senate Economics References Committee, *Interest Rates and Informed Choice in the Australian Credit Card Market*, Commonwealth of Australia, 16 December 2015

Australian Securities & Investments Commission, *Report 580: Credit Card Lending in Australia*, July 2018

AlphaBeta, *How Millennials Manage Money: Facts on the Spending Habits of Young Australians*, Report commissioned by Afterpay, 2019

Lance Blockley, 'Australian credit cards enter their twilight years', The Initiatives Group, September 2019

John Kehoe, Misa Han & Jonathan Shapiro, 'Afterpay share plunge probe explores Chinese whispers', *The Australian Financial Review*, 21 February 2019

Colin Kruger & Patrick Hatch, 'Millennial masterstroke: All credit to Afterpay in generation grab', *The Sydney Morning Herald*, 2 March 2019

Colin Kruger, 'Afterpay spikes after big growth in the US', *The Sydney Morning Herald*, 5 June 2019

AUSTRAC, 'AUSTRAC orders audit of Afterpay's compliance with financial crime legislation', Media release, 13 June 2019, <www.austrac.gov.au/austrac-orders-audit-afterpays-compliance-financial-crime-legislation>

**Chapter 13**

Sebastian Mallaby, *More Money than God: Hedge Funds and the Making of a New Elite*, New York: The Penguin Press, 2010

Brook Turner, 'Lunch with the AFR: Julian Robertson', *The Australian Financial Review,* 19 July 2013

Hema Parmar, Melissa Karsh & Sophie Alexander, 'Quiet achiever: The 44-year-old investing genius with a $6.6 billion fortune', *The Sydney Morning Herald,* 28 June 2019

Ivan Dogan, 'Lone Pine Capital 2019 Q2 Investor Letter', *Insider Monkey,* 23 August 2019, <www.insidermonkey.com/blog/lone-pine-capital-2019-q2-investor-letter-768888>

David Allingham, 'Afterpay: What's a billion-dollar revenue line worth?', *Livewire,* 27 March 2019, <www.livewiremarkets.com/wires/afterpay-what-s-a-billion-dollar-revenue-line-worth>

Marc Whittaker, 'How different is it this time?', *Investors Mutual Ltd,* 18 July 2019, <https://iml.com.au/news-and-views/insights/how-different-it-time>

Joe Aston, 'Former Afterpay CFO in $48 million options haul', *The Australian Financial Review,* 2 February 2021

Jonathan Shapiro & James Eyers, 'Disclosure cloud over Afterpay's US growth push', *The Australian Financial Review,* 17 April 2019

Adam Creighton, 'Afterpay goes to top of class at Harvard', *The Australian,* 1 June 2019

James Eyers, 'Afterpay CEO dismisses threat from CBA's big investment', *The Australian Financial Review,* 12 August 2019

Tony Boyd, 'Afterpay snares ASIC's buy now, pay later guru', *The Australian Financial Review,* 1 August 2019

James Eyers, 'Larry Summers: Why I joined Afterpay', *The Australian Financial Review,* 17 October 2019

Parliament of Australia, *Journals of the Senate,* no. 14, 11 September 2019

Antonio Moreno, Donald Ngwe & George Gonzalez, 'Afterpay U.S.: The omnichannel dilemma', Harvard Business School Case 519-086, 9 April 2019

James Samson, '5 Things to watch for Afterpay investors', Ownership Matters, 14 March 2019

Joe Aston, 'Afterpay's PR guy gifted 800,000 reasons to defend it', *The Australian Financial Review,* 17 November 2019

Nathan Vardi, 'The hedge fund manager who became a billionaire from tech', *Forbes,* 3 May 2018

Jonathan Shapiro, 'Afterpay's ASIC hire shocks consumer groups',
  *The Australian Financial Review*, 2 August 2019

Tom Beadle & Jonathan Mott, 'If you don't buy now, could you pay less later?',
  UBS research initiation of coverage report on Afterpay, 16 October 2019

James Thomson, 'How Afterpay hooked the big fish of investing',
  *The Australian Financial Review*, 13 November 2019

**Chapter 14**

CEDA annual dinner, Transcript of Q&A, published in *The Australian
  Financial Review*, 17 November 2020

James Eyers, 'Consumers join retailers in war on Afterpay', *The Australian
  Financial Review*, 5 February 2020

Reserve Bank of Australia, 'Submissions on Review of Retail Payments
  Regulation', 3 February 2020, <www.rba.gov.au/payments-and-
  infrastructure/submissions/review-of-retail-payments-regulation/index.html>

Court documents filed in the Supreme Court of Victoria, Cleevecorp Pty
  Cleeve Group v Wendy Sze Teng Ng S CI 2018 00897, Writ filed
  (13 March 2018), Amended Statement of Claim (21 June 2019),
  Defence (9 July 2019), Summons (1 November 2019), Affidavit
  (10 March 2020), Judge Signed Order (11 March 2020)

Senate Select Committee on Financial Technology and Regulatory
  Technology, *Committee Hansard*, Sydney, 20 February 2020

James Eyers, 'Afterpay tells RBA it's "not a payments system"', *The Australian
  Financial Review*, 6 February 2020

Guy Debelle, 'The global financial crisis', 13 March 2019, <www.rba.gov.au/
  education/resources/videos.html>

Julie-anne Sprague, 'Why a walk in the park beats Zoom, says Alex Waislitz',
  *The Australian Financial Review*, 9 June 2020

Marc Kennis & Chen Ge, *The Buy Now, Pay Later Revolution*, Stocks Down
  Under research report, 25 August 2020

James Daggar-Nickson, 'Why global expansion makes most sense now for
  Afterpay', *The Australian Financial Review*, 30 June 2020

Chris Farrell, 'You can have fun in the stock market, but keep sums small',
  *Star Tribune*, 20 June 2020

Marcus Padley, 'The Afterpay bubble', *Livewire*, 11 July 2020, <www.
  livewiremarkets.com/wires/the-afterpay-bubble>

Susie Cagle, 'Would you take out a loan for a pair of jeans?', *Racked*, 29 November 2017

Scott Galloway, *The Prof G Show* (podcast), 3 December 2020

James Eyers, 'Afterpay urges ASIC to focus on its low bad debts', *The Australian Financial Review*, 28 August 2020

Senate Select Committee on Financial Technology and Regulatory Technology, *Interim Report*, Commonwealth of Australia, September 2020

House of Representatives Economics Committee, 'Review of the Four Major Banks', *Committee Hansard*, Sydney, 4 September 2020

James Eyers, 'Reserve Bank, ASIC urged to keep pressure on Afterpay', *The Australian Financial Review*, 14 September 2020

Supratim Adhikari, 'I was wrong on Afterpay: Big tech's fiercest critic lauds buy now, pay later darling', *The Sydney Morning Herald*, 28 October 2020

Juliet Chung, 'Covid-19 caused chaos for investors in 2020. These hedge funds earned billions', *The Wall Street Journal*, 25 December 2020

Robin Wigglesworth, '"Tiger cub" hedge fund Coatue surges to 52% gain', *The Financial Times*, 2 December 2020

Tom Maloney & Hema Parmar, 'Coleman leads $23 billion payday for 15 hedge fund earners', *Bloomberg*, 15 February 2021

Stephen Taub, 'The 20th annual Rich List, the definitive ranking of what hedge fund managers earned in 2020', *Institutional Investor*, 22 February 2021

Simon Mawhinney & Allan Gray, 'Afterpay —buy now, pain later?', *Livewire,* 12 November 2020, <www.livewiremarkets.com/wires/afterpay-buy-now-pain-later>

Anton Tagliaferro & Daniel Moore, 'Investor series: Is the sharemarket correctly pricing in fundamentals?', *Investors Mutual Ltd*, 12 November 2020, <https://iml.com.au/news-and-views/insights/sharemarket-correctly-pricing-fundamentals>

David Speers, 'The cost of coronavirus', *Four Corners*, ABC TV, 20 April 2020, <www.abc.net.au/4corners/4cs_economy_2004/12165974>

Jonathan Shapiro, 'Meet the sharemarket's corona generation', *The Australian Financial Review*, 13 June 2020

Andrei Stadnik, Jenny Hau, Richard Wiles, Sona Fernandes, 'Afterpay upgrade to OW: Building a global BNPL platform', Morgan Stanley, 8 July 2020

Jonathan Higgins, *Buy into 1Q21 results—QuadPay likely to be fastest growing US BNPL*, Shaw and Partners report, 29 September 2020

**Chapter 15**
The Treasury, *Review of the Australian Payments System*, 21 October 2020
The Treasury, *Payments System Review: Issues Paper*, November 2020
James Eyers, 'ASIC to call out buy now, pay later "harms that we continue to see"', *The Australian Financial Review*, 13 November 2020
Australian Securities & Investments Commission, *REP 672: Buy Now Pay Later: An Industry Update*, 16 November 2020
The Australian Financial Review Banking & Wealth Summit, transcript, 18 November 2020
Prime Minister of Australia, Speech to the Singapore Fintech Festival, 8 December 2020, <www.pm.gov.au/media/virtual-speech-singapore-fintech-festival>

**Chapter 16**
Lauren Sams, 'In Vogue', *The Australian Financial Review Magazine*, 26 March 2021
Natasha Gillezeau, 'Afterpay underscores fashion links in TikTok campaign', *The Australian Financial Review*, 2 November 2020
Nicholas Reimann, 'AOC calls Reddit-fueled GameStop frenzy similar to movement that put her in Congress', *Forbes*, 30 January 2021
Dutch Authority for the Financial Markets (AFM), net short positions archive, <www.afm.nl>
'Robinhood trader "sticking it to the man"', *Reuters Now*, 30 January 2021, <www.reuters.com/video/watch/idPWzc?now=true>
'Affirm: The morality of money', *The Generalist*, 10 December 2020, <https://thegeneralist.substack.com/p/affirm-the-morality-of-money>
WWD & PayPal, *The Power of Later*, Research report, 17 March 2021
Donna Fuscaldo, 'Struggling online lender OnDeck sold to Enova International', *Forbes*, 29 July 2020
Sarah Thompson, Anthony Macdonald & Tim Boyd, 'Zip Co goes shopping for US investors, mulls second listing', *The Australian Financial Review*, 7 February 2021

Tom Richardson, 'Zip valuation frustrates boss after "absolutely cracking" quarter', *The Australian Financial Review*, 21 January 2021

Jeff Kaufli, 'Inside the billion-dollar plan to kill credit cards', *Forbes*, 8 February 2021

Thea de Gallier, Harvey Day & Hannah Price, 'Influencer: "Why I stopped working with Klarna"', BBC, 11 February 2021

HM Treasury, 'Buy-now-pay-later products to be regulated', 2 February 2021, <www.gov.uk/government/news/buy-now-pay-later-products-to-be-regulated>

Simon English, 'City watchdog launches clampdown on buy-now-pay-later loans', *Evening Standard*, 2 February 2021

Julia Kollewe & Kalyeena Makortoff, 'Buy now pay later firms such as Klarna to face FCA regulation', *The Guardian*, 3 February 2021

Hans van Leeuwen & James Eyers, 'Britain wields regulator's rod on buy now, pay later firms', *The Australian Financial Review*, 3 February 2021

Danielle Wightman-Stone, 'London Fashion Week names Clearpay as principal partner', *FashionUnited*, 10 February 2021

Danielle Wightman-Stone, 'MPs criticise London Fashion Week sponsorship deal with Clearpay', *FashionUnited*, 22 February 2021

James Eyers, 'ASIC lashes buy now, pay later code of conduct', *The Australian Financial Review*, 10 June 2020

John Kehoe, 'Responsible lending laws to be axed', *The Australian Financial Review*, 24 September 2020

Consumers' Federation of Australia, 'Joint Consumer Submission: Australian Finance Industry Association (AFIA) Buy Now Pay Later Code of Practice', 6 May 2020, <http://consumersfederation.org.au/wp-content/uploads/2020/05/20200506-FINAL-Submission.pdf>

Tom Richardson, 'PayPal flags extraordinary demand in buy now, pay later space', *The Australian Financial Review*, 3 November 2020

Ashwini Chandra, *Some observations on US BNPL from PYPL's 4Q20*, Goldman Sachs research report, 4 February 2021

Tom Beadle, 'PayPal's entry into "Pay in 4": Running the scenarios', UBS Global Research, 10 September 2020

Tim Piper, *BNPL: Payments giant PayPal enters "Pay in 4"*, RBC Capital Markets report, 6 September 2020

James Eyers, 'Consumer groups attack the new buy now, pay later code of conduct', *The Australian Financial Review*, 24 February 2021

**Chapter 17**

Matthew Wilson & Nikolai Dale, 'Afterpay: Launched by Gen Y, embraced by Gen Z, positioning for Gen Alpha', E&P Financial, 25 February 2021

Richard Henderson, 'Nowhere to hide from market's growth traps', *The Australian Financial Review*, 9 March 2021

James Eyers, 'Afterpay readies for battle with CBA', *The Australian Financial Review*, 18 March 2021

Credit Suisse, 'Research bulletin', 17 March 2021

Macquarie Research, 24 March 2021

Tony Boyd, 'Buy now, pay later has an image problem', *The Australian Financial Review*, 16 March 2021

Michael Roddan & Jonathan Shapiro, 'ASIC will test new powers on buy now, pay later', *The Australian Financial Review*, 10 March 2021

Chay Fisher, Cara Holland & Tim West, 'Developments in the buy now, pay later market', *RBA Bulletin*, March 2021

Karen Maley, 'Bringing an end to the buy now, pay later lunacy', *The Australian Financial Review*, 22 March 2021

Lucy Maken, 'Afterpay's Nick Molnar makes like a billionaire, buys block next door for $18.5m', *Domain*, 20 March 2021

Senate Select Committee on Financial Technology and Regulatory Technology, 'Australia as a Technology and Financial Centre', *Committee Hansard*, Sydney, 11 February 2021

Lauren Sams, 'In Vogue', *The Australian Financial Review Magazine*, 26 March 2021

# INDEX

375

Made in the USA
Monee, IL
28 November 2021